inside

JAVA™

WORKSHOP™

THE SUNSOFT PRESS
JAVA SERIES

▼ **_Core Java,_ _Second Edition_**
Gary Cornell & Cay S. Horstmann

▼ **_Graphic Java_**
David M. Geary & Alan L. McClellan

▼ **_Inside Java WorkShop_**
Lynn Weaver & Bob Jervis

▼ **_Instant Java,_ _Second Edition_**
John A. Pew

▼ **_Java by Example,_ _Second Edition_**
Jerry R. Jackson & Alan L. McClellan

▼ **_Just Java,_ _Second Edition_**
Peter van der Linden

inside

JAVA™

WorkShop™

LYNN WEAVER • BOB JERVIS

Sun Microsystems Press
A Prentice Hall Title

The publisher offers discounts on this book when ordered in bulk quantities.
For more information, contact Corporate Sales Department, Prentice Hall PTR,
One Lake Street, Upper Saddle River, NJ 07458. Phone: 800-382-3419; FAX: 201- 236-7141.
E-mail: corpsales@prenhall.com.

Editorial/production supervision: *Patti Guerrieri*
Cover design director: *Jerry Votta*
Cover designer: *Talar Agasyan*
Cover illustration: *Karen Strelecki*
Manufacturing manager: *Alexis R. Heydt*
Marketing manager: *Stephen Solomon*
Acquisitions editor: *Gregory G. Doench*
Sun Microsystems Press publisher: *Rachel Borden*

10 9 8 7 6 5 4 3 2 1

ISBN 0-13-858234-3

Sun Microsystems Press
A Prentice Hall Title

To all the great teachers, especially
Frances and Claire.
Lynn

To my wife Sheila, who's been forced to
share me with Java WorkShop.
Bob

Contents

Part 2   A Working Tour of Java WorkShop

Chapter 2

Java WorkShop Basics, 19

Part 3 Java WorkShop: Advanced Topics

Part 4   What Next?

Chapter 13
Watching Java Developments, 173

Part 5   Appendixes

Authors' Notes

It has been exciting to watch a programming language excite content developers as much as it does application developers. Even people outside of the world of Internet content and software development are talking about Java. As someone who has written programming guides but lives nearer to the content end of the development spectrum, I am interested in tools that make the language more accessible, easier to understand, and easier to use. Java's suitability for travel on the Internet and its ability to handle a variety of media will, I hope, continue to drive the making of Java development tools for all levels of Internet programmers.

No sophisticated language is easy to use right out of the box. Help is near at hand (as close as the software on the *Inside Java WorkShop* CD-ROM) for command-line Java programmers who have waited patiently (or not) for the time when Java tools would make programming easier. I imagine that everyone, even the few, the proud, the most elite of programmers, welcomes tools that provide the opportunity to spend less time on mechanical coding tasks and more time on high-value activities like designing powerful and usable software. Java WorkShop is just such a tool. It's a powerful, integrated, development environment, written in and for Java, that is especially suited for the serious Internet programmer.

The folks who brought you the Java WorkShop, and who have enthusiastic plans for its future, have been involved in the development of this book. They have read drafts, offered suggestions and advice, and provided information, examples, and some of the tips you'll find inside. I am especially pleased that Bob Jervis, the engineering project leader for the first release of Java WorkShop, has provided the material in Chapter 1. Bob's perspective and information about how to approach Java development inside Java Workshop will improve your understanding of and success with Java WorkShop.

One of the rewards of writing this book has been working with so many gifted and committed colleagues inside and outside of Sun. I appreciate what their ideas, suggestions, encouragement, support, and review have added to these pages. I am especially grateful to Kelly Rogers for her inspired leadership in making the idea for the book a reality, and for doing so with an uncommon blend of intellect, enthusiasm, insight, and warmth. I have been lucky to have these people on my team— Susan Najour who believed in me and gracefully cleared a path, Mike Boyer, Don Miller, and Dan O'Leary, who helped with key examples and reviews, Gail Chappell who offered good ideas and a strong commitment to helping people use Java WorkShop, and Thu Trinh who tested examples and pulled everything together for the CD-ROM. To the many others who provided information, perspectives, and reviews—especially Jeff Anders, Lee Bieber, Samuel Chen, Linda Gallops, Larry Hoffman, and Lynn McConnell—I could not have done it without your help. I'd also like to thank our wonderful editor, Mary Lou Nohr whose intelligence and clarity made this a better book. I'm obliged to our publishers, Rachel Borden at Sun Microsystems Press and Greg Doench at Prentice Hall, for identifying the need for this book and managing its delivery. Thanks, too, to John Bortner at Sun, and to Lisa Iarkowski and Patti Guerrieri at Prentice Hall. Last, but not least, I offer my heartfelt thanks to Barbara Wood whose patience, faith, encouragement, good humor, and excellent cooking sustained me throughout.

—Lynn Weaver
Mountain View, California
January 1997

The most common reaction inside Sun Microsystems to the Java phenomenon has been profound, albeit pleasant, surprise. No one has seen the kind of passionate embrace given to any other new technology, especially a programming language. As I write this, two years ago Java was just getting its official name. It was one of at least four different programming language research projects then running in different parts of Sun and so didn't grab much attention inside the company. A year ago it had already helped scuttle Microsoft's networking strategy and push the giant to endorse the Internet. Not a single commercial product had been released for sale that incorporated Java technology. Today, more than 80 percent of Internet browsers in use support the running of Java applets. Java applications can run on almost all computer systems. The first two press runs of the Java WorkShop product CDs were gone so quickly from our warehouses that we in the development team couldn't get copies of our own package for weeks!

Engineers put their hearts into a project in the belief that what they are doing is intellectually right. We make guesses about what that rightness is and then build our products to incorporate it. The research engineers who labored for years creating Java believed in what they did. But belief in your own product isn't enough for success, and no technology in the history of computing has had the immediate excitement and overwhelming acceptance that Java has enjoyed.

When we started Java WorkShop, the wave was just starting to rise. We thought a lot about who was interested in using Java and why. That thinking informed our design from the beginning to the final shipment. The chapter "The Java Workshop Model" illuminates our ideas and, we hope, gives you insight into how we think Java WorkShop can best be used. Of course, ultimately what matters about Java is what you do with it, and not what we think you do. Since Java WorkShop is a living, growing product, you can help us by letting us know where we've gotten the story wrong or left something out. We are constantly looking for ways to make Java WorkShop better, and the feedback we have gotten from customers during the early-access period has already improved it. It's a shared adventure; we invite you to join in the fun.

I would like to acknowledge the hard work and commitment of the entire Java WorkShop team, from development engineers to Webmasters, without whom Java WorkShop would not exist today. It was a superb effort and I am grateful to have been a part of that team.

—Bob Jervis
Mountain View, California
January 1997

Preface

This book doesn't attempt to teach you Java™, although it also does not assume firsthand knowledge of some aspects of the language, like the Abstract Windowing Toolkit (AWT) or threads. There are plenty of excellent texts for learning about Java, including those in the rest of the Java Series. Instead of teaching Java through a development environment, we chose to focus on maximizing your understanding of this particular development environment. Of course, we are talking about a *Java* development environment, so there are Java examples and some discussion of Java concepts where required. You'll find *Inside Java WorkShop* most useful if you already have some Java experience.

How to Use Inside Java WorkShop

The book is divided into parts that become increasingly more detailed or advanced. *Inside Java WorkShop* begins with practical concepts, shows how they are implemented in the tools that make up Java WorkShop™, and then moves on to spend extra time on the more challenging and essential topics of debugging and GUI building. It ends with a chapter on Java developments and resources. For added convenience, appendixes contain reference material that you can keep at hand as you work.

Experienced programmers might want to read and use selected chapters. Begin with Part I, in which the mental model for developing with Java WorkShop is described. That's where you'll learn how to think about the application problem you want to solve—before you start working with the tool. Then you can choose how much of Part II you need and move on to Part III.

Part II is a working tour of every tool in Java WorkShop. Java WorkShop is the only Java development environment that uses a browser model, so programmers familiar with other development environments might want to spend time on the working tour to familiarize themselves with each tool before getting into more serious work with any one of them.

Part III revisits the more complex topics of debugging and GUI building. That is why you'll see two chapters about the Debugger and Visual Java™ (the GUI builder) in the table of contents. In Part II, the debugging and GUI building chapters provide a first level of basics so that you are prepared to handle the advanced debugging and GUI building chapters in Part III.

Part IV looks at some Java developments and sources for more information. The number of Java technologies that are emerging is staggering. Future developments chapters get out of date before you can finish reading them. So we've created a Java developments chapter to give you a vocabulary of Java movements and to list the resources that you can track to find out more and stay up to date.

Finally, Part V contains appendixes of keyboard shortcuts, Visual Java component attributes, frequently asked Java WorkShop questions and answers, and source code listings for the examples in the book.

Conventions Used in This Book

Table P-1 shows the typographic conventions used in this book.

Table P-1   Typographic Conventions

Typeface or Symbol	Description
	Indicates information to make a note of as you work with Java WorkShop.
	Denotes a tip to make your work in Java WorkShop easier.

Table P-1 Typographic Conventions (Continued)

Typeface or Symbol	Description
![CAUTION]	Indicates a warning to heed before or while you do something in Java WorkShop.
`courier`	Indicates a command, directory, file name, environment variable, class name, method, argument, Java keyword, HTML tag, file content, or code excerpt.
bold courier	Indicates a sample command line entry or illustrates code example text that you change during an exercise in the book.
italics	Indicates a new term that is defined when it is introduced, emphasis, a book title, a variable that you should replace with a valid value, or the name of a Java WorkShop project or portfolio.

Using the Inside Java WorkShop CD-ROM

The companion CD-ROM contains the Java WorkShop portfolios and projects used in this book and an HTML page with URLs for Java resources. It also contains "Try and Buy" free trial software for Java WorkShop. This is the full Java WorkShop development environment with the Java Developers Kit™ (JDK) 1.0.2. It is not a "light" version of the product. You can use it to do real work.

The examples in this book are on the CD-ROM, but with one exception they are offered as solutions to exercises in the book. This gives you the option to do the exercises in the book and create your own Java WorkShop projects or to just import the sample projects and follow along in the exercises. The exception is the *TumbleItem* project, which should be imported for the debugging exercise in Chapter 11.

Platform Requirements

To use Java WorkShop 1.0, your platform should meet these requirements:

- Windows 95™ or Windows NT™ 3.5.1
  - 486 100 MHz or higher
  - 16 Mbytes memory minimum, 24 Mbytes recommended
  - 15 Mbytes free disk space
- Solaris® 2.4 or higher
  - SPARCsystem™
  - 486 100 MHz or higher

- 32 Mbytes memory
- 15 Mbytes free disk space

To install Java WorkShop on Windows 95 and Windows NT:

NOTE: This CD was designed to work with a 100% compatible Windows 95/NT system. Some of the files use long file names, which is one of the features of Windows 95. If you are unable to see the long file names on the CD, then your system may not be 100 percent compatible with Windows 95/NT. Windows 95/NT 4.0 users can check for compatibility by double-clicking on the "System" icon in the Control Panel and then clicking on the "Performance" tab. If the "Performance" section does not indicate that "Your system is configured for optimal performance" then you have some sort of system conflict that should be resolved. Consult Windows Help or contact Microsoft Technical Support for further assistance.

1. Insert the Inside Java WorkShop CD into your CD-ROM drive.

2. Double click on `setupws.exe`[1] to launch the installation program. The installer will uncompress and copy all the necessary files to your hard drive. The default directory is `C:\Java-WorkShop`. You can specify a different directory by clicking the Browse button in the installation dialog.

3. Follow the installation by clicking the appropriate buttons and entering the installation directory when, and if, needed.

4. After the installation is complete, double click on the Java WorkShop icon to start the Workshop. (The installation creates a program group containing all the icons.)

5. When Java WorkShop loads for the first time, you will be prompted to enter a serial number. Click on the "30-day trial" button and a serial number will be entered automatically.

6. To uninstall Java WorkShop, double-click the uninstall icon in the Java WorkShop program group.

7. To install the examples provided on the CD-ROM, follow the directions in"To install and use the Inside Java WorkShop example projects:" on page xxvi.

---

1. The file appears as Setupws.exe on Windows 95, and SETUPWS.EXE on Windows NT.

To install Java WorkShop on Solaris 2.x:

1. Insert the Inside Java WorkShop CD into your CD-ROM drive.

2. If Volume Manager is running on your machine, the CD-ROM is automatically mounted to the /cdrom/insidejws directory. Skip to step 3.

    If the Volume Manager is NOT running on your machine, create a directory called /cdrom/insidejws and mount the CD-ROM manually by becoming root and typing:
    ```
    # mkdir -p /cdrom/insidejws
    # mount -rF hsfs /dev/dsk/c0t6d0s0 /cdrom/insidejws
    ```

3. Change to the directory where you intend to install the Java WorkShop files:
    ```
    % cd /<destination_directory>
    ```

4. Extract the Java WorkShop files by typing:
    ```
    % tar -xvf /cdrom/insidejws/jw-<platform>.tar
    ```
    Where <platform> is either "sparc-S2" or "intel-S2" depending on whether you use a SPARC or Intel system.

    Note: This command is entered all on one line, but printing limitations mean we show it on two lines.

5. If you mounted the CD-ROM manually, unmount the drive by becoming root and typing:
    ```
    # cd /
    # umount /dev/dsk/c0t6d0s0
    ```
    Otherwise, go to Step 6.

6. Eject the CD by typing:
    ```
    % cd /
    % eject
    ```
    You can now use Java WorkShop.

7. Start Java WorkShop by typing:
    ```
    % /<destination_directory>/JWS/<platform>-S2/bin/jws &
    ```
    For example, if you installed Java WorkShop in a directory named /home/lynnw/JavaWorkShop on a SPARC, the command for running the product would be:
    ```
    % /home/lynnw/JavaWorkShop/JWS/sparc-S2/bin/jws &
    ```
    Java WorkShop starts up with a license window. Click on the "30-day trial" button and a serial number will be entered automatically.

8. To copy the examples provided on the CD-ROM, follow the directions in"To install and use the Inside Java WorkShop example projects:" on page xxvi.

To install and use the Inside Java WorkShop example projects:

The `insidejws/Examples` directory on the CD-ROM contains the sample projects from the book. In the `Examples` directory there is a directory for each project.

Solaris users: Copy the `Examples` directory to your hard drive.

Windows users: Click on `EXAMPLES.EXE` to install the examples. By default, `EXAMPLES.EXE` places the files in a top-level directory named `insidejws`. You can specify a different directory by clicking the Browse button in the installation dialog.

Because Java WorkShop organizes files into projects, the files must be imported into Java WorkShop if you want to use them in Java WorkShop. You could also create a new project instead of importing one and use just the source files in the Examples directory. Of course, you have the option of actually doing each exercise and creating your own project and source files as you go. The projects on the CD are examples of what your completed projects would be like. See Chapter 4 for information about how to import and use projects. You'll find instructions there for bringing your own source files into a Java WorkShop project, too.

The CD-ROM contains sample projects that run on Windows 95, Windows NT and Solaris, but the illustrations in this book are from a PC running Windows 95. We use Windows-style path names in the illustrations. Because you are creating or using your own project directories, your path names will be different, regardless of whether you are working in a Unix or Windows environment.

To use the Inside Java WorkShop Resources Web page, copy `resource.html` to your hard drive and open it in a browser.

PART ONE

CHAPTER

1

- A Brief History of Software Development

- The Java WorkShop Way

- Applets and the Web

- Projects—The Basic Unit Of Work

- The Great Cycles: Edit-Compile and Edit-Compile-Debug

- Using Visual Java

- Tips and Tricks

The Java WorkShop Model

This chapter puts you in the picture that the Java WorkShop team envisioned during development of the first release and shows how you can use the team's development experiences in your own work. First, though, let's briefly review our programming origins.

A Brief History of Software Development

We still deal with programming a line at a time because of the days when programs were written as a pile of cards and the cards were run through a card reader. In those days, programs executed as the cards were read, and program editing consisted of adding and removing cards. More sophisticated mainframes stored the cards temporarily on disk before they were run. Since computers were expensive and operating systems were primitive, they had to be shared among many people, one person at a time. Programs had to be designed to run and complete so the next user could have the machine.

Online systems came next. Even though the first online systems were designed for mainframes, time-sharing was normally associated with minicomputers running operating systems like UNIX. Interactive programming was born. Programs were still written in text in line-oriented text editors like ed. As printing terminals gave way to video displays, real editors like Emacs and vi appeared.

The UNIX development environment consisted of a shell, a bag of utility programs like `diff`, `grep`, `lint`, and `adb`, and a compiler like `cc`. Specialized tools like `yacc` made it easy to write sophisticated parsers. The 64-kilobyte memory limit of early minicomputers encouraged a small-is-beautiful approach. The programmer had to figure out clever ways to combine the UNIX utilities to get the job done. Fortunately, programming was much simpler in those days, since a single program couldn't contain more than a few thousand lines of code and user interfaces were rarely more sophisticated than a simple conversational typewriter-like scheme.

The personal computer revolution spawned its own editors; for example, WordStar (really a word processor) provided many programmers with a useful tool. Otherwise, the early personal computers were too much like early minicomputers to allow for much innovation in development tools. The pervasiveness of low-resolution graphics capabilities in these early PCs did lead to the creation of more graphic programs with very different demands on programming tools. Little could be done, however, to expand the kinds of tools being used—until 1981, when the IBM PC, with more than 64 kilobytes of RAM, marked the entry of affordable machines in the market.

The revolutionary Borland development environment, TurboPascal, was first released in 1983. This was the first combined text editor and fast compiler in one product. Through a succession of releases, Borland extended and perfected the concept of the integrated development environment. By the release of TurboC 2.0 in 1988, the environment included projects to build multifile programs, an integrated editor, debugger, compiler, and online help with a finely tuned, text-based, windowing user interface. Everything about the product was engineered to make the mechanics of building and testing a program effortless.

Integrated environments came late to the UNIX world because as UNIX has evolved, programmers have assembled and integrated their own environment. They use high-powered workstations with numerous windows running different tasks. Although there's more typing involved, an ingenious UNIX hacker can customize shell scripts and makefiles to do almost anything. The flexibility is unbounded, even if it does take a long time to put it all together.

Integrated environments, in contrast, use an all-in-one approach, and if you don't like one of the tools, you really can't move easily to another tool without switching the whole environment. Years of tool development, however, have made the PC environments very effective and easy to use.

The Java WorkShop design draws from the combined wisdom of the UNIX and the PC worlds. Here, Java has proven itself invaluable. Because Java WorkShop is written in Java, tools written as applets can share project information, allowing for sophisticated integration. Adding new tools is as easy as writing a new applet. Collaborative groups of applets can leverage the capabilities of Java to bring all kinds of new functionality to you. What you see today is only the beginning.

The Java WorkShop Way

Java WorkShop is about helping you create a user experience. That user experience is created out of a combination of Web pages, multimedia, Java applets, and server code. Today, Java WorkShop provides a complete set of tools, integrated into a single environment, for managing the Java programming part of this problem. Most importantly, Java WorkShop uses a highly modular structure that enables you to easily plug new tools into the overall structure.

The real genius of Java lies not in its features per se, which were carefully selected from earlier languages, but in the way in which those features interact with the Internet. By providing a common programming interface for networking, graphical user interfaces, and multithreading, Java makes it possible for you to write the kinds of applications that are most needed on the Internet. By a lucky coincidence, corporate computing divisions all over the world have realized that most of their networking needs can be met by intranets, private computing microcosms that use Internet protocols.

So, whether you are writing code for the Internet or your own corporate intranet, we believe that you are most likely to be trying to create network-aware software and a related Web site. As a language, Java is well suited for general-purpose programming, but the current implementations are still not as fast as C++ for many tasks. This disadvantage is only temporary and grows smaller every day, so Java WorkShop lets you develop standalone programs as well as applets.

One important lesson we learned from the experience of making Java WorkShop is that we were right to commit to Web technologies as the foundation of our toolset, but we're still learning how to make Web software. We started relatively modestly in our support of Web content, but we see that as a key area for expansion.

Of Tools

If you are developing applets, you need to debug them in a browser environment, and Java WorkShop was the first to let you do that. We experienced this need as we developed Java WorkShop itself. Even though the WorkShop is a standalone application, we chose to use a browser look-and-feel, in part because the best way for us to understand the problems you face is to face them ourselves. Also, since we agree that the Web enables new ways of making software work, we needed to create an environment that exploited the Web as much as possible. It didn't make sense to preach the value of the Web and then to ignore it in our own tools.

The Web browser you are using in 1997 still uses a design model that was created for visiting static pages of information. Java applets introduce a new set of issues, as you now are visiting a whole set of active applications that live on for a while after you stop looking at their page. All of a sudden it matters how you got to a specific page in the Web and, even more, how you return to it later on.

We also found, when we began shipping Java WorkShop, that people want to have a Stop button on their tools, but browsers don't do that for applets. Applets live and die with their page, and most people have no idea when a page "dies" in a browser or how to kill one. Sooner or later, this observation will translate into better Java applet support in browsers and in Java WorkShop. *Meanwhile, when you create a Java applet, make sure there is a way to stop it running and release whatever system resources it has grabbed; don't rely on the destroy method to do it for you.*

Of Teams

The Web has also contributed to a trend begun by graphical user interfaces—a development team must include many more skills than ever before. Our own development team comprises programmers, writers, graphic artists, interaction engineers, human interface engineers, testers, translators, and evangelists. Software created for internal corporate use may not be quite as intense in its use of production values, but programming long ago ceased being a solitary activity. *Java WorkShop provides support for easily sharing projects over the Web and also for version control integrated with your source editor.* While these facilities help programmers specifically, we plan to provide better support for all members of the development team, not just the programmers.

Applets and the Web

Applets are a new concept introduced by Java. An *applet* is simply a visual component that is placed on a Web page. Whenever the page is brought into a Java-enabled browser, the applet is started running.

Security

Because applets run on the machine of the browser, they need to be carefully secured so they do no harm. Security policy is a tricky business that is evolving rapidly on the Web. Today, applets are not allowed to do very much. They have no access to the local disk of the machine they run on—so no local data caching, and no local storage of program state of any kind. An applet can only connect back through the network to talk to the host it came from. It can't start native programs running or even inspect properties that would describe what the local machine is like.

This situation will change over time, but we don't know yet exactly what the security policies will be. Network computers—which have no local disk storage and hence no local file system to access—play a role here. Eventually, we may have conventions for how to locate and use persistent storage for a user.*Meanwhile, write your applet software to use URLs and networking to manipulate data.*

Server

A lot of the early applets that people published were small programs that didn't do much. These really give a fairly trivial view of what applets can do. The secret of getting the most out of applets lies with the server—the applet comes from a server and belongs to it. This means that applets really are different from conventional GUI programs. They are intrinsically network oriented.

When combined with an interesting server component, an applet becomes a powerful front end for a client/server application. The industry is rapidly evolving to use Java on the server side of the equation as well. It is easy to write software for communications among Java modules, because you don't have to think about the differences between client and server operating systems, CPU, or data format. Because the server side is still changing rapidly, today's Java WorkShop does not give you much help there. Nevertheless, the picture is becoming much clearer every day, and we will provide you with the facilities to get the job done.

For now, Java WorkShop can help you with your applet code. When you develop an applet with Java WorkShop, we give you a test environment that enforces applet security and gives you a complete Web browser operational environment. That way, you'll see how your applet will behave in the browser your user will eventually use.

Projects

One of the concepts pioneered by PC development environments and used in Java WorkShop is the *project*. Projects are the primary mechanism for organizing your work. All the tools of the environment store their persistent information in a project. It's the way the tools integrate with one another. We talk about ways to take advantage of the project concept in "Tips and Tricks" on page 13 and throughout the book.

We also designed in the notion of a project type. The types for standalone applications, applets, and packages are fairly obvious. Image projects are not terribly useful yet. You can paste them into HTML source files, and that's about it for now.

Eventually, you'll be able to do all sorts of image processing on them. Remote applet projects turn out to be not all that interesting; you can do just about as much with a portfolio of remote applet projects as you can with a simple links page but with less control over the layout and display. (We used remote applet projects to set up our demo portfolios of JavaSoft applets, so that we could just point at them and not ship them with our product.)

Very early on, we instituted the notion that projects can be nested inside one another. Java WorkShop itself is represented as a collection of projects. One stand-alone application project contains the sun.jws package, and each of the other packages is set up as a subproject. We can then build or debug the standalone project or build each of the subprojects. Altogether, seventeen projects make up Java WorkShop 1.0.

As we worked with the project structure, some not so obvious consequences emerged. Because of the way that Java source files import information from other classes, files can have implicit dependencies on one another. The closest equivalent in C or C++ is the way that object files not only depend on the source file, but also depend on each of the include files that are included in compiling the object file. C and C++ environments can automatically track how include files are used and can correctly rebuild affected object files in a project. We couldn't get the Java WorkShop builder to fully track the dependencies of Java classes automatically in the first release. And because native methods are written in C or C++, Java Work-Shop cannot be used to build them. *Each operating system platform will require need a somewhat different approach to building your native methods.*

The way we decided to have the builder work also imposes a constraint on the way you organize your packages. Since the packages must be built one at a time, packages can depend only on other packages that have already been built. One of the indirect consequences of this was beneficial to Java WorkShop. We have organized our integration architecture around a base of environment code that knows nothing about the individual tools. The tools, built later in the process, can use the integration framework but know little or nothing about each other. *This structure enables you to design your application with layered interfaces, with each layer corresponding to one package.*

Java packages are more than just layering devices. By limiting the scope of fields and methods, you can impose security constraints or encapsulate information as a way to limit complexity. As a result, the current constraints on package order in the build must be relaxed. Rather than build one package at a time, in the future you will be able to build groups of packages as a unit. The builder and the compiler will carefully track all explicit and implicit dependencies, so you will be able to control the layering of your programs much more effectively.

The Great Cycles: Edit-Compile and Edit-Compile-Debug

When we thought about how to organize the Java WorkShop, we used the idea of two great cycles that a programmer goes through in creating a program. Most frequently, we cycle between editing our program and compiling it to discover compile-time errors. We can move on to the second cycle, editing, compiling, and debugging only when all the compile-time errors are gone. For example, if you use many compiles, you might put small amounts of new code into a program for each compile. It's easier to fix the errors, and then when you run tests, it's also easier to discover the causes of the runtime bugs. Different people have different styles, but integrated environments help cut the mechanical effort involved in working through the cycles. Rather than having to remember an assortment of commands, you let the environment take care of them for you.

If you're not accustomed to an integrated environment, using an error browser may feel a little odd at first. You may have trained yourself to work your way through the bugs from the bottom up because error messages with line numbers in them get out of sync with your editor if you work from the top down. However, an error browser will track your edits in the editor, and so when you link to the next error, it will still be pointing at the actual location of the error, not at the original numbered line.

Compilers are designed to diagnose as many distinct errors as possible in a source program. But how many distinct errors are in a program? If you made a mistake in the declaration of a variable, is each of the references to the variable also in error or just the result of the mistake in the declaration? If the compiler encounters an undefined variable name in the program, is the mistake a typo in the reference or in the original declaration? Only the programmer knows which spelling is correct. Eventually, you learn how a compiler responds. The common thread is usually some completely inexplicable error message complaining about what looks like a perfectly good statement or declaration.

All of this goes to explain why you will sometimes fix one problem and another diagnostic suddenly appears in the next compile, or why some seemingly innocuous error will generate a whole cascade of inaccurate diagnostics. Ultimately, it is an insoluble problem. We can only find ways to analyze the circumstances of a failure and devise clearer diagnostics. *In Java, many of the errors and diagnostics are quite similar to those of a C or C++ compiler, and the corrective action is the same.*

Java diagnostics differ from C or C++ in the area of importing classes. With C or C++, include files are sources, so they are all present or not, and the order in which you compile source files doesn't really matter. In Java, since imports work off previously compiled class files, there are a number of ways in which the current builder can report that class files don't exist but on a recompile, the diagnostics go away. This is usually due to some sort of ordering error in the build. Most of the time, the `javac` compiler doesn't care about the order in which you list the source files on the command line, but occasionally it does matter. *Usually when this happens, repeating the build resolves the problem.*

Sometimes a diagnostic shows up during a complete rebuild of your project. This is usually due to a hidden dependency that was only detected when the original class files were deleted and the sources were recompiled, for example, when there are circular dependencies among packages, so that a class in one package depends on the interface of a class in another package, and so on, until you get back to where you started from. *The only way to satisfy the dependency is to make sure that all the source files in the cycle are compiled together. You may have to add source files to a package project that are not part of the package in order to do this.*

In the future, we will correct these deficiencies. They don't arise very often, especially in a small- to medium-sized program. Even in a product as large as Java WorkShop (over 100,000 lines of source code), this sort of problem only occasionally arises and only when we have done major restructurings of the source code.

Using Visual Java

Graphical interfaces are easier to create and modify when you can actually view the interface as you work. Of course, Java WorkShop lets you write your code entirely in the Java language if you want to—the AWT library is easy to use, compared to other GUI systems. Even so, a GUI application can be difficult to write in Java. That's when you turn to Visual Java.

Visual Java is not a perfect visual programming environment, at least not yet, especially in terms of some less obvious aspects of its user interface, but it is worth getting to know. It contains a cornucopia of neat stuff with which you can create some pretty effective window layouts. And Visual Java makes it easy to experiment with the layout as you design it, always a better way to design a GUI. Visual Java is easy to use once you get the hang of things. Good online help is out there, and in this book, Chapter 7 gives you basics of the interface and some conceptual background, and Chapter 12 deepens your understanding with a hands-on exercise and coverage of advanced topics. So go for it!

There are two parts to a GUI program you create in Visual Java. The first part is the visual layout, the appearance of the program. The second part is the behavior, the code to execute when you press a button or select a checkbox. Visual Java effectively separates the two aspects of the program. You can freely rearrange components and not have to alter the Java code at all.

GUI Layout

Let's start with the visual layout part of the program. When you create an applet in Java WorkShop, by default the environment first opens a Visual Java display screen. If you are accustomed to PC layout programs, the Visual Java layout screen may appear odd at first.

AWT is designed to run on many different systems. An applet you write can work on the Macintosh, Windows PC, Solaris, Linux, and almost any other Java system. This means that your applet will run on a wide variety of screen sizes and font sizes and, in the future, with a variety of foreign languages. This means that you can't easily predict the exact sizes of labels and buttons. AWT solves this problem by using layout managers. A layout manager lets you specify the relative placement of the various components you group in a window, without having to fix them to specific locations on the screen. The most flexible layout manager in AWT is called the GridBag. When Visual Java starts on a new window, that's the layout manager you start with.

Start out by sketching the basic outline of each window. Break the window down into groups of display areas and controls. Try using a few horizontal or vertical bands subregions. That way, as you rearrange the controls within each band, the other parts of the window hold their shape pretty well. Thinking out how you want things grouped can make it easier to make changes later.

Chapter 12 describes how to use Visual Java to place your components and manipulate them once they're there, so let's assume you've learned enough of that to let you create your layout. The GridBag layout is very much like a spreadsheet in structure, and you have a great deal of control over the width or height of cells, as well as how they respond to resizing the window.

Techniques vary. Some people put a minimum of controls into a GUI before wiring up the controls and experimenting with the behavior. Other people like to fill out the whole screen first. Either way, you eventually get to a point where you are ready to start writing code.

GUI Behavior

There are two ways to write the code for a Visual Java GUI. If you are accustomed to writing AWT code in Java, you'll probably find writing code in a Group class more familiar. On the other hand, you can save yourself the effort of writing boilerplate code by writing Visual Java operations. The down side of operations is that they may be a little harder to debug.

How does defining GUI behavior in Visual Java work? Visual Java generates up to four kinds of files from your GUI layout: Main, Root, Ops, and Group. (If you don't write operations in Visual Java, the tool doesn't generate an Ops file.) You generate the Group file once, and the rest every time you change the GUI. As a result, you never touch the contents of the Main, Root, or Ops files directly, which can be confusing when you are debugging an operation. For example, if you fix a bug in the Ops file, the fix will get blown away on the next build. *You have to remember to go back to the original window where you entered the operation's Java code.* Again, Chapter 12 is helpful in showing how to reload operations code in Visual Java.

GUI Design for Large Applications

If you are using Visual Java to create a really big application, you ought to start thinking about how to exploit Group files. Groups allow you to do two things: organize the flow of information through your GUI and create reusable components or dialogs. For example, you can add pop-up dialogs this way and build powerful GUI programs by just repeating this process for each window in the application.

Groups stemmed from some of our early experience writing GUIs in Java. One of the ways our Web-centric approach affected the way we designed Java WorkShop is that we allowed buttons and links in many parts of the application to communicate with tools that were far away. For example, you can bring up the Debugger and ask to see the source code for a breakpoint. That causes the Point and Click Editor to load the file or, if the file is already in a window, to scroll to the desired location.

The important issue here is how to get the button press event to trigger something in the editor. We exploited the event structure of AWT to accomplish this. For instance, when you press the Show Source button in the Breakpoints card of the Debugger, the event handler for that window responds directly to the button press. However, all it does is check the currently selected breakpoint and send an event off to some central event dispatcher. In the early days of the project, we created a haphazard set of event registries where environment services like the editor or the help browser could publish their interest in classes of events. After some initial variations, we arrived at a fairly regular structure. When the GUI builder project started, the team created the concept of a Group to manage the flow of events through the system. The ability to create a nested tree of Groups allows a Visual Java application to grow quite large.

Tips and Tricks

As you use Java Workshop, you'll devise clever ways to accomplish your Java programming goals. Here are some of our tricks (and rationale) for:

- Editing multiple files

- Starting up projects and portfolios

- Sharing code

- Organizing projects

- Using portfolios for Web offerings

- Doing business

Editing Multiple Files

Java WorkShop can easily edit numerous source files at the same time. On a Solaris or Windows NT 3.51 desktop, an easy way to manage the editing of multiple files is to iconify them and place the icons in a group. By moving the mouse cursor over the icons, you can then locate the file you are looking for. Often, you can put all the files you are currently working on in editors and switch among them by iconifying and deiconifying different editors.

Starting Up Portfolios and Projects

If you are developing code just for your own use, you can forget about portfolios. Portfolios come into play only when you are working in groups, publishing, or browsing for somebody else's work. You can use the free portfolio you get when you install Java WorkShop or you can create your own. We talk about portfolios later in this section and in detail in Chapter 3 and Chapter 4.

A project in its easiest form is just an applet or a standalone application. You can create and modify projects to your heart's content. As with a portfolio, you don't have to start from scratch with a project. If you have an applet (or anything else written in Java, for that matter), you can create a project around it. Because we collect some extra information to help in debugging, if you want to debug a program that you created elsewhere, you'll have to rebuild it under Java WorkShop.

Sharing Code by Means of the Source Editor and Projects

Sharing code with others is always cumbersome. In designing Java WorkShop, we thought a lot about several scenarios:

- People working on a project in a team (like us)

- People publishing applets and applications code over an intranet

- People publishing applets and applications code over the Internet

For people working in a team, the problem is how to manage needed changes in such a way that people can't clobber each other's changes. For this, Java Work-Shop provides the version control interface in the Source Editor.

On larger programs, most of the time you will need to modify only a few files to fix a bug or add a new feature. As a result, you're probably in a situation where the source files are checked in to your version control system (such as PVCS on Windows or SCCS or RCS on Solaris). So, when you are running the debugger to find a problem, odds are that the buggy file hasn't been checked out. With Java WorkShop, if you see a bug in the source and try to change it, the Source Editor will ask you to check out the file before you make the change. Later, when you're satisfied that the change works properly, you can check the file back in right from the Source Editor. Your version control commands are all in one place.

The Source Editor is also very useful for putting debugging code into the program temporarily. For example, you can check out a file and add some print statements or some extra, temporary checks. Then, when you've found the problem, you can just uncheckout the file with the Source Editor, discarding all the temporary hacks in one step.

We designed the project file contents very carefully to include information that the whole team could use. As long as your source files are located in the same directory (or in some subdirectory underneath it) as the project file itself, you can move the whole project to different places on your disk and still have everything work. Thus, if you use a code management system like Sun WorkShop™ Team-Ware™, where each member of a team makes a local copy of the project, you don't have to be careful about preserving the exact same path names on every team member's machine.

You can use file management facilities (like Windows Explorer, for example) to copy the files around to your team. As long as you don't forget any important files, the project file contains the information needed to preserve the relationships between different files. Most important, you can move the files between Solaris and Windows machines, as we do all the time for our own development. (Some of our team members prefer using a PC for their day-to-day work, and others prefer Sun workstations. Either way, we can share our projects.)

Java WorkShop provides through its publishing mechanisms ways of copying projects from place to place that are probably more reliable than using the system's file manager or batch scripts. You can not only specify the Java source files for a project, but you can add any number of supporting data files into the project definition. This sort of information isn't necessary for normal building or testing of your code, but when you give someone else a copy of the project, it can be vital. This is where portfolios become interesting.

Organizing Projects by Means of Portfolios

A *portfolio* is just a bag of projects. The projects in a portfolio can be located anywhere, not just under the same directory as the portfolio. As with projects, if all the projects in a portfolio are located in the same directory or in a subdirectory underneath the portfolio file's directory, you gain some advantages.

Although there are advantages to putting all the files of a project under the same directory on your disk, there may be times when that isn't possible and we do allow distributed files. However, sharing the project with others is much easier if you keep things well organized.

So what do you gain from keeping things together? You can use the Java Work-Shop to copy whole projects around to your team. In one operation you can copy all the files of a project from one place to another without having to remember which files to copy or without having to maintain two copies of the list of files. See "Moving Projects Between Portfolios" on page 42 for the mechanics of how to do this. Once you set up this organization, you can use portfolios in all your sharing situations.

For a team, you can create an integration portfolio on some network drive to which you all have access. Then, team members import that portfolio into their Java WorkShop. Team members can then copy projects to or from the integration area as they do their work. We didn't provide anything special in Java WorkShop to avoid collisions in that integration area, so using your version control system on the portfolio or project files themselves is probably the best way to handle the situation. For example, to modify a project on the integration portfolio, first check out the project file there, then copy it into your local space for actual work. That way, no one else can touch the project until you check the project file back in.

Using Portfolios for Web Offerings

If you work in a large corporation that has an intranet, you aren't limited to having direct access to the file servers holding a project using Netware or Solaris NFS®. All you need is access to a Web site on your intranet, because you can browse the net, using Java WorkShop to locate the portfolio you want to access. Any time the Java WorkShop browser follows a link that has a URL that names a portfolio, the portfolio can be loaded directly into the Portfolio Manager, from which you can copy projects.

One point about copying projects that may not be immediately obvious: Java Workshop offers the option to copy the source files for a project whenever you copy the project. When working within a development team, you will, of course, answer yes. But when you want to provide interesting applets to your company at large, or even more importantly, when you want to expose code to the Internet, you may not want to share the source code.

Unless you don't mind the entire Internet seeing your work in progress, you will probably want to use a staging area. In a "staging" model, your projects are in your development area (probably in your personal portfolio). Then, you create another portfolio in your Web site area. When you are ready to publish something, you copy the project to the Web site, at which time you decide whether to exclude source files in that copy. That way, the Web site includes only the source files you do want to share with the world, or enterprise, at large.

In a big company with significant security concerns about putting things on the Web, there may be another layer between you and the actual Web site. In the "layer" or "firewall" model, there is a staging area, not visible to the Web, that the Webmaster periodically pushes out to the Web. You place your portfolio in the staging area and copy your published code to this portfolio. Your Webmaster can then copy the files to the real Web site without needing to know that some of the files are Java WorkShop files.

The beauty of storing data the way we did is that any of these configurations are supported with just a few simple operations.

Doing Business

The only thing we didn't put in this release was a charge meter on the portfolio. The comment is offered purely in jest, but it does suggest an additional use for publishing things in portfolios. If and when commerce on the Net becomes standardized, we may well provide support for the complications of charging money for stuff you publish, but for now you'll have to devise your own way of doing business.

PART TWO

A Working Tour of Java WorkShop

CHAPTER

2

- Java WorkShop Tools

- Java WorkShop Browser

- Browser Preferences

- Java WorkShop Files and Directories

- Printing

Java
WorkShop
Basics

J ava WorkShop has been designed as an Internet development tool. Although there are now alternatives to developing Java programs from the command line with the Java Development Kit (JDK), Java WorkShop is unique in that it is a fully integrated, Web-based, Java development and deployment environment written in Java. Java WorkShop is also the first Java development environment that was not recast from an existing C++ environment. One of the advantages from developing the WorkShop with Java in an Internet development environment (the WorkShop itself) is that enhancements and extensions can be developed and deployed more quickly than with traditional tools. You'll experience this advantage with your applications, too.

A brief tour of some of the basic tools and features of Java WorkShop should give you an idea of what all this means to you as you develop your Java programs.

Java WorkShop Tools

Java WorkShop uses a Web browser model. Each tool in the development environment is an HTML file that contains a Java applet. The browser model means that you can move around in the environment just as you do in any browser. Every time you click an icon representing one of the tools, Java WorkShop loads an HTML file for that tool into the Browser. The tools themselves are Java applets. This might give you some idea of the kinds of applications you can create by using Java and Java WorkShop. Java WorkShop is itself an example of what it can create. It's a tool for developing on and for the Web, and it is built using Web technology.

The integrated tools of Java WorkShop, in the order they appear on the Browser tool bar (see Figure 2–1) are Portfolio Manager, Project Manager, Source Editor, Build Manager, Visual Java, Source Browser, Debugger, Project Tester, and Help. All of the tools listed here are described throughout this part of the book.

Figure 2–1 Java WorkShop Tool Bar

- **Portfolio Manager** — The tool for creating, organizing, and operating on projects. A project file holds and keeps track of the information and the various files needed to build, browse, run, and debug a Java project. Projects are grouped together into portfolios. Projects can be applets, standalone programs, images, remote applets, and Java packages. Portfolio Manager is not only useful for keeping projects organized, but it also supports deployment of applets on an internal and or external Web.

- **Project Manager** — The tool for creating, importing, and managing projects. Project manager also supports editing the settings for compiling, debugging, publishing, and running projects. These settings define the individual characteristics of the project, such as how it appears on a Web page or how it is to be compiled.

- **Source Editor** — A point-and-click source code editor. The Source Editor is a general-purpose editor, and a source display used by various Java WorkShop tools. As you would expect, it's integrated with other tools, so, for example, you can move from compilation errors displayed in Build Manager directly to the source code where the error occurs.

  Source Editor also provides controls for the most often used debugging functions, such as setting a breakpoint and single-stepping through source code.

- **Build Manager** — The tool for making and compiling projects. Build Manager invokes the `javac` compiler and runs that tool within a graphical interface. It also provides an interface for managing files and settings for builds. Because source files are organized into projects, Build Manager supports compiling all project files or just the parts of the project modified since the last build. If your project contains errors, the Build Manager reports the errors and provides links to your source code.

- **Visual Java** — Java WorkShop's graphical user interface (GUI) builder. Visual Java is a visual programming tool that provides both an interactive interface and an API for working with the Java Abstract Windowing Toolkit (AWT). The classes in the AWT package define graphics, components, and layouts. With Visual Java, you can click on visual counterparts to these GUI elements on a palette and place them on a layout grid. You can change their attributes with an Attribute Editor. The Attribute Editor also provides support for adding operations to GUI components. Operations provide a way to generate code for common actions and events interactively. You can write application-specific event handling code using the same interactive interface, and Java WorkShop will insert it in your source files. Once you have laid out the GUI, Visual Java generates the Java code for it.

  Visual Java Runtime Classes: Java WorkShop includes Visual Java runtime classes that you can reproduce for distribution with your applications. Visual Java runtime classes enable you to run the applets you create using Visual Java outside of the Java WorkShop environment.

- **Source Browser** — The tool for browsing classes, methods, and API (Application Programming Interface) documentation for the source files that make up a project. Source Browser also lets you search for strings and follow links to the first occurrence of the string in the source code.

- **Debugger** — The tool for locating and correcting bugs in your code. From the Debugger, you can start, run, single-step, and stop a program. Java Work-Shop's Debugger includes the ability to debug multiple threads. You can also set breakpoints, evaluate variables, catch and ignore exceptions, and examine the packages and classes in your program. The Debugger appears as a six-tabbed window within the Java WorkShop Browser. There's a tab for threads and stack frames, variables, breakpoints, exceptions, classes, and messages (where you can see messages from the Debugger).

- **Project Tester** — The tool for running applets or programs. Project Tester creates an HTML file for the project and runs your applet in a browser. If your project is a standalone program, the Project Tester runs it outside the Web browser. If your project is an image, the image is displayed in the Web browser.

- **Online Help, Documentation, and Tutorials** — Covers tasks and tools and is displayed in a separate browser window.

  Help: Available from the Help control (the question mark) on the Java Work-Shop tool bar, from within tools (use the F1 key or click the Help button in the tool's window), and from the Java WorkShop menu. Context-sensitive help is available in most windows and dialog boxes. The Help button within a window summons help on that part of Java WorkShop. From the help menu, you can open Workshop Task Help for an index, table of contents, and links to help on tasks. Other useful commands in the Help menu are:

- WorkShop Web Browser — Elements of the Java Workshop Browser user interface.

- Release Notes — The most recent information about the current release.

- Send Comments — A direct line of communication to the Java WorkShop product team.

- Java API Documentation (1.0) — Links to the Java standard API.

- Java JDK Website — A link to the Java Developer's Kit web page, from JavaSoft.

Online documentation: Includes an active table of contents created with Java applets. When you click on a book icon, the "book" opens to reveal another level of contents.

Java WorkShop Help Table of Contents (doc:/lib/html/help/toc.html) is a good page to bookmark. From here you can easily see and use the whole structure of Java WorkShop online assistance.

Tutorials: Java WorkShop help includes nine tutorials designed to help you become familiar with the environment. The tutorials are: Introducing the Java WorkShop, Creating a Project, Editing Project Attributes, Fixing Errors in Source Code, Browsing a Project, Debugging a Project, Publishing a Project, Customizing a Run Page, and Creating a GUI.

Java WorkShop Browser

The Browser is the center of Java WorkShop. Each tool appears in the Browser window, and other windows and dialog boxes that support development activities are launched from the Browser as Java applets.

Within the Java WorkShop Browser window, multifaceted tools are designed as tabbed "pages," so that you can easily move from one kind of operation or one element, such as a project, to another. Building the tools around a browser model provides a number of benefits, including giving programmers a familiar paradigm, providing linked navigation between tools and files, developing programs in the environment where users will run them, and easily deploying them to the world or to another developer anywhere on an internal web or the World Wide Web.

Figure 2–2 shows the tabbed pages in the Java WorkShop Project Manager. There is a tab for each phase of project development, as well as a tab for adding a description and an icon for how the project appears in Portfolio Manager.

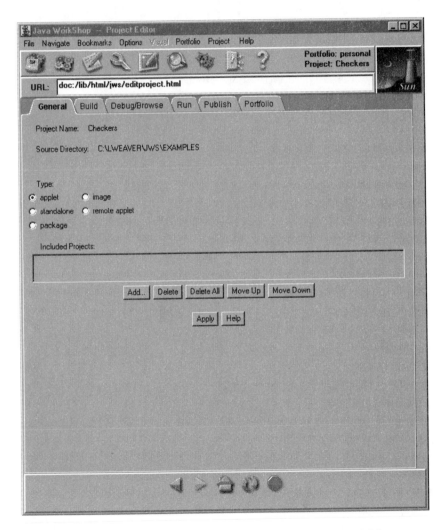

Figure 2–2 Tabbed Pages in Java WorkShop's Project Manager

You have probably used one or more Web browsers before, so Java WorkShop will look familiar in many respects. This section shows you what areas you should notice and describes those parts of Java WorkShop that may be less familiar.

The Tool and Menu Bars

Java WorkShop's tool bar is the primary launch point for tools. To give you alternatives, there are also commands on the Browser menu bar that launch some tools. Half of the menu bar is devoted to general Browser activities—the menus and commands that control the Browser—and the other half contains commands for handling projects and portfolios in Java WorkShop, including running projects. The tool bar is a series of icon-based controls for quickly moving from tool to tool from anywhere in Java WorkShop. The tool bar also displays the current portfolio and project. Figure 2–1 on page 20 shows the tool bar.

As you pass the cursor over the icons in the tool bar, Java WorkShop displays the tool's name in the Browser footer. The Browser footer is the space at the bottom of the Browser to the left of the navigation icons. Watch this space for messages, too. This capability exists throughout Java WorkShop. As long as an icon on a tool bar or a palette is *active* (that means available), you can read a description of it in the Browser footer. When icons or menus appear fuzzy, or what used to be called "grayed out" when monochrome monitors were the rule, that tool or command is not available.

Browser Navigation Icons

Navigation icons in the Browser footer (Figure 2–3) provide an alternative to the commands in the Navigation menu. They provide the usual navigational choices: Back, Forward, Home, Reload, and Stop. Home is the splash page you see when you first open Java WorkShop. You can make a different page the Home page by using the Options menu. Because each tool in Java WorkShop operates in its own Browser page, the navigation icons offer a useful way to move among the tools you have been using. For example, you might build a project in Build Manager and then move to the Debugger. After some work in the Debugger, you want to rebuild the project or a file. Clicking the Back icon will return the Debugger.

Figure 2–3 Browser Footer with Navigation Icons

Browser Header and URL Bar

Two last items that will help orient you in the Java WorkShop Browser environment are the header and the URL display. Java WorkShop Browser displays the name of the tool that you are using in the title bar, or Browser header. Like other browsers, it displays the current page in the URL bar. You can specify a different URL and press Return to go elsewhere. Figure 2–4 shows the Browser header.

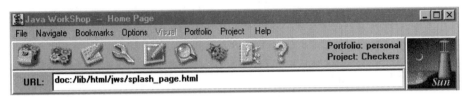

Figure 2–4 Java WorkShop Browser Header and URL Bar

Browser Preferences

You can change the default font for text displayed in the Browser. You can also specify a Home page that Java WorkShop uses when you start it. Both of these options and two others—network paths and proxies, and version control—are available from the Options menu. To start Java WorkShop with a preferred tool, use the Path command and then copy and paste the tool's URL into the URL field. Whenever you start Java WorkShop or click on the Home footer button, that tool is loaded. To change to one of four font sizes, use the Font command.

Java WorkShop Messages

In addition to displaying status messages and icon names in the Browser footer, Java WorkShop opens message dialog boxes for WorkShop confirmations and warnings. There's also a Console Output Window to display user messages from running applets, and error messages from applets and Java WorkShop. The console window displays text that would otherwise be sent to standard output (the destination to which your system usually sends text).

A visual status message is provided by the lighthouse in the upper-right corner of the Java WorkShop Browser. Naturally, it is an applet. When Java WorkShop is performing a task, such as loading a URL, the light on the lighthouse turns. It's a visual version of the old and familiar text-based "Working. . .working" messages.

Java WorkShop Files and Directories

Source files in Java WorkShop are handled by the Project Manager, freeing you to specify project names instead of individual file names when you want to build, run, or debug a program. (You still have the option to build files individually if you want.) The context of a current project is maintained until you switch projects.

Projects are grouped into portfolios, so it's useful to think of a portfolio as a sort of super project. Portfolio file names take the form *portfolioname.psf*, and project names take the form *projectname.prj*. You won't operate on the `.psf` and `.prj` files directly. Projects and portfolios just provide a context for your work in Java WorkShop and give you the opportunity to operate at a higher level than specific files. Although you are not required to organize files and directories in any particular way, there are some recommendations. You'll find those in "Putting Projects and Portfolios to Work" (Chapter 4).

Java WorkShop source file naming conventions are based on the Java programming language conventions. (For example, Java source files and class files must have the same name.) Java WorkShop itself is case sensitive, so if you use the examples shipped with Java WorkShop or from the *Inside Java WorkShop* CD-ROM, enter the names of projects, portfolios, and `.java` and `.class` files just as they are. You'll notice that if you do the Java WorkShop online tutorial exercise "Creating a Project," you are asked to enter the project name *Blink* with the capital "B."

Printing

Java WorkShop does not currently support printing from the Browser, so you'll have to use your system's print utilities to print source listings. You can print online help pages in a browser that supports printing.

To print online help:

1. Open a different browser (such as Netscape Navigator).

2. Determine the URL of a help page by loading the help page you want in the Java WorkShop Browser. Note the URL of the page.

    URLs for online help start with the `doc:` protocol, followed by the path name of the help page. This path is relative to the name of the directory where you installed Java WorkShop. You'll need to include this path name in the URL.

3. Concatenate this information—installation directory, doc path name— with the `file:` protocol.

Let's say that you installed Java WorkShop in the default directory that the installation program uses for Windows 95 or Windows NT (`c:\Java-WorkShop`) and you want to print the tutorial page on using the Class Browser to view the methods in a project: (`doc:/lib/html/help/start/method.html`).

The URL you would supply to your browser of choice would be:

`file:/Java-WorkShop/lib/html/help/start/method.html`

4. Load the help page in the alternate browser and print it.

Compatible Products

Java WorkShop is compatible with Sun Visual WorkShop for C++, Java applets based on JDK 1.0 or later, and these version control systems:

*   Sun WorkShop TeamWare

*   SCCS

*   RCS

*   PVCS

Summary

In this first stop on the Java WorkShop tour, you spent some time:

*   Seeing the tools that make up Java WorkShop

*   Learning about Visual Java runtime classes

*   Learning how to get help on Java WorkShop tools and tasks

*   Finding out about Java WorkShop tutorials

*   Exploring the Java WorkShop browser environment

*   Discovering where to look for messages

*   Learning about Java WorkShop files and directories

*   Discovering how to print help and tutorials

CHAPTER

3

- What Is a Java WorkShop Project?
- Types of Projects
- Projects Within Projects
- Organizing Projects
- What Is a Portfolio?
- Doing More with Projects and Portfolios

Projects and Portfolios

Java WorkShop includes two tools for managing the files you create and use when building Java applications and World Wide Web pages: the Project Manager and the Portfolio Manager. Together they provide a level of organization that helps you understand and control development efforts, whether you are working alone or as part of a team. This chapter defines Java WorkShop projects and portfolios and describes what you can do with them. Its companion chapter, "Putting Projects and Portfolios to Work," uses examples to start you working with projects and portfolios.

What Is a Java WorkShop Project?

A file is the basic building block in a Java program. In Java WorkShop, the *project* is the basic building block. Using projects enables you to organize the files required to produce an applet, a standalone program, a Java Package, an HTML image, or a remote applet. A project also includes information that defines the project's individual characteristics, such as the project's name and main class file.

Organizing files in projects enables you to operate on a set of related files as a whole. For example, an applet would require at least these files: the Java source code (.java), the compiled class file (.class), a mapping file used by Java WorkShop (.map), and the HTML file (.html) to hold the applet. Your project might contain several applets, each of which has several files associated with it. You can compile this project as a whole, including all of the Java source files in it.

For example, the *Checkers* project that comes with Java WorkShop contains the files illustrated in Figure 3–1.

Project File	`Checkers.prj`
Java WorkShop Mapping File (created by Project Manager)	`Checkers.map`
Program Source File (created in Source Editor)	`CheckersGame.java`
Compiled File (from Build Manager)	`CheckersGame.class`
Image Files	`blackChecker.gif`
	`blackCheckerKing.gif`
	`redChecker.gif`
	`redCheckerKing.gif`
Page for Running Checkers Applet (automatically generated)	`Checkers.tmp.html`

Figure 3–1 Java WorkShop Project Files: An Example

A project establishes a context for your work with all of the tools in Java Work-Shop. You supply a project name where required in different tools, so that you don't have to locate and specify individual file names. Also, Java WorkShop maintains a current project, and that context is changed only when you choose a different project.

When you create an applet, Java WorkShop automatically creates a project file and gives it the file type `.prj`. You can specify a name for it. Remember that you don't edit project files directly, but handle them using Project Manager.

You also might want to specify how you want a project to be displayed on an HTML page, or which compiler options to use to build the project. You set these and other attributes for the whole project in Java WorkShop's Project Manager.

How Projects Are Created

If you have created an applet by using the Java Development Kit (JDK), you probably opened a text editor and began typing in lines of Java code. With Java Work-Shop, you write applets or applications in the context of a project. In fact, if you want to create an applet, you open the Project menu and choose the command for creating an applet (**Create ⟹ Applet**). You automatically start your work at a higher level, the project level. In this case, you would be working on an applet project.

Types of Projects

There is a project type for anything you might want to create with Java Work-Shop. Java WorkShop Project types are summarized in Table 3-1.

Table 3-1 Types of Projects

Types of Projects	Description
Applet	A program written in Java that runs within a Java-enabled Web browser, such as HotJava.
Standalone Program	A program written in the Java language that runs outside a Web browser, usually from a command line.
Java Package	A group of classes declared with the same package name.
Image	An HTML image, usually a .gif or a .jpeg file, to be used in the HTML tag <img>.
Remote Applet	An applet that resides elsewhere on the Internet.

Projects Within Projects

Projects can be included inside other projects. This is a handy way of capturing dependencies between files without makefiles. Let's say that you have written your own packages and standalone programs that work with the packages. You can treat the package project and the program project as a unit by including one within the other. Java WorkShop calls this arrangement a *nested project*.

Java WorkShop itself is an application made with nested projects. The super project is a standalone application that contains the main Java WorkShop package (sun.jws), and the remaining packages are subprojects within it. Nested projects are good organizing tools for large applications.

Including C and C++ Source Files in Projects

Java allows you to declare methods to be native, meaning that they are implemented by a language other than Java. There may be some areas of native functionality not yet covered by the Java APIs for which you need to use C or C++ code. (Java APIs are constantly being extended, so check the URLs listed in Chapter 13, "Watching Java Developments" for current API information.) You can include C or C++ files in a Java WorkShop project. You'll be able to use Project Tester on applications with native code, but you'll have to compile the C and/or C++ files outside of Java WorkShop.

Operations on Projects

In addition to creating or selecting projects, Java WorkShop supports the following operations on projects:

Import   For adding an existing project to a portfolio. You must have write permission for the portfolio. You can import a project by copying all of its files into the portfolio or by creating just a reference to the project.

Edit   For editing project attributes such as options for compiling, debugging, browsing, publishing, and running the project.

Remove   For eliminating a project from a portfolio. Java WorkShop just removes the project from the portfolio; it doesn't delete the project file from the file system. You can import it again later if you change your mind.

Of course, you can't remove a project from read-only portfolios.

Copy   For putting a copy of a project on the Java WorkShop clipboard. Once on the clipboard, a project is available for pasting.

Paste   For pasting the project into another portfolio or into the Source Editor.

Organizing Projects

When you create an applet and, by default, a project, Java WorkShop places your project within a portfolio. By default, it puts new projects into the current portfolio. When you start using Java WorkShop, the provided portfolio named *personal* is the default current portfolio. Portfolios represent another, higher level for organizing your work. A portfolio is a "super project" because it can hold one or more projects of one or more types.

You can use the *personal* portfolio that comes with Java WorkShop as a holder for your projects; then, when you want to structure them, use copy and paste to move them into different portfolios or nest them in projects.

What Is a Portfolio?

A portfolio is a collection of projects. Portfolios are useful tools for organizing projects for a development team and for publishing projects. When you create a new project, it is automatically added to the current portfolio. By default, when you first use Java WorkShop, it opens a portfolio named *personal* as the current portfolio. Whenever you exit from Java WorkShop and reopen it, it loads the project you were working on last.

Personal is one of three portfolios that come with Java WorkShop. By the way, the *personal* portfolio also includes a sample project called *Checkers* for you to build, run, and debug.

The other two portfolios that come with Java WorkShop are read-only:

- *jdk* —Java Developer's Kit portfolio. This portfolio contains sample applets from the Java Developer's Kit (JDK).

- *awt* —Abstract Windowing Toolkit (AWT) portfolio. This portfolio contains some test applets from the JDK that use the AWT.

Operations on Portfolios

There is a lot more that you can do with portfolios. Using the Portfolio menu on the Java WorkShop tool bar, you can perform the following operations:

- Create a portfolio.

- Make your portfolio available to other WorkShop users on the Internet.

- Import a portfolio from your local file system or the Internet.

- Change the current portfolio.

- Remove a portfolio from Java WorkShop.

Doing More with Projects and Portfolios

"Putting Projects and Portfolios to Work" on page 35 gives you some hands-on experience with Java WorkShop projects and portfolios.

Summary

By now you should understand the basic building blocks for Java WorkShop development, including:

- Types and contents of projects

- Portfolios as collections of projects

- How to organize projects

- Operations you can perform on portfolios

CHAPTER
4

Putting Projects and Portfolios to Work

People approach program development in different ways. If you prefer to think of your work in terms of how you are going to organize the effort, you could start by creating a portfolio and projects. Or you might prefer to start writing an applet or its graphical user interface (GUI), using the Source Editor or Visual Java. Java WorkShop supports either approach but enforces the notion of a project by starting a project file any time you choose to create an applet, standalone program, or another file supported by Java WorkShop.

For team efforts, Java WorkShop supports version control from within the Source Editor. We'll talk about it in the next chapter because it happens at the file level; it's not something you set at the project or portfolio level.

Getting Started with Java WorkShop

If you have existing Java applets or standalone programs and you want to work on them in Java WorkShop, you should start by creating a portfolio and project and then adding your existing source files to it. In fact, these exercises assume you probably have written a Java applet already. If not, you'll find examples on the companion CD-ROM or at the Web site for *Inside Java WorkShop*. And, as you are probably well aware, there are lots of applets available for free on the World Wide Web. Chapter 13 lists some of the URLs for applets, or you can load the HTML version of that chapter into a browser. It's available on the CD-ROM in `resource.html`.

When you start work on a new applet, you'll have a choice of using Visual Java or the Source Editor. If you work first on the graphical user interface (GUI) for your applet and would like to use the GUI builder, select Visual Java, described in Chapter 7. To begin writing source code, select Source Editor, described in Chapter 5. If you want to jump ahead and start creating source files, see those chapters.

This part of the tour of Java WorkShop shows you how to create a project to hold existing source files. It also uses projects that come with Java WorkShop to show you how to manage projects.

Java WorkShop Files and Directories

When you install Java WorkShop, it creates directories for the WorkShop itself and the Java Development Kit (JDK) that is shipped with it. Java WorkShop comes with a slightly enhanced version of JDK 1.0.2. You can use source files created with the regular version of JDK 1.0.2 in the WorkShop. Wherever you choose to install Java WorkShop, it will create two subdirectories—JWS and JDK.

Unless you specify otherwise, the Windows setup program for Java WorkShop installs the product and related files on C:\Java-Workshop. Solaris users unzip a compressed file and use the tar command to move the Java WorkShop files to a directory they specify. If you don't change the default installation directory or specify a different directory when you create portfolios and projects, Java WorkShop stores projects and portfolios in the default installation directory.

Projects keep track of source files as well as the files that Java WorkShop creates or generates. There are several types of files in the latter category that you should not modify directly: .map, .prj, .psf, jws.properties, and the Main, Ops, and Root files generated by the Visual Java GUI builder. Files generated by Visual Java either begin with a line that tells you not to modify the file or a line stating that the file is a template that can be edited. Project and portfolio files can be kept anywhere, but it will help to organize your work if you keep portfolios in a single directory, and create a directory for each project. The project files, both source and others, could be kept in the project directory.

Class Paths

Java WorkShop, when started, ignores the CLASSPATH environment variable. If you want to designate a directory of classes when you start Java WorkShop from the command line, you can use:

```
jws -classpath <your_class_directory>
```

For multiple directories, separate the directory names by colons. Java WorkShop adds the directories specified in the CLASSPATH when it starts running.

The JDK that ships with Java WorkShop is a version of JDK 1.0.2 enhanced to work with Java WorkShop. Ignoring the CLASSPATH variable prevents Java WorkShop from using any other version of JDK that you might have installed on your system. Java WorkShop sets up a class path in a private process.

Creating a Portfolio

To build a program starting at the portfolio level, you can choose an existing portfolio and add to it, or you can create a new one. Java WorkShop provides one portfolio with write access (*personal*) and two read-only portfolios (*jdk* and *awt*). So you will probably want to create some of your own.

In this chapter, you will create a portfolio to hold the projects that you will make or use in this book and then import, cut, paste, remove, and create some projects.

For the rest of this book, expect menu-command sequences to appear like this **Portfolio** ⟶ **Choose** ⟶ **personal**. The first item is the main menu entry, followed by the command from that menu, and finally the submenu for that command.

To create a portfolio:

1. Choose **Portfolio** ⟶ **Create**.

    Java WorkShop opens a dialog box with a field for the portfolio name.

    Enter a name for portfolio to use with the examples in this book, but don't change the .psf file extension. Java WorkShop uses that for all portfolio files. Call yours *insidejws*.

    You can specify a directory path name or just a portfolio name. To give other Java WorkShop users on the Internet access to your portfolio, you could enter a path name that is accessible by your HTTP server.

2. Click the Create button.

Java WorkShop creates the portfolio file in the directory you specified. If you do not specify a path name, Java WorkShop creates the portfolio in the default directory created when you installed Java WorkShop. The new portfolio becomes the current portfolio. You should see its name displayed in the tool bar. Java Work-Shop also adds the name of the portfolio you just created to the Choose and Remove submenus in the Portfolio menu.

Creating an Applet Project

For now, you're going to create a new applet project. You can use this first project to bring existing sources into Java WorkShop.

As you'll soon see, Java WorkShop doesn't require you to keep source files with project files. As long as the source files are in a directory that is relative to the project file's directory, you can even move both around in your file system. When you need to build, run, or debug, you'll just specify a project name, and Java WorkShop will find the files that are in that project. Java WorkShop online help recommends that you keep a project in its own directory. This makes a lot of sense, especially when you have many different source files in a project.

By default, Java WorkShop uses the .jws directory created when you run Java WorkShop the first time. To keep the organization of projects and portfolios and source files clear, the examples on the CD-ROM do follow the recommendation by having a separate directory for every project.

Note: A nice feature of Java WorkShop is that you can create directories for your projects as you go. When you create projects, specify a directory names in the Source Directory field and Java WorkShop will create the directory.

To create an applet project:

1. Select a portfolio.

    If you created a portfolio for the exercise in "Creating a Portfolio", your current portfolio is *insidejws*. If it's not your current portfolio, use **Portfolio ⟶Choose ⟶ insidejws** to make it the current portfolio.

2. Choose **Project ⟶Create ⟶ Applet**.

    The Java WorkShop Create Project window opens with tabbed pages for each type of project. The Applet tab is on top. Java WorkShop has supplied a default project name, *untitled1*.

3. Give the project a name by placing the cursor in the Project Name field and erasing the default name. Highlight it and type over it, or backspace to delete character by character. For ease of following along in the examples, call your project *Chapter4*.

Once you have named a project in Java WorkShop, it won't be easy to change it, so choose project names you can live with. For now, Java WorkShop doesn't support renaming projects. Later on, we'll look at ways to work around this.

The Create Project window is shown in Figure 4–1. If you change your mind about what you want to create, or if you'd like to create several different projects in one sitting, just click another one of the Create Project tabs to bring it to the front.'

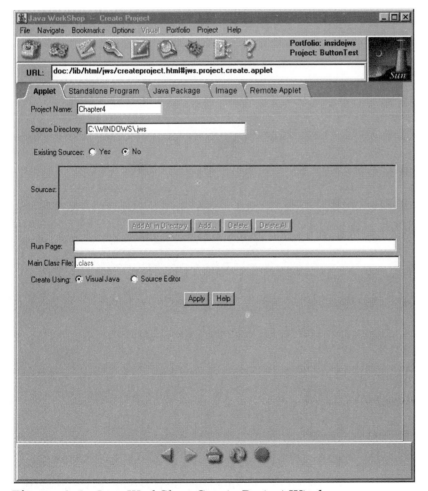

Figure 4–1 Java WorkShop Create Project Window

4. Check the directory named in the Source Directory field to be sure you are working in the directory you want and click the Yes radio button to indicate that you want to use existing sources. (If you don't add source files when you click Yes, Java WorkShop won't create a project.)

5. Click Apply.

6. Notice the "Apply succeeded" message that appears in the Browser footer. The footer displays useful status messages as you work, so it's a good idea to check this area when you perform operations in Java WorkShop.

   Be sure to click the Apply button when you have made settings in a window, dialog, or tabbed page. If you move to another tool without clicking Apply, your settings will be lost.

That's it. You now have a project file that contains the location of your source files. You can use your project file to build, run, and debug your applet in Java Work-Shop. Here are the names of your Java WorkShop creations so far:

- **Portfolio:** *insidejws* (stored as `insidejws.psf`)
- **Project:** *Chapter4* (stored as `Chapter4.prj`)

Your project directory should also contain the mapping file used by Java Work-Shop (`Chapter4.map`).

If you want to include images in an applet project, you have to follow an additional step. Java WorkShop doesn't import image files. You specify their location in an applet parameter. "Using the Run Tab to Include Applet Images" on page 49 disrobes how.

Creating a Package Project

A package is a group of classes declared with the same package name. You can make a project that contains your package and use Java WorkShop to build and browse it. Of course, you can also include packages within other projects. The steps for creating a package project are basically the same as for creating an applet or standalone project:

1. Select a portfolio.

2. Choose **Project ⇒Create ⇒Java Package**.

3. Enter a name for the project in the Project Name field.

4. Type the name of the package in the Package Name field.

5. Type the root directory of the class hierarchy in the Root Directory field.

   This field is equivalent to the -d option to the `javac` command.[1]

6. Enter a directory name for the project in the Source Directory field.

The directory does not have to exist; Java WorkShop will create it.

7. Click yes or no to Existing source files for the package.

8. Click Apply.

Java WorkShop creates a package project that you can build and browse or nest within another project.

Creating a Nested Project

To nest one or more projects inside another project:

1. Make current the project that you want to be the "super project."

2. Choose **Project** ➠ **Edit**.

3. In the General tab, go to the Included Projects list and use the Add button to add each "subproject." There's a file chooser button (the one with the ellipsis. . .) next to this field so that you can browse directories for the projects you want to add.

    Figure 4–2 shows the General tab for a nested project.

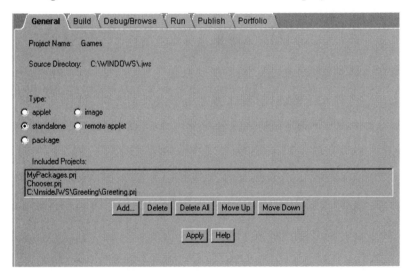

Figure 4–2 Adding Projects to a Project in the General Tab

1. The -d option specifies a directory. By default javac places .class files in the same directory as the .java source file. The -d option causes javac to treat the specified directory as the root directory of the class hierarchy and to store the .class file in that directory.

Note that the order in which projects are listed here is the order used by the Build Manager to build them. To change the build order, select a project in the list and use the Move Up and Move Down buttons.

Some good uses for nested projects are described in "Projects Within Projects" on page 31 and "Using Groups to Better Advantage" on page 167.

Populating Portfolios with Projects

There are several ways to put projects into portfolios. You can start with existing projects or make new ones:

- Copy or cut a project from one portfolio and paste it into another.

- Choose a portfolio and create a new project within it.

- Choose a portfolio and import projects into it.

Let's look at cutting, pasting, and importing projects.

Moving Projects Between Portfolios

To copy a project from one portfolio to another, open Portfolio Manager. If you completed the exercise before this one ("Creating a Portfolio"), your current portfolio is *insidejws*. We'll copy the *Checkers* project from the *personal* portfolio into the *insidejws* portfolio.

Before we start, let's take a look at the Paste Project dialog box (Figure 4–3) and the accompanying description,Table 4-1, which lists the options that appear in both the Paste Project and Import Project dialog boxes.

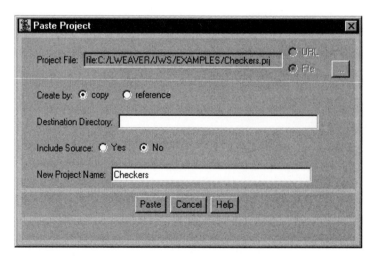

Figure 4–3 The Paste Project Dialog

Table 4-1   Paste and Import Dialog Box Fields and Buttons

Field/Button	Description
Project File	The path name of the project file you want to paste or import, including the extension `.prj`.
URL and File Buttons	Choose a project in a file system or one on the World Wide Web.
Browse Files Button	If you choose File, the Browse button opens a list dialog box where you can move around in the file system to find the directory and project file you want.
Create by	Choose between the copy and reference radio buttons. Copy copies the files into a destination directory; reference just stores the project's file name and maintains a link between the portfolio and the pasted or imported project.
Destination Directory	Enter the absolute path name of the directory where you want to store the project files. For clarity, you should store the project files in their own directory. If you decide to paste or import by reference, you won't have to specify a destination directory.
Include Source	Use the Yes or No radio buttons to specify whether or not to copy the `.java` source files into the destination directory. Naturally, if you are pasting or importing by reference, you won't have a choice to copy the source files.
New Project Name	The name you want the project to have in the portfolio where you have pasted or imported it. It can be the same name as the original.
Paste/Import	Paste (in Paste Project dialog) or Import (in the Import Project dialog) puts the project into the current portfolio and makes it available to the commands in the Project menu.
Cancel	Closes the dialog box without applying any of the options you specified. The project is not pasted or imported.
Help	Displays task help for the dialog box.

Now, let's begin. We'll add comments as we go.

1.   Choose **Portfolio** ➠ **Choose** ➠ **personal**.

     You could have performed those steps in reverse order, too. That is, you could go to Portfolio Manager first and then choose a current portfolio.

When you are in Portfolio Manager, you'll see the project icon for *Checkers* displayed.

2.   Click on the *Checkers* project icon. A highlight square around the icon indicates that it is selected.

You can write descriptive comments for projects and make them available to others who might be browsing through a portfolio to see what projects are in it. Notice that if you move the cursor over the *Checkers* project icon, the Browser footer displays a brief description of the project, "The game of checkers implemented in Java."

Adding such comments to your projects is something you can do later in this chapter when you edit project attributes.

3.   Choose **Project** ➠ **Copy** or click on the Copy icon in the Portfolio Manager toolbar.

Now that you have the *Checkers* project on the Java WorkShop clipboard, you could also copy it into the Source Editor as well as another portfolio. For now, you're going to copy it into *insidejws*.

4.   Choose **Portfolio** ➠ **Choose** ➠ **insidejws**.

5.   When you have Portfolio Manager open to *insidejws*, choose **Project** ➠ **Paste** or use the Paste icon.

Java WorkShop opens the Project Paste dialog box. Figure 4–3 on page 42 shows the Paste Project dialog.

Java WorkShop allows you to select various paste options besides the destination directory. For example, you'll have a choice between pasting the project into the portfolio by copy or reference:

If you click the copy button, Java WorkShop stores copies of the project files (`.prj` file, source files, and data files) in the destination directory. When you copy directly, you have the option to also include source files.

If you click reference, Java WorkShop stores only the project file name in the portfolio and maintains a link between the project in the portfolio and the project file.

6.   Let's save disk space. Click reference.

7.   Click the Paste button.

Checkers is pasted into the new portfolio, *insidejws*. You can remove a copied project from its original portfolio if you want a single copy, or develop it along different lines and use the two portfolios to distinguish the two projects. The copy and paste operation is a way to rename a project or reuse and change it.

If you are working on a large programming effort or with a team, you'll be better able to keep track of things if you organize projects into portfolios. By choosing the "Paste by reference" option for pasting the project, you keep the files for the project in one place, but allow different portfolios to include them.

The fields and buttons in the Paste Project are the same ones you will encounter when you import a project (described next). Table 4-1 on page 43 offers a handy reference for the settings in both dialogs.

Importing Projects

Let's start with importing a local project and then move on to importing a remote project. *Local* means that the project is on your file system. *Remote* means that the project is in a file system other than your local file system.

Importing a Local Project. You can import a project even if it is not contained in another portfolio. You can also import a project that you have removed from Java WorkShop if you haven't deleted the project file from your file system. Just as in the cut and paste method for moving a project, you can import the project by reference or by actually copying it into a directory.

Let's remove a project from Java WorkShop and then import it back. To remove the project:

1. Choose the *personal* portfolio.

2. Choose **Project ⟶ Remove ⟶ Checkers**.

3. Choose the portfolio into which you want the project to go.

    At this point you could change portfolios and import (rescue) the project into that portfolio, or import it back into the current portfolio (*personal*).

To import the project:

1. Choose **Project ⟶ Import ⟶ Checkers**.

2. Java WorkShop opens the Import Project dialog box. The dialog should look familiar if you tried pasting a project into a portfolio.

3. In the Project File field, enter the absolute path name of the *Checkers* project file. Remember that if you removed the project, the project file should still be available on the file system, even if it's not visible to Java WorkShop.

If you haven't changed the Java WorkShop default directories, *Checkers* is in an `examples` subdirectory of the directory where you installed Java Work-Shop (`\examples\checkers\Checkers.prj` for Windows users, and `/examples/checkers/Checkers.prj` for Solaris users).

4.   Choose import by reference.

(We'll try the copy option when we import a remote project.)

5.   Click the Import button.

Java WorkShop imports *Checkers* into the current portfolio and adds its name to the Project submenus.

Importing a Project from the Web. Here's another instance of Java WorkShop's unique status as an Internet development environment for Java. If you were working with other people linked by an internal Web or through the World Wide Web itself, you could get and deploy projects and portfolios without leaving the development environment.

You'll recall that both the Paste Project and Import Project dialog boxes give you the option to use projects from a file system or a URL. (See Table 4-1 on page 43.) If you are connected to an internal or external Web, you can try importing a remote project.

The steps for importing a project from an internal web or the World Wide Web are as easy as importing a local project. The difference is that you specify a URL instead of a path name. When Java WorkShop opens the Import Project dialog box, enter a URL. You'll probably want to copy the actual project file, instead of just creating a link (reference) to it, and include the source files. Specify a destination directory and click the Import button. The project and the source files it contains are all available for your use now.

Importing a Visual Java Project. When you import a project created in the Visual Java GUI builder, you can import just the generated GUI file, or all of the project files. To import the GUI file alone, open Visual Java and choose **Visual ⟶ Import** from the Browser menu. To import all of the project files, follow the instructions for importing a project using **Project ⟶ Import**.

Publishing Projects on the Web

When you publish a project, you simply make it available to an HTTP server so that developers or users on the Internet can copy it or run it remotely. There is no publish tool or command, because you are just using a regular Java WorkShop portfolio that happens to be visible to the HTTP server.

For example, suppose you have a portfolio named *examples* in a directory
\myname\JWS\myexamples. You created the project *Chapter4* in
\myname\JWS\myexamples. These path names are local to your file system and
only local users can access them. Now you want to go public with your work. So
you create a portfolio and call it *public* and put it in a directory that is visible to
your HTTP server— \users\myname\public_html. All you have to do is
copy the project that you want to publish, *Chapter4*, and paste it in the portfolio
you named *public*. With that, you're on the Internet, where other users have access
to your project. They can run the published project or they can copy and paste it
into their own local portfolio and work with it locally.

Users at the receiving end will have the Java WorkShop files copied into their file
system if they decide to copy and paste the *Chapter4* project. The copy and paste
operation puts the following files into the destination file system:

- The project file; in our example, Chapter4.prj

- The .class files created at build time

- An HTML file that displays the project

- A .gui file, if the project was built with a GUI created in the Java WorkShop
  GUI builder (Visual Java)

- A .map file used internally by Java WorkShop

- Any other data files (for example, .gif and .au files) that the project needs
  and that the user specified when setting up the project with the Project Manager

- The source files for the project; .java source code files are copied only if the
  original project location contains source files and the user specifies that the
  sources be copied

Now, about making a portfolio a public portfolio: it's as easy as 1, 2, 3:

1. Choose **Portfolio ⟱ Create**.

2. In the Portfolio dialog box, enter a portfolio path name that you know is
    accessible to an HTTP server. Remember that a portfolio name must end in
    the extension .psf.

3. Click the Create button.

Editing Project Attributes

Another benefit of using projects is that you can operate on all of the files necessary for a program without having to use makefiles. You might be familiar with using visual tools to set preferences for how projects are compiled. Java WorkShop supports setting preferences for building programs, too, but because it is an internet development environment, it also includes settings for running applets in a browser, as well as publishing, debugging, browsing, and more.

Here are the project attributes you can set in Java WorkShop:

- **General** — Information about the project, including name, type, and source directory.

- **Build** — Information required to compile the project.

- **Debug/Browse** — Information required to debug and browse the project source files.

- **Run** — Information required to execute the project or run it in an HTML page. The fields in this tab depend on the project type. For applet projects, the Run tab contains fields for specifying <applet> tag arguments and defining <param> tags.

- **Publish** — Information required to publish the project. When you publish a project, you copy it into a portfolio visible to an HTTP server so Java WorkShop users on the Internet can either copy the project or run it remotely.

- **Portfolio** — Information required to view the project in a portfolio.

Setting Attributes

One of the advantages of the project concept is that you can set different attributes for each project. And you can edit any project at any time by choosing **Project** ➟ **Edit** ➟ *projectname* from the Java WorkShop menu. It doesn't even have to be the current project.

You supply values for some attributes when you create the project; the Java WorkShop supplies default values for all other attributes. To view or modify these attributes, you'll use the Project Manager.

In Chapter 6 you'll set Build attributes, and in Chapter 8, you'll edit the Run attributes for a sample project. Here's a general description of how to edit the Publish attribute to set up a project for publication to other Java WorkShop users on the Web. *Publish* means to copy a project into a portfolio visible to an HTTP server so other Java WorkShop users on the Internet can either copy the project or run it remotely.

1.   Open the Project Manager by clicking the Project Manager icon in the tool
     bar or by using the **Project ⁕ Edit ⁕ Checkers** menu-command sequence.

     Java WorkShop opens the Project Editor with its six tabbed pages, one for
     each attribute area.

2.   Click on the Publish tab.

3.   In the list of files, click the names of files that you want to publish.

     You don't need to specify the `.class`, `.map`, `.gui`, or `.html` files. Java
     WorkShop publishes these automatically when you publish a project. You
     can delete a file from the list by selecting the file name and clicking the
     Delete button.

4.   Type the name of the person adding the project to the portfolio in the Sub-
     mitter's Name field.

5.   Type the email address of the person adding the project to the portfolio in
     the Submitter's E-Mail field.

6.   Type the Web page address of the person adding the project to the portfolio
     in the Submitter's URL field.

     Remember that when you change an input field in a tab, you must click the
     Apply button to enter the changes before moving to another tab or leaving
     the Project Editor.

Using the Run Tab to Include Applet Images

If your applet uses images, you must make them available to the applet. To get
this parameter from the HTML page in which the applet runs, you can use the
Run tab to specify the `img` parameter value. The `<param>` tag as it would appear
in an HTML page is:

```
<param name=img value="images/tumble">
```

Here's an example of setting this parameter interactively in the Run tab for the
TumbleItem project that you will use later in this book:

1.   Choose **Project ⁕ Edit ⁕ TumbleItem**.

2.   Click the Run tab.

3.   Enter the following in the Parameter Name and Value fields: `img` and
     `"/images/tumble"`. See Figure 4–4.

Parameters:		
img="images/tumble"	Name:	img
	Value:	"images/tumble"

Figure 4–4 Defining the Parameter for Applet Images in the Run Tab

Renaming Projects

The easiest way to give a project a new name is to copy it and give it another name when you paste it. The Paste dialog box has a field for a new name. An alternative is to import the project and give it a new name in the Import project dialog box.

Listing or Changing the Source Files in a Project

Projects keep track of source files used by your application and files used by Java WorkShop to manage projects. To see all of the files in a project directory, such as image files used by an applet, list the directory contents as you would for any directory on your system. To see the source files used by Java WorkShop for any project, make the project the current project and then look at the files listed in the Build tab of the Project Editor. You can add or remove source files from a project by using the Add and Delete buttons in this tab.

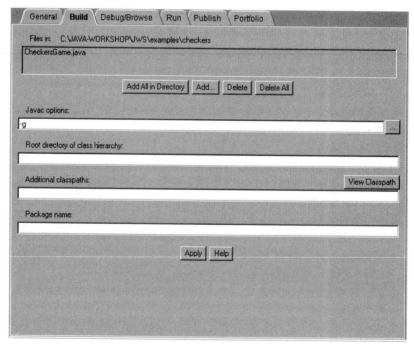

Figure 4–5 Listing Files in the Build Tab

Source files and project files must be on the same drive. To add a source file from another drive, copy the file to the drive where the project resides and then include it in the project. Projects and portfolios use relative path names. A path name that includes a drive name cannot be relative to a different drive.

Summary

In this part of the Java WorkShop tour you saw the tools and steps for:

- Creating portfolios
- Creating projects
- Getting projects into portfolios
- Moving projects between portfolios
- Importing local and remote projects
- Editing project attributes
- Renaming projects
- Listing the files in a project
- Adding or deleting files in a project

CHAPTER
5

- Starting the Source Editor

- Editing Source Code

- Basic File Operations

- Basic Text Operations

- Source Editor Extras

- Setting How the Source Editor Is Used for Tools Display

- Using Version Control

Editing Source Files

Java WorkShop's Source Editor is a basic tool for creating or editing source files written in Java or HTML. The Source Editor is easy to use and uses some familiar keyboard shortcuts for things like cut/paste and search/replace operations. The Source Editor is also the interactive display for source files when you are browsing source, tracking down compiler errors, or debugging.

About the Source Editor

The Java Workshop Source Editor supports version control, multiple editor windows, indicators for line and column position indicators, file change status, and access status (read/write). And it's integrated with the Build Manager, Source Browser, and Debugger. However, in Version 1.0, the Source Editor doesn't support searches for regular expressions or highlight Java syntax. Given the Java WorkShop team's responsiveness to user feedback asking for features like these, you can expect improvements.

There's no restriction on what editor you use to create the existing source files you might bring into Java WorkShop, so you can use another editor and then create a project that uses existing sources. You can continue work on those files in the Source Editor. In fact you'll probably want to do so when you are fixing build errors, because the Source Editor opens to the errors that appear in the Build Manager.

The Java WorkShop Source Editor:

- Is integrated with other Java WorkShop tools

- Opens multiple windows

- Allows string searches

- Enhances its utility as a team development tool with version control support

Starting the Source Editor

You can open, or move to, the Source Editor from its icon on the Tool Bar. Don't be fooled by the Edit command in the Project menu. That command takes you to the Project Editor where you can edit the project's attributes, not source files. The quickest route to the Source Editor is to click the Source Editor icon.

The Source Editor is also available as one of the tools of choice for starting to work on a new project that has no source files yet. (Visual Java is the other.) Figure 5–1 shows the radio button for starting new project source files with the Source Editor.

The Source Editor is also opened by any tool that needs to display source code. For example, when you start a debugging session, Java WorkShop opens the Source Editor. In the debugging role, the Source Editor becomes a powerful tool for setting and removing breakpoints, stepping into or over methods, resuming threads, and moving through calls. During a debugging session, Java WorkShop uses multiple editing windows so you can see the source for all of the classes used by your program. You'll see the Source Editor in this mode when you read the debugging chapters.

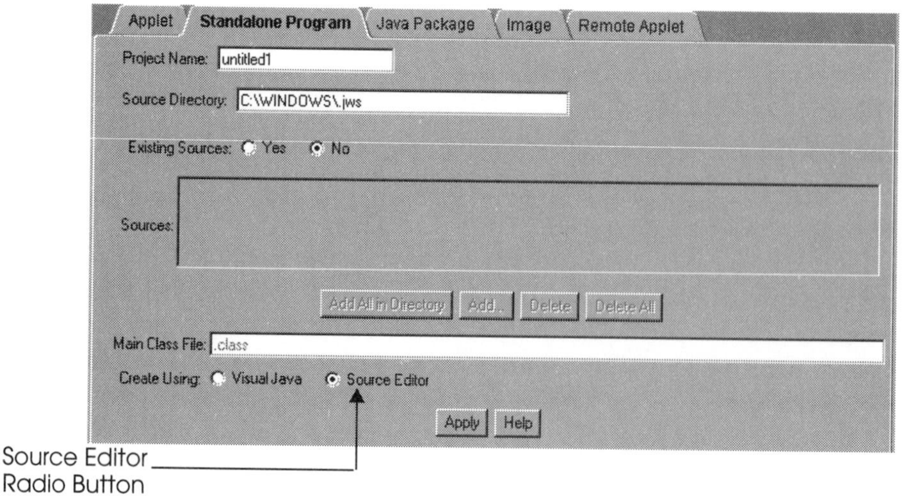

Source Editor
Radio Button

Figure 5–1 Starting a New Project with the Source Editor

Projects with Source Files

Because projects provide the context for your work in Java WorkShop, clicking on the Source Editor icon opens the editor with the main file in the current project already loaded. However, this is only true when you haven't edited any other source files. The Source Editor keeps the last edited source file in its window unless you close it or load a new file.

Projects with No Source Files

What if you have a project with no source files in it yet? When you start a new applet or standalone project with no existing source files, you have the choice of starting your work with Visual Java or the Source Editor. If you choose the Source Editor, Java WorkShop opens the editor with a default name for the project and the applet source file. Of course, you can change the default names by supplying your own project name before you move to the Source Editor. *In fact, you should give projects meaningful names right from the start because Java WorkShop currently doesn't support renaming projects.*

Editing Source Code

Let's create a standalone application project and use the Source Editor to create the source file. This project is for a file dialog box that allows users to choose directories and files from scrolling lists. We're making it a standalone application because applet security restrictions don't allow file access.

If you created an applet project in Chapter 4, you already know these steps. Here's a review for those who might have skipped that exercise:

1. Select a portfolio. We'll use *insidejws*. **Portfolio** ⟶ **Choose** ⟶ **insidejws**.

2. Choose **Project** ⟶ **Create** ⟶ **Standalone Program**.
    The Java WorkShop Create Project window opens to the Standalone Program tab.

3. Give the project a name. We'll use *Chooser*. If you want to create a directory for the project, enter a name for it now in the Source Directory field.

4. Click No at Existing Sources.

5. Click Create Using Source Editor.

Java WorkShop opens a new file in the editor and provides the skeleton code for an application —a class declaration for a class named `Chooser` or whatever name you have given your project, a constructor for the class, and a `main()` method. Notice that the class is declared with the same name as the project, and, following Java conventions, the file is given the same name as the class. Of course, the application file name includes the `.java` file extension.

Figure 5–2 shows the Source Editor with basic code for a new application.

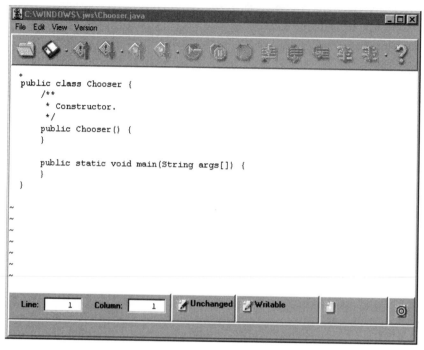

Figure 5–2 Source Editor with New Program File

As you can see, only two icons are available in this editing session: Open and Save. The remaining icons on the tool bar are dimmed. They become active when you use the Source Editor with the Build Manager or Debugger. Later on in this chapter, we'll look at Source Browser integration with other Java WorkShop tools. For now, here's a quick tour of the basic file and text-editing operations available in the editor. Later you'll edit the `Chooser.java` file in the Source Editor.

Basic File Operations

The Source Editor File menu supports all of the basic file operations. Because you can open multiple editing windows, the menu adds a command for saving all of the files you have open. Table 5-1 lists the File menu commands.

Table 5-1 Source Editor File Menu Commands

Commands	Description
New	Clears the editor for you to start a new file. If there's a file in the editor that you have not saved, Java WorkShop prompts you to save it (or not).
Open	Brings an existing file into the editor. You can also open with the Open icon (the file folder icon on the tool bar).
Reload	Reloads a file from disk, discarding any edits you've made since the last saved version. (Behaves like a "Revert to last saved" command.)
Save	Writes the file to disk. You can also save with the Save icon (the one that looks like a disk).
Save As	Writes the file to disk under a new name that you specify.
Save All	Saves the contents of all open editor windows.
Close	Closes the window but prompts you to save if you have made any changes since the last save.

If you'd rather learn text editing operations as you go, you might want to skip the next section and move on to some of the special aspects of Java WorkShop's Source Editor or to the hands-on exercise in "Editing the Chooser Source File" on page 59.

Basic Text Operations

The Source Editor supports inserting, deleting, selecting, cutting, copying, pasting, searching, and replacing text.

Inserting Text

Move the cursor to any location in the text and start typing. You can move around in text by using either the mouse or the arrow keys. The Source Editor also supports inserting whole files. Choose Insert A File from the Edit menu.

Deleting Text

All of the following types of deletion are supported:

- Delete one character to the left of the cursor with the Backspace key.

- Delete one character to the right of the cursor with the Delete key.
- Delete selected text with the Delete key.
- Delete the current line with <Ctrl+D>.

Selecting Text

Select text with one of these methods:

- Drag through the text you want to select.
- Click at the beginning of a selection and Shift-click at the end of the selection.
- Double-click on a word.
- Triple-click on a line.
- Use Shift-arrow keys to select text (Windows 95/NT only).

Operating on Selected Text

To copy or cut and paste text:

1. Select the text.
2. Copy the text to the clipboard. Choose **Edit ➠ Copy** or use <Ctrl+C>, or cut the text: **Edit ➠ Cut** or <Ctrl+X>.
3. Move the cursor to where you want the text to go.
4. Choose **Edit ➠ Paste** or use <Ctrl+V>.

To overstrike existing text with new text:

1. Select the text.
2. Type while the text is highlighted.

Searching and Replacing Text Strings

Java WorkShop doesn't currently support regular expressions (substitution characters), but you can search for and replace text strings.

To search for a text string and replace it:

1. Choose **Edit ➠ Find** or use<Ctrl+F> to open the Search dialog box.
2. Choose **Edit ➠ Replace** or use <Ctrl+R> to open the Replace dialog box.

To repeat a search or replace operation:

- Choose **Edit ➠ Repeat Last** or use <Ctrl+A>.

That covers most of the text editing operations except for undo, redo, and inserting a file. Those three operations are also available from the Edit menu:

- Undo—Reverses the editing operations you've performed. Undo reverses one operation at a time from the last up to the first operation. Of course, you can't undo a save operation.

- Redo—Reverses a series of Undo commands, one at a time.

- Insert a File—Opens a file dialog box and inserts the selected file at the cursor position.

Editing the Chooser Source File

You should still have the skeleton for a Chooser class in the Source Editor. Let's edit it now to create a file dialog box.

Use the editor to make the changes and additions necessary to supply the code for a file dialog called "Applications." The program is shown in Example 5-1.

```
import java.awt.*;

public class Chooser {
    static Frame f = new Frame ("Applications");

    public static void main(String[] a) {
        FileDialog Chooser = new FileDialog(f, "Applications");
        Chooser.show();
        f.add(Chooser);
        f.show ();
    }
}
```

Example 5-1 Chooser.java

The program imports the Java Abstract Windowing Toolkit (AWT) package, the package containing graphical user interface (GUI) components, including the FileDialog class, and creates a simple file dialog object. There are a lot more things you would need to do to make a useful file dialog, but this one takes fewer keystrokes to create. Because the Java API documentation is accessible from within Java WorkShop, you could look at the constructors and other methods available to you while you are editing source code. The Help menu contains a Java API Documentation item. Because the Help menu is available from any tool in Java WorkShop, so is the API documentation.

Building and Running the Chooser Project

Java WorkShop's Build Manager is described in Chapter 6. We'll give a sneak preview of it here so that you can see your file dialog in action.

1. Open Build Manager by clicking on the Build Manager icon.

2. Click the Project radio button.

3. Start the build by clicking the build icon (the wrench) in the Build Manager tool bar.

    Chooser should build with no errors if you entered it correctly in the Source Editor. If not, you'll see compilation errors. They'll be highlighted because they're browser links to the code in the Source Editor.

4. Now click the Tester icon to run the program.

You should see the file dialog box named "Applications" displayed in a separate window. Figure 5–3 shows the Chooser project as it would look on Windows 95. When you are done, just quit the program as you would any other.

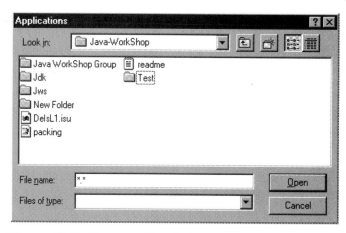

Figure 5–3 Chooser Standalone Program Project

Source Editor Extras

So far, we've described editor basics. Now let's take a look at some additional features of the Source Editor. First, let's see what the last two menus on the Source Editor Menu bar offer.

The Source Editor's View menu has just two commands, one for opening a new window and the other for setting (or unsetting) the editor as a display for other Java WorkShop tools. As you would expect, **View ➡ New Window** opens another editor window so that you can edit multiple source files. The Version menu allows you to specify what, if any, version control system you want to use on your source files.

Setting How the Source Editor Is Used for Tools Display

The Use for Tools Display command toggles between setting the editor to edit source files or setting it to be available for Java WorkShop to use when debugging, browsing source, and building projects. It could get a little confusing here about who's in charge of your editing windows, you or Java WorkShop. Besides, you might not want your work to be interrupted, which is what will happen if a Java WorkShop tool expects to be able to use the editor window and you have unsaved changes. If you want to control how the editor is used for display, read on.

What You Should Know About Tools Display. Some caveats are associated with using the Source Editor for tools display:

- If you have unsaved changes in the editor window when another tool uses it to display a file, Java WorkShop warns you in a dialog box that gives you a choice to open another Source Editor window or to save the file.

- When you have multiple editing windows, only one can be set for Tools Display. By default, Java WorkShop opens the Source Editor in Use For Tools Display mode. The bull's-eye graphic on the right side of the editor's footer indicates that this mode is set.

- To keep Java WorkShop from replacing the contents of the file loaded in the editor, turn off the Use For Tools Display setting. Java WorkShop will open a new editor window for display when required.

The bottom line? If you plan to be editing other files while debugging, consider turning off Use For Tools Display. Java WorkShop will go ahead and open one in Use For Tools Display mode when necessary, and this way it won't interrupt the editing you have in progress. You'll know that the window is all yours because the bull's-eye will be replaced by the multiple files icon.

Using Version Control

Java WorkShop currently supports the following version control systems:

PVCS	Microsoft Windows 95/NT, Solaris
RCS	Solaris
SCCS	Solaris

Java WorkShop doesn't have its own version control system but integrates with some common ones. If you find that you can't work with one of the supported systems, make sure that the version control system is in your execution path.

To use a version control system with Java WorkShop, choose **Options ⟶ Version Control**. Java WorkShop opens a preferences window with a tab for Paths, Proxies and Ports, and Version Control. By default, None is the active choice for version control. After you choose a version control tool, return to the Source Editor. Now you can use any of the version control commands for checking in or checking out files. Table 5-2 describes the Version menu.

Table 5-2 Version Control Commands

Command	Description
Check out	Checks out the file that is open in the Source Editor and makes the file writable.
Check In	Checks in the file that is open and makes the file read-only.
Check In New	Places the open file under version control and makes it read-only.
Uncheckout	Undoes a check out. Uncheckout deletes any changes that you made to the file and checks the file in to the version control system. Makes the file read-only. Use Uncheckout to roll back changes to a file.

Troubleshooting PVCS in Java WorkShop.

You should be using the version of Intersolv PVCS for Windows 95/NT. The older version for DOS doesn't support long file names and doesn't work with .java files. Once you are sure you're running the right version, check to see that the directory for the PVCS commands is in your PATH definition before you start Windows and Java WorkShop. Check AUTOEXEC.BAT for the PATH. Restart Windows if you make changes. After you have completed these steps, choose **Options ⟶ Version Control ⟶ PVCS** and then click Apply.

Now you need to open the source file you want in the Source Editor. (If the file was loaded while you did the troubleshooting steps above, close it and open it again.) You should see active version control commands in the Version Control menu: Check out, Check In, Check in New, Uncheckout.

Reading the Status Display

How can you tell if a file is already checked out? Look at the status area.

• **Version control status area**—Indicates whether the file is checked in or out. If the version commands are inactive, version control is not in effect. If the version status icon shows a check mark on the document icon, the file is under version control and is checked in.

Figure 5–4 shows the status area when a file is under version control and is checked in.

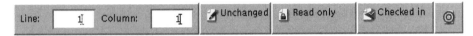

Figure 5–4 Source Editor Status Indicators

• **Line and Column** — These fields tell you where in the source file the cursor is focused. You can enter new values here to change the location of the cursor. Put in a new line value, press Return, and the cursor is moved to the new line.

• **Change status area** — Tells you whether a file is new (has not been opened in the Source Editor). After you save a file and before you make any more changes, Unchanged indicates that the file opened in the editor has not been modified. The status changes to Changed when you edit the file.

• **Read/Write Status**—Lets you know if the file is writable, meaning that you can save any editing that you've done, or if it is Read-only. Read-only status may simply mean that a file under version control is not checked out. You can edit a read-only file but to save the changes, you'll have to use the Save as command and save the file under a different name. It's a good idea to check the permission status before you make modifications to your program. That way, you can avoid any file gymnastics later.

Summary

In this chapter, we talked about:

• Starting the Source Editor in various ways

• Handling files and editing text

• Searching and replacing text strings

• Building and running the project that we created

• Source Editor extras

• Using version control

CHAPTER
6

- Building an Applet

- Setting Build Options

- Building Projects or Building Files

- Handling Build Errors

- Stopping a Build in Progress

- Going from Compiler Errors to Source Code

- Running the Applet

Building Projects

If you've compiled Java applets and standalone applications using the Java Developer's Kit (JDK), you've used the `javac` command with any one or more of the seven or so options to invoke the Java compiler. Java WorkShop's Build Manager supports all of these compiler options.

In this chapter, we create a simple Java applet and build it, using some of the build options.

Building an Applet

We'll make a project called *Greeting*. It contains a simple applet that welcomes visitors to a home page. Using Build manager, we'll compile it and then use the Project Tester to run it and create a basic HTML page for it.

If you would prefer to import the finished sample project included on the CD-ROM, follow the instructions in "Importing Projects" on page 45.

1. Choose the *insidejws* portfolio. **Portfolio** ⟶ **Choose** ⟶ **insidejws**.

2. Choose **Create** ⟶ **Project** ⟶ **Applet**.

3. Name the Project *Greeting*. Enter a directory name in the Source Directory field to have Java WorkShop create a directory for you.

4. Click No for Existing Sources.

5. Click the Source Editor radio button.

Because you're starting a new file, Source Editor opens with some placeholder Java code, including a class declaration based on the Project name:

```
public class Greeting extends Applet {
// methods
}
```

When the Source Editor opens, enter the applet code in Example 6-1, or use an applet of your own. Feel free to enter a different greeting string.

```
import java.awt.*;
import java.applet.*;

public class Greeting extends Applet {
    Font welcome = new Font("TimesRoman", Font.ITALIC, 24);
    public void init() {
        resize(600,100);
    }
    public void paint(Graphics g) {
        g.setFont(welcome);
        setBackground(Color.blue);
        g.drawString("Welcome to Inside Java WorkShop",140,50);
        }
}
```

Example 6-1 Greeting.java

The applet will display the text in a Times Roman italic font against a blue background. It's not a very interesting applet, but it does improve upon the capabilities of a plain HTML page. For one thing, you control the font, point size, and style of the text to get the exact results that you want instead of depending on the user's browser. In Chapter 8 we'll show you how to use the Project Editor to change, on-the-fly, some of the applet parameters for the *Greeting* project.

Naturally, applets can do a lot more. We kept this one simple to make it easier to edit. For now, save it in the Source Editor and get ready to edit the project attributes for building *Greeting*.

Setting Build Options

When you create a project, Java WorkShop supplies default project attributes, including the compiler debug option:

```
javac -g
```

To use Java WorkShop's Debugger, build with the debug option.

Let's change the compiler option to add the verbose option. The verbose option causes javac to print messages stating what source files are being compiled and what class files are loaded.

1.   Click the Project Manager icon.

2.   Choose the Build tab in the Project Editor.

3.   If the file Greeting.java is not listed in the files list at the top of the Build tab, use the Add button to add it there. (See Figure 6–1.)

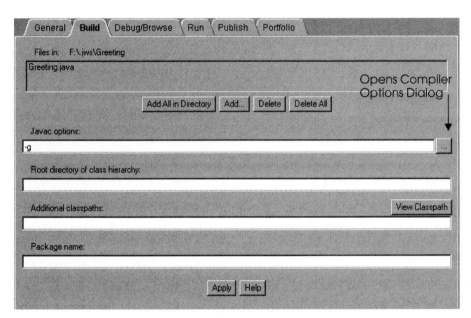

Figure 6–1 Editing Build Options in the Project Editor

4.   At the Javac options field you will see the -g (debug) option already listed. At the end of the Javac options field is a Java WorkShop chooser button. Click on it to open the Java Compiler Options dialog:

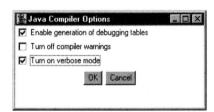

Figure 6–2 Compiler Options Dialog Box

Only three options are listed in the dialog. Remaining compiler options are available from fields on the Build tab itself. The options in the dialog box are equivalent to these javac options: -g, -nowarn, and -verbose. You might find it easier just to enter options in the Javac options field. Choose

"Turn on verbose mode" or just enter `verbose` in the field. Consider this field an extension of the `javac` command and enter options as you would at the command line.

5. Remember to click Apply to save Build settings in the Project Editor.

Which compiler options did I choose?

Some development environments require you to verify build settings by looking in a dialog box. When you build a project in Java WorkShop, compiler output, including the options used, is displayed in the Build Manager itself. One of the first pieces of compiler feedback you'll see is the `javac` command line that was used.

If you are building a nested project, you should also check the General tab to see how the projects included within the project are listed. Build Manager builds the projects in a nested project in the order in which they are listed here. If you want to change the order, use the Move Up or Move Down buttons. Select a project in the Included Projects list and move it up or down the list. Figure 6–3 shows the build order for a nested project.

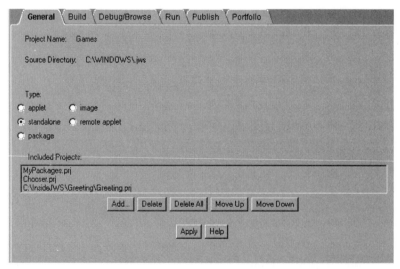

Figure 6–3 Setting the Build Order for a Nested Project

Using the Build Manager

Because a project is Java WorkShop's basic unit of development, you have the option to build a project or a single file. In our case, we are using a fairly simple project that has just one buildable file in it, Greeting.java.

Building Projects or Building Files

You'll have two choices to make before you build your project. The first choice is the kind of build: whether to build the files that have changed or to build all files. The single wrench icon starts an incremental build, the double wrench builds all files. Once you have built a project, you'll find the Build Manager works faster when you are compiling only the changes.

The second choice is whether to build a project or a single file.

Here's a summary of the differences between building a file and building a project.

If you're building a project:

- The current project is named in the Project or File field. The file chooser is inactive. To change project names, enter a new name in the field.

- If you build a project, all of the information used to build it (source files, compiler options, class paths, package to use) comes from the project definition.

If you're building a file:

- The chooser opens a file chooser. You can choose any file to build, even a file that is not in the current project.

- Build Manager checks these factors to determine how to build the file:

  - The compiler options specified for the current project

  - The path name for the classes directory (CLASSPATH) taken from the project source directory, the necessary Java Development Kit (JDK) directories, and any directories you add in the Project Manager's Build tab. (To see the setting for CLASSPATH, click the View Classpath button on the Build tab.)

The compiled class file is placed in the same directory as the source file.

Building entire projects becomes most useful when you have multiple files in a project, or nested projects (projects within projects).

Building the Greeting Project

The Build Manager window is quite simple.

1. Open it now by clicking on the Build Manager icon (the wrench) in the tool bar.

2. Decide whether you are building a project or a single file. Let's build the project.

3. Start the build by clicking the build icon (the single wrench) in the Build Manager tool bar.

    This step can be a little confusing. You might think you have started the build by just invoking Build Manager from the Java WorkShop tool bar. The intermediate step of clicking the single or double wrench in the Build Manager is there so that you can make a choice about what to build (only the changed files or all files).

The main body of the Build Manager window is an output area for displaying messages, starting with the expanded `javac` command in use and including the path names of the class directories that are used and the names of the source files being compiled. Of course, if there are build errors, this window displays those, too. If not, the last status message in the window is "Done."

If the build completes without encountering any errors, the message "Build Succeeded" is displayed just above the build output display.

The build of *Greeting* should have been successful. Let's consider the other possible outcome and how to handle it.

Handling Build Errors

If the build is not successful, Build Manager displays a list of compiler errors. The errors are Browser links to the source code. You may recall from the Source Editor chapter that one of its uses is to serve as a display for other tools. If you click on a compiler error, Java WorkShop opens the Source Editor with the line where the error occurred highlighted in yellow.

Let's make a mistake and see this at work. You probably still have the file `Greeting.java` loaded in the Source Editor. If not, load it now.

1. In the Source Editor, delete the semicolon from the end of the applet package `import` statement:

    ```
    import java.applet.*
    ```

2. Save the file.

3. Build it.

You should see two related errors. Your Build Manager window should contain messages like those in Figure 6–4. (Your path names will differ.) The first error indicates the missing semicolon. The second indicates that you have defined a class with no known superclass. Of course, you'd get the second error because the `import` statement for the applet package wasn't valid. (You may have to resize the window or scroll right to see long path names in compiler messages.)

Building Project Greeting ...

```
C:\LWEAVER\JDK\bin\javac -g -verbose -d C:\LWEAVER\JDK\bin\InsideJWS\Greeting
-classpath
C:\LWEAVER\JWS\classes;C:\LWEAVER\JDK\bin\InsideJWS\Greeting;C:\LWEAVER\JDK\classe
C:\LWEAVER\JDK\bin\InsideJWS\Greeting\Greeting.java
[parsed C:\LWEAVER\JDK\bin\InsideJWS\Greeting\Greeting.java in 1100ms]
Greeting.java:2 ';' expected.
import java.applet.*
                   ^
[checking class Greeting]
Greeting.java:4 Superclass Applet of class Greeting not found.
public class Greeting extends Applet {
             ^
2 errors
```

Figure 6–4 Build Manager Output with Compiler Errors

4. Click on the first error.

    Java WorkShop displays the source code in the Source Editor. The first error is highlighted (Figure 6–5).

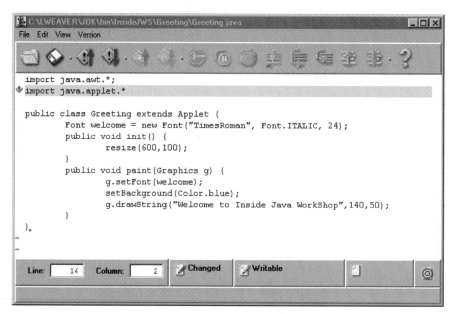

```
import java.awt.*;
import java.applet.*;

public class Greeting extends Applet {
        Font welcome = new Font("TimesRoman", Font.ITALIC, 24);
        public void init() {
                resize(600,100);
        }
        public void paint(Graphics g) {
                g.setFont(welcome);
                setBackground(Color.blue);
                g.drawString("Welcome to Inside Java WorkShop",140,50);
        }
},
```

Figure 6–5 Error Highlighting in the Source Editor

You can step through the other errors by using the next and previous icons in the Source Editor tool bar.

Go to Next Error Icon

Go to Previous Error Icon

You know, of course, that if you fix the first error, Greeting.java will compile successfully.

By the way, the other icons in the Source Editor become active if you start the Debugger and use the Source Editor to fix your code. You can toggle breakpoints, start and stop execution, and so on. Chapter 10 describes using the Source Editor during debugging.

Stopping a Build in Progress

What if we had a more complex program that was generating errors? If you saw the error that was causing others, you could stop the build rather than waiting for it to compile everything. To stop a build before it completes, just click on the Stop icon in the Build Manager tool bar. The build output stops and the message "Stopped" appears.

Running the Applet

Now that your applet compiles successfully, you'll probably want to run it. Let's run the *Greeting* project now so you can see it in use and discover how easy it is to display it on a Java WorkShop Browser page.

There are two ways to run the project:

- From the Java WorkShop main menu, choose **Project** ⇒ **Run** ⇒ **Greeting**.

- On the tool bar, click the Project Tester icon (the light switch).

The applet itself is not terribly dramatic, but there it is in a Web page. Java Work-Shop uses an HTML page to run projects in the Browser. It calls this HTML page a run page. When you run the applet, Java WorkShop creates a temporary HTML file in the project's directory: `Greeting.tmp.html`. Example 6-2 shows the temporary HTM file.

```
<applet
   name="Greeting"
   code="Greeting.class"
   codebase="\LWEAVER\InsideJWS\Greeting"
   width="500"
   height="600"
   align="Top"
   alt="If you had a java-enabled browser, you would see an applet
here."
>      <hr>If your browser recognized the applet tag,
       you would see an applet here.<hr>
</applet>
```

Example 6-2 Greeting Project Run Page

Note that the path name for your `codebase` will differ from the example.

You could use this file as a starting point for your own applet Web page and tell Java WorkShop to use it as the run page for the project. If you want to change it and use it, be sure to rename it. You can edit the `.html` file in the Source Editor.

Anytime you run an applet project, Java WorkShop creates the file *projectname*`.tmp.html` in your project directory. If you edit this file, you must save it under a different file name; otherwise, Java WorkShop will overwrite it the next time you run the applet. To have Java WorkShop use this file as a run page, specify its name where it says Existing Run Page URL in the Run tab of the Project Editor.

Running projects, setting Run attributes, and editing run pages are all discussed in Chapter 8.

Summary

This chapter and the example you created have given you all the background you need to build Java WorkShop projects, including:

- Setting Build options in the Project Editor
- Stopping a build in progress
- Finding build errors in source code
- Seeing how Java WorkShop creates an HTML page for running the applets you build

Now, because the edit-build-run process is so simple, you just need to remember to save and build every time you make changes. This becomes especially important when you build GUIs because you are "editing" the interface interactively and you have to save the layout before the build. The GUI builder is next on the tour of Java WorkShop.

CHAPTER
7

- Building Your First GUI

- GUI Building Basics

- Files Created by the GUI Builder

- The Visual Menu and Tool Bar

- GUI Attribute Editor

Building GUIs

Visual Java is a powerful tool for designing and building graphical user interfaces (GUIs) and then generating the code for the GUI elements. It's a visual interface to Java's Abstract Windowing Toolkit (AWT). It spares you some programmatic details so that you can focus on application needs. You can create a GUI layout with mouse clicks, and you can also achieve basic event handling by making choices in dialog boxes. Then you generate GUI code. Visual Java helps you create, operate on, and understand the interaction between GUI objects.

You can use Java WorkShop's GUI builder to:

- Construct user interfaces for applets or standalone applications.

- Define operations to generate code for callbacks.

- Edit the common and specialized attributes of components.

- Generate Java source code.

- Preview and run your project.

There is so much going on in Visual Java that it warrants a second, advanced topics chapter later in this book. In this chapter, we'll dive right into GUI building with Visual Java, using a simple GUI example that creates a list box for selecting a color from among several choices. Then we'll offer a quick refresher on Java GUI objects and describe some Visual Java basics.

Building Your First GUI

You'll create a new project, lay out a simple list box, generate the source code, then build and run the project.

Create a new project using Visual Java:

1. Choose **Portfolio** ➡ **Choose** ➡ **insidejws**.
2. Choose **Project** ➡ **Create** ➡ **Applet**.
3. In the Create Project window, enter the project name *FirstGUI*.
4. Click No to Existing Sources.
5. Click the Visual Java radio button.
6. Click Apply.

Java WorkShop loads the Visual Java page in the Browser (Figure 7–1).

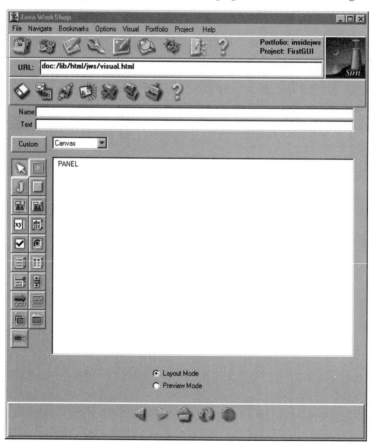

Figure 7–1 Visual Java Page

Notice that the Visual menu, usually inactive, is now active. You'll use this menu to generate the Java code for the GUI. The word PANEL appears in the container list in the Visual Java page (Figure 7–1). A Panel is one of three types of GUI containers that you can create with Visual Java. For a description of all three, see "Containers in Visual Java" on page 85.

Java WorkShop also opens a separate layout window with a 12-cell grid in it (Figure 7–2). Because you are creating an applet project, the default container is a Panel.

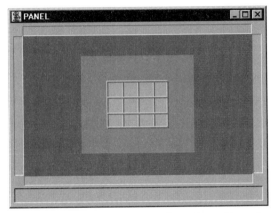

Figure 7–2 Layout Window for a Panel

If you are familiar with the AWT, you know that a Panel is a container that can be used in other containers, such as an application window, or by itself in a browser window. The Panel in this example is quite simple and might be used within another component. You could use a series of Checkboxes to implement the same capability, but where there are more than a few choices, placing them in a list is a simpler and more attractive alternative to multiple check boxes.

Laying Out the GUI Components

Let's set up the grid and lay out the list component. You'll use the layout window and the palette. Items on the palette are analogous to the components in the Abstract Windowing Toolkit (AWT). If you put the wrong component in a cell, just select it and use the Delete key to delete it. It's impossible to delete a component in a cell without first selecting the component.

Figure 7–3 illustrates the component palette. You'll use the List component in this exercise.

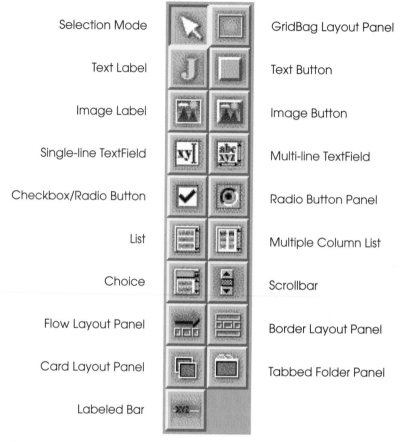

Selection Mode			GridBag Layout Panel
Text Label			Text Button
Image Label			Image Button
Single-line TextField			Multi-line TextField
Checkbox/Radio Button			Radio Button Panel
List			Multiple Column List
Choice			Scrollbar
Flow Layout Panel			Border Layout Panel
Card Layout Panel			Tabbed Folder Panel
Labeled Bar			

Figure 7–3 Visual Java Palette

If the layout window is behind another window, bring it to the front by clicking the word PANEL in the component list.

1. Make a grid with one cell. Delete cells by clicking in them and pressing the Delete key. If you make a mistake and need to add cells, click in a cell and press the arrow keys: left or right arrows to add columns, up and down arrows to add rows.

2. Find the List component on the palette (left side of Visual Java window). You can move the mouse pointer over a component on the palette and see its name displayed in the Status bar (in the Browser footer).

3. Click the List button on the palette.

4. Move the cursor to the cell in the layout window. Click again.

You should have a List component in the cell with a couple of default list items in it:

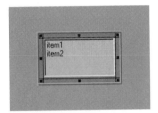

5. To define properties or attributes for the List component, open the Attribute Editor.[1]

   The Attribute Editor is not just for setting component attributes; it is also used to create event handlers (callbacks). We'll look at using the editor to create callbacks in Chapter 12.

6. Enter this list of items in the items text field, separating each item with a comma (no spaces): Red, Yellow, Blue.

   Figure 7–4 shows the fields in the Attribute Editor.

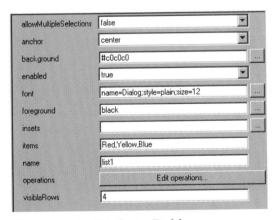

Figure 7–4 Attribute Fields

7. Click the Apply button. Now see what happens if the list is longer than the space you've allowed for this component. Go back to the Attribute Editor and add at least two more items. We added Orange, Green, and Purple. Because the number of items exceeds the space in the default component, the list includes a scroll bar now.

---

1. For quick access to the Attribute Editor, click the right mouse button in the selected component's border (where its handles are). To be sure you have the correct component for editing, look at the component name in the name field.

You can set the visibleRow attribute to control how much of the list is visible without scrolling.

8.   Save the GUI by clicking the Save icon (the disk) on the Visual Java tool bar. Check the Browser footer for a status message.

Visual Java creates a file named `FirstGUI.gui`. To see what your work will look like, go to the bottom of the Visual Java window and click the Preview Mode radio button.

As it is, the list is not very useful. You'll certainly want to attach actions to it, and you might want to change its appearance. In "Editing Operations" on page 149, you'll learn how to create code for user interface actions. There are a number of tools in Visual Java to help you make some basic GUI components operable and useful without having to write code. Of course, you can always work on GUI component attributes programmatically if you prefer.

Generating Source Code

Before you build a GUI, you must save it. You can generate the code for it now, but this is not required because the Build Manager will generate it when you build the project. To generate source code for your finished GUI:

*   Choose **Visual** ➠ **Generate**.

It is not always obvious when code generation is completed. Watch the Browser footer for a status message that says "Saved file <*your_filename*>.gui." When you generate source code for a GUI, Visual Java saves the layout (if you have not saved it already) and creates these files:

*   `FirstGUI.gui`

*   `FirstGUI.java`

*   `FirstGUIMain.java`

*   `FirstGUIRoot.java`

Appendix D contains listings for all of these files. The purpose of each file is explained in "Files Created by the GUI Builder" on page 88. The only source file that you would work with is the `FirstGUI.java` file; the others are created and updated for you. Even though the `.gui` file is generated, you can modify it, too. For example, you might want to add action methods to it.

Building and Running the Project

Of course, to run the GUI, you'll have to build it. *Save the layout before you build it. Without this step, Java WorkShop won't include your layout in the build.Build Manager will automatically generate the .gui file, so that step is not required before building.*

Use the Build Manager to compile the *FirstGUI* project:

1. Click the Build Manager icon.

2. In the Build Manager tool bar, click the Initiate a build icon (the single wrench).

In addition to the files mentioned above, you now have three `.class` files:

```
FirstGUI.class

FirstGUIMain.class

FirstGUIRoot.class
```

After a successful build, you can run the project by clicking the Tester icon. You'll see your GUI in the Browser (Figure 7–5). Because Java WorkShop is a Browser-based development tool, you can see exactly how your applet will look without leaving the environment where you created it.

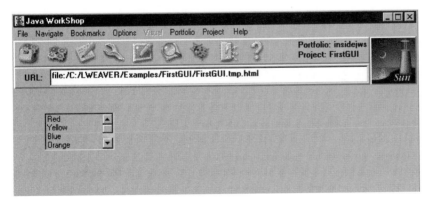

Figure 7–5 The FirstGUI Applet

To get the list to do anything besides scroll, you'd have to define operations for it. You can do this by editing the applet source file, or interactively in the Visual Java Attribute Editor. You'll see how to define operations in Chapter 12. The rest of this chapter gives you the background for doing more with the Visual Java GUI builder.

Importing Visual Java Projects

Importing a Visual Java is just like importing any other project. But you can also import just the GUI file created in Visual Java and then generate and build the project. If you want only the GUI from a project:

1.   Create a new project, click No to existing sources, and Create Using Visual Java.

2.   Choose **Visual** ⟶ **Import**. Select the .gui file from the file chooser.

    Visual Java loads the layout. You can work on it or just generate and build it.

3.   Choose **Visual** ⟶ **Generate**.

4.   Build the project.

5.   Run the project.

GUI Building Basics

If you've written Java GUIs before and are familiar with the AWT, you might prefer to skip this part. It's a brief definition of the AWT triumvirate: *components, containers*, and *layout managers* in the context of Java WorkShop.

Components by any other name. . .

What Java calls components, you may know as controls or widgets, depending on where you got your GUI programming experience. We'll call them components, as Java WorkShop does, to maintain consistency with Java terminology.

GUI Components in Visual Java

In general terms, a *component* is simply a visual object. In Java language terms, components are classes for such objects and they are the core of the AWT. More than half of the classes in the AWT are derived from the Component class. Component is an abstract class. That means that many of its methods are to be implemented when you create a subclass that inherits from Component. (In Visual

Java, components actually inherit from a class called ShadowComponent. Shadow classes are an interface to the AWT classes and are described in the advanced GUI building chapter, Chapter 12.)

The components you use in Visual Java include the ones you can use programmatically in Java as well as some that do not appear in the AWT. Components not in the AWT are called custom components. If you know the AWT, you'll notice that Java WorkShop has added a Tabbed Folder Panel like the one used in the Java WorkShop interface. You can extend the palette with custom components that you create or buy. Then you have the choice of just using your component once by importing it, making it available on the palette, or including it in the Custom Choice menu. "Adding Custom Components and Windows" on page 163 describes how.

All of the GUI components are available graphically in the palette, from a choice menu adjacent to the Custom button on the Visual Java page, and from the Visual menu. Table 7-1 describes each of these areas for selecting components.

Table 7-1 Component Selection Areas

To use a component from:	Do:
Palette	Click on a component in the palette and move the mouse cursor to a cell in the layout grid. Click in a cell to place the component.
Custom Choice Menu	Choose the component from the choice menu (next to the Custom button) and click the Custom button. This is the equivalent of clicking an item in the visual palette. Click in a cell in the layout grid to place the component.
Visual Menu	Choose New Window from the Visual menu in the Browser menu bar. Visual Java opens a dialog with a list of components.

Containers in Visual Java

Remember that when you started an applet project and chose Visual Java, Visual Java opened with a PANEL in the component list? Visual Java opened your applet project with a Panel because a Panel is a kind of container suited for an applet:

- Panels don't create their own windows. You can use Panels inside another container, such as a browser Frame or an application window.

- Panels are useful for grouping visual objects that are related.

Visual Java supports two other kinds of container: Frames and Dialog Boxes. Frames can exist outside a browser and are typically used for application windows. Dialogs, are, well, dialog boxes. Dialogs are like Frames except that they can be modal. Modal means that the Dialog can be used to halt input to any other container until some action is performed in the Dialog. Frames, Dialogs, and Panels are the three containers supported in the Java AWT. All of them allow you to group components together.

A container is an extension of a component and can contain many components. When you build GUIs you group components into one or more of the three containers (Frames, Dialogs, Panels). (In Java language terms, the `Container` class extends `Component`. In fact, all AWT components extend the `Component` class.) The `Container` class implements a `Component` that can hold other components. Table 7-2 describes the three containers.

Table 7-2 Visual Java Containers

Container	Description
Frames	Application windows for GUIs that can exist outside a browser. You can add menu bars to Frames but not to other containers. A Frame is the main container for standalone applications.
Panels	The main container for an applet's GUI, but can also be used in application windows. Useful for grouping related components.
Dialog Boxes	Pop-up windows that can be activated both from Frames and Panels.

Layout Managers in Visual Java

The business of positioning and shaping the components in a container falls to a layout manager. `LayoutManager` is an interface that defines the methods that arrange components in a container. A number of classes implement the Layout Manager interface, many of which will be familiar to anyone who has used the AWT:

- `BorderLayout`
- `CardLayout`
- `FlowLayout`
- `GridBagConstraints`
- `GridBagLayout`
- `GridLayout`

The outermost layout manager is always GridBagLayout. Other layout managers can be placed in the cells of GridBagLayout. GridBagLayout implements the AWT LayoutManager interface to lay out Component objects in a Container.

Visual Java's grid-based system uses a layout model in which GUI components are laid out relative to each other. That means that your applets are better equipped for multi-platform display, and, given the capabilities of Java, you will probably want your work to appear on more than one platform. Some systems lay out components in absolute positions. Java WorkShop's relative layout enables predictable behavior when different native window toolkits cause components to vary in size and appearance.

While important to use to preserve the good looks of your application across platforms and window sizes, layout managers are difficult to program. Visual Java automates the effective use of complex layout managers, such as GridBagLayout.

Groups and Shadows

Visual Java uses groups and shadows as an interface to the AWT. A group is a generic container. A shadow wraps an AWT class. These are implemented as classes created especially for Java WorkShop—Group is the base class for the components you use in the GUI builder, and Shadow is the base class for the wrappers. These classes are used by Java WorkShop to present the AWT components to you at design time and to the user at runtime.

"Programming with Groups and Shadows" on page 157 describes how to use group and shadow classes.

Using Custom Components in Visual Java

If you've written a component and you want to add it to the palette or otherwise reuse it, Visual Java provides a way. Next to the Custom component button above the component palette is a choice menu. If you pull it down, you'll find additional components that you can use in Visual Java: Canvas, Generic, Multi-line Label, Scrolling Panel, and Text List. You can use these components in your GUI; their attributes are described in "Custom Components and their Attributes" on page 199.

Note: The Generic component is of special interest to those who have created components and want to use them in their GUIs in Java WorkShop. The Generic component is your door to importing any custom component class that you write. You'll see how to use it "Importing Custom Components" on page 163.

To add one of the components on the choice menu to a layout:

1.   Choose the component from the choice menu (next to the Custom button.)

2.   Click the Custom button.

3.   Click in a cell in the layout window where you want the component to go.

In other words, it is the same basic process as using the palette components, except you pick the component from a menu instead of the palette.

Files Created by the GUI Builder

The GUI Builder places the following source file types in your project directory when you build a GUI.

- *<ProjectName>*.gui — Contains the code that describes the GUI. This file is updated (or created) whenever you save the layout. One .gui file is generated per group.

- *<ProjectName>*Root.java — Contains the code for initializing the components for the group.

- *<ProjectName>*Ops.java — Contains the operations for the group. This file is generated only if you have defined operations on one or more of the components in the group.

- *<ProjectName>*Main.java — Contains the main() method that is used to run the group as a standalone application. This is where the program starts.

- *<ProjectName>*.java — Contains a template for the group. This file is generated only once. You modify it to implement event handlers, action handlers, and other functionality.

"Class Dependencies" on page 169 describes the dependencies between the classes created when you build these source files.

The Visual Menu and Tool Bar

The Visual menu becomes active only when Visual Java is active. It provides an alternative to some of the operations in the Visual Java tool bar, giving you the choice to use either icons or menu commands to do your work. The Visual Java menu includes additional capabilities, such as commands that support importing files and adding components.

The Visual menu is described in Table 7-3.

Table 7-3 Visual Menu Commands

Command	Description
Import	Imports `.gui` files that contain Visual Java windows that you want to include in your application.
Import URL	Just like **Import** except that you can specify a URL for the `.gui` file.
Generate	Generates Java source code from your layout.
Save	Saves your layout to disk in the file *<ProjectName>*`.gui`.
Cut	Deletes the selected component or window and puts it on the Java WorkShop clipboard. You can paste the component or window to another location in the layout.
Copy	Copies the selected component or window to the clipboard. You can paste the copied component or window from the clipboard to another cell in the layout
Paste	Pastes the component or window that is on the clipboard to the cell you select in the layout.
Delete	Deletes the selected component or window. **Delete** does not place a copy on the clipboard and cannot be undone.
Edit Attributes	Opens the Attribute Editor or makes it the active window if it is already open. The attributes of the selected component or window are loaded in the attribute fields.
New Window	Activates the New Window dialog box. Use the New Window dialog box to add a new Frame, Dialog, or generic window to your application.
Nested Panel	Nests (in place) the selected component within a GridBag Layout Panel component.
Main Container	Activates the Main Container dialog. Use the Main Container dialog to change the type of a main container to a Frame or a Panel.
Edit Palette	Activates the Palette Editor. Use the Palette Editor to add, delete, and rearrange items in the Component Palette, Custom Menu, or New Windows dialog box.
Open Palette	Opens a previously saved version of the component palette. Displays a file chooser for you to select a saved palette.
Save Palette	Saves a copy of the component palette to a named file. Displays a file chooser for you to name the palette.

GUI Attribute Editor

You already used the Attribute Editor to add items to the list in the exercise at the beginning of this chapter. Here's a summary of how to use it, plus another exercise that will familiarize you with setting attributes and using the save-generate/build-run cycles of GUI building.

The GUI builder makes specifying and changing the attributes[2] of components easier by making these development tasks available interactively. Using the editor and its dialogs, you can:

- Change the attributes of GUI components, including Frames, Panels, and Dialogs.

- Set background colors, fonts, placement, and size of GUI components.

- Rename components.

- Define borders.

- Set insets.

- Add callbacks to components.

As usual, there are alternative ways to open the Attribute Editor:

- From within the layout window, click the right mouse button while the cursor is in the area between the component and its cell border. This is the most practical way, especially if you have a number of components. You can select a component, click the right mouse button, edit attributes and apply them, and then click the next component. The Attribute Editor changes context to the new component.

- Select the component, then click on the Attribute Editor icon in the Visual Java tool bar.

- Select the component, then choose **Visual** ⟹ **Edit Attributes** from the Java WorkShop menu.

---

2. PC developers are more familiar with the term "properties." Because Java WorkShop uses the term attributes, we'll use attributes in this book. Attributes are the same as properties.

GUI components have their own specialized attributes, but some attributes are common to all. For the special attributes of each component, see Appendix B. The common attributes are described in Table 7-4.

Table 7-4 **Attributes Common to All GUI Components**

Attribute	Purpose
anchor	Determines where the component is anchored within the layout cell.
background	Changes the color of the component's background. Java WorkShop opens a color chooser.
borderLabel	Adds a text label to the Panel border.
borderRelief	Adds a graphical border around the edge of the Panel.
borderWidth	Sets the width of borderRelief.
operations	Opens the Operations dialog box. Use the Operations dialog box to add callbacks to components.
font	Changes the font to use in the component if it is a component that contains text. Java WorkShop opens a font chooser.
foreground	Specifies the color of the font. Java WorkShop opens a color chooser.
insets	Specifies the distance in pixels from the left, right, top, or bottom edge of the layout cell. A dialog box is opened for you to enter the values.
enabled	Controls whether the component is initially in the enabled or disabled state.
name	Lists the name of the component. All components are uniquely named when you create them (i.e., place them in the layout). You can change the name by using this attribute. Be sure that all component names within a group are unique. Alternatively, you can quickly change the name of a selected component by typing in the Name field at the top of the Visual Java main window.
text	Specifies the text to be displayed on the component. Enter the text you want on the component here. Alternatively, you can quickly change the text on a selected component by typing in the Text field at the top of the Visual Java main window.

More Attribute Editing

If you'd like to experiment with changing other attributes and observing the effect in both the Layout Mode and Preview Mode, go back to the *FirstGUI* project and try some of these:

- Change the enabled attribute from true to false. You'll see that the items in the list are grayed out.

- Change the visibleRows attribute to 10. You might have to resize the layout or preview window to see the bottom of the list component.

- Change the background color. If you know a supported applet color by its number (for example, #64c0c0), enter it in the background attribute. The pound sign (#) is part of the number, so enter it, too, or else you'll get an error message. To create your own color, click the chooser button to open a color chooser and change the red, green, and blue values until you get the color you want.

- Change the anchor attribute to northwest or northeast. This moves the applet out of the center of the browser and into the upper left or upper right corner respectively.

To see what effect these changes have on the applet:

1. Click Apply after you make changes in the Attribute Editor.
2. Save the GUI.

   When you save a layout in Visual Java, you are saving the attributes that you set, too.

3. Generate the code.
4. Build the project.
5. Run the project.

Note: If you make and save changes to *FirstGUI* now, your project won't look exactly like the one from the CD-ROM. The project's generated source files won't match the source code listings in Appendix D, either. However, experimentation is encouraged, so go ahead and apply the changes and save the layout. Then you can compare the new .gui file to the one on page 213 to see how attributes are saved.

If you want to know what an attribute does, see the attribute reference appendix, Appendix B.

By now you have seen how much coding the Attribute Editor saves you. It also saves time and lets you focus on design because you can see your changes immediately in the layout window, Preview Mode, or the Browser.

Additional Attribute Editor Features

The Attribute Editor also includes an Operations Editor for adding event handling to components. You'll use the Operations Editor in Chapter 12. If you are editing a Frame, you are also presented with an attribute called "menubar." Instead of a field, you get a button here that opens the Menu Editor. You'll use the Menu Editor in Chapter 12, too.

Summary

This first of two chapters on GUI building should have given you some understanding of the concepts and parts of Visual Java:

- Building a simple GUI

- Generating source code

- Building and running a project created with Visual Java

- Using the Visual menu and tool bar

- Editing GUI attributes

We've started with something simple to acquaint you with Visual Java. Chapter 12, "Doing More with the GUI Builder," offers a complete example to illustrate the features of Visual Java.

CHAPTER

8

Running Projects

Running projects in Java WorkShop is pretty straightforward. Because Java WorkShop is itself a Browser, you can run applets right in the development environment. Of course, if you run a standalone program, it runs in its own window.

Note that you can try out your applets in another browser. For example, Windows 95 users can drag and drop the HTML file used as a run page for their applets to Netscape Navigator. Be aware, however, that some platform and browser combinations handle user interface actions differently at runtime. Consult Table B-1 on page 201 when you are defining actions for GUI components. See "Visual Java Runtime Classes" on page 162 for additional information on running applications created with the Visual Java GUI builder outside of Java WorkShop.

Running an Applet Project

There are two ways to run a project. When you are ready for a test run, just flip the light switch icon (Tester) in the Browser tool bar. Or you can use the run command in the Project menu.

We've already tried both ways, once when we looked at the Source Editor and once when we used the Build Manager, but we'll run another project here and change some of the attributes that affect how it runs.

When you run a project, Java WorkShop uses the attributes you set in the Run tab in the Project Editor. The first time you run an applet project, Java WorkShop also creates an HTML page for the applet to run in. This page is called a run page; you can modify it or use another one in its place. We'll work with that file later.

For now, let's run one of the projects that comes with Java WorkShop.

1.   Choose **Portfolio** ➠ **Choose** ➠ **personal**.

2.   Choose **Project** ➠ **Choose** ➠ **Blink**.

3.   Click the Tester icon.

4.   Java WorkShop loads an HTML page with the applet in it

To stop a project that is running, load another page in the Browser by clicking on any tool in the Browser tool bar or return to the previous page by clicking the Previous icon in the navigation bar.

The HTML file that Java WorkShop uses to run your applet is determined by the settings you make when you edit a project's run attributes. If you have specified an HTML page, Java WorkShop uses that one. If you haven't specified a run page, Java WorkShop creates a temporary file in which to run the project. For the *Blink* project, Java WorkShop created a file named `Blink.tmp.html`, shown in Example 8-1.

```
<applet
    name="Blink"
    code="Blink.class"
    codebase="\JAVA-WORKSOP\JWS\examples\Blink"
    width="500"
    height="600"
    align="Top"
    alt="If you had a java-enabled browser, you would see an applet
here."
>       <hr>If your browser recognized the applet tag,
        you would see an applet here.<hr>
</applet>
```

Example 8-1 Temporary HTML File

The temporary file offers the bare bones of a Web page but gives you a starting point for making your own page. You might want to create one that offers more and then specify it as the run page so you can see how it looks in the Browser as you work on the project.

Editing the HTML Run Page

To make your own HTML run page, edit the temporary file in the Source Editor or another HTML editor. Save it under a different name and specify its name in the Run Page attribute in the Project Editor.

If you do edit the temporary HTML file or supply one of your own, be sure that Java WorkShop knows which HTML page to use for running and testing the applet.

To specify the run page for a project, edit the project's Run attribute:

1. Choose **Project** ➠ **Edit** ➠ *<project_name>*. (A faster way to edit projects, assuming the project that you want to edit is the current project, is to click the Project Manager icon.)

2. Click the Run tab in the Project Editor.

3. In the Existing Run Page URL Field, enter the name of the new HTML file.

Running Other Project Types

Having specified a run page, you can run standalone programs, image projects, and remote applet projects.

- **Running a standalone program**

  Execute these steps, as, for example, with the *Chooser* project:

  1. Choose **Portfolio** ➠ **Choose** ➠ **insidejws**.

  2. Choose **Project** ➠ **Run** ➠ **Chooser**.

  Java WorkShop creates an MS-DOS command window (or a shell tool in the UNIX operating environment) and runs the program. You can edit the Run attribute to specify any arguments to pass to the program's `main()` method.

- **Running an image project**

  Make it the active project and click the Project Tester icon. Java WorkShop creates a temporary HTML file containing the `<img>` tag and loads it into the browser.

- **Running a remote applet project**

  Same as running an applet project, except that Java WorkShop loads the HTML file containing an `<applet>` tag with a URL into the browser and runs the applet.

Running Visual Java Projects

Applets and applications created in Visual Java require the Visual Java runtime classes. You can redistribute the Visual Java runtime classes with your applications. Copy them into the directory containing your application's main class file so that they can be downloaded by the applet class loader of the browser or viewer, or install them locally where your programs will run and specify them in the CLASSPATH variable.

To copy the runtime classes into an application directory, copy the contents of <install_dir_path>/JWS/classes/sunsoft

into the directory that contains the main applet class. On a Unix system, you can make a link to the sunsoft classes directory rather than an actual copy.

Changing Run Attributes

In addition to changing the run page, you can modify default settings for running any kind of Java WorkShop project. You can get online help in Java WorkShop for all of the available run attributes for each project type. We'll describe the most elaborate set of run attributes here, the attributes you can set for the most common project type—applets.

Remember, to edit project attributes:

1. Choose **Project** ⁗➡ **Edit** ⁗➡ *<project_name>*.

2. Click on the Run tab.

3. Click Apply to save your changes.

Applets run in browsers, of course, so the run attributes for applets, shown in Table 8-1, provide an interactive method for handling how the applet displays on the page. Defining applet parameters in the Run tab provides some HTML page wizardry in the absence of a dedicated HTML editor.

Table 8-1 Run Attributes for Applets

Attribute	Description
Existing Run Page URL	Specification for URL. If you have your own HTML page, select Yes and enter its URL here.
Main Class File	The user-specified .class file where the init() method is defined.
Codebase	The base URL or file name of the applet. The applet code is relative to this URL or file name. By default, Java WorkShop uses the URL or file name of the document in which the applet appears.
Width	The initial width, in pixels, needed to display the applet.

Table 8-1 Run Attributes for Applets (Continued)

Attribute	Description
Height	The initial height, in pixels, needed to display the applet.
Horizontal Space	Number of pixels on each side of the applet.
Vertical Space	Number of pixels above and below the applet.
Instance Name	Name for the applet instance. This name makes it possible for applets running on the same page to communicate with one another.
Alignment	The alignment of the applet on the page. Possible values are Top, Bottom, Middle, Left, Right, TextTop, Absmiddle, Baseline, and Absbottom.
Parameters	Parameters to be passed to the applet. Here you supply any arguments you might make to the HTML `<param>` tag. `<param>` tag arguments are specified in the format `name=value`. For example, `TxFont=Courier`.
	In Java WorkShop, simply enter the name of the parameter in the Name field and its value in the Value field. Then click the Add button. You can easily delete a parameter by selecting it and clicking the Delete button.
Alternate Text	Alternate text to be displayed by browsers that are not Java-enabled (i.e., they can't run applets).
Alternate HTML	Alternate HTML code to be displayed by browsers that do not recognize the `<applet>` tag.

Setting the run attributes in the Project Editor is a handy method for trying out different ways of presenting an applet without editing HTML source files. The `<applet>` tag requires arguments that specify the applet's name and dimensions. You can change these dimensions in the Run tab, and you can also specify values for the optional `<param>` tag. First we'll look at changing the arguments to the `<applet>` tag by using the Run tab.

Changing Applet Arguments

When we created the *Greeting* project in Chapter 6, we didn't set any run attributes, so the default `Greeting.tmp.html` file looked like the one shown (your `codebase` path name will differ):

```
<applet
    name="Greeting"
    code="Greeting.class"
    codebase="\LWEAVER\InsideJWS\Greeting"
    width="500"
    height="600"
    align="Top"
    alt="If you had a java-enabled browser, you would see an applet
here."
>       <hr>If your browser recognized the applet tag,
        you would see an applet here.<hr>
</applet>
```

The `<applet>` tag requires you to specify values for width and height. You can set those values by editing the HTML file, or interactively in the Run tab.

1. Click the Project Manager icon.

2. Click on the Run tab.

3. Enter some new values in the fields for Width and Height. We used a value of 600 for Width and 60 for Height.

4. Change the alignment to be Middle.

5. Apply the changes.

6. Run the applet.

The HTML file that Java WorkShop generates if you changed the run attributes for Width, Height, and Alignment looks like this (with new settings shown in **bold** type):

```
<applet
    name="Greeting"
    code="Greeting.class"
 codebase="\LWEAVER\InsideJWS\Greeting"
    width="600"
    height="60"
    align="Middle"
    alt="If you had a java-enabled browser, you would see an applet
here."
>       <hr>If your browser recognized the applet tag,
        you would see an applet here.<hr>
</applet>
```

Setting and Changing Parameters

In addition to supplying values on-the-fly for arguments to the applet tag, you can use the Run tab to try out different arguments for the <param> tag. When you set parameters in an HTML file, you edit the file to include the <param> tag and its arguments (name, value). The Run tab gives you fields for setting name and value interactively. After you enter values in these fields and click the Add button, the parameter is listed in the Parameters field. You can click on any parameter in the list and delete it or change it. Figure 8–1 shows the addition of a parameter for setting the background color of the applet to white.

Figure 8–1 Adding Parameters in the Run Tab

For an applet to get a parameter from the HTML page, it has to have a getParameter method defined. The *Greeting* project does not use the getParameter method. The applet in the *TumbleItem* example project uses getParameter to get the location of image files, among other things. You'll see how to set a value for the img parameter in the Run tab when you import that project in Chapter 11.

In summary, when you use the Run tab to make changes to how an applet will run, you repeat the following steps until you see the applet displayed the way you want it:

1. Open the Project Manager.

2. Change applet arguments or parameters.

3. Choose **Project ➠ Run ➠** *<project_name>*.

Summary

In this chapter, we've looked at some of the basics of running projects:

- Running an applet project

- Using and modifying HTML files to use as run pages

- Running other types of projects, including projects you create with Visual Java

- Editing Run attributes in the Project Editor

- Interactively changing <applet> tag and <param> tag arguments for your applet's HTML page

CHAPTER
9

- Browsing the Class Hierarchy

- Browsing Source Code

- Viewing the Java APIs

- Customizing Your Own API Documentation

- Searching for Strings

Browsing
Source Files

T he Java WorkShop Source Browser has two components: a Class Browser and a String Searcher. Each component has a tabbed page in the Source Browser.

If you have used the Java Developer's Kit, you might be familiar with the java-doc program and its output, the Java API (Application Programming Interface) documentation. When you use the Class Browser, Java WorkShop uses javadoc to generate an HTML page that offers a similar view of your code. Together, these constitute the classes you can browse in the Class Browser: your own code and the Java APIs.

The Source Browser helps you understand the architecture of your program, right down to the variables used. The Source Browser enables you to:

- See where classes are derived.

- Follow links to the superclasses.

- Display a list of the methods used in your projects and follow links to their definitions in source files.

- View comments included in code.

- View the output of your own javadoc tags in your APIs.

Browsing the Class Hierarchy

Let's browse one of the examples available with Java WorkShop, the Checkers project.

To browse the *Checkers* project:

1. Choose **Portfolio** ➤ **Choose** ➤ **personal**.

2. Choose **Project** ➤ **Choose** ➤ **Checkers**.

3. Open the Source Browser (the magnifying glass icon in the tool bar).

4. The source file for *Checkers* should be listed.

5. Click on the file name.

    Clicking on the file name starts the browsing. While the Browser is loading, you'll see the status message "Browsing."

    The Source Browser displays the API documentation for `CheckersGame.java`.

6. Follow any link to view information in the source file.

When you follow links, Java WorkShop displays the source code in the Source Editor.

Click on a method name and go to that method in the source file. While you are looking around, notice that *Checkers* has a `main()` method, which means *Checkers* can be run as a standalone application as well as an applet. To see how the constructor for this applet was implemented, click on `CheckersGame` under "Constructors" in the API documentation.

Figure 9–1 shows the result of browsing the Checkers project:

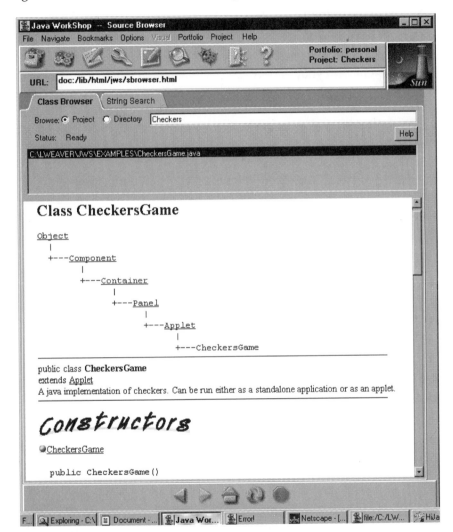

Figure 9–1 Source Browser With *Checkers* Project Loaded

Java API Documentation

The API documentation for Java packages is available from the Java WorkShop Help menu:

Help ➠ Java API Documentation 1.0.

For Java API additions and changes since JDK 1.0, check Sun's Java Web page:

```
http://java.sun.com
```

Of course, you view the Java APIs in the context of your own projects when you use the Java WorkShop Source Browser.

Doing More with Your Own API Documentation

Java WorkShop uses the `javadoc` tool to generate your API documentation. If you'd like to do more with your project API documentation when it is generated in the Source Browser, check out the reference pages for `javadoc` at:

```
http://java.sun.com/products/JDK/tools/win32/javadoc.html
http://java.sun.com/products/JDK/tools/solaris/javadoc.html
```

The reference pages will tell you what kinds of tags you can add to your own source (`.java`) files. We'll describe the `javadoc` doc tag here and show how you can add comments that will appear both in the source file and the generated HTML pages.

How `javadoc` works. The `javadoc` tool reformats and displays all public and protected declarations for:

- Classes and interfaces
- Methods
- Variables

`javadoc` also supports the use of special tags for comments in code so you can augment your own API documentation by putting API comments in code. The tag is called a doc tag and it starts with an @. There are a number of doc tags, for example, specific tags that support the generation of an author line or a version line as well as "see also" links.

Doc tags should come after the last `import` statement and must be within a special delimiter for comments that will be included automatically in generated documentation. The delimiters for documentation comments begin with /** and end with */. You can embed standard HTML tags within a doc comment, but the JDK tools documentation recommends that you avoid using heading tags (<h1>, <h2>, and so on) or the horizontal rule tag (<hr>) because these tags interfere with the structured document created by `javadoc`. Doc tags must start at the beginning of a line.

Here's a sample API comment that includes two of the available doc tags:

```
/**
 * I wrote this to show you how to add comments.
 *
 * @version 0.1 of a file chooser.
 * @author Your Name Here.
 *

 */
```

If you'd like to try this yourself:

1. Choose the *insidejws* portfolio and the *Chooser* project.

2. In the Source Editor, change `Chooser.java` to add the API comments and doc tags in the sample above.

```
import java.awt.*;

/**
 * I wrote this to show you how to add comments.
 *
 * @version 0.1 of a file chooser.
 * @author Your Name Here.
 *
 */

public class Chooser {
    /**
     * Constructor.
     */
    static Frame f = new Frame ("Applications");

    public static void main (String[] a) {
      FileDialog Chooser = new FileDialog(f, "Applications");
        Chooser.show();
        f.add(Chooser);
        f.show ();
    }
}
```

3. Save the file.

4. Open the Source Browser and browse the `Chooser` class.

The Source Browser should display a page like this, with the API comments you have just added:

Class Chooser

```
Object
  |
  +---Chooser
```

---

public class **Chooser**
extends <u>Object</u>
I wrote this to show you how to add comments.
Version:
　0.1 of a file chooser.
Author:
　Your Name Here.

Constructors

<u>Chooser</u>

```
public Chooser()
```

Methods

<u>main</u>

```
public static void main(String a[])
```

Searching for Strings

In the first release of Java WorkShop, the Source Browser supports searches for specified strings and nothing more—no wildcard characters or other regular substitutions.

The scope of the search can be either a directory or a project. The Source Browser will also let you specify what file types to search (`.java`, `.html`, `.h`, `.c` and so on). Searching a project limits the search to those source files that you created or included when you made the project. Searching a directory limits the search to the files in a named directory and its subdirectories. The Source Browser won't assume that you mean it to search the directory for the current project; you'll have to enter a directory name explicitly.

Take a look at Figure 9–2 to see the basic parts of the Source Browser String Searcher before we try it out.

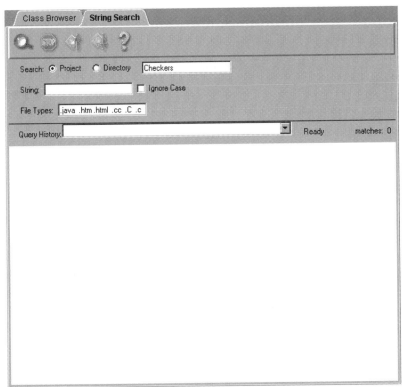

Figure 9–2 Source Browser String Search

The String Search tool bar contains icons for (left to right in Figure 9–3) finding matches, stopping the search, finding the next match, finding the previous match, and getting Help.

Figure 9–3 String Search Tool Bar

To search for a string:

1. Open the Source Browser.

2. Set the scope of your search to either a project or a directory. By default, the String Searcher is going to search the current project, but you can enter another project name or a directory name in the Search field.

3. Enter a string in the String field.

110

4. To narrow the search to certain types of files, delete or add file types to the list in the File Types field. Separate the items in the list by a space.

5. Click on the Find Matches icon in the String Search tool bar.

    You could also start searching by pressing Return after you enter the string in the String field.

The Source Browser displays the search results with links to the code where the string appears. Figure 9–4 illustrates the results of a search for the string "paint" in the Checkers project.

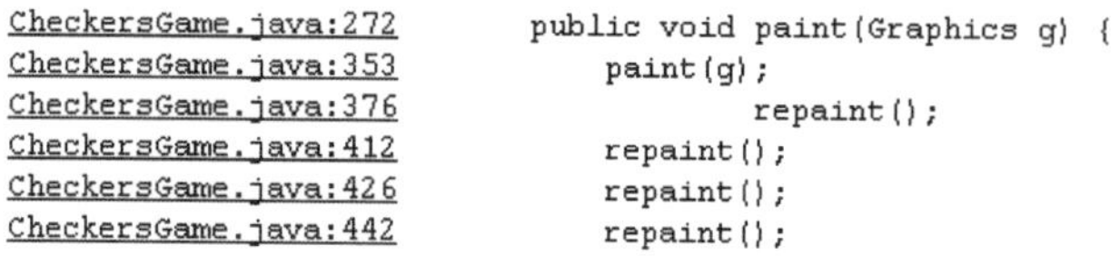

```
CheckersGame.java:272      public void paint(Graphics g) {
CheckersGame.java:353          paint(g);
CheckersGame.java:376              repaint();
CheckersGame.java:412      repaint();
CheckersGame.java:426      repaint();
CheckersGame.java:442      repaint();
```

Figure 9–4 Source Browser Search Results

Clicking on a link takes you to the source code displayed in the Source Editor.

Search results consist of:

*   The file that contains the string

*   The line number

*   The text of the line where the match occurred

The Next and Previous icons in the Source Browser tool bar enable you to move from match to match without having to click on the file name.

Source Browser keeps a Query History list in a pulldown menu. To repeat a search, select it from the Query History list. The Query History lists every query and the types of files included in the search, even if you switched portfolios and projects. Figure 9–5 illustrates the Query History list.

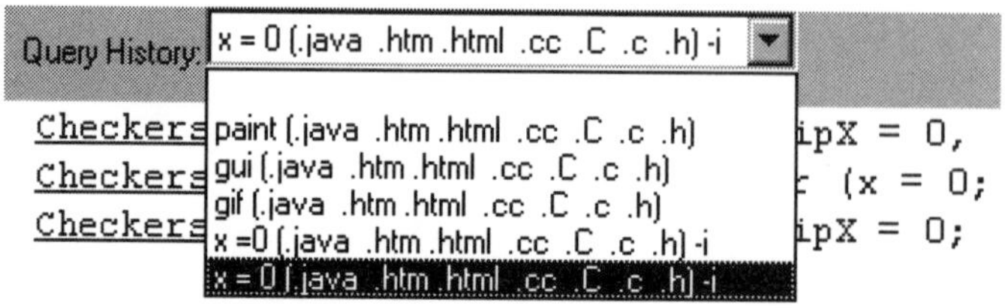

Query History: | x = 0 (.java .htm .html .cc .C .c .h) -i ▼ |

```
Checkers  paint (.java .htm .html .cc .C .c .h)       pX = 0,
Checkers  gui (.java .htm .html .cc .C .c .h)         (x = 0;
Checkers  gif (.java .htm .html .cc .C .c .h)         pX = 0;
          x =0 (.java .htm .html .cc .C .c .h) -i
          x = 0 (.java .htm .html .cc .C .c .h) -i
```

Figure 9–5 Query History List

Another way to repeat a query if you don't want to find it in the pulldown list is to enter enough characters to identify the string in the Query History field. For example, entering the character "p" uniquely identifies the "paint" string. The String Search tab again displays the results for the "paint" search.

Summary

In the tour of the Source Browser, we discussed:

- Browsing the class hierarchy, including the classes you created and the Java classes used
- Finding Java API documentation
- Adding `javadoc` tags to your own source code
- Searching for strings
- Using the String Search Query History list

CHAPTER 10

Debugging Projects

The Java WorkShop Debugger is a powerful tool for examining and debugging Java applets and standalone programs. The Debugger employs the by now familiar tabbed metaphor, with a tab for each of the debugging areas you want to examine or set: Threads/Stack, Variables, Breakpoints, Exceptions, Classes, and Messages. Each tab has a Help button to provide a ready online reference for every element and option in that tab.

Here are some of the things you can do with the Debugger:

- List, inspect, suspend, and resume threads.

- Evaluate local or class variables.

- Set, view, and clear breakpoints.

- Control how exceptions are handled in a debugging session.

- Examine the packages, classes, and methods in the current project and expand objects and arrays to show all embedded variables.

- View console input and output for the project being debugged.

- Move between Source Editor and Debugger windows.

- Examine all of the source files used by your program.

- Run the applet you are debugging in a Browser window or the Applet Viewer.

There is a lot you can do with the Debugger, so we have devoted two chapters to it. This one introduces the Debugger and offers a simple exercise. We'll save the heavy-duty debugging for Chapter 11. But you should take this part of the tour to familiarize yourself with the Debugger tool.

Figure 10–1 shows the Debugger in the Browser window.

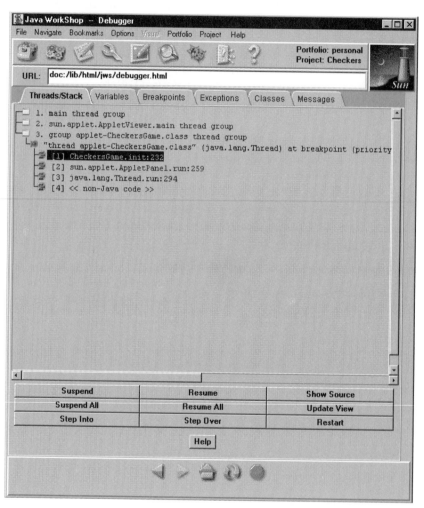

Figure 10–1 The Tabbed Pages of the Debugger

Setting Debug Attributes

One of the advantages of the project concept is that you can set and save different attributes for each project. And you can edit any project at any time by choosing **Project** ⇒ **Edit** ⇒ *projectname* from the Java WorkShop menu. It doesn't even have to be the current project.

Remember the Project Editor we described in "Editing Project Attributes" on page 48? One of the project attributes that you can edit is Debug/Browse.

You can set the following attributes for a debugging session:

- **Source paths to prepend to default:** Additional paths to add to the source path. To view the default entries, click the View Source Path button.

- **Main class file:** The .class file in which the init() method (applets) or main() method (standalone programs) is defined.

- **Run page:** The URL of the HTML file that contains the applet when you run it in Java WorkShop. You can use the default run page created by Java Work-Shop or develop your own HTML file on-the-fly.

- **Java interpreter options:** The options to pass to the java interpreter, such as -classpath or -verbose. (Standalone programs only.)

- **For applet debugging use:** Radio buttons for choosing where to display the applet you are debugging: in the Applet Viewer or in the Java WorkShop Browser. Applet Viewer is the default, but Browser lets you display applets other than the one you are debugging, as well as view the entire HTML page that contains the applet or applets.

Later in this chapter you can follow an exercise that uses the Debugger. For ease of following along, set the Debug attribute for applet debugging to be the Browser and click the Apply button.

Building in Debug Mode

Before you debug, you should have compiled the applet or program with the debug option. This is one of the options you would have set when you edited the Build attributes in the Project Editor. It causes Build Manager to run the compiler with the -g option:

```
javac -g
```

If you haven't used the Build Manager yet, see "Using the Build Manager" on page 69.

Starting A Debugging Session

Choose the Project you want to debug and then launch the Debugger:

• Click the Debugger icon—the ladybug—on the Java WorkShop tool bar.

Here's what Java WorkShop does when you launch the Debugger:

• Opens the Debugger to the Threads tab with the thread groups for the project displayed.

• Opens the Source Editor to display the code you are debugging.

• Starts a debugging session.

• Sets a breakpoint in the first line of the `init()` method if your project is an applet or `main()` if your project is a standalone program. The line where the breakpoint is set is highlighted in red.

• Runs the project to the breakpoint, then stops execution. The breakpoint high-lighting changes from red to green so you know where execution stopped.

• Of course, if you haven't defined an `init()` or `main()` you'll get a warning message instead of an initial breakpoint.

• For applet projects, Java WorkShop launches a second Browser or an Applet Viewer for running the project you are debugging, depending on the Debug attribute you set.

Windows 95 and NT developers:

If the applet is suspended at a breakpoint, the Browser or Applet Viewer will not respond to window operations (move, close, resize, and so on). You'll have to handle window operations by using these tricks:

• Press Alt-Tab to bring the Browser window to the front.
• Click the Resume button in the Source Editor.
• Press Control-Alt-Delete to pop up the task list.
• Move the Browser to a location that you like before you start debugging the applet. That way, you won't have to move it.

Quitting a Debugging Session

Ending a debugging session is a little awkward in Java WorkShop. If you try to switch projects, a warning message advises you that you are in the middle of a debugging session. If you try to open another tool, you won't receive the warning. In short, the only way to quit a debugging session is to switch projects and watch for a prompt. For example, let's say that you are debugging the *Blink* project. To end the debugging session, you could choose **Project** ⇒ **Choose** ⇒ **Greeting** or any project other than *Blink*. Java WorkShop opens a dialog box asking if you want to kill the current debugging session. Click the Yes button. That's it; the debugging session is ended.

Using the Debugger

Let's load one of the sample projects you created and built earlier into the Debugger. If you didn't create and build the *Chooser* project, you can find the files for it on the CD-ROM.

1. Choose **Portfolio** ⇒ **Choose** ⇒ **insidejws** from the Java WorkShop menu.

2. Choose **Project** ⇒ **Choose** ⇒ **Chooser**.

3. Click the Debugger icon on the tool bar.

    Java WorkShop opens the Debugger with the Threads/Stack tab on top. This tab lists the thread groups in your program. In our example, there are no threads except those used by the Debugger itself.

    Java WorkShop also opens the Source Editor with the code for Chooser.java loaded and the first breakpoint highlighted.

4. Click the Resume button in the Threads/Stack tab.

    Java WorkShop launches the *Chooser* project in a separate window. The Threads/Stack tab is updated.

Each of the Debugger's six tabs offers a view of some aspect of your program. The Threads/Stack tab lists the threads in the current project. To expand a thread group to get more information, click on the glyph (little icon) to its left. The first expansion shows the stack frames. Expanding the glyph next to the stack frame shows the variables local to that stack. There are buttons in the Threads/Stack tab for suspending and resuming one or all of your program threads, single stepping through a method a statement at a time, or stepping into a method, and so on. We'll try these operations on an animated applet in Chapter 11.

The Variables tab enables you to evaluate local or global variables that are within the scope of the object whose method you are stopped in. By entering the variable's name in the evaluate field you display its value at the current time. You can also expand objects and arrays to show all embedded variables.

The Breakpoints tab is one place where you set breakpoints (the source editor and Classes tabs are two others). To set a breakpoint, specify a class and the method name or line number where you want the breakpoint to be set. You can also set a breakpoint in the Source Editor by using the Toggle Breakpoint icon.

The Classes tab displays the packages, classes, and methods in the current project. You can also set breakpoints in this tab.

The Messages tab is used by the Debugger to display warning messages during the debugging session, as well as program output as you debug your applet or application.

The Exceptions tab is where you control how the Debugger should handle exceptions when you run your applet or application during a debugging session. We'll spend more time using the Threads/Stack, Variables, Breakpoints, and Classes tabs in Chapter 11, so let's look at the Exceptions tab in more detail now to see what you can do with it.

Click the Exceptions tab now and look at the exceptions list. The list includes the predefined exceptions from the JDK. If you want to include any exceptions that you used in your program, you have to add them here. We didn't include exceptions in the `Chooser` program, so all of the exceptions listed are from the JDK.

All of the exceptions listed are set to "break uncaught." This is the default. You can use the exceptions buttons (Break on Uncaught, Break Always, and Ignore) to change the setting on each exception. The Break on Uncaught setting causes the Debugger to stop when the exception is thrown, just as if you had set a breakpoint. Break Always does the same thing (stops as if at a breakpoint) even if you have caught and handled the exception in your program. Ignore does just what it says: it causes the Debugger to ignore the selected exception or exceptions. The last button in this area, Show Source, loads the source code of the selected exception into the Source Editor.

If there is an exception in your code that you want to add to the list, use the Exception field at the bottom of the tab. Enter the exception name and include the package, for example, `java.lang.NumberFormatException`. The Debugger adds this to the top of the exceptions list. Now you can control how the Debugger handles the exception from your code.

Updating Debugger Information

Each tab provides information about an aspect of your program. They also work together. The Threads/Stack tab is updated automatically as you run to breakpoints or suspend and resume threads. The Variables tab can also be updated, but you control the updates by clicking the Evaluate button to refresh the tab with current variable values. A more global updating option is the Restart button, available from both the Threads/Stack tab and the Source Editor. Restart begins the debugging session, but it does not clear away any breakpoints that you have set. To clear breakpoints, use the Clear buttons in the Breakpoints tab.

In Chapter 11, you'll use these tools in a debugging exercise with an animated applet.

Summary

Java WorkShop debugging features are extensive enough for the Java WorkShop online documentation to devote both a tutorial with six exercises and about two dozen task-oriented help pages to them. If you want more experience with the Debugger interface before you try the exercise in Chapter 11, the URL for the tutorial is:

`doc:/lib/html/help/start/simpledebug.html.`

In this first look at debugging projects in Java WorkShop, we discussed:

- Building projects in debug mode
- Setting debugging attributes
- Starting and ending a debugging session
- Using the Debugger tabs to get information about your program

PART THREE

CHAPTER 11

- Debugging an Applet Project

- Looking at What Threads Do

- Viewing Threads and Call Stacks

- Setting and Removing Breakpoints

- Evaluating Variables with the Threads/Stack Tab

- Tips for Using the Debugger

Doing More with the Debugger

In this chapter you'll use Java WorkShop's Debugger to:

- Find an error in an applet project that uses animation
- Set and clear breakpoints
- Stop and resume threads
- View threads
- Examine call stacks
- Go from the Debugger to source code
- Display and evaluate variables

The debugging exercise in this chapter is meant to be done as a unit. Topic headings are used to indicate specific task areas along the way, such as viewing threads and setting breakpoints.

Debugging an Applet Project

The *TumbleItem* project from the CD-ROM examples contains an applet with some simple animation. You'll use the Debugger to stop and resume threads and examine the state of variables in this project.

TumbleItem consists of one Java source file and sixteen images (.gif files) that are loaded in a sequence that produces an animation of the Java mascot, Duke, tumbling across the top of your browser or applet viewer. Duke's routine varies as the program loops through the complete sequence of images. There is an error in the source code that allows the program to compile but causes the animation to behave in an unexpected way. You'll use the Debugger to track down the problem and fix it, and then you'll run the project to see the result.

Here are the files for *TumbleItem*:

- `TumbleItem.prj`
- `TumbleItem.class`
- `TumbleItem.java`
- `TumbleItem.map`
- `images\tumble\` (for Windows; `images/tumble` for Solaris)
- `TumbleItem.html`

The first step is to get the project into Java WorkShop. You'll import the project and give it the same name, *TumbleItem*.

▼ To import the *TumbleItem* project, choose **Portfolio** ⟶**Choose** ⟶ **insidejws** to make *insidejws* the current portfolio, and then choose **Import** ⟶ **Project**. In the Import Project Dialog, enter the directory where you copied *TumbleItem* from the CD-ROM. Create by copy or reference. Enter a destination directory. Click Yes at Include Source. Enter the project name (use *TumbleItem* and omit the `.prj` suffix) and click Import.

There's one more step to make sure that you get the project's images in the right place. The HTML run page that comes with the project defines the value of the `img` parameter to be "images/tumble." If you copied the `images` directory when you copied the project directory and you put it at the same level as the project files, you're all set.

▼ To change the `img` parameter to point to a different directory, use the Run tab in the Project Editor to make that change or edit the HTML file itself. If you need to specify a different directory name in the `img` parameter, choose **Project** ⟶**Edit** ⟶**TumbleItem**. Click the Run tab. Enter the directory for the images in the Parameter Name and Value fields.

When we set up the example, we specified img and "/images/tumble" in the Parameters fields, as shown in Figure 11–1.

Parameters:

img="images/tumble"

Name: img

Value: "images/tumble"

Figure 11–1 Using the Run Tab to Include Images in an Applet Project

Note: To debug a program in Java WorkShop, you should have built the program in Java WorkShop. The *TumbleItem* project was build with the Build Manager.

If you don't need any background on threads before you get into the debugging exercise, skip ahead to "Debugging the Applet" on page 126.

Looking at What Threads Do

A *thread* is an independent execution sequence within a program. In Java programs, multiple threads can run at the same time. Many Java programmers are using applets to create animation or writing applets that run at the same time on a Web page. They are using threads because threads allow an applet to run through a stack of images (animate) without interfering with other resources, or to start, stop, and run at the same time as other applets. If you have ever had to stop an applet by using the brute force technique of quitting a browser or other applet viewer, you appreciate a programmer who knows how to use threads.

The TumbleItem applet has three thread groups: a group that handles user interactions within the Browser while the applet is running, a group for the Browser or Applet Viewer itself, and a group that is particular to the applet. This last thread group is the one controlling the animation.

Threads are good practice for things besides looping through a set of images. For example, if you have written code that will take some time to execute and you want the user to be able to interact with your program at the same time, you should use multiple threads. Every program has a main thread to take care of user interface actions. This is the thread that notices when a user clicks on a button to stop the applet while another thread takes care of animation. In Java, you put a concurrent execution sequence under the control of a thread by deriving a class from the Thread class and implementing the run() method.

The Java WorkShop Debugger helps you to observe the behavior of threads as they are running. Threads have states. They can be running, sleeping, suspended, waiting for a condition, stopped, zombie, or undetermined. The state of a thread is indicated by the glyph next to it in the Threads/Stack tab and by the text accompanying it, for example:

```
"Thread-4" (java.lang.thread) suspended (priority 7)
```

When a thread is stopped, you can view the stack of calls that make up the thread. You can also view the call stack of a running thread, but you see only the last snapshot of the thread. The call stack includes all methods that have been called but have not returned to the caller. The methods in the call stack are listed in the order in which they were called by your program; at the top of the stack is the method that was executing when the program stopped.

A stack frame in Java is like a stack frame in a procedural language—it just holds the state for a method call as opposed to a function call.

Using the Threads/Stack tab, you can view:

- Threads in a thread group

- Stack frames in a thread

- Variables local to each stack frame

- Variables within objects and arrays

You'll use the Threads/Stack tab to keep track of the value of a variable while you step through your code.

Debugging the Applet

▼ With *TumbleItem* the current project, click the Debugger icon.

Java WorkShop loads the Debugger tool into the Browser with the Threads/Stack tab on top, opens the Source Editor with `TumbleItem.java` loaded and a breakpoint set at the `init()` method (Figure 11–2), and creates a separate Debugging HTML Browser page for running the applet.

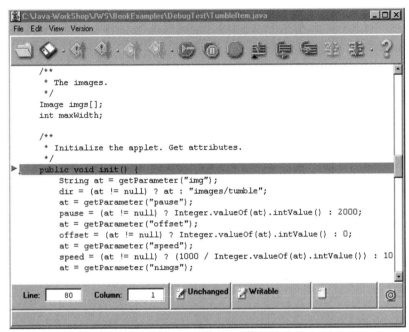

Figure 11–2 Source Editor with Breakpoint Set at init()

The Source Editor's debug icons are active. The buttons in the Threads/Stack tab have counterparts in the Source Editor debug icons. You can step over or into methods, set and remove breakpoints, suspend and resume threads, and restart the debugging session in either tool. The Restart button or icon offers easy ways to start a debugging session over again if you have tried a number of debugging techniques that you want to clear away without leaving the Debugger. Breakpoint settings are retained after you restart the session. If you want to clear those before or after restarting, click the Clear All button in the Breakpoints tab.

Because this is a ready-made project, a number of project attributes have already been set in the Project Editor. These options were used:

- Debug option (-g) — Set in the Build tab

- Java WorkShop Browser as the execution environment for debugging — Set in the Debug/Browse tab

- Run page (TumbleItem.html) — Set in the Run tab

- The directory for the images — Set in the Run tab

You can change any of these settings, but the debug option is required for debugging. You might try to examine a local variable only to see the message "No local variables. Try debugging with -g."

To show you the Browser Debugging window, we chose to debug using the Browser, but the Applet Viewer is probably a lot faster for most applets. The Browser Debugging window does get faster after the applet has been loaded the first time.

Let's view the thread groups in the *TumbleItem* project (Figure 11–3 shows all of the thread groups expanded).

```
Threads/Stack | Variables | Breakpoints | Exceptions | Classes | Messages

1. main thread group
  "main" (java.lang.Thread) cond. waiting (priority 1)
  "Debugger agent" (java.lang.Thread) running (priority 10)
  "Screen Updater" (sun.awt.ScreenUpdater) cond. waiting (priority 4)
  "Image Fetcher 0" (sun.awt.image.ImageFetcher) cond. waiting (priority 8)
  "Image Fetcher 1" (sun.awt.image.ImageFetcher) cond. waiting (priority 8)
  "Image Fetcher 2" (sun.awt.image.ImageFetcher) cond. waiting (priority 8)
  "Image Fetcher 3" (sun.awt.image.ImageFetcher) cond. waiting (priority 8)
2. sun.applet.AppletViewer.main thread group
  "AWT-Win32" (java.lang.Thread) running (priority 5)
  "AWT-Callback-Win32" (java.lang.Thread) running (priority 5)
3. group applet-TumbleItem.class thread group
  "thread applet-TumbleItem.class" (java.lang.Thread) cond. waiting (priority
    [1] java.lang.Object.wait:152
    [2] sun.applet.AppletPanel.getNextEvent:185
    [3] sun.applet.AppletPanel.run:216
    [4] java.lang.Thread.run:294
    [5] << non-Java code >>
  "Thread-3" (java.lang.Thread) running (priority 4)
```

Figure 11–3 Thread/Stack for the Animation Applet

Viewing Threads and Call Stacks

The Threads/Stack tab lists all the thread groups in the *TumbleItem* project. Because the Debugger automatically sets a breakpoint in the init() method, you won't see any other threads until you resume the program from the breakpoint. The reason is simple—with the program stopped at the init() method, none of the other threads have been created yet. You should see all the threads used by your program after you click the Resume All button either in the Threads/Stack tab or the Source Editor.

Notice the glyphs next to the thread groups.

▼ To expand any item in the page, click the glyph next to it once and only once. To condense the items, click the glyph again.

Three thread groups should be listed in the Threads/Stack tab:

- "main" (java.lang.Thread)

  For handling user keyboard actions.

- sun.jws.main.Main thread group

  Depending on whether you choose to debug in a browser window or the Applet Viewer, you'll see the thread group that represents the browser (the sun.jws.Main thread group) or the Applet Viewer (the sun.applet.Applet-Viewer.main thread group).

  Applets run in multiple threads with the init(), start(), and stop() methods running under one thread, and paint() and handleEvent() running under another—AWT-Motif on Solaris, or AWT-CallBack-Win32 on Windows NT and Windows 95.

- applet-TumbleItem.class thread group

  This is the thread group for the applet itself.

The glyph accompanying a thread is an additional clue to the state of the thread. The glyphs for each of the seven states are illustrated in online help (Figure 11–4).

The glyph accompanying a thread is an additional clue as to the state of the thread. In all, a thread can be in one of seven states.

- The state of the thread cannot be determined.

- Thread is a zombie (has been exited, but has not yet been reaped or has been constructed but not yet started).

- Thread is running.

- Thread is sleeping.

- Thread is waiting on a conditional variable.

- Thread is suspended.

- Thread is stopped at a breakpoint.

Figure 11–4 Thread Glyphs

Setting and Removing Breakpoints

The TumbleItem.class thread group should be expanded already because it holds the init() method, which is the default breakpoint when you start a debugging session. It's also the default breakpoint when you restart a debugging session.

▼ So that you can see Duke tumble in the Debugging HTML Browser, set a new breakpoint at the `run()` method and then run the program to that point.

You can set the new breakpoint in one of several ways.

To set a breakpoint by using the Breakpoints tab:

- Enter the class and method names (`TumbleItem`, `run`) and click the Stop In button.

- Enter the class and line number (`TumbleItem`, 99) and click the Stop At button.

To set a breakpoint by using the Source Editor:

- Use the Find command in the Edit menu (or use the keyboard shortcut <Ctrl+F>) to search for the string "run." Click the Toggle Breakpoint icon when you find the line containing the `run()` method.

- Enter the line number in the status bar. Click the Toggle Breakpoint icon on the line with the `run()` method.

The Debugger often provides alternate ways of performing tasks. Many developers prefer to use the Source Editor to set breakpoints, but we'll describe the alternatives when we introduce a step so you can decide on the method you prefer.

Now that you know how to set a breakpoint, you should know how to clear it. Clear the current breakpoint in one of these ways:

- Use the Breakpoints tab and click Clear all or select a breakpoint from the list and click Clear.

- Use the Source Editor and click the Toggle Breakpoint icon.

Note: You must have the Debugger running your program to examine variables in the Variables tab. The variables you can evaluate in the Variables tab are in the thread's scope, so be sure to select a new thread in the Threads/Stack tab to examine the variables in the scope of that thread. If you try to set a breakpoint without a selected thread, you might not be aware of why you can't set a breakpoint, because the error message from Java WorkShop appears in the Messages tab. Java WorkShop displays the message in the bottom half of the Messages tab, the section reserved for Debugger messages. In this case, look for the message `No thread selected, select a thread from the Threads list`.

▼ Now that you have a breakpoint set at the `run()` method, click the Resume all icon in the Source Editor.

Duke begins tumbling.

This applet is programmed with a variety of images to give Duke's routine some variety. The current version of the source code for *TumbleItem* is deliberately written with an error that causes Duke to tumble using only some of the available images. The result is a choppy animation that repeats just several images. Let's find out why and restore some variety to Duke's routine.

If you had written this applet, you would probably know immediately where to begin looking for the problem. Consider where someone who was not familiar with the code might begin to investigate the applet. Unless you were very patient or compulsive, you wouldn't start by stepping through lines or methods beginning at the `init()` method. You might begin by looking at the `run()` or `paint()` methods instead and examining the changes to the variables used in those methods. Or you might start at a higher level by finding the thread that controls the animation.

There is only one applet-specific thread group in the example, so you shouldn't have much trouble guessing which thread group to examine.

▼ Select the applet's thread group—the `TumbleItem.class` thread group—and click on the glyph next to it to see what threads are in it. Click on the first thread to display its call stack.

There are two methods of interest to the current mystery, a `wait()` method and a `run()` method.

▼ Suspend the thread with the `wait()` method in it.

The Threads/Stack tab updates the status of the thread to display "Thread-#" (`java.lang.Thread`) suspended.

Look at the Debugging HTML Browser and you'll see that Duke is still tumbling. This looks like the thread that controls Duke's sleeping moments, not the one that controls his tumbling.

▼ Resume the thread. Select the next thread and suspend that one.

Duke stops tumbling. This is the thread that controls Duke's tumbling.

▼ You have your thread now, so expand it to see the call stack for it. There's a call on the stack for `TumbleItem.run`. Expand this call stack. You know that there must be a method that loops through the images and that the loop probably increments a variable. Click the glyph next to `this = TumbleItem` to display the variables in this object. Examine the list of variables until you see likely candidates. The `loopslot` and `nimgs` variables seem to have something to do with the images and the loop, so let's narrow our search to one of them and evaluate it at different stages of the applet as it runs.

At any stage you might find it more expedient to go to the Source Editor and search for methods or variables by name to see what role they are playing. You might also use the Source Browser. However, to show you the kind of dynamic information you can get from the Threads/Stack, we are deliberately deferring those approaches.

Evaluating Variables with the Threads/Stack Tab

You can examine the values of variables dynamically in the Threads/Stack tab or evaluate them in the Variables Tab. The Threads/Stack is more dynamic because it is updated as the state of the program changes. Try running Duke and observing variable values in the Threads/Stack tab at the same time.

▼ Step into the `run()` method while the Threads/Stack tab is open. Arrange your desktop so that you see the Debugging HTML Browser and the Threads/Stack tab at the same time. The Threads/Stack tab automatically updates itself with the current state of a thread, but you can also click the Update View button.

Watch the values for the `loopslot` and `nimgs` variables in the Threads/Stack tab as Duke tumbles. The value of `nimgs` remains at 16. The value of `loopslot` increments, but only from 10 to 15, not from 0 to 15 as we would expect if every image was being used by the program. Now is a good time to look at how these variables are used in the program.

Viewing Source

To go from the Threads/Stack tab to the code in the Source Editor, select a call in the call stack and click the View Source button.

▼ To expand a call, click its glyph. To select it, put the mouse cursor in its name. If it is highlighted, it is selected. Select `TumbleItem.run`. When it is highlighted, click View Source.

Figure 11–5 illustrates the code in the Source Editor.

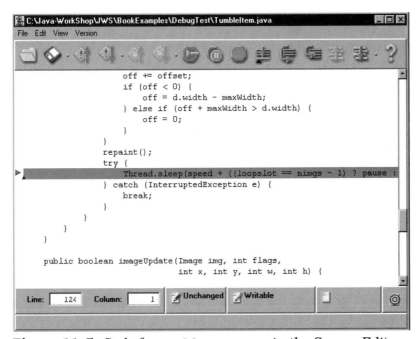

Figure 11–5 Code for `TumbleItem.run` in the Source Editor

Without too much looking around, we can see that there is an `if` statement that controls the looping of images (Example 11-1).

```
        if (++loopslot >= nimgs) {
            loopslot = 10;
            off += offset;
            if (off < 0) {
            off = d.width - maxWidth;
            } else if (off + maxWidth > d.width) {
            off = 0;
            }
        }
        repaint();
        try {
            Thread.sleep(speed + ((loopslot == nimgs - 1) ? pause :
0));
        } catch (InterruptedException e) {
            break;
        }
```

Example 11-1 Image Loop in **TumbleItem.java**

Because of a typographical error, the value of `loopslot` is set to 10, not 0 as intended. That's it; you've solved the problem.

▼ Correct the error now, save the file, and rebuild the project. When the build is done, return to the Debugger. You'll have to use the Restart button to restart the debugging session.

Now when you run *TumbleItem* in the Debugger or by using Project Tester, you can see that Duke does some handstands in his tumbling routine. The missing images are being used in the program.

Evaluating Variables with the Variables Tab

We might have used the Variables tab to observe variable values, too. It is not dynamic like the Threads/Stack tab, but you can use it to check a variable after you have stopped a program at different points in its execution.

▼ To use the Variables tab, enter the name of the variable in the Evaluate field. Click Evaluate. You can try evaluating the value of `loopslot` at different stages. To update the variables tab, click Evaluate again.

Try running the program to a breakpoint and then evaluating `loopslot` again. The value of `loopslot` changes; we can see that it uses all 16 frames in Duke's animation. Figure 11–6 shows the results in the Variables tab.

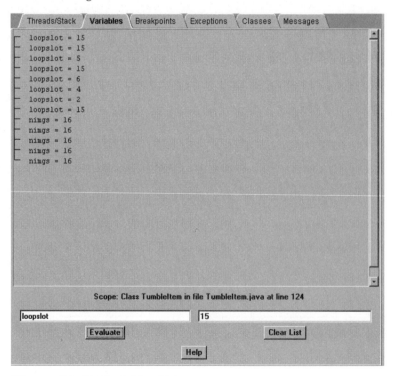

Figure 11–6 Variables Tab

Notice that the Variables tab footer shows the scope of the variable being evaluated, in our case, Scope: Class TumbleItem in file TumbleItem.java at line 124. Local variables become active when the method they appear in becomes active and remain active as long as its method is on the call stack and the execution is within the scope of the variable declaration.

Incidentally, the value of nimgs could be set in the program or the HTML page that holds the applet. If you look at the file TumbleItem.html, you'll see that the number of images to use, as well as other parameters, is passed in to the applet from the applet tag in the HTML page (Example 11-2).

```
<title>Tumbling Duke</title>
<hr>
<applet code="TumbleItem.class" width=600 height=95>
<param name=speed value="10">
<param name=maxwidth value="120">
<param name=nimgs value="16">
<param name=offset value="-57">
<param name=img value="images/tumble">
</applet>
<hr>
<a href="TumbleItem.java">The source.</a>
```

Example 11-2 HTML Code for TumbleItem

To review how to suspend and resume threads, try suspending and resuming the thread that controls Duke's animation until you can stop Duke at the handstand image that was missing when we started the debugging exercise.

▼ Select the applet's thread group in the Thread/Stack tab. Make sure it is running. Watch Duke until you think he's about to stand on his hands and then click Suspend. It might take a few tries to catch him in the act.

Checking the value of the loopslot variable now tells us that this image appears when loopslot=6.

Tips for Using the Debugger

Here are some tips to help you move between tools and know where you are in source code during a Debugging session.

Navigating. You can move between tools in Java WorkShop by using the Browser navigation buttons in the Browser footer, but this only applies to HTML pages. It works for the tools because each tool runs in its own Browser page. Tabs are a different story. To move between tabs in the Debugger, click on the tab you want. To go to the last-used tool, click the Back icon or just choose a new tool from the Browser menu bar.

Reloading the page. If you reload the Debugger page, with the Reload icon or by choosing **File ➠ Reload** from the menu bar, you reset the debugging session to the beginning and will lose any debugging steps you might have taken.

Losing your way in source code. Your view of your program as you work in the Debugger includes the Java base classes or any other classes that your program uses. That is, if Java WorkShop can find the classes. If the Debugger can't find the source code for the frame at the top of the call stack, it goes to the first frame for which it does find source and highlights the line in purple. That's your clue that you are in what has been dubbed "purple hell." In fact, things are not that bad. If you see a line highlighted in purple, check for an error message in the Browser footer. It will probably display a message saying that it can't find the source code. If you really do have source code for the method in the call stack, try adding the path for it to the project. Use the Project Editor's Debug/Browse tab to view the path or add to it.

Assuming that all of the required source paths have been identified for Java WorkShop, you are able to navigate through all of the Java code that your program calls. This is expected and required behavior for coherent debugging, but you might not be aware when it is happening unless you pay attention to the color highlighting in the Source Editor.

Table 11-1 offers a reference to the color highlighting used in the Source Editor during debugging.

Table 11-1 Source Editor Debugging Highlights

Highlight Color	Description
Green	Indicates the line that was executing when the program stopped.
Red	Indicates that a breakpoint is set in the line.
Yellow	Indicates that the line contains an error.
Purple	Indicates one of several things:
	A method for which the source code was not available.
	The method call of the current stack frame.
	Code viewed from the Source Browser. When you are browsing source and you click on a link in the Source Browser, the selected method is highlighted in purple in the Source Editor.
Blue	Indicates a Source Browser match.

Summary

In this chapter you acquired more hands-on experience with the Debugger and learned about:

- Debugging an applet project
- Viewing threads and call stacks
- Setting and removing breakpoints
- Evaluating variables
- Moving between source files while debugging
- Using and updating the information in the Debugger tabs during a debugging session

CHAPTER
12

- Building a GUI: An Extended Example

- Creating the Rolo Project

- Laying Out The Rolo Project

- Editing the GUI Component Attributes

- Previewing the GUI

- Adding Callbacks Interactively

- Building and Running the Rolo Project

- Creating Menus

- Programming with Groups and Shadows

- Visual Java Runtime Classes

- Visual Java Class Hierarchy

- Using the Visual Java API

- Adding Custom Components and Windows

- GUI Building Tips

Doing More with the GUI Builder

Visual Java enables you to lay out your program's user interface, view the results, make changes, and see the effects immediately. This is a far sight easier than using the AWT, compiling the program, running it, and then rewriting code. But creating the interface, while a significant part of the effort, is still just a part of what you'll be doing.

You can run the Visual Java program, but it will just display the user interface (as with the *Chooser* example in Chapter 5). You still have to create the code that will enable your program to respond to and handle events, whether the event is a simple user event, like a mouse click on a button, or a window event, like scrolling or closing a window. Creating the event handling code is less automated, of course, but Visual Java does offer a little wizardry in the form of dialogs for setting filters and actions. Another feature of Visual Java is that you can enter code for callbacks without having to go to the Source Editor. The code is written to your source files when you generate the GUI.

Chapter 7 ("Building GUIs") gave you a tour of the Visual Java interface, including the component palette, the layout grid and window, the Attribute Editor, and the filter and action dialog boxes. In this chapter, you'll take a second look at GUI building with Visual Java and go through a GUI building scenario. You'll also see how to create menus, import and add components, and use groups and shadow classes.

Building a GUI: An Extended Example

You are going to use the GUI builder to create an online name and telephone index (a "scrollodex," if you will). The project is named *Rolo*. The result will be a GUI that looks similar to Figure 12–1, depending on your platform.

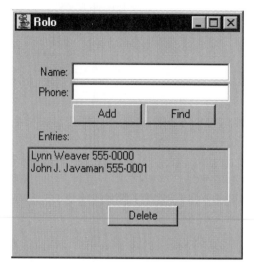

Figure 12–1 Preview of the Rolo Project

With the *Rolo* application, the user can:

- Enter text in Name and Phone fields

- Add the text entries from the two fields to a list

- Delete entries from the list

- Search the list

You'll use the following GUI components[1] and write callbacks for them:

- Text Label

- Single-line TextField

- Text Button

- List

---

1. Visual Java uses the term components for the GUI elements that you might know by the terms "controls" or "widgets." To be consistent with Visual Java terminology, we refer to them as components in the discussions of GUI building.

Creating the Rolo Project

Start by creating a standalone program project named *Rolo*, and choose Visual Java as the tool for creating the project:

▼ Choose **Portfolio** ⁙⁙➤**Choose** ⁙⁙➤ **insidejws**. Choose **Project** ⁙⁙➤**Create** ⁙⁙➤ **Standalone Program**. In the Standalone Program Project Tab, click No to Existing Sources and click the Visual Java radio button to start the project in the GUI builder.

Figure 12–2 shows the Standalone Program tab at the start of the *Rolo* project.

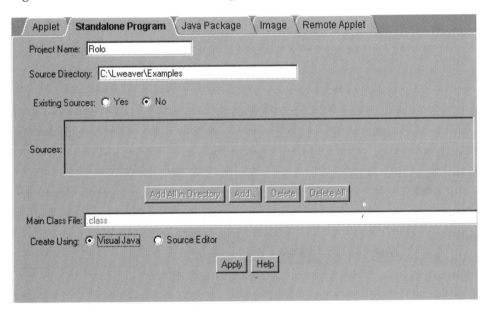

Figure 12–2 Creating the Rolo Project

When Visual Java opens, the default main container is the Panel. You need to change this to a Frame because the application is a standalone program. Recall that a Frame is the main container for a standalone application and a Panel is the main container for an applet.

▼ Choose **Visual Main** ⁙⁙➤ **Container**. In the Main Container dialog box, click the Frame radio button. Click Apply to make the change and then click Ok to close the dialog.

Visual Java displays "Unnamed Frame" in the component list instead of PANEL. You can name the Frame at any time. This name will be displayed in the title bar of your application. Let's name the Frame now to refresh your memory about how to use the Attribute Editor.

▼ With "Unnamed Frame" selected in the component list, open the Attribute Editor by clicking the Attribute Editor icon or clicking the right mouse button. In the Title field for the component, enter "Rolo." Click Apply and you will see the named Frame listed in the component list. The Title field is where you name the window, so the name you supply here is the name you'll see in the window's title bar.

It's entirely up to you whether you lay out components first and then edit their attributes or edit attributes for each component as you add it to the GUI. For some designs, it might make more sense to edit the attributes when you are reasonably confident that you have the basic GUI that you want. We'll lay out the components first and then edit the attributes.

Laying Out The Rolo Project

You'll need a layout grid that is four cells wide by six cells high.[2]

▼ To add rows to the default grid, use the arrow keys. The default grid is four cells (or columns) wide and three cells (or rows) long. Press the Up or Down arrow keys to add rows until you have four columns and six rows. (The Left and Right arrow keys add columns.)

▼ To delete a row or column, click in it and press the Delete key.

Now create labels for the data entry fields. There are two fields, one for a name and the other for a phone number.

▼ To create the Text Label for the name field, click the Text Label component in the Visual Java palette and then the cell in the layout grid where you want the component to go. Repeat this step to create the Text Label for the phone field.

You'll put the first Text Label in the cell at row 1, column 1. The next Text Label goes directly below the first (row 2, column 1). Figure 12–3 shows the placement of the two Text Labels.

2.   If you would prefer to skip the layout steps, you can use the GUI from the CD-ROM Examples. Follow the first three steps in "Using the Rolo Project Example from the CD-ROM" on page 153. The benefit of doing this part of the exercise, of course, is that you familiarize yourself with creating layouts in Visual Java.

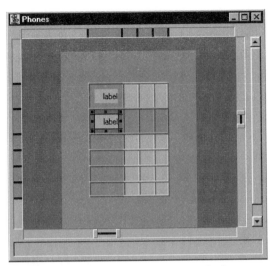

Figure 12–3 Grid with Text Labels

Another way to use a component multiple times is to copy the component and paste it into cells, using the commands on the Visual menu or the tool bar. For convenience and speed, we'll use the Visual Java tool bar, shown in Figure 12–4. From left to right, the icons are Save GUI file, Save GUI and generate source, Attribute Editor, Create a new window, Cut, Copy, Paste, and Help.

Figure 12–4 Visual Java Tool Bar

▼ Select the component and click the Copy icon. Move to the cell where you want the component and click Paste.

Another way to copy a selected component is to hold down the Control key and click in the cells where you want to duplicate the component.

Now let's add the components for entering data in the fields. The component to add is Single-line TextField. Add one to the right of each label. The text fields are probably not large enough to handle most names, so we are going to widen both and have them each straddle all the rows to the right of its label.

▼ To straddle cells, "grab" one of the handles of the component and drag it until it spans the cells you want.

The handles are the small black squares that surround the component (Figure 12–5). **Note:** You can straddle in two dimensions at the same time by grabbing the corner handles and moving down across rows and over columns at the same time.

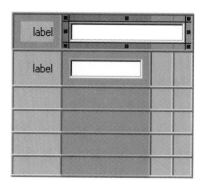

Figure 12–5 Straddling Cells

Now you'll add three buttons that enable the user to add, find, or delete the names entered in the text fields. We'll start by putting the two Text Buttons for the add and find operations into the grid.

▼ Put a Text Button in the cell at row 3, column 2 (below the bottom Single-line TextField) and another Text Button in the cell at row 3, column 3 (to the right of the first Text Button). Add a Text Label to the cell at row 4, column 1. This label is for the list that we'll create next.

The scrolling list comes next. The List component is nonscrolling until you add elements to the list. Once the default size is exceeded, the list becomes a scrolling list. You can change the point at which it begins to scroll by changing the default size in the visibleRow attribute.

▼ Click the List component and put it into any of the four cells below the Text Buttons. Exact placement doesn't matter because we want this component to straddle all four cells. Grab the component by a corner handle and drag the handle until the component straddles all four columns.

You can tell how many cells your component takes up by looking at the faint gray grid lines that appear where the cell grid lines used to be.

Now add the last of the three Text Buttons. This one is for the Delete operation. Because it will be used less and we wouldn't want the user to click it by mistake, we are placing it by itself at the bottom of the Frame.

▼ Click the Text Button in the palette and place it in one of the two middle cells in the last row. To center the Delete button in the design, make this last Text Button straddle the two middle rows.

Figure 12–6 shows the GUI layout we have so far.

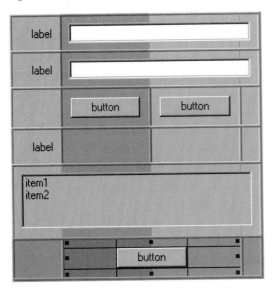

Figure 12–6 GUI Layout for *Rolo* Project

▼ Save the layout by clicking the Save icon in the tool bar or choosing Save from the Visual menu.

Editing the GUI Component Attributes

We have the basic layout for the GUI, but none of the GUI elements have been given a name we want, the Text Buttons and Text Labels have default (and not yet useful) labels, and no operations are defined for any of the elements. It's time to use the Attribute Editor to define these attributes.[3]

Let's start at the top of the interface again and look at the first Text Label and Single-line TextField in the Attribute Editor. Select the first label. Put the mouse cursor in the label's border and click the right mouse button to open the Attribute Editor.

By default Java WorkShop gives GUI components names that are based on the component type. For example, our unnamed label is called `label1`. The second label is called `label2`.

---

3. In Visual Java parlance, attributes are what PC developers know as "properties." Because Java WorkShop uses the term attributes, we'll use the term attributes in this book.

To make our program more understandable, we are going to change all of the default component names in the Attribute Editor to names that describe the roles the components play. The first Text Label is for the name field, so call it nameLabel. The name field is the third from the bottom in the Attribute Editor. Don't confuse it with the text field, which is where you enter the string that you want to appear on the label.

▼ Enter the string Name: in the text field. Click Apply to save the changes.

Table 12-1 summarizes the name and text attributes that you are going to set for the whole GUI. A blank means that the attribute does not apply to the named component. The name field is where you name the component, and the text field is where you enter the text that appears as a label for that component.

Table 12-1 Names and Text Labels for the Rolo GUI

Default Component Name	Component Name	Component Text
label1	nameLabel	Name:
label2	phoneLabel	Phone:
textField1	nameTextField	
textField2	phoneTextField	
button1	addButton	Add
button2	findButton	Find
label3	listLabel	Entries:
button3	deleteButton	Delete

The results of your attribute settings show immediately in the Layout Window.

You could change any of the other attributes for the Text Labels now, but our example takes the defaults for all but the name and text fields mentioned. (Appendix B is a reference for all of the GUI component attributes.)

▼ Leaving the Attribute Editor open and within view on your desktop, change the name and text fields for the next Text Label. Call this one phoneLabel and enter Phone: in the text field. Click Apply.

Repeat this for each Text Label and Text Button in the GUI. Click Apply to save the attributes for each component you edit.

You can leave the Attribute Editor open and visible and just select each component to edit it. The Attribute Editor changes its display to show the attributes for that component.

To provide some data in the list of entries, use the Attribute Editor to change the default items in the list (`item1`, `item2`) to some real names. Data would really come from user entries when the program is run, but enter some values now to see if you have properly sized the Single-line TextFields.

▼ In the items field, enter some names, separating them by commas without preceding and succeeding spaces. You can resize the Attribute Editor so that you can see longer entries. When you have finished naming and labeling components, save the GUI.

For example, we entered these two items in the items field:

items	Lynn Weaver 555-0000,John J. Javaman 555-0001

The spaces separate the text for name from the phone number within the entry; the comma (with no intervening space) separates items.

In the next section, you'll see how to preview the interface you have created. If you are happy with what you see, you can generate the source code for the *Rolo* project and run it.

Previewing the GUI

One of the great benefits of using Visual Java to create GUIs is that you can see the results of your interface design, modify it, preview it again, and repeat this process until you are satisfied with the results—without having to repeat source editing and compile cycles.

▼ To preview your *Rolo* standalone program GUI now, click the Preview radio button at the bottom of the Visual Java page.

The result should look like the preview of the application in Figure 12–1 on page 140.

If you build and run the *Rolo* project now, the application will appear on the desktop, but it won't do anything yet. There's a way to define actions for the GUI without leaving Visual Java.

Adding Callbacks Interactively

We're going to use the Attribute Editor to define how the program responds to user actions.

▼ To look at the code generated for the GUI components first, choose **Visual ⟶ Generate** or click the Save and generate icon.

The file to look at is `Rolo.gui`.

The `Rolo.gui` file contains the definitions for the components and the attributes you set in the Attribute Editor. The components are defined as children of a parent shadow class. (Shadows are described in "GUI Building Tips" on page 167.) For instance, Example 12-1 is the definition for the `nameLabel`.

```
java.awt.LabelShadow nameLabel {
    GBC GBConstraints x=0;y=0
    java.lang.String text Name:
}
```

Example 12-1   nameLabel Definition

You could have set these attributes programmatically instead of interactively, but the Attribute Editor spares you that effort. Having said that, it is also important to note that there are some attributes that are not available in the Attribute Editor. If you are in doubt, check the attributes listed in the Editor against the API for the component you're working with. For example, of you look at the `ListShadow` component, you'll see that `getSelectedItems` is available in the API but not the Attribute Editor. You have to get items from a list programmatically.

You could also write callbacks in your source, but once you are working on the GUI in Visual Java, it's easier to create some types of *operations* for GUI components by using Visual Java.

Visual Java Operations. In Visual Java parlance, operations are "specialized callbacks." In procedural language terms, a callback is a function you register somewhere so that it can be called later. The word callback has endured, and we'll use it in the object-oriented context of Java because it's easier to say "create a callback" than it is to say "capture an event and pass it the handler that you wrote earlier." But the latter is essentially what you are doing when you handle events in the user interface you create.

Visual Java helps automate the writing of callbacks for some common actions and events through the Operations Editor, which is a part of the Attribute Editor. With the Attribute Editor open and a particular component loaded in it, you edit operations for that component. You'll find that you can use the Operations Editor for all or most of your callbacks.

An operation consists of two parts: a *filter* and an *action*. Use filters to specify "when" and use an action to specify "what." For example, *when* a user clicks the mouse, the action (*what*) could be to send a message to the handler of the event. Visual Java ultimately writes the operations that you define to a file named <*ProjectName*>Ops.java. This is an automatically generated file that you should not edit. The actual code that executes is written to a file named <*Project-Name*>.gui. This file is editable and is used, along with the .java source file, to create the executable program.

The files created when you generate a Visual Java program are described in Table 12-2.

Table 12-2 Visual Java Files

File	Description
`<ProjectName>.gui`	The file that describes the GUI. A `.gui` file is generated for each group. Visual Java updates this file whenever you save a layout.
`<ProjectName>Root.java`	The file that contains the code to initialize the components in a group. Don't make changes to this file; it is automatically generated.
`<ProjectName>Ops.java`	The file that contains the operations you define. Visual Java generates the file only if you define operations. Don't make changes to this file; it is automatically generated.
`<ProjectName>Main.java`	The file that contains the `main()` method. Don't make changes to this file; it is automatically generated.
`<ProjectName>.java`	The group file. This is a template for defining a group class. Visual Java generates this file once; you modify it to add action methods, event handlers, and other application logic.

The dependencies between the classes that are built from these files are described in "Class Dependencies" on page 169 of this chapter.

Editing Operations. The first time you edit an operation, you might find it a little confusing because the buttons and fields in the dialog boxes are all inactive. Until you insert an operation, you can't do anything in these dialogs. So, the first step is to create the operation (Op1, by default), then define filters and actions.

These are the general steps for adding an operation to a user interface component:

1. Select a component in the Layout Window.
2. Open the Attribute Editor.
3. Click the Edit operations button in the Attribute Editor.
4. Create a new operation by clicking the Insert button.

    The Delete button removes an operation from the list.

    There is no undo operation, so you cannot undo changes once you click Apply. You can use Reset to restore the last applied (saved) changes.

    Each time you click Insert, Visual Java adds an operation to the list and gives it a unique name. You can edit that name in the Op Name field.
5. Click the Filter button to open the Filter dialog box.

There are two types of filters, event filters and message filters. To create your own event types, you would use message filters. This version of Java Work-Shop doesn't automatically generate messages. You can use the operations dialog box to specify the names of incoming messages and the actions that they trigger when they are received.

Event filters are for standard events handling one action, like a mouse click on a button. For an event that does something a little more complicated, like applying all of the changes in a dialog, you would probably create an Apply button to capture all of the data and send a message.

6.   Click on the Action button to open the Action dialog.

Visual Java supports some common actions such as showing and hiding a component, exiting an application, and setting an attribute on a component. Our action requires us to write code.

▼ To add callback code to the *Rolo* project, switch back to Layout Mode and make sure that the Attribute Editor is open and visible. Start with the Add button. Select it in the Layout Window and then click the Edit operations bar in the Attribute Editor. The Operations Editor opens.

Click the Insert button to put an operation on the operations list. Visual Java gives the operation the default name, Op1.

Once you have a named operation inserted, you are ready to define the action for it.

▼ In the Operations Editor, click the Action button to open the Actions dialog. For Action Type, choose Execute Code.

You are going to create three actions, one for each button: Add, Find, and Delete. The Add button action concatenates the text entered in the Name and Phone fields of the *Rolo* application and enters those values in the Entries list.

▼ To write this callback for the addButton component, choose Execute Code from the choice menu in the Action dialog. Enter code to:

- Create an object (gui.addButton) that is an instance of a button shadow class.

- Use the get() method to get the values of the two text fields (the value of the "items" attribute).

- Operate on that text (concatenate it into a string called newItem).

- Use the put() method to add this data to the list.

After you enter code, Click Apply.

Example 12-2 shows the code entered in the Execute Code text area for the first callback in the *Rolo* example. If you don't want to type it in, you can copy the `Rolo.gui` file from the CD-ROM and use it instead. "Using the Rolo Project Example from the CD-ROM" on page 153 describes how.

```
String[] listContents = (String []) gui.namesList.get("items");
String newItem = (String) gui.nameTextfield.get("text") + " " +
                         (String) gui.phoneTextfield.get("text");
int len = listContents.length;
String[] newContents = new String[len + 1];
int i = 0;

for (i=0; i < len; i++) {
  newContents[i] = listContents[i];
}
newContents[len] = newItem;
gui.namesList.set("items",  newContents);}
```

Example 12-2 The Callback Code for add**Button**

In the addButton code, as well as the examples to follow, we have written the code required to perform the basic operations of the program just to show how the components work together. For example, we have omitted the application logic that would check for valid values. Your application code might differ in many ways from the example. The point illustrated is that you can enter code in the Execute Code text area, apply it, generate a GUI, and build a program that includes the code.

▼ To write callback code for the next component, select the component in the Layout Window and choose Execute Code from the choice menu in the Action dialog. Then, enter code in the text area and click Apply.

The callback code for findButton gets the value entered in the name field and uses it as a search key (Example 12-3).

```
List listBody = (List) gui.namesList.getBody();
 int numItems = listBody.countItems();
 String nameToFind = (String) gui.nameTextfield.get("text");
 String currentName = "";
 int i = 0;
 int j = 0;
 int len = 0;
 int nameLen = nameToFind.length();

 for (i=0; i < numItems; i++) {
   currentName = listBody.getItem(i);
   len = currentName.length();
   if (len >= nameLen &&
       len != 0 &&
       nameLen != 0) {
     for (j=0; j < len - nameLen + 1; j++) {
        if (currentName.regionMatches(true,
                                      j,
                                      nameToFind,
                                      0,
                                      nameLen) == true) {
              listBody.select(i);
              return;
         }
      }
    }
  }
}
```

Example 12-3 The Callback Code for findButton

The callback code for the last GUI component, `deleteButton`, is the simplest
(Example 12-4). It also omits the kind of application-specific coding that you
might include to prompt the user to verify the delete operation. It gets the list
Body, the index of the selected item, and deletes the item. Notice that an `import`
statement starts the code block. When you generate code for this statement, Visual
Java places the `import` statement at the top of the source.

```
{import java.awt.List;
List listBody = (List) gui.namesList.getBody();
int selectedIndex = listBody.getSelectedIndex();

listBody.delItem(selectedIndex);
}
```

Example 12-4 The Callback Code for deleteButton

Building and Running the Rolo Project

▼ Click the Save and generate icon in the Visual Java tool bar. Build the *Rolo* project by using the Build Manager and then run the project.

You can test some filters and actions directly in Visual Java in the Layout Window. However, the effects of the code you add in the Action dialog box are visible only when you run the application in or out of Java WorkShop, not in the Layout Window. Use the Project Tester to see those results.

Using the Rolo Project Example from the CD-ROM

Visual Java allows you to import any layout created in Visual Java. If you don't want to create the Rolo example from scratch, copy the `Rolo.gui` file from the CD-ROM to a directory on your drive and follow these steps to import it and use it:

1. Create a project directory for *Rolo*. For the sake of clarity, give the directory the same name as the project.

2. Create a standalone project named *Rolo*. Click No to existing sources. At Create Using, click the Visual Java radio button.

3. Choose **Visual** ⟶ **Import**. Select the `Rolo.gui` file from the file chooser.

    You should find `Rolo.gui` in the directory to which you copied it from the CD-ROM. After you import it into Visual Java, you should see the *Rolo* GUI in the Layout Window.

    If there was a default component in the component list (such as PANEL, or Unnamed Frame) when you imported the GUI, delete the component by selecting it and choosing Visual ⟶ Delete. Rolo should be the only component in the list.

4. Choose **Visual** ⟶ **Generate**.

5. Build the project.

6. Run the project.

These are the same steps you would follow to use any GUI file created in Java WorkShop in a new project.

Creating Menus

Not all GUI components are created with the layout grid. To create menus, you use the Visual Java Menu Editor. Menus are defined by using the Attribute Editor to edit attributes for a Frame. One of the attributes for a Frame is the menu bar attribute. Instead of editing a field for this attribute, you click the Edit menu bar button to open a dialog for creating a menu bar. Figure 12–7 shows the attributes for a Frame, including the menu bar button.

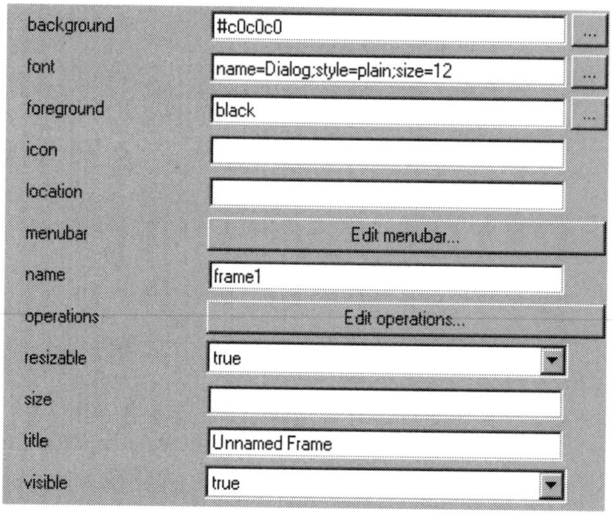

background	#c0c0c0
font	name=Dialog;style=plain;size=12
foreground	black
icon	
location	
menubar	Edit menubar...
name	frame1
operations	Edit operations...
resizable	true
size	
title	Unnamed Frame
visible	true

Figure 12–7   Frame Attributes

The first thing you have to do is create a Frame. By default, Visual Java opens with a Panel selected as the main container.

▼ Change to a Frame with the Main Container command, then apply changes to the Frame in the Attribute Editor. Choose **Visual** ⟶ **Main Container**. When the Main Container dialog box opens, click the Frame radio button.

Now you have a Frame to which you can add a menu bar.

▼ Just select the Unnamed Frame in the container list in Visual Java's main window and open the Attribute Editor. Click the Edit menu bar button to open the Menu Editor (Figure 12–8).

Note: When you have a Frame selected, the Attribute Editor includes a button for editing menus as well as one for editing operations.

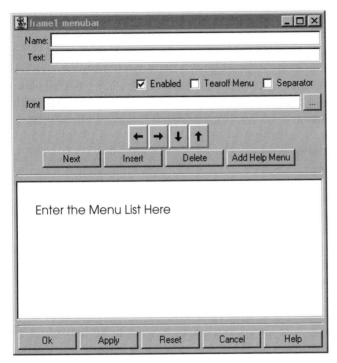

Figure 12–8 Menu Editor

Use the Menu Editor to describe the menus you want to include in a menu bar. When you click Apply, the menus are added to your Frame.

Although you can't see them, there are columns for the menu list. You'll see a cursor marking your place when you start editing a menu list. Here's how you use the columns:

- Items that begin in the first column are menus on the menu bar.

- Items that begin in the second column are items within a menu.

- Items that begin in subsequent columns are pull-right items.

- Separators are added at the same hierarchical level as the items they separate.

Figure 12–9 presents an example showing the start of a menu bar.

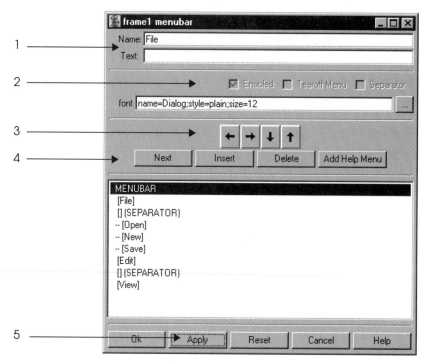

Figure 12–9 Creating a Menu List

Use the controls shown in Figure 12–9 to create the Menu Editor list:

1. To name the item, enter text in the name field. To provide the text for the menu item, use the Text and font fields.

2. To enable a menu by default or to add a space between items, use the Enabled and Separator radio buttons. The Tear-off menu button is not yet implemented.

3. To move menu items in the menu list to different columns or up and down in the list, use the arrow buttons.

4. To move to the next item in the list, insert a new item, or delete an item, use the Next, Insert, or Delete buttons. Use the Help button to add a Help menu. The Help menu is automatically placed on the right of the menu bar as it is in standard user interfaces. Use the Help button last, or move the Help menu to the last position if you add anything after it. Help must be the last item on the menu bar.

5. Click Apply to see your changes take effect.

Editing Operations for Menu Items

Your menu-in-progress appears in the Layout Window.

▼ Pull down the menu and select the item you want to edit. Open the Attribute Editor. You edit the menu item attributes as you would any other component, including adding operations for it.

Click the Edit operations button to add a callback.

Insert an operation as you would for any other component that also requires an action event. Open the Filter dialog and choose the Event Filter Type. Finally, open the Action dialog and select Execute Code. Enter a callback for the menu item in the text area.

Programming with Groups and Shadows

Most of the GUI building activities that we've done so far we did interactively, but there is still a lot you have to do programmatically to make your application useful and powerful. What you get with a GUI building tool is the ability to lay out components, see what they look like, change their properties, eliminate some, add others, and preview it all interactively, without writing AWT code. This visual programming has trade-offs, however. One of them is that to properly manage and present the AWT components to you during design and at runtime, Visual Java had to interpose an interface between you and the AWT. The result is an interface API made up of something that Visual Java calls *groups* and *shadows*, the source code for which is shipped with the product and can be redistributed with your programs for use at runtime.

What are groups and shadows? They are a lot less mysterious than they sound. A *group* is a generic container. Groups provide public interfaces and base classes that allow Visual Java GUIs to be included in other Visual Java GUIs. A *shadow* is a wrapper for an AWT class. That is, Visual Java uses shadow classes to "wrap" AWT components for presentation to you at design time and to your users at runtime. The result is that when you are working in Visual Java, you are not working directly with AWT components. The use of these wrapper classes represents a pre-Java Beans implementation solution for visual programming. Had Java beans been available when Java WorkShop 1.0 was developed, you would probably not have to program with groups and shadows. But for now, you do, so it might help to familiarize yourself with some basics about groups and shadows.

If you are familiar with the AWT programming model, then groups and shadows will not represent a challenge. They are just classes that correspond to AWT components. Instead of programming to the AWT, you program (both interactively in Visual Java and programmatically by writing custom code) with the classes in this interface. In the example you did in "Building a GUI: An Extended Example" starting on page 140, you took a List from the Visual Java palette, put it on the layout grid, and generated a GUI. When you did this, you programmed to a shadow of the AWT List component. Your list component (`namesList`) is a child of a shadow parent (`java.awt.ListShadow`).

As wrapper classes for AWT components, shadows do several things:

- Map component methods to attributes (component properties)

- Delay the instantiation of AWT components

- Propagate AWT events to groups

(Shadow classes also provide a number of workarounds for AWT limitations that make it possible for you to build complex applications that work on both Windows and Solaris systems.)

A group encapsulates a set of shadows and subgroups. When you build a GUI in Visual Java you are defining new groups out of existing shadows and groups. New groups can be imported into the Visual Java palette and can then be incorporated into other groups.

Groups that are included inside other groups are called subgroups. The top-level group is called the base group. Your program uses the tree of groups while it is running. Messages sent by subgroups propagate up toward the top of the tree until they are handled or until they reach the base group. From an external viewpoint, a group is a single component that has a set of attributes, public methods, and messages. These attributes, methods, and messages are described in Table 12-3.

Table 12-3 Group Attributes, Methods, and Messages

Attributes	Attributes for a group are defined in the constructor and are handled by means of the `getOnGroup` and `setOnGroup` methods. Support is provided for forwarding a set of attributes to one or more children of the group—a child being either a shadow or a subgroup.
Methods	Most methods are custom methods written by the author of the group. Some useful methods, such as the `get`/`set` attribute methods, are defined in the `Group` class itself.
Messages	A group will create messages and post them to the parent groups. A group does not need to have any knowledge of its parent. Instead, the parent can listen for a particular message from its subgroup and perform an action based on the message.

Visual Java Class Hierarchy

To take a look at the class hierarchy for the Visual Java interface to the AWT, point the Java WorkShop Browser to: `doc:lib/visual/api/tree.html`.

Figure 12–10 illustrates a simplified view of part of the Visual Java API tree.

```
Object
        AttributeManager
                Root
                Group
                Shadow
                        ComponentShadow
                        CanvasShadow
                                ColumnListShadow
```

Figure 12–10 Simplified View of the Visual Java API Tree

You'll see that the `AttributeManager` class is the base class for objects that have attributes. Below `AttributeManager` in the class hierarchy are the `Root`, `Group`, and `Shadow` classes. Instances of `Root` are used for the root class of a group's shadow tree. Child shadows of the `Root` object are typically the top-level window of an application or a top-level Panel for an applet. `Group` extends `AttributeManager` and is the base class for every kind of group. `Shadow` extends `AttributeManager` and is the class you must subclass if you want to add an object to the Visual Java palette.

Going further down the tree, you'll see that `ComponentShadow` extends `Shadow` and is the class that wraps the AWT Component class. All shadow classes, except for the ones related to the menu component, include the attributes from `ComponentShadow` as well as their own.

Using the Visual Java API

Another way to look at groups and shadows is as specialized components that you program using Visual Java. To write your own class, start with what is already available in the Visual Java API, looking in the tree for a class close to yours to implement. The documentation for the Visual Java API is at this URL: `doc:/lib/visual/api/packages.htm`

You can include custom functionality in your shadow classes, in fact you'll have to do so if you want to set and get attributes and handle events. In the callback example for the Rolo project, we needed to determine which item in a list was selected for deletion. The list component (namesList) is a child of a shadow parent (java.awt.ListShadow). To get the items in the list, you would use:

gui.namesList.getBody().getSelectedItems()

This call points to the AWT object from a shadow class. In *general*, it is better to use the shadow class for the get and set methods rather than methods that access the AWT component directly.

Rules for Writing Groups and Shadows

Java WorkShop online documentation recommends that you follow certain rules for writing a group. We've included the rules here for your convenience:

- Define attributes in the constructor method. Call these methods in the constructor to add a set of forwarded attributes to the group—addComponentAttributes, addFrameAttributes, and addDialogAttributes.

- In general, handle the attributes that you define in the getOnGroup() and setOnGroup() methods. Any attributes that are not handled should be passed up the hierarchy, using a call to super.

- You can call super.setOnGroup() with an attribute, even if the attribute is already being handled by your setOnGroup() method. This type of call causes the attribute value to be stored in the group's list of attributes. Then getOnGroup() looks up this attribute's value from the list. Make sure that any attributes that are handled in setOnGroup() without calling super are also handled in getOnGroup().

- The initRoot() method has to be overriden in group classes to initialize the root of the application. When you generate code, the default generated group contains an initRoot() method that does this.

- You can override the startGroup() and stopGroup() methods to request notification when an applet starts and stops. Also, startGroup() is called when standalone applications are finished initializing. This call can be useful if you want to do something that may cause an error, and you want to immediately pop up an error dialog box.

- Override the handleMessage() and handleEvent() methods to receive AWT events from the root children. For AWT events, the target of the message is the shadow corresponding to the AWT component that sent the event.

The target of the AWT event is the AWT component itself. For AWT components that do not have a shadow, the target of the message will be the AWT component itself.

- Be careful about delayed instantiation. The getOnGroup() and setOn-Group() methods will not be invoked until the group has been initialized. When the group is initialized, setOnGroup() will be invoked for all the attributes. However, any custom methods you write need to handle the case of the group not being initialized or created. This isn't a problem if the user of the group is careful not to call the group's methods until it is initialized—but better safe than sorry. Dealing with the group not being initialized almost always consists of doing a null check on the gui instance variable.

Here are the recommended rules for writing a shadow:

- Declare the attributes in the constructor. Add or remove attributes in the constructor.

- Handle attributes with the getOnBody() and setOnBody() methods in the shadow class where they are declared (attributes flagged with NONBODY are the exception to this rule).[4]

- getOnBody() and setOnBody() should invoke super for all attributes that aren't handled in that particular shadow class.

- You can override the default value of an attribute in a shadow class. Overriding the default value means that you have to handle the attribute in the overriding shadow. The attribute can be handled by the class in which it was originally declared.

- In general, attributes do not need any flags. If you use an attribute flag, be sure that you know what it does. (To find out what attributes have flags, consult the Visual Java API documentation for the classes you are interested in.)

---

4. Flags are a Visual Java construct and do not appear in the Java language. If you look at the Visual Java API documentation, you will see that attribute flags are declared as variables. These variables use all uppercase characters, so you will be able to recognize them. For example, in the AttributeManager class, there are flags named "CONTAINER," "HIDDEN," READONLY," and so on. Consult the API documentation for descriptions of what the flags do.

Visual Java Runtime Classes

You can reproduce and distribute Visual Java runtime classes so that the applets and application programs that you create with Visual Java will run outside the Java WorkShop environment. The alternative would be to duplicate runtime code in your applications.

To see the Visual Java API, enter this URL in the Java WorkShop Browser: `doc:/lib/visual/api/packages.html`.

By default, the runtime classes are installed on Windows in:

`<install_dir_path>/JWS/classes/sunsoft/jws/visual/rt`

On Solaris in:

`<install_dir_path>/JWS/classes/sunsoft/jws/visual/rt`

Visual Java applets run in any Java-enabled browser or viewer that supports JDK version 1.0.2 or later.

The Visual Java runtime classes consist of the shadow and base classes, type converters, and custom components. *Type converters* convert any type to a type `string` and a `string` type to another type. A *custom component* is a component that is not standard in the AWT, such as the Tabbed Folder Panel, Image Label, and Multiple Column List components.

Running Visual Java Applets in Netscape Navigator

Netscape Navigator searches the CLASSPATH when it loads classes. For local applets, include the runtime classes directory in your CLASSPATH variable. For users who run your applet elsewhere on the Internet (or an internet) and don't have local copies of the runtime classes, include the runtime classes in the same directory path that you specify in the CODEBASE parameter. That is, for remote applets, put the runtime classes in the same directory as the applet. Although it would be nice if you could specify multiple directories in the CODEBASE parameter, or include a CLASSPATH value in a parameter to the applet tag, applet tags do not allow either approach.

You can also distribute the runtime classes with your applet. Copy the classes to the same directory as the main `.class` file or to a directory in the user's CLASSPATH. Copy the `sunsoft` directory and the directories below it, not just the Java WorkShop runtime classes directory.

Adding Custom Components and Windows

If you have already written your own AWT classes, there are a couple of ways to use them inside Java WorkShop. One way is to import the component for a single use; the other is to incorporate the component into Java WorkShop by making it an element in the Custom choice menu or the palette. Naturally, the importing method is easier, but you may want to share or reuse the component often enough that it should be brought in to the Custom menu or the palette.

There are two simple rules for using components that you write:

- You must write your component with a null constructor.

- The component must be a subclass of `java.awt.ComponentShadow`.

Importing Custom Components

To use your custom component in a layout in Visual Java, use the built-in Generic Component from the Custom menu.

▼ To import your own component, click the Custom button and choose the Generic component from the choice menu (Figure 12–11) to its right. Then click in a cell to place the component where you want it.

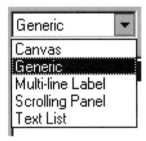

Figure 12–11 Custom Choice Menu

▼ Next, place the Generic component in a layout cell and then open the Attribute Editor. Use the class attribute to specify your custom component by its full package and class name. You'll have to highlight and type over the default package and class name, `java.awt.Button`. Click Apply.

Your component will appear in the layout grid.

Putting Your Component on the Menu

Do you want to add your component to the Custom menu? Having it on the menu enables you to select it more easily. This might be the best approach if you expect other Java WorkShop users to use the component or if you plan to reuse it yourself without having to specify the package and class name. This step takes you to another Visual Java tool, one that you have not used yet—the Palette Editor.

▼   From the Java WorkShop menu, choose **Visual ➠ Edit Palette**. When the Palette Editor (shown in Figure 12–12) opens, pull down the choice menu and choose Custom Menu.

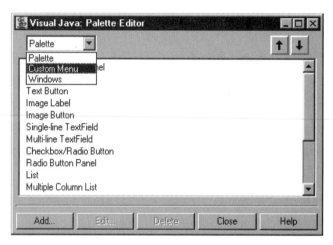

Figure 12–12   The Palette Editor

▼   Click the Add button to open the dialog box shown in Figure 12–13.

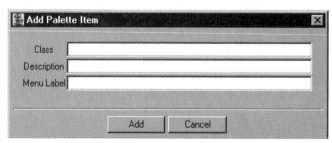

Figure 12–13   Add Palette Item Dialog

▼ Enter values for the text fields described below and click Add:

Class
: The full package and class name of your component.

Description
: The description of the component that is displayed in the browser footer when you select the component and move the mouse cursor over the Custom button. Use this to indicate to others, or to remind yourself what the component does.

Menu Label
: The name of the component as you want it to appear in the Custom choice menu.

When you write a custom component and add new shadow classes or group classes, all of the standard component attributes are available (for example, foreground, background colors, font), because any new shadow or group class extends an already existing class. Any new attributes specific to the custom component are also available in the Attribute Editor.

Putting Your Component on the Palette

To add your component to the component palette, use the Palette Editor, but this time, choose Palette instead of Custom Menu.

▼ Click Add, enter the text fields, and, instead of entering a menu label, enter a path name for the icon you want to have appear for your component in the palette.

The path name for the icon can be a URL or a path name relative to the codebase of the applet. If your applet's `.class` file and image files are in the same directory, you can enter the file name without the path.

There is a simple rule for the image:

• Icon images should be GIF files that are 24 x 24 pixels.

Adding Custom Windows

To add a custom window, follow almost the same basic steps as adding a component.

▼ Choose **Visual** ➠ **New Window** instead of opening the Palette Editor. Choose Generic Window from the list shown in Figure 12–14 and click the Create button.

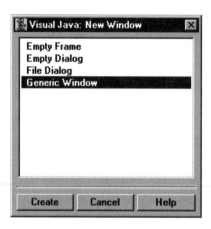

Figure 12–14 New Window Dialog

You'll find your new Generic Window listed in the component list on the Visual Java page of the Browser.

A right mouse click on the name of the component opens the Attribute Editor, where you can enter the class and package name. Enter the package and class name for your Generic Window by highlighting the default name (sunsoft.jws.visual.rt.awt.RootFrame) and typing over it.

Of course, there is a simple rule for this component, too.

• The class for your custom window must be a subclass of one of these Visual Java runtime classes:
```
sunsoft.jws.visual.rt.awt.RootFrame
sunsoft.jws.visual.rt.awt.RootDialog
```

GUI Building Tips

Here are some tips for programming with Visual Java, including using groups, using the event choices in the Filter dialog, and understanding Visual Java class dependencies.

Using Groups to Better Advantage

When you program with Visual Java, you are programming with groups. To make your programs more efficient and easier to understand and maintain, consider putting any pieces of the GUI that can be independent units into their own groups. Use a top-level group class for every major component in the GUI and then create a subgroup for each of the related components in that group. The Visual Java Attribute Editor is a good example of this approach. The Attribute Editor group is the top-level group, and the Operations Editor and each of its dialogs are a group—there is a subgroup for the Filter dialog and another for the Action dialog. Taken altogether these subgroups are part of the Attribute Editor group. This technique makes it easier to edit the interface, too, because you don't have one monolithic .gui file.

As you organize these groups into projects, remember that each .gui file defines a group, and each project can have one .gui file. That means each group must have its own project. You should organize your groups, using a top-level project for the top-level group and nested projects for the subgroups.

Reloading and Editing Code in the Operations Editor

The <project_name>Ops.java file is generated whenever you generate the GUI, so you can't edit it directly. If you did, your changes would be lost when you generated the GUI again. So, it's helpful to know how to reload an operation in the Operations Editor.

When you select Execute Code as the Action Type in the Action dialog, Visual Java opens a dialog with a text area to enter code. It might not be obvious how to reload and change the code that you wrote for an operation in this text area; here's how to reload what you entered in the text area:

▼ In the layout window, select the component you wrote the operation for. Open the Attribute Editor. Click Edit operations.

Visual Java opens the Operations Editor with a list of the operations that you defined on this component. Click the operation you want and then click Action.

Visual Java loads the code frame for the operation in the Execute Code text area.

You can try this now with the *Rolo* project.

▼ Open Visual Java to the *Rolo* project and select the Add button in the layout window. Open the Attribute Editor and then the Operations Editor. There is only one operation defined on this component, so it is already selected. Click the Action button. You'll see the callback code for the Add button in the text area.

You can also cut and paste text from the desktop to the text area. For example, if you're a Solaris user and you list a file in a shell by using `cat` or `more`, you can use the keyboard Cut, Copy, and Paste buttons to take text from the listing and put it in the Execute Code text area. If you're a Windows user, note that this text area is a TextArea widget, so it works with other Windows TextArea widgets. Windows users can use <Ctrl+C> and <Ctrl+V> to cut from a widget like the NotePad or WordPad and paste to the Execute Code text area.

Choosing Operations

You might have noticed that the choice menu for events in the Filter dialog contains events for a variety of components. The list is inclusive and not categorized by component. The Java AWT API itself is not especially clear about what events to associate with what components. Here are some categories that will help you associate events in the choice menu with the proper component.

The Action Event is for generic actions and is what you use for any component that requires some action that must be handled with custom code, such as writing a file when a user clicks a Save button or, as in the *Rolo* example, when text entered has to be written to another component.

The Key events (Key Press and Key Release, for example) are for actions in which a user uses the keyboard while over or in a component. This event is typically received by text components, such as a TextField. The events beginning with "Mouse" are all related, and your program can receive these over just about any component except those where an action event is important. For example, a button doesn't "see" a Mouse Down or Mouse Up event, but receives an action event instead. Mouse Move events, however, can be received by most components. Mouse Enter and Mouse Exit events receive the user actions of entering or leaving a component such as a window. Mouse Enter/Exit events are typically received and handled for a mouse over a text field where you might want to indicate a Mouse Enter event by highlighting the text in the field.

Got Focus and Lost Focus are typically used for text components (things that have focus) where a key might be pressed, for example, in the case where the user presses the Tab key in a text field to move the focus to another text field or uses a key to complete the text entry.

The five Window events listed in the choice menu are generated by actions taken on a window and apply only to Frames or Dialogs. For example, when a window's menu allows the user to quit the window, the window receives a Window Destroy event.

Scroll events are received only by the Scrollbar component. List events are received by Lists, Multiple Column Lists, and scrolling Lists. These events apply to lists only, and to single-click actions in the lists. Double-click actions require an Action Event because double clicks require something to happen, whereas single clicks just indicate a selection.

Load and Save apply to File Dialogs. Recall that to use the File Dialog component in Visual Java, you choose **Visual ➠New Window** and select File Dialog from the list that opens.

Class Dependencies

For the *Rolo* project, Visual Java created these classes: Rolo, RoloMain, RoloOps, and RoloRoot. Rolo extends the base Group class, which initializes RoloRoot (the root class). If there is an operation defined in RoloOps your program calls it before the Group class handles it.The class dependencies for these classes are illustrated in Figure 12–15.

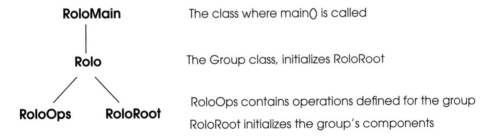

The class where main() is called

The Group class, initializes RoloRoot

RoloOps contains operations defined for the group

RoloRoot initializes the group's components

Figure 12–15 Visual Java Class Dependencies

Summary

In this chapter you built a GUI, edited its attributes, and learned about:

- Laying out a GUI
- Editing GUI attributes
- Using operations to add callbacks for GUI components
- Generating code for GUIs
- Importing Visual Java projects
- Creating menus
- Programming with groups and shadows
- Using the Visual Java API
- Adding custom components and windows
- Using groups to better advantage
- Reloading code in the Operations Editor

PART FOUR

What Next?

CHAPTER 13

- The Java Platform

- Java Resources

- Further Reading

Watching Java Developments

Because the Java world is constantly changing, this chapter offers a working vocabulary for some Java developments so that you know some areas to watch and where to find out more about them. There is a companion HTML page on the CD-ROM—`resource.html`, which contains links to the World Wide Web URLs mentioned here.

The Java Platform

Java Development Kit (JDK) users are familiar with the JDK 1.0 Java Application Programming Interface (API) as that set of Java base classes that provide basic programming capabilities—the language, I/O, network, Abstract Windowing Toolkit (AWT), utilities, and applet packages.

The Java API is changing as new capabilities are added both by Sun and other vendors who are extending Java. These extensions are all happening at a rapid rate, but in the public eye in the form of published API specifications.

Java APIs

Java APIs are characterized as core or standard extension APIs.

A *core API* is an API that you can assume has been published, reviewed, and incorporated into implementations of the Java Platform. The list of core APIs continues to grow as the APIs are implemented in releases of the JDK. The next core API will be based on what is in JDK 1.1.

A *standard extension API* is an API that is not yet in the core, and may not make it into the core, but has been published, reviewed, and defined as standard. Most standard extensions to the API make their way into the core as the Java Platform develops, but it is possible to use them now along with the core APIs. Some standard APIs may not become part of the core simply because they are not used by enough applications and may not be guaranteed to be on every platform.

Here's a list of some of the areas in which APIs have either been published or are coming soon and a brief description of their functionality:

- Java Enterprise APIs — connectivity to enterprise databases and legacy applications

- Java Server API — the Java "servlet" technology, a framework for developing network (Internet and intranet) servers

- Java Security API — digital signature, encryption, and authentication capabilities

- Java Beans™ API — for software components

- Java Commerce API (Java Wallet) — client-side framework for electronic commerce

- Java Management API — for developing enterprise network management applets. The JMAPI enables a variety of managements services to be performed from a browser-based console from anywhere in the network. Following the "write once, run anywhere" paradigm, it enables writing once and deploying and managing applications and devices anywhere.

- Java Media APIs —2D, 3D audio, video, telephony, and application sharing for collaborative tools like electronic white boards

- Java Embedded API —how to subset the Java APIs for devices that can't support the core set

We'll look at a couple of API areas to be included in JDK 1.1. See "The Java Language and APIs" on page 177 for the URL that provides dates and information for the others.

An Enterprise API for Database Connectivity. JavaSoft (an operating company of Sun Microsystems) published the specification for the Java Database Connectivity (JDBC™) API in March 1996. This API is a core API in JDK 1.1. Some vendors have created proprietary connectivity interfaces; the Java JDBC specification sets a standard for Java database connectivity, a standard that was informed by the input of a number of large database and database tools vendors who have a high level of interest in Java-to-database connections (Oracle, Sybase, IBM, Borland, to name a few).

Microsoft's Open Database Connectivity (ODBC) has become the standard for PCs and local area networks. The JDBC standard is comparable and, like the ODBC, is based on the X/Open SQL Call Level Interface. It will also use URLs for database addressing and will allow bridging to existing ODBC implementations.

Java Beans APIs. A number of vendors of component architectures have vied for the attention of independent software vendors (ISVs) who are making component-based applications. These are applications that, unlike monolithic applications that take a long time to get to market and contain unused features, are delivered as pieces that end users can use to construct the complete set of software tools they want. Sun's Java entry into this market is Java Beans, the component architecture for Java programmers. Java Beans will enable developers to make reusable software components that end users can hook together, using visual application building tools.

The Java Beans APIs cover various aspects of component development—events (an extension of the AWT event model), attributes (color, font, etc.), persistence, introspection at the type and design levels, and application builder support—as defined in Sun's Java Beans component architecture.

If you develop software components that use the Java Beans APIs, your software will be portable to containers, including Internet Explorer, Netscape Navigator, HotJava™, a variety of other development tools, and applications that are built with compatible component architectures. Java WorkShop has anticipated this technology and will be there to use to your advantage. You should expect Sun to have entries in the visual application builder field, too.

The Java Beans Developers Kit should be available by the time you read this.

Just in Time Compilers

One of the few negatives voiced by Java developers is concern about performance, both at compile time and runtime. Java is interpreted, therefore much is made of its performance relative to C, which is compiled. Java is up to the tasks for which it is especially suited—interactive, multimedia, networked, GUI applications, but support for performance-critical applications is coming in a variety of forms. Java Just in Time compilers (JITs) are one response to the performance issue. The Java compiler generates byte codes instead of native machine code (like C). This gives Java its remarkable portability. JITs translate Java byte codes into machine language for a particular machine (CPU) at runtime. JITs should lower the price in performance that developers pay for the architectural neutrality of Java. Of course, Java WorkShop will take advantage of any gains made with JITs or any optimizations of the Java Virtual Machine.

Java Resources

This list of World Wide Web and print resources should help you establish your own Java knowledge base, keep an eye on what's coming in Java developments and find out what the news means to you, as well as provide information about how to use the language and tools. An HTML version of this section is available on the CD-ROM. It's called `resource.html`. You can use it to navigate to the URLs described here.

Java WorkShop

- http://www.sun.com/workshop/java/literature/Product-Guide/WSjava_tech.html

  Sun's Java WorkShop product specification.

- http://www.sun.com/workshop/java/literature/idc.html

  Java WorkShop white paper by the International Data Corporation's Evan Quinn. IDC is an information technology market research organization.

- http://www.sun.com/workshop/java/link

  Information about how to qualify for linking your Java WorkShop applications to the Java WorkShop page with the official Java WorkShop link icon. The icon is free, but there are requirements for using it.

- http://www.sun.com/workshop/java/technical/FAQ.html

  The Java WorkShop frequently asked questions link.

- http://www.sun.com/workshop/java/literature/cookbook2

  Example programs for some GUI building tasks. This material was written before the final release of Java WorkShop 1.0, so it doesn't address Visual Java operations. However, the page will be updated. One recent addition worth noting is the Multiple Column List applet mentioned in Appendix C.

- http://www.sun.com/java/list.html

  Java products, training and related services. Links to early access products. At the time this book went to press, the early access products included ICE-T, a development and deployment solution for Java (front end) to C/C++ (back end) client/server applications.

Inside Java WorkShop

- **http://www.prenhall.com/divisions/ptr/ptr_home.html**

  The Web site for the Prentice Hall Professional Technical Reference book catalog.

- **http:// http://www.sun.com/books**

  The Sun Microsystems Press (formerly SunSoft Press) list of current and upcoming titles in the Java Series.

The Java Language and APIs

- **http://java.sun.com**

  The main site for Sun's Java developments, products, programs, documentation, and white papers. There's even a link to the Java store for those who want Java mugs and tees.

- **http://java.sun.com/products/JDK/1.1/designspecs/index.html**

  Design specification for JDK 1.1.

- **http://www.sun.com/961029/JES/whitepapers**

  Java enterprise computing white papers from Sun.

- **http://www.sun.com/javacomputing**

  Papers describing how to put Java to work in enterprise computing. This link takes you directly to three of the whitepapers that are on the linked list at "http://www.sun.com/961029/JES/whitepapers" above. The three whitepapers here describe strategic applications of Java for IS managers, with an example from the finance area.

- **http://java.sun.com/nav/read/apis.html**

  A list of Java Application Programming Interfaces (APIs) that are standard or on their way to becoming standard, with their availability dates and links to Web pages for each API.

- **http://splash.javasoft.com/beans**

  The Java Beans home page from Sun.

- **http://splash.javasoft.com/beans/download.html**

  The Java Beans specification available for downloading in PostScript or Adobe Acrobat formats.

- **http://www-net.com/java/faq**

  Frequently asked questions, and some answers, from the people who use Java and Java tools. This mega-FAQ site has links to other FAQ pages.

- **http://www.javasoft.com/doc/programmer.html**

  Programmer documentation for Java.

- **http://splash.javasoft.com/jdbc**

  Sun's Java Database Connectivity (JDBC) home page, with links to the vendors who endorse it, available JDBC drivers, and API documentation.

- **http://www.professionals.com/~cmcmanis/java**

  Chuck McManis' Java resources Web page. McManis was a member of the Java development group in its early days.

- **http://www.artweb.co.uk/javaweb/javaweb.html**

  A site that argues for Java as the language of choice for application development and not just an Internet language. With examples.

Just in Time Compiler Technology

- **http://www.javacats.com/us/articles/chuckmcmanis091696.html**

  An article about Just in Time compiler technology by Chuck McManis, a former member of the original Java Platform development team.

- **http://www.sun.com/workshop/java/jit**

  Sun's Java JIT site.

Java Applets and News

- **http://www.gamelan.com**

  Well-known and oft-cited collection of Java applets and news from Earth-Web. By declaration of JavaSoft (an operating company of Sun Microsystems), Gamelan (pronounced Gamma-lahn) is the "Official Directory for Java."

- **http://www.io.org/~mentor/jnIndex.html**

  The Digital Espresso site by Mentor Software Solutions. Weekly summaries of Java newsgroups and mailing lists. Searchable. Interesting collections of white papers, references to commercial sites, and, most useful, a lot of discussions by developers about developer experiences and solutions.

- **http://www.javaworld.com**

  "IDG's magazine for the Java community" contains news, tips and tricks, applet reviews, new product information, and links to other Java resources.

- **http://www.javaworld.com/netnews.html**

  Java World's daily compilation of links to other Java sources on the Web.

- **http://www.sigma.net/javasig**

  Software Forum's Java SIG page. Information about events of interest to Java developers. Software Forum (formerly the Software Entrepreneurs Forum) is a non-profit, member-managed organization located in Palo Alto, California.

Hypertext Markup Language (HTML)

- http://www.ncsa.uiuc.edu/General/Internet/WWW/HTMLPrimer.html

    "A Beginner's Guide to HTML" with links to other HTML resources.

- http://www.sandia.gov/sci_compute/elements.html

    A complete description of all RFC 1866 HTML elements, their attributes, and enhancements. RFC 1866 is the official specification of HTML Version 2.0. Includes descriptions of the `<applet>` and `<param>` tags.

Further Reading

Inside Java WorkShop is part of a series of Java books published by Sun Microsystems Press (formerly SunSoft Press) and Prentice Hall. The Java series addresses different audiences for Java, including programmers of Web pages (*Instant Java*), graphics programmers (*Graphic Java*), programmers writing full-scale Java applications (*Core Java* and *Just Java*), and programmers who are new to Java and looking for basic techniques (*Java by Example*).

Core Java, 2nd Edition
by Gary Cornell and Cay S. Horstmann
CD-ROM included

ISBN 0-13-596891-7

For programmers with a solid background in C, C++, or Visual Basic who want to put Java to work in serious applications.

Graphic Java: Mastering the AWT
by David M. Geary and Alan L. McClellan
CD-ROM included

ISBN 0-13-565847-0

For Java programmers who want to get right to work using and extending the AWT.

Instant Java, 2nd Edition
by John A. Pew
CD-ROM included

ISBN 0-13-272287-9

The title is meant to suggest kinship with instant coffee. For applet programmers who don't want to understand the mechanics of grinding and brewing but want to begin serving up applets immediately. This is an applet cookbook with lots of recipes in print and on CD-ROM, with reference tables for applet parameters.

Java by Example, 2nd Edition
by Jerry R. Jackson and Alan L. McClellan
CD-ROM included

ISBN 0-13-272295-X

A pragmatic and illustrative approach to the basics of the Java language and techniques for applet writing for programmers new to the language.

Just Java, 2nd Edition
by Peter van der Linden
CD-ROM included

ISBN 0-13-272303-4

A lively and clear guide to the essential features of the Java language by the author of *Expert C Programming: Deep C Secrets*.

Here are some additional books that address application areas, such as object-oriented design, interface design, and client/server development.

Java Programming for the Internet
by Michael D. Thomas, Pratik R. Patel, Alan D. Hudson, Donald A. Ball, Jr.
published by Ventana Communications Group

ISBN 1-56604-355-7

Java programming guide with a section of Internet application examples. Examples are available on a companion CD-ROM and at the book's Web site (http://http://www.vmedia.com/java.html).

The Essential Client/Server Survival Guide, 2nd Edition
by Robert Orfali, Dan Harkey, Jeri Edwards
published by John Wiley and Sons

ISBN 0471153257

Good "big picture" background in a very readable form for enterprise-technology decision makers and application developers alike. It provides history and context for understanding client/server trends, with definitions, views of what different vendors are doing in the client/server arena, and product names and capabilities. The second edition updates the book to include the role of the Internet and the World Wide Web in client/server technologies.

Design Patterns: Elements of Reusable Object-Oriented Software
by Erich Gamma, Richard Helm, Ralph Johnson, and John Vlissides

published by Addison-Wesley

ISBN 0-201-63361-2

Although it doesn't address Java specifically, this is a very useful guide for thinking about object-oriented design solutions to typical application problems. It includes a catalog of design patterns derived from experience in developing object-oriented solutions.

Designing Visual Interfaces
by Kevin Mullet and Darrel Sano

published by SunSoft Press-Prentice Hall

ISBN 0-13-303389-9

For anyone involved in user interface design, including graphic designers and user interface developers. This isn't a straightforward topic to teach, especially given the range of people in the interface community who need to know about it. The book describes fundamental techniques without being bound to the language or concepts of any one discipline.

PART FIVE

Appendixes

APPENDIX A

- **Java WorkShop Browser Keyboard Shortcuts**

Keyboard Shortcuts

Browser Keyboard Accelerators

You can use the keys described in Table A-1 to navigate between and within Java WorkShop Browser pages.

Table A-1 Browser Keyboard Accelerators

Key	Action
F1	Loads the help page for whichever WorkShop tool has cursor focus (is active).
Home	Moves to the top of the Browser page.
End	Moves to the end of the Browser page. This is handy for moving quickly to the end of help pages.
PageUp	Scrolls the contents of the Browser window up one screen.
PageDown	Scrolls the contents of the Browser window down one screen.
UpArrow	Scrolls the Browser display up one line.
DownArrow	Scrolls the Browser display down one line.
LeftArrow	Scrolls the Browser display left one character.
RightArrow	Scrolls the Browser display right one character.

APPENDIX

B

- Attributes Common to Most Components

- Special Attributes

- Custom Components and their Attributes

- Differences in GUI Actions at Runtime

GUI Component Attributes

This appendix provides an easy reference for the GUI component attributes that you can set interactively or programmatically. Use it as a companion to the chapters about GUI building (Chapter 7, "Building GUIs" and Chapter 12, "Doing More with the GUI Builder").

Pay special attention to Table B-1 on page 201. It can help you avoid some of the pitfalls in defining actions for GUI components.

Attributes Common to Most Components

Many Visual Java components share common attributes. Those attributes are listed here, followed by a section that lists the attributes that are special to each component.

anchor

> Determines where the component is anchored within the cell.

background

> Changes the color of the component's background. Visual Java provides a color chooser dialog box for you to enter a color by number or create one.

borderLabel

> Adds a text label to the Panel border.

borderRelief

Adds a graphical border around the edge of the Panel.

borderWidth

Sets the width of borderRelief.

enabled

Controls whether the component is initially in the enabled or disabled state.

font

Changes font to use in the component (if it contains text). A font chooser dialog box is provided.

foreground

Changes the color of the font. A color chooser dialog is provided.

insets

The distance (in pixels) from the left, right, top, or bottom edge of the cell. A dialog box is provided for entering the values.

name

The name of the component. All components are uniquely named by Visual Java when they are created. You can change the name by means of this attribute. Be sure that all component names within a group are unique.

You can quickly change the name of a selected component by typing in the Name field at the top of the Visual Java page.

operations

Activates the Operations dialog box. Use the Operations dialog box to add callbacks to components. See Operations Dialog Box for details.

text

Text displayed on the component. You can quickly add or change the text of a selected component by typing it in the Text field at the top of the Visual Java page.

Special Attributes

The AWT standard components, represented in Visual Java's palette and the Visual menu, and their special attributes are described here. Custom (non-standard) component attributes are described in "Custom Components and their Attributes" on page 199.

Visual Java Containers

Visual Java supports these three containers:

- Dialog Box
- Frame
- Panel

Dialog Box

A pop-up windows that is activated from a Frame or Panel. The Dialog component is available by choosing **Visual** ➞ **New Window** and selecting Empty Dialog or File Dialog from the list of New Window choices.

location

Sets the initial coordinates of the dialog box on the screen.

modal

Determines whether or not the dialog box has modes.

resizable

Determines whether the size of the dialog box can be changed by the user.

size

Sets the initial size of the dialog box.

visible

Determines whether the dialog box is initially visible.

Frame

Top-level application window with a title and a border. Use a Frame as the main container for a standalone application or for an applet with a GUI that runs outside the browser page. Frames are the only types of containers to which you can add menu bars. To use a Frame choose **Visual ➡ Main Container** and click the Frame radio button.

icon

Specifies the path name of the file that contains the image for the icon. Enter a path name followed by a semicolon followed by the size of the image in pixels.

The path name for the image file can be a URL or (preferably) a path name relative to the codebase of the applet. If the applet `.class` file and image files are in the same directory, only the file name is required.

location

Sets the initial coordinates of the Frame on the screen.

menubar

Invokes the Menu Editor.

resizable

Determines if the size of the Frame can be changed by the user.

size

Sets the initial size of the Frame.

visible

Determines whether the Frame is initially visible.

Panel

A container that does not create a separate window. Use Panels as the main container for applets whose GUIs run in a browser page or applet viewer.

labelAlignment

Sets the position (left, right, center) of the borderLabel on the top edge of the Panel.

Visual Java Components

This section describes the items on the palette (in alphabetical order) and their attributes.

Figure B-1 illustrates the component palette.

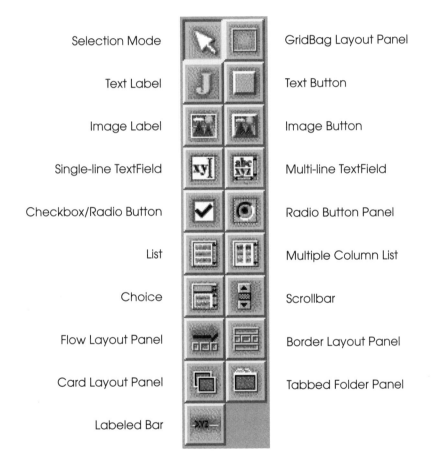

Selection Mode — GridBag Layout Panel

Text Label — Text Button

Image Label — Image Button

Single-line TextField — Multi-line TextField

Checkbox/Radio Button — Radio Button Panel

List — Multiple Column List

Choice — Scrollbar

Flow Layout Panel — Border Layout Panel

Card Layout Panel — Tabbed Folder Panel

Labeled Bar

Figure B-1 Component Palette

Border Layout Panel

Use the Border Layout Panel to position four components against the four edges of the Panel and position another component in the center. The center component receives all remaining space in the Panel.

labelAlignment

Sets the position (left, right, center) of the borderLabel on the top edge of the Panel

useCenter

Removes or includes the center cell in the Panel.

useEast

Removes or includes the east cell in the Panel.

useNorth

Removes or includes the north cell in the Panel.

useSouth

Removes or includes the south cell in the Panel.

useWest

Removes or includes the west cell in the Panel.

Card Layout Panel

Use the Card Layout Panel to create a stack of Panels that can be displayed one at a time.

cards

Invokes the Cards dialog box. Use the Cards dialog box to add, delete, name, and label the stack of Panels (cards).

delayedCreation

If set to true, delays creation of the component until it is requested by the program.

labelAlignment

Sets the position (left, right, center) of the borderLabel on the top edge of the Panel.

Checkbox/Radio Button

Use the Checkbox/Radio Button to maintain a toggle (Boolean) state—whether it is checked or not.

state

Sets the initial state of the checkbox.

Choice

Use the Choice component to display an options menu that drops down from a button.

Flow Layout Panel

Use the Flow Layout Panel component to arrange components from left to right in rows. It fits as many components in the row as possible before creating additional rows.

hgap

The horizontal distance (in pixels) between components. Also controls the distance of the leftmost and rightmost components from the edges of the Panel.

items

A dialog box that enables you to add and delete Panels from the Flow Layout Panel and to change the names of those Panels.

labelAlignment

Sets the position (left, right, center) of the borderLabel on the top edge of the Panel.

vgap

The vertical distance (in pixels) between rows of components. Also controls the distance between components and the top and bottom edges of the Panel.

GridBag Layout Panel

Use the GridBag Layout Panel component to nest a Layout Panel inside an existing cell. Here's a shortcut for placing a component into a GridBag Layout Panel:

a.   Select a component you have already inserted into the layout grid.

b.   Choose **Visual ⟹ Nested Panel**.

Visual Java places the component within a GridBag Layout Panel.

Image Button

Use the Image Button to add a button that contains an image. Specify the image path name in the Attribute Editor.

image

The path name of the image for the button. The path name can be a URL or (preferably) a path name relative to the applet's codebase. If the .class file and image file are in the same directory, you can use the file name.

pressMovement

The number of pixels down and to the left that the image moves when the button is clicked.

lineWidth

The width of the button bevel (in pixels).

padWidth

The number of pixels between the edge of the button and the image displayed within it.

Image Label

Use the Image Label component to add a graphic label in the GUI.

image

The path name of the file for the image to be contained in the label. The path to the image can be a URL or (preferably) a path name relative to the codebase of the applet. If the .class file and image files are in the same directory, only the file name is required.

padWidth

Sets the number of pixels between the edge of the label component and the image displayed within it.

Labeled Bar

Use the Labeled Bar component to add a horizontal rule that contains a text label.

alignment

Aligns text to the left, right, or center of the bar.

textOffsetFromEdge

Number of pixels the text is offset from the edge of the cell.

List

Use the List component to create a list of string items.

listContents

Adds strings to the list.

visibleRows

Sets the number of rows in the list.

Multiple Column List

Use the Multiple Column List component to create a columnar list of strings with headers.

autowidth

Causes a column to automatically become wider to accommodate a new piece of data that doesn't fit within the current width of the column.

displayRows

Sets the minimum number of rows displayed in the list.

headers

Inserts the names of column headers.

highlightItems

When highlightItems is set to true and you later programmatically change the values in one of the rows in the column list, that row will be highlighted for a moment and then gradually fade. Useful for demos or applications where you want to draw attention to the arrival of new information in the list.

selectable

Sets items in the list as selectable by users.

showHeaders

Determines whether column headers are displayed.

Multi-line TextField

Use the Multi-line Text Field component to add a text field for user input and/or displaying text generated by the application.

editable

Sets the field to be writable by the user.

numColumns

Sets the minimum width of the field to accommodate the specified number of characters.

numRows

Sets the minimum height of the field to accommodate the specified number of rows.

Radio Button Panel

Use the Radio Button Panel to enforce mutual exclusion ("radio button" behavior) among any number of checkbox/radio button components.

labelAlignment

Sets the position (left, right, center) of the borderLabel on the top edge of the Panel.

Scrollbar

Use the Scrollbar component to scroll GUI objects horizontally or vertically.

minimum/maximum

Scrollbars have an integer value associated with them that represents the location of the slider/thumb in the scrolled object. Use minimum and maximum to determine the range of those values. For example, if minimum and maximum are set to 0 and 100, then when the slider/thumb is in the middle of the displayed object, its value is 50. This value is available to the programmer to manipulate the scrolled object.

lineIncrement

The number added or subtracted from the location value when the user clicks on the arrows at the ends of the Scrollbar.

orientation

Determines whether the Scrollbar is oriented horizontally or vertically.

pageIncrement

> The number added to or subtracted from the location value when the user clicks in the area between the slider/thumb and the arrows at each end of the scrollbar.

value

> The integer value that represents the initial position of the slider/thumb relative to the values of minimum and maximum.

visiblePageSize

> The initial length (in value units) of the slider/thumb. This length usually indicates the percentage of the entire document that can be viewed in the window that the scrollbar controls.

Selection Mode

Use the selection mode to select cells and components in the layout grid. When you select a cell, the available operations are:

- Add new rows and columns to the grid.
- Add components from the palette to the selected cell.

When you select components in the layout grid you can:

- Change their attributes.
- Change their size.
- Extend them across other cells.
- Delete them.
- Copy them to the clipboard.
- Cut them to the clipboard.

Single-Line Text Field

Use the Single-line Text Field component to add a one-line text field. Use a Single-line Text Field for user input and/or to display text generated by the application.

editable

> Sets the field to be writable by the user.

numColumns

> Sets the minimum width of the field to accommodate the specified number of characters.

Tabbed Folder Panel

Use the Tabbed Folder Panel to create a stack of tabbed Panels that can be displayed one at a time. A Tabbed Folder Panel is a variant of the Card Layout Panel, in which each Panel has a labeled tab that is used to select the Panel from the stack.

cards

Invokes the Cards dialog box. Use the Cards dialog box to add, delete, name, and label the stack of Panels. The string in the Label field is displayed on the folder's tab.

delayedCreation

If set to true, delays creation of the component until it is requested by the program.

labelAlignment

Sets the position (left, right, center) of the borderLabel on the top edge of the Panel.

Text Button

Use the Text Button component to add a button with a text label.

standard

When set to true, the component sizes to a standard button size. Use this attribute when you have a row of buttons with varying amounts of text and you want the button size to be uniform.

Text Label

Use the Text Label component to add text labels to your GUI.

alignment

You can align text to the left side, right side, or center of the label.

Custom Components and their Attributes

Custom components and their attributes are described here. "GUI Components in Visual Java" on page 84 describes how to use them in Java WorkShop.

Canvas

The Canvas component is a subclass (VJCanvas) of the AWT Canvas class. You can draw objects in it programmatically. It will send these events when the paint() and update() methods are called: VJCanvas.PAINT_EVENT and VJCanvas.UPDATE_EVENT.

minHeight

> Minimum height (in pixels) of the canvas.

minWidth

> Minimum width (in pixels) of the canvas.

Generic

Use the Generic component to import any custom AWT component class that you write.

Multi-line Label

Use the multi-line label to add text labels of more than one line to your GUI.

Scrolling Panel

The Scrolling Panel provides a Panel with scrollbars for AWT components. If there is not enough space in the cells of the Panel to display components you've added, scrollbars are automatically added.

scrollAreaHeight

> Height (in pixels) of the scroll area of the Panel.

scrollAreaInsets

> Space (in pixels) between the edge of the Panel and its display area.

scrollAreaWidth

> Width (in pixels) of the scroll area of the Panel.

Text List

The Text List component is similar to the standard AWT List component in its behavior, with the exception that it won't allow multiple selections. The major difference between the two components is the programmatic interface. The Text List component uses a vector to track its list elements, and you can access this vector directly. The Text List component can also be much faster and more convenient to use than the standard List interface, especially with really long lists.

`visibleRows`

Sets the number or rows in the list.

Differences in GUI Actions at Runtime

You can interactively attach actions to GUI components in Java WorkShop's GUI builder (described in Chapter 7 and in more detail in Chapter 12). In the current release of Java WorkShop, the entire list of events is active for all components, even though some events don't apply to some components. This means that at design time you need to know which events are possible for a component because they vary, depending on the runtime environment.

To avoid problems, consult Table B-1 to see the events generated on different platforms and browser combinations. You might want to keep a copy of the table handy when you are adding operations to GUI components.

Table B-1 Runtime Differences for User Interface Actions

	Applet (PC)	Applet (Mac)	Application (PC)	Application (Mac)	Netscape Navigator 3.0 (PC)	Netscape Navigator 3.0 (Mac)	Internet Explorer (PC)
action	BCLRT	BCLRT	BCLRT	BCLRT	BCLRT	BCLRT	BCLRT
keyPress	T	T	BCLRT	T	ABCLPRT	T	BCLRT
keyRelease	T		BCLRT		ABCLPRT	T	BCLRT
gotFocus		T	P	T	ABCLRT	T	
lostFocus		T	P	T	ABCLRT	T	
mouseDown	I	I	IP	I	ABCILPRT	I	I
mouseUp	I	I	IP	I	ABCILPRT	IL	I
mouseEnter	IP	ABCLPRT	IP	ABCLPRT	ABCLPRT	ABCLPRT	P
mouseExit	IP	ABCLPRT	IP	ABCLPRT	ABCLPRT	ABCLPRT	P
mouseMove	IP	ABCLPRT	IP	ABCLRT	ABCILPRT	ABCILPRT	IP
mouseDrag	I	I	IP	I	ABCILPRT	IL	I

Legend:

A = Label	B = Button	C = Choice	I = Image (Canvas)
L = List	P = Panel	R = RadioButton	T = TextArea

APPENDIX C

- Managing Projects

- Editing Source Files

- Running Applets

- Building GUIs

- Working in the Java WorkShop Environment

Java
WorkShop
Questions and
Answers

This appendix answers some of the questions that users ask the Java WorkShop team. It covers areas where there is a critical mass of questions. Some of the topics in the questions have been answered in a different form elsewhere in this book but are included here to highlight them. The Java WorkShop Web site maintains a more complete list of Frequently Asked Questions (FAQs) about Java WorkShop. The URL for the Java WorkShop FAQ is:

`http://www.sun.com/workshop/java/technical/FAQ.html.`

Managing Projects

How can I see what source files are in a project?

You can list a project's source files and add or delete files for a project by using the Build Tab in the Project Editor. Choose a project and click the Project Manager icon. Click the Build tab and look at the scrolling list of source files. Use the Add or Delete buttons to change the source files in a project.

How do I build a project with multiple packages?

If you want to build a project that uses multiple packages, it is best to use nested projects. Create a project for each package, then create a "super project" that includes each of the package projects. (This is how Java WorkShop itself is built.) When you build the super project, Java WorkShop builds all of the package projects included in it.

How do I know if there are projects within projects?

You can tell if a project is a nested project and see a list of all of the projects contained within it by looking at the General tab in the Project Editor. This tab lists "Included Projects" (if there are any) for the current project.

How do I let Java WorkShop know that I have moved project files to a new directory?

Java WorkShop currently does not support renaming projects. Moving projects from one directory to another changes the project's name, so you'll have to import the project, including the source files, from the directory where you moved it. In general, it's easier to move projects by cutting and pasting them. When you paste the project back into a portfolio you can specify a destination directory.

Editing Source Files

How do I edit multiple source files with the Source Editor?

Use the New Window command on the Source Editor's View menu. Java WorkShop opens a file chooser for you to specify the file to be loaded in the new window.

Note that this is different from using the New command in the Source Editor File menu. The New command clears the file in the Source Editor; it does not open a new window.

Running Applets

What's required to run the applets that I created in Java WorkShop in Netscape Navigator?

You can open the HTML page for your Java WorkShop applet in other browsers. If Navigator fails to find the Visual Java runtime classes required to run your applet outside of Java WorkShop, you will probably see one of the following error messages:

- ```
  Applet can't start: class <class_name> got a security
  violation: method verification error.
  ```

- ```
  Applet can't start: error.java.lang.NoClassDefFoundError.
  ```

"Running Visual Java Applets in Netscape Navigator" on page 162 describes how to set the CLASSPATH variable so that Netscape Navigator can find the runtime classes. If Navigator fails to find the classes, you may need to restart Navigator after the CLASSPATH variable has been defined.

Building GUIs

How do I get the values from a List?

When you create a list in Visual Java, you are creating a shadow class for the AWT List component. The class is called `ListShadow`. The AWT List object has two members for getting the selected item and the selected items in a list. `ListShadow` does provide access to the first of these members, but not the second. The selected items member comes into play when the `ListShadow` allowMultipleSelections attribute is set to true. You have to get selected items programmatically.

The `getBody()` method allows access to the methods of the classes on which shadow classes are based. In other words, it bypasses the shadow classes themselves. For a `ListShadow` object, you could use `getBody` to return the AWT component for the shadow, the List object. The `getBody` method returns an Object, so the caller has to cast it to an appropriate AWT type. Here, then, is the call that returns the selected items in a list that you created in Visual Java:

```
((List) listShadowObject.getBody()).getSelectedItems()
```

It helps if you recall that shadow classes are wrappers for AWT classes. It also helps to remember that shadows are the tools that make visual programming possible in Java WorkShop, which sometimes makes them more useful to Java WorkShop than to you. There are a number of ways to find out which attributes are available in the Attribute Editor (because they are wrapped by the shadow class for the component) and which are not. The easiest thing to do is to look at the attributes listed for any component when you are editing the component in the Attribute Editor and compare that to the API for the class.

Once you grasp the basic idea that shadows wrap AWT components and that there are occasions when you access the AWT components directly, you'll find the API documentation tells you what you need to know. The API documentation is at the URL `doc:/lib/visual/api/packages.html`.

How do I access items in a Multiple Column List?

You'll find a sample applet on one of the Java WorkShop Web pages that illustrates a Multiple Column List component. We'll look at two pieces of the applet code that illustrate approaches to common Multiple Column List questions. For the complete applet see this URL:

```
http://www.sun.com/workshop/java/literature/cookbook2
```

Click on the link named Multi-Column List.

This site contains a number of Visual Java programming examples that show how to get and set component attributes programmatically. Many of the examples were written for the early development releases of Java WorkShop, but the example at the Multi-Column List link was created with Java WorkShop 1.0. Follow the link to run or download the applet named MULTIC. For your convenience, the source code for the applet is included in Appendix D.

MULTIC uses a number of components created in Java WorkShop, including the Multiple Column List. Here's a code snippet from the applet that illustrates adding items in a Multiple Column List component named addressColumnList. This is one approach; you might prefer to use a loop for the calls that add items.

```
String data[][] = {{"Boyer","3567 Benton","Santa Clara",
"CA","95051","555-1212"},
    {"Smith","123 Easy Street","Los Angeles",  "CA","80333","555-
2222"},
    {"Miller","7 Main, Apt 4","San Francisco",  "CA","91111","555-
3333"}};
```

```
((ColumnList)
gui.addressColumnList.getBody()).addItem(data[0],true);
((ColumnList)
gui.addressColumnList.getBody()).addItem(data[1],true);
((ColumnList)
gui.addressColumnList.getBody()).addItem(data[2],true);
```

Here's a code snippet that illustrates how to determine the selected row:

```
//Selecting a row causes a LIST_SELECT event to occur

    if (evt.id == Event.LIST_SELECT) {

    //row number is returned in evt.arg

    Integer intObject =  (Integer)evt.arg;
    int row = intObject.intValue();
    currentRow = row;
```

How do I access Applet methods from a group class created in Visual Java?

For access to Applet methods, call getApplet() from your group subclass. The example given in online help is for editing an operation to add code that gets the applet parameter for the blink rate for the *Blink* project:

```
Applet ap = getApplet();
String param = ap.getParameter("blinkrate");
```

Here's another example that calls getApplet() from a subclass of Group. Say you have a button named button1 in your GUI and you want it to get a URL to display an HTML page. You can add the following code to the group subclass generated for your GUI. (See Chapter 12 for information about using groups. Rolo.java in Appendix D is an example of a generated group class.)

```
public boolean action (Message msg, Event evt, Object what) {

    if (msg.target == gui.button1) {
        System.out.println("Got press on button1");
        Applet ap = getApplet();

        // getApplet returns null if you are not running
        // under a browser, so check
        if (ap == null)
            System.out.println("Cannot show a document without a
browser.");
        else {
            try {
                URL u = new URL("http://www.sun.com");
                // or, a file if you want:
                // URL u = new URL("file://Blink.html");
                ap.getAppletContext().showDocument(u);
            } catch (java.net.MalformedURLException x) {
            }
        }
    }
    return true;

}
```

Working in the Java WorkShop Environment

How can I copy and paste text between Java WorkShop and other tools?

Java WorkShop does not currently support cutting and pasting between Java WorkShop and your desktop. For example, you can't cut text from a source listing in your system's text editor or command window and paste it into the Source Editor or a field in one of the Java WorkShop tabs.

You can use cut and paste between Source Editor windows and within a Source Editor window, and you can use copy/cut/paste between fields in Java WorkShop tabs. For example, the Windows shortcuts for copying and pasting (<Ctrl+C>and <Ctrl+V>, respectively) will work if you want to copy a run page name from the Existing Run Page field in the Run tab to the Run Page field in the Debug tab.

You can also use the cut/copy/paste operations on projects to move them between portfolios.

How can I control where the .jws directory is created?

When you start Java WorkShop, it uses the value of the HOME environment variable to determine where to create the .jws directory. Windows 95 users usually set the HOME environment variable in the autoexec.bat file. Windows NT users can go to the Control Panel and click on the System icon to make changes to environment variables. Reboot the machine after you make the changes. Java WorkShop will pick up the new HOME setting after that.

Solaris users can also set the value of the HOME environment variable and restart Java WorkShop.

What if I installed earlier releases of Java WorkShop?

If you install Java WorkShop 1.0 without uninstalling earlier development releases you might have been testing (referred to as Dev# releases, for example "Dev6"), you could encounter problems because of the older JWS class files. Windows 95 and Windows NT users could encounter problems when Java WorkShop 1.0 looks for class files at startup. For the current release, the best advice is to uninstall the old development releases before you install Java WorkShop 1.0.

How can I print online help pages?

There's no printing from the current version of the Java WorkShop Browser, so you'll have to open the help pages you want in another browser that does support printing.

For example, suppose you installed Java WorkShop in c:\Java-WorkShop and you want to print the top-level Visual Java help page (doc:/lib/html/help/visual/visual.html).

- Open Netscape Navigator.

- Take the URL of the help page from Java WorkShop minus the *doc:* protocol. To the front of it, add the *file:* protocol plus the installation directory name.

  The URL you would enter in Netscape Navigator would be:
  file:/Java-WorkShop/lib/html/help/visual/visual.html

APPENDIX
D

- Chooser.java

- Greeting.java

- FirstGUI.gui

- FirstGUI.java

- FirstGUIMain.java

- FirstGUIRoot.java

- TumbleItem.java

- Rolo.gui

- Rolo.java

- RoloMain.java

- RoloOps.java

- RoloRoot.java

- MULTIC.java

Code Listings

Chooser.java

```java
import java.awt.*;

/**
 * I wrote this to show you how to add comments.
 *
 * @version 0.1 of a file chooser.
 * @author Your Name Here.
 *
 */
public class Chooser {
    /**
     * Constructor.
     */
    static Frame f = new Frame ("Applications");

    public static void main (String[] a) {
        FileDialog Chooser = new FileDialog(f, "Applications");
        Chooser.show();
        f.add(Chooser);
        f.show ();
    }
}
```

Greeting.java

```java
import java.awt.*;
import java.applet.*;

public class Greeting extends Applet {
    Font welcome = new Font("TimesRoman", Font.ITALIC, 24);
    public void init() {
        resize(600,100);
    }
    public void paint(Graphics g) {
        g.setFont(welcome);
        setBackground(Color.blue);
        g.drawString("Welcome to Inside Java WorkShop",140,50);
        }
}
```

FirstGUI.gui

```
GUI DESCRIPTION VERSION 6[1]
Root root1 {
  java.awt.Dimension appletSize width=229;height=162
  java.lang.Boolean willGenerateGroup true
  java.lang.String groupType Panel
  java.lang.String generateClass FirstGUI
  child list {
    GBPanelShadow gbpanel1 {
      [I rowHeights 14
      GBC GBConstraints x=0;y=0;fill=both
      [I columnWidths 14
      [D rowWeights 0
      java.awt.Dimension layoutSize width=400;height=300
      [D columnWeights 0
      java.awt.Point layoutLocation x=15;y=35
      child list {
        java.awt.ListShadow list1 {
          [Ljava.lang.String; items Red,Yellow,Blue,Orange,Green,Purple
          GBC GBConstraints x=0;y=0;fill=both
        }
      }
    }
  }
}
```

---

1. GUI files are generated files, but you can edit them.

FirstGUI.java

```
/**
 * This is a template.  You can modify this file.
 *
 * Runtime vendor: SunSoft, Inc.
 * Runtime version: 1
 *
 * Visual vendor: SunSoft, Inc.
 * Visual version: 1
 */


import sunsoft.jws.visual.rt.base.*;
import sunsoft.jws.visual.rt.shadow.java.awt.*;
import java.awt.*;


public class FirstGUI extends Group {
  private FirstGUIRoot gui;

  /**
   * Sample method call ordering during a group's lifetime:
   *
   * Constructor
   * initRoot
   * initGroup
   * (setOnGroup and getOnGroup can be called at any time in any
   *  order after initGroup has been called)
   * createGroup
   * showGroup/hideGroup + startGroup/stopGroup
   * destroyGroup
   */

  /**
   * All the attributes used by the group must be defined in the
   * constructor.  setOnGroup is called at initialization for all
   * the attributes.  If the attribute has not been set prior to
   * initialization, setOnGroup is called with the default value.
   */
  public FirstGUI() {
    /**
     * Define the group's custom attributes here.
     *
     * For example:
     *
     * attributes.add("customString", "java.lang.String",
```

```
    *           "Default String", 0);
    */

   /**
    * This method defines the attributes that will be forwarded to
    * the main child (either a window or a panel).  All attributes
    * defined by this method are marked with the FORWARD flag.
    */
   addForwardedAttributes();
}


/**
 * initRoot must be overridden in group subclasses to initialize
 * the shadow tree.  The return value must be the root of the
 * newly initialized shadow tree.
 */
protected Root initRoot() {
  /**
   * Initialize the gui components
   */
  gui = new FirstGUIRoot(this);

  /**
   * This method registers an attribute manager with the group, such
   * that attributes marked with the FORWARD flag will be sent to
   * this attribute manager.
   */
  addAttributeForward(gui.getMainChild());

  return gui;
}


/**
 * initGroup is called during initialization.  It is called just after
 * initRoot is called, but before the subgroups are initialized and
 * before the attributes are sent to the setOnGroup method.
 *
 * initGroup is only called once in the lifetime of the Group.
 * This is because groups cannot be uninitialized.  Anything that
 * needs to be cleaned up should be created in createGroup instead
 * of initGroup and then can be cleaned up in destroyGroup.
 * createGroup and destroyGroup can be called multiple times during
 * the lifetime of a group.
 */
protected void initGroup() { }

  /**
   * showGroup can be overridden by group subclasses that want
```

```
 * to know when the group becomes visible.  It is called just before
 * the group becomes visible.  The group will already be initialized
 * and created at this point.
 */
protected void showGroup() { }


/**
 * hideGroup can be overridden by group subclasses that want
 * to know when the group becomes nonvisible.  It is called just
 * before the group becomes nonvisible.
 */
protected void hideGroup() { }


/**
 * createGroup is called during group creation.  Groups can be
 * created and destroyed multiple times during their lifetime.
 * Anything that is created in createGroup should be cleaned up
 * in destroyGroup.  createGroup is called just after the group
 * has been created.  Anything that needs to be done before the
 * group is created should be done in initGroup.
 */
protected void createGroup() { }


/**
 * destroyGroup is called during the destroy operation.  Groups can
 * be created and destroyed multiple times during their lifetime.
 * Anything that has been created in createGroup should be cleaned up
 * in destroyGroup.  destroyGroup is called just before the group
 * is destroyed.
 */
protected void destroyGroup() { }


/**
 * This method can be overridden by group subclasses that want
 * to be informed when the application is starting.  This method is
 * only called after the entire application has been initialized and
 * created.
 *
 * For applets, startGroup is called whenever start is called on the
 * applet.
 */
protected void startGroup() { }


/**
 * This method can be overridden by group subclasses that want
 * to be informed when the application is stopping.  This method
 * will be called before a destroy is done.
 *
```

```
 * For applets, stopGroup is called whenever stop is called on the
 * applet.
 */
protected void stopGroup() { }

/**
 * "getOnGroup" can be overridden by subgroups that
 * store attribute values themselves, and do not depend on the
 * group superclass to store them.  This method should be overridden
 * instead of "get".  Any attributes handled in setOnGroup where
 * super.setOnGroup is not called must also be handled in getOnGroup.
 *
 * The default implementation of getOnGroup retrieves the value
 * from the attribute table.
 *
 * The reason that "getOnGroup" should be overridden instead
 * of "get" is that "getOnGroup" is guaranteed not to be called
 * until the group class is initialized.  This means that initRoot
 * will always be called before any calls to getOnGroup are made.
 *
 * Also, this method is only for attributes that are defined in the
 * subgroups.  It is not called for forwarded attributes.
 */
protected Object getOnGroup(String key) {
  return super.getOnGroup(key);
}

/**
 * "setOnGroup" can be overridden by subgroups that
 * want notification when attributes are changed.  This method
 * should be overridden instead of "set".  Any attributes handled
 * in setOnGroup where super.setOnGroup is not called must also be
 * handled in getOnGroup.
 *
 * The default implementation of setOnGroup puts the value
 * in the attribute table.
 *
 * The reason that "setOnGroup" should be overridden instead
 * of "set" is that "setOnGroup" is guaranteed not to be called
 * until the group class is initialized.  This means that initRoot
 * will always be called before any calls to setOnGroup are made.
 *
 * During initialization, "setOnGroup" will be called for all
 * the group's attributes even if they have not been changed from
 * the default value.  But for attributes that have the DEFAULT
 * flag set, "setOnGroup" will only be called if the value
 * of the attribute has changed from the default.
 *
```

```
 * Also, this method is only called when attributes defined in the
 * subgroups are updated.  It is not called for forwarded attributes.
 */
protected void setOnGroup(String key, Object value) {
  super.setOnGroup(key, value);
}


/**
 * handleMessage can be overridden by subclasses that want to act
 * on messages that are sent to the group.  Typically, messages are
 * either AWT events that have been translated to messages, or they
 * are messages that have been sent by other groups.
 * super.handleMessage should be called for any messages that aren't
 * handled.  If super.handleMessage is not called, then handleEvent
 * will not be called.
 *
 * The default implementation of handleMessage returns "true".  This
 * means that no events will be passed up the group tree, unless a
 * subclass overrides this method to return "false".  AWT events are
 * not propagated, regardless of the return value from handleEvent.
 *
 * If you want a message to go to the parent group, override
 * handleMessage to return false for that message.
 *
 * If you want an AWT event to go to the parent group, you need to
 * call postMessageToParent() with the event message.
 */
public boolean handleMessage(Message msg) {
  return super.handleMessage(msg);
}


/**
 * handleEvent can be overridden by subclasses that want to get
 * notified when AWT events are sent by the gui components.
 * The return value should be true for handled events, and
 * super.handleEvent should be called for unhandled events.
 * If super.handleEvent is not called, then the specific event
 * handling methods will not be called.
 *
 * The message's target is set to the shadow that sent the event.
 * The event's target is set to the AWT component that sent the event.
 *
 *
 * The following specific event handling methods can also be
overridden:
 *
 * public boolean mouseDown(Message msg, Event evt, int x, int y);
 * public boolean mouseDrag(Message msg, Event evt, int x, int y);
```

```
 * public boolean mouseUp(Message msg, Event evt, int x, int y);
 * public boolean mouseMove(Message msg, Event evt, int x, int y);
 * public boolean mouseEnter(Message msg, Event evt, int x, int y);
 * public boolean mouseExit(Message msg, Event evt, int x, int y);
 * public boolean keyDown(Message msg, Event evt, int key);
 * public boolean keyUp(Message msg, Event evt, int key);
 * public boolean action(Message msg, Event evt, Object what);
 * public boolean gotFocus(Message msg, Event evt, Object what);
 * public boolean lostFocus(Message msg, Event evt, Object what);
 */
public boolean handleEvent(Message msg, Event evt) {
  return super.handleEvent(msg, evt);
}
}
```

FirstGUIMain.java

```
/**
 * This file was automatically generated.  Do not manually modify this
 file.
 *
 * Runtime vendor: SunSoft, Inc.
 * Runtime version: 1
 *
 * Visual vendor: SunSoft, Inc.
 * Visual version: 1
 */

import sunsoft.jws.visual.rt.base.Group;
import sunsoft.jws.visual.rt.base.MainHelper;
import java.applet.Applet;

/**
 * Generated Main class
 *
 * @version 1.20, 05/21/96
 */
public class FirstGUIMain extends Applet {
  /**
   * Helper class for the generated main class.  This variable is only
   * used when we are running as an applet.
   */
  private MainHelper helper;

  /**
   * Called when application is run from the command line.
   */
  public static void main(String args[]) {
    MainHelper helper = new MainHelper();
    helper.checkVersion(1);

    Group group = new FirstGUI();
    helper.main(group, args);
  }

  /**
   * Called when the applet is loaded.
   */
  public void init() {
    helper = new MainHelper();
    helper.checkVersion(1);
```

```java
    Group group = new FirstGUI();
    helper.init(this, group);
  }

  /**
   * Called whenever the applet's page is visited.
   */
  public void start(){
    helper.start();
  }

  /**
   * Called by the browser when the user leaves the page.
   */
  public void stop() {
    helper.stop();
  }

  /**
   * Called by the browser when the applet should be destroyed.
   */
  public void destroy() {
    helper.destroy();
  }
}
```

FirstGUIRoot.java

```java
/**
 * This file was automatically generated.  Do not manually modify this
file.
 *
 * Runtime vendor: SunSoft, Inc.
 * Runtime version: 1
 *
 * Visual vendor: SunSoft, Inc.
 * Visual version: 1
 */


import sunsoft.jws.visual.rt.awt.GBConstraints;
import sunsoft.jws.visual.rt.base.*;
import sunsoft.jws.visual.rt.shadow.*;
import sunsoft.jws.visual.rt.shadow.java.awt.*;
import sunsoft.jws.visual.rt.type.*;


public class FirstGUIRoot extends Root {
   public GBPanelShadow gbpanel1;
   public ListShadow list1;
   public Root root1;

   public FirstGUIRoot(Group group) {
     setGroup(group);

     gbpanel1 = new GBPanelShadow();
     gbpanel1.set("name", "gbpanel1");
     add(gbpanel1);
     {
       int _tmp[] = {14};
       gbpanel1.set("rowHeights", _tmp);
     }
     gbpanel1.set("GBConstraints", new
GBConstraints("x=0;y=0;fill=both"));
     {
       int _tmp[] = {14};
       gbpanel1.set("columnWidths", _tmp);
     }
     gbpanel1.set("layoutSize", new java.awt.Dimension(400, 300));
     {
       double _tmp[] = {0};
       gbpanel1.set("rowWeights", _tmp);
     }
```

```
    {
      double _tmp[] = {0};
      gbpanel1.set("columnWeights", _tmp);
    }
    gbpanel1.set("layoutLocation", new java.awt.Point(15, 35));

    list1 = new ListShadow();
    list1.set("name", "list1");
    gbpanel1.add(list1);
    list1.set("items", convert("[Ljava.lang.String;",
"Red,Yellow,Blue,Orange,Green,Purple"));
    list1.set("GBConstraints", new GBConstraints("x=0;y=0;fill=both"));
  }

  // methods from lib/visual/gen/methods.java

  /**
   * Converts a string to the specified type.
   */
  private Object convert(String type, String value) {
    return(Converter.getConverter(type).convertFromString(value));
  }
}
```

TumbleItem.java

```
/*
 * @(#)Tumble.java
 *
 * Copyright (c) 1994-1995 Sun Microsystems, Inc. All Rights Reserved.
 *
 * Permission to use, copy, modify, and distribute this software
 * and its documentation for NON-COMMERCIAL or COMMERCIAL purposes and
 * without fee is hereby granted.
 * Please refer to the file http://java.sun.com/copy_trademarks.html
 * for further important copyright and trademark information and to
 * http://java.sun.com/licensing.html for further important licensing
 * information for the Java (tm) Technology.
 *
 * SUN MAKES NO REPRESENTATIONS OR WARRANTIES ABOUT THE SUITABILITY OF
 * THE SOFTWARE, EITHER EXPRESS OR IMPLIED, INCLUDING BUT NOT LIMITED
 * TO THE IMPLIED WARRANTIES OF MERCHANTABILITY, FITNESS FOR A
 * PARTICULAR PURPOSE, OR NON-INFRINGEMENT. SUN SHALL NOT BE LIABLE FOR
 * ANY DAMAGES SUFFERED BY LICENSEE AS A RESULT OF USING, MODIFYING OR
 * DISTRIBUTING THIS SOFTWARE OR ITS DERIVATIVES.
 *
 * THIS SOFTWARE IS NOT DESIGNED OR INTENDED FOR USE OR RESALE AS ON-LINE
 * CONTROL EQUIPMENT IN HAZARDOUS ENVIRONMENTS REQUIRING FAIL-SAFE
 * PERFORMANCE, SUCH AS IN THE OPERATION OF NUCLEAR FACILITIES, AIRCRAFT
 * NAVIGATION OR COMMUNICATION SYSTEMS, AIR TRAFFIC CONTROL, DIRECT LIFE
 * SUPPORT MACHINES, OR WEAPONS SYSTEMS, IN WHICH THE FAILURE OF THE
 * SOFTWARE COULD LEAD DIRECTLY TO DEATH, PERSONAL INJURY, OR SEVERE
 * PHYSICAL OR ENVIRONMENTAL DAMAGE ("HIGH RISK ACTIVITIES").  SUN
 * SPECIFICALLY DISCLAIMS ANY EXPRESS OR IMPLIED WARRANTY OF FITNESS FOR
 * HIGH RISK ACTIVITIES.
 */

import java.io.InputStream;
import java.applet.Applet;
import java.awt.*;
import java.net.*;

/**
 * A simple Item class to play an image loop.  The "img" tag parameter
 * indicates what image loop to play.
 *
 * @author James Gosling
 * @version 1.17, 31 Jan 1995
 */
public
class TumbleItem extends Applet implements Runnable {
```

```
/**
 * The current loop slot.
 */
int loopslot = 0;

/**
 * The directory or URL from which the images are loaded
 */
String dir;

/**
 * The thread animating the images.
 */
Thread kicker = null;

/**
 * The length of the pause between revs.
 */
int pause;

int offset;
int off;
int speed;
int nimgs;

/**
 * The images.
 */
Image imgs[];
int maxWidth;

/**
 * Initialize the applet. Get attributes.
 */
 public void init() {
String at = getParameter("img");
dir = (at != null) ? at : "images/tumble";
at = getParameter("pause");
pause = (at != null) ? Integer.valueOf(at).intValue() : 2000;
at = getParameter("offset");
offset = (at != null) ? Integer.valueOf(at).intValue() : 0;
at = getParameter("speed");
speed = (at != null) ? (1000 / Integer.valueOf(at).intValue()) : 100;
at = getParameter("nimgs");
nimgs = (at != null) ? Integer.valueOf(at).intValue() : 16;
at = getParameter("maxwidth");
maxWidth = (at != null) ? Integer.valueOf(at).intValue() : 0;
 }
```

```
    /**
     * Run the image loop. This method is called by class Thread.
     * @see java.lang.Thread
     */
    public void run() {
    Thread.currentThread().setPriority(Thread.NORM_PRIORITY-1);
    imgs = new Image[nimgs];
    for (int i = 1 ; i < nimgs; i++) {
        imgs[i] = getImage(getDocumentBase(), dir + "/T" + i + ".gif");
    }

    Dimension d = size();
    if (nimgs > 1) {
        if (offset < 0) {
        off = d.width - maxWidth;
        }
        while (kicker != null) {
        //System.out.println("frame = " +  loopslot);
        if (++loopslot >= nimgs) {
            loopslot = 10;
            off += offset;
            if (off < 0) {
            off = d.width - maxWidth;
            } else if (off + maxWidth > d.width) {
            off = 0;
            }
        }
        repaint();
        try {
            Thread.sleep(speed + ((loopslot == nimgs - 1) ? pause : 0));
        } catch (InterruptedException e) {
            break;
        }
        }
    }
    }

    public boolean imageUpdate(Image img, int flags,
                int x, int y, int w, int h) {
    if ((flags & (SOMEBITS|FRAMEBITS|ALLBITS)) != 0) {
        if ((imgs != null) && (loopslot < nimgs) && (imgs[loopslot] ==
img)) {
        repaint(100);
        }
    }
    return (flags & (ALLBITS|ERROR)) == 0;
    }
```

```java
    /**
     * Paint the current frame.
     */
    public void paint(Graphics g) {
    //System.out.println("paint");
    if ((imgs != null) && (loopslot < nimgs) && (imgs[loopslot] != null))
{
        g.drawImage(imgs[loopslot], off, 0, this);
    }
    }

    /**
     * Start the applet by forking an animation thread.
     */
    public void start() {
    if (kicker == null) {
        kicker = new Thread(this);
        kicker.start();
    }
    }

    /**
     * Stop the applet. The thread will exit because kicker is set to
null.
     */
    public void stop() {
    if (kicker != null) {
        kicker.stop();
        kicker = null;
    }
    }
}
```

Rolo.gui

```
GUI DESCRIPTION VERSION 6²
Root root1 {
  java.awt.Dimension appletSize width=316;height=324
  java.lang.String groupType Frame
  java.lang.String generateClass Rolo
  child list {
    java.awt.FrameShadow RoloFrame {
      java.lang.String title Rolo
      java.awt.Dimension layoutSize width=457;height=570
      java.awt.Point layoutLocation x=55;y=174
      child list {
        GBPanelShadow gbpanel2 {
          [I rowHeights 14,14,14,14,14,14
          GBC GBConstraints x=0;y=0;fill=both
          [I columnWidths 14,14,14,14
          [D rowWeights 0,0,0,0,0,0
          [D columnWeights 0,0,0,0
          child list {
            java.awt.LabelShadow nameLabel {
              GBC GBConstraints x=0;y=0
              java.lang.String text Name:
              [Lsunsoft.jws.visual.rt.type.Op; operations {
                {
                  name Op1
                  filter {
                    filterType EVENT
                    id 1001
                  }
                  action {
                    actionType CODE
                    code {}
                  }
                }
              }
            }
            java.awt.ListShadow namesList {
              [Ljava.lang.String; items "Lynn Weaver 555-0000,John J.
Javaman 555-0001"
              GBC GBConstraints x=0;y=4;width=4;fill=both
            }
            java.awt.TextFieldShadow nameTextfield {
              GBC GBConstraints x=1;y=0;width=3;fill=horizontal
            }
```

2.   GUI files are generated files, but you can edit them.

```
java.awt.LabelShadow phoneLabel {
  GBC GBConstraints x=0;y=1
  java.lang.String text Phone:
}
java.awt.TextFieldShadow phoneTextfield {
  GBC GBConstraints x=1;y=1;width=3;fill=horizontal
}
java.awt.ButtonShadow addButton {
  GBC GBConstraints x=1;y=2
  java.lang.String text Add
  [Lsunsoft.jws.visual.rt.type.Op; operations {
    {
      name Op1
      filter {
        filterType EVENT
        id 1001
      }
      action {
        actionType CODE
        code {String[] listContents = (String [])
gui.namesList.get("items");
String newItem = (String) gui.nameTextfield.get("text") + " " +
                       (String) gui.phoneTextfield.get("text");
int len = listContents.length;
String[] newContents = new String[len + 1];
int i = 0;

for (i=0; i < len; i++) {
  newContents[i] = listContents[i];
}
newContents[len] = newItem;
gui.namesList.set("items",  newContents);}
      }
    }
  }
}
java.awt.ButtonShadow findButton {
  GBC GBConstraints x=2;y=2
  java.lang.String text Find
  [Lsunsoft.jws.visual.rt.type.Op; operations {
    {
      name Op1
      filter {
        filterType EVENT
        id 1001
      }
```

```
                    action {
                      actionType CODE
                    code {List listBody = (List) gui.namesList.getBody();
                            int numItems = listBody.countItems();
                            String nameToFind = (String)
gui.nameTextfield.get("text");
                            String currentName = "";
                            int i = 0;
                            int j = 0;
                            int len = 0;
                            int nameLen = nameToFind.length();

                            for (i=0; i < numItems; i++) {
                                currentName = listBody.getItem(i);
                                len = currentName.length();
                                if (len >= nameLen &&
                                    len != 0 &&
                                    nameLen != 0) {
                                  for (j=0; j < len - nameLen + 1; j++) {
                                    if (currentName.regionMatches(true,
                                                                  j,
                                                            nameToFind,
                                                                   0,
                                                  nameLen) == true) {
                                      listBody.select(i);
                                      return;
                                    }
                                  }
                                }
                            }
                    }
                  }
                }
              }
            java.awt.ButtonShadow deleteButton {
              GBC GBConstraints x=1;y=5;width=2
              java.lang.String text Delete
              [Lsunsoft.jws.visual.rt.type.Op; operations {
                {
                  name Op1
                  filter {
                    filterType EVENT
                    id 1001
                  }
                  action {
                    actionType CODE
                    code {import java.awt.List;
```

```
List listBody = (List) gui.namesList.getBody();
int selectedIndex = listBody.getSelectedIndex();

listBody.delItem(selectedIndex);
}
                    }
                }
            }
        }
        java.awt.LabelShadow listLabel {
            GBC GBConstraints x=0;y=3
            java.lang.String text Entries:
        }
      }
    }
  }
 }
}
```

Rolo.java

```java
/**
 * This is a template.  You can modify this file.
 *
 * Runtime vendor: SunSoft, Inc.
 * Runtime version: 1
 *
 * Visual vendor: SunSoft, Inc.
 * Visual version: 1
 */


import sunsoft.jws.visual.rt.base.*;
import sunsoft.jws.visual.rt.shadow.java.awt.*;
import java.awt.*;


public class Rolo extends Group {
  private RoloRoot gui;

  /**
    * Sample method call ordering during a group's lifetime:
    *
    * Constructor
    * initRoot
    * initGroup
    * (setOnGroup and getOnGroup can be called at any time in any
    *  order after initGroup has been called)
    * createGroup
    * showGroup/hideGroup + startGroup/stopGroup
    * destroyGroup
    */

  /**
    * All the attributes used by the group must be defined in the
    * constructor.  setOnGroup is called at initialization for all
    * the attributes.  If the attribute has not been set prior to
    * initialization, setOnGroup is called with the default value.
    */
  public Rolo() {
    /**
      * Define the group's custom attributes here.
      *
      * For example:
      *
      * attributes.add("customString", "java.lang.String",
```

```
 *         "Default String", 0);
 */

/**
 * This method defines the attributes that will be forwarded to
 * the main child (either a window or a panel).  All attributes
 * defined by this method are marked with the FORWARD flag.
 */
addForwardedAttributes();
}

/**
 * initRoot must be overridden in group subclasses to initialize
 * the shadow tree.  The return value must be the root of the
 * newly initialized shadow tree.
 */
protected Root initRoot() {
  /**
   * Initialize the gui components
   */
  gui = new RoloRoot(this);

  /**
   * This method registers an attribute manager with the group, such
   * that attributes marked with the FORWARD flag will be sent to
   * this attribute manager.
   */
  addAttributeForward(gui.getMainChild());

  return gui;
}

/**
 * initGroup is called during initialization.  It is called just after
 * initRoot is called, but before the subgroups are initialized and
 * before the attributes are sent to the setOnGroup method.
 *
 * initGroup is only called once in the lifetime of the Group.
 * This is because groups cannot be uninitialized.  Anything that
 * needs to be cleaned up should be created in createGroup instead
 * of initGroup and then can be cleaned up in destroyGroup.
 * createGroup and destroyGroup can be called multiple times during
 * the lifetime of a group.
 */
protected void initGroup() { }

/**
 * showGroup can be overridden by group subclasses that want
```

```
 * to know when the group becomes visible.  It is called just before
 * the group becomes visible.  The group will already be initialized
 * and created at this point.
 */
protected void showGroup() { }


/**
 * hideGroup can be overridden by group subclasses that want
 * to know when the group becomes nonvisible.  It is called just
 * before the group becomes nonvisible.
 */
protected void hideGroup() { }


/**
 * createGroup is called during group creation.  Groups can be
 * created and destroyed multiple times during their lifetime.
 * Anything that is created in createGroup should be cleaned up
 * in destroyGroup.  createGroup is called just after the group
 * has been created.  Anything that needs to be done before the
 * group is created should be done in initGroup.
 */
protected void createGroup() { }


/**
 * destroyGroup is called during the destroy operation.  Groups can
 * be created and destroyed multiple times during their lifetime.
 * Anything that has been created in createGroup should be cleaned up
 * in destroyGroup.  destroyGroup is called just before the group
 * is destroyed.
 */
protected void destroyGroup() { }


/**
 * This method can be overridden by group subclasses that want
 * to be informed when the application is starting.  This method is
 * only called after the entire application has been initialized and
 * created.
 *
 * For applets, startGroup is called whenever start is called on the
 * applet.
 */
protected void startGroup() { }


/**
 * This method can be overridden by group subclasses that want
 * to be informed when the application is stopping.  This method
 * will be called before a destroy is done.
 *
```

```
 * For applets, stopGroup is called whenever stop is called on the
 * applet.
 */
protected void stopGroup() { }

/**
 * "getOnGroup" can be overridden by subgroups that
 * store attribute values themselves and do not depend on the
 * group superclass to store them.  This method should be overridden
 * instead of "get".  Any attributes handled in setOnGroup where
 * super.setOnGroup is not called must also be handled in getOnGroup.
 *
 * The default implementation of getOnGroup retrieves the value
 * from the attribute table.
 *
 * The reason that "getOnGroup" should be overridden instead
 * of "get" is that "getOnGroup" is guaranteed not to be called
 * until the group class is initialized.  This means that initRoot
 * will always be called before any calls to getOnGroup are made.
 *
 * Also, this method is only for attributes that are defined in the
 * subgroups.  It is not called for forwarded attributes.
 */
protected Object getOnGroup(String key) {
  return super.getOnGroup(key);
}

/**
 * "setOnGroup" can be overridden by subgroups that
 * want notification when attributes are changed.  This method
 * should be overridden instead of "set".  Any attributes handled
 * in setOnGroup where super.setOnGroup is not called must also be
 * handled in getOnGroup.
 *
 * The default implementation of setOnGroup puts the value
 * in the attribute table.
 *
 * The reason that "setOnGroup" should be overridden instead
 * of "set" is that "setOnGroup" is guaranteed not to be called
 * until the group class is initialized.  This means that initRoot
 * will always be called before any calls to setOnGroup are made.
 *
 * During initialization, "setOnGroup" will be called for all
 * the group's attributes even if they have not been changed from
 * the default value.  But for attributes that have the DEFAULT
 * flag set, "setOnGroup" will only be called if the value
 * of the attribute has changed from the default.
 *
```

```
 * Also, this method is only called when attributes defined in the
 * subgroups are updated.  It is not called for forwarded attributes.
 */
protected void setOnGroup(String key, Object value) {
  super.setOnGroup(key, value);
}


/**
 * handleMessage can be overridden by subclasses that want to act
 * on messages that are sent to the group.  Typically, messages are
 * either AWT events that have been translated to messages, or they
 * are messages that have been sent by other groups.
 * super.handleMessage should be called for any messages that aren't
 * handled.  If super.handleMessage is not called, then handleEvent
 * will not be called.
 *
 * The default implementation of handleMessage returns "true".  This
 * means that no events will be passed up the group tree, unless a
 * subclass overrides this method to return "false".  AWT events are
 * not propagated, regardless of the return value from handleEvent.
 *
 * If you want a message to go to the parent group, override
 * handleMessage to return false for that message.
 *
 * If you want an AWT event to go to the parent group,
 * call postMessageToParent() with the event message.
 */
public boolean handleMessage(Message msg) {
  return super.handleMessage(msg);
}


/**
 * handleEvent can be overridden by subclasses that want to get
 * notified when AWT events are sent by the gui components.
 * The return value should be true for handled events, and
 * super.handleEvent should be called for unhandled events.
 * If super.handleEvent is not called, then the specific event
 * handling methods will not be called.
 *
 * The message's target is set to the shadow that sent the event.
 * The event's target is set to the AWT component that sent the event.
 *
 *
 * The following specific event handling methods can also be
overridden:
 *
 * public boolean mouseDown(Message msg, Event evt, int x, int y);
 * public boolean mouseDrag(Message msg, Event evt, int x, int y);
```

```
 * public boolean mouseUp(Message msg, Event evt, int x, int y);
 * public boolean mouseMove(Message msg, Event evt, int x, int y);
 * public boolean mouseEnter(Message msg, Event evt, int x, int y);
 * public boolean mouseExit(Message msg, Event evt, int x, int y);
 * public boolean keyDown(Message msg, Event evt, int key);
 * public boolean keyUp(Message msg, Event evt, int key);
 * public boolean action(Message msg, Event evt, Object what);
 * public boolean gotFocus(Message msg, Event evt, Object what);
 * public boolean lostFocus(Message msg, Event evt, Object what);
 */
public boolean handleEvent(Message msg, Event evt) {
  return super.handleEvent(msg, evt);
}
}
```

RoloMain.java

```java
/**
 * This file was automatically generated.  Do not manually modify this
 * file.
 *
 * Runtime vendor: SunSoft, Inc.
 * Runtime version: 1
 *
 * Visual vendor: SunSoft, Inc.
 * Visual version: 1
 */



import sunsoft.jws.visual.rt.base.Group;
import sunsoft.jws.visual.rt.base.MainHelper;
import java.applet.Applet;

/**
 * Generated Main class
 *
 * @version 1.20, 05/21/96
 */
public class RoloMain extends Applet {
  /**
   * Helper class for the generated main class.  This variable is only
   * used when we are running as an applet.
   */
  private MainHelper helper;

  /**
   * Called when application is run from the command line.
   */
  public static void main(String args[]) {
    MainHelper helper = new MainHelper();
    helper.checkVersion(1);

    Group group = new Rolo();
    helper.main(group, args);
  }

  /**
   * Called when the applet is loaded.
   */
```

```java
public void init() {
  helper = new MainHelper();
  helper.checkVersion(1);

  Group group = new Rolo();
  helper.init(this, group);
}

/**
 * Called whenever the applet's page is visited.
 */
public void start(){
  helper.start();
}

/**
 * Called by the browser when the user leaves the page.
 */
public void stop() {
  helper.stop();
}

/**
 * Called by the browser when the applet should be destroyed.
 */
public void destroy() {
  helper.destroy();
}
}
```

RoloOps.java

```
/**
 * This file was automatically generated. Do not modify this file.
 *
 * Runtime vendor: SunSoft, Inc.
 * Runtime version: 1
 *
 * Visual vendor: SunSoft, Inc.
 * Visual version: 1
 */

import sunsoft.jws.visual.rt.base.*;
import sunsoft.jws.visual.rt.type.*;
import java.awt.Event;
import java.awt.List;

public class RoloOps extends Operations {
  private Op ops[];

  private Rolo group;
  private RoloRoot gui;

  public void setGroup(Group group) {
    this.group = (Rolo)group;
  }

  public void setRoot(Root root) {
    this.gui = (RoloRoot)root;
    if (ops == null)
      initializeOps();
  }

  public boolean handleMessage(Message msg) {
    for (int i=0; i<ops.length; i++) {
      if (ops[i].hasCode()) {
   if (ops[i].matchMessage(msg)) {
     handleCallback(i, msg, (msg.isAWT ? (Event)msg.arg : null));
   }
      }
      else {
   ops[i].handleMessage(msg);
      }
    }

    return false;
  }
```

```
private void initializeOps() {
  ops = new Op[4];

  ops[0] = new Op(gui);
  ops[0].name = "Op1";
  ops[0].filter = new OpFilter();
  ops[0].filter.filterType = OpFilter.EVENT;
  ops[0].filter.target = gui.nameLabel;
  ops[0].filter.id = 1001;
  ops[0].action = new OpAction();
  ops[0].action.actionType = OpAction.CODE;

  ops[1] = new Op(gui);
  ops[1].name = "Op1";
  ops[1].filter = new OpFilter();
  ops[1].filter.filterType = OpFilter.EVENT;
  ops[1].filter.target = gui.addButton;
  ops[1].filter.id = 1001;
  ops[1].action = new OpAction();
  ops[1].action.actionType = OpAction.CODE;

  ops[2] = new Op(gui);
  ops[2].name = "Op1";
  ops[2].filter = new OpFilter();
  ops[2].filter.filterType = OpFilter.EVENT;
  ops[2].filter.target = gui.findButton;
  ops[2].filter.id = 1001;
  ops[2].action = new OpAction();
  ops[2].action.actionType = OpAction.CODE;

  ops[3] = new Op(gui);
  ops[3].name = "Op1";
  ops[3].filter = new OpFilter();
  ops[3].filter.filterType = OpFilter.EVENT;
  ops[3].filter.target = gui.deleteButton;
  ops[3].filter.id = 1001;
  ops[3].action = new OpAction();
  ops[3].action.actionType = OpAction.CODE;
}

private void handleCallback(int index, Message msg, Event evt) {
  switch (index) {
  case 0:
    {
    }
    break;
```

```
        case 1:
          {
String[] listContents = (String []) gui.namesList.get("items");
String newItem = (String) gui.nameTextfield.get("text") + " " +
                            (String) gui.phoneTextfield.get("text");
int len = listContents.length;
String[] newContents = new String[len + 1];
int i = 0;
for (i=0; i < len; i++) {
  newContents[i] = listContents[i];
}
newContents[len] = newItem;
gui.namesList.set("items",  newContents);
          }
        break;
        case 2:
          {
List listBody = (List) gui.namesList.getBody();
                        int numItems = listBody.countItems();
                        String nameToFind = (String)
gui.nameTextfield.get("text");
                        String currentName = "";
                        int i = 0;
                        int j = 0;
                        int len = 0;
                        int nameLen = nameToFind.length();

                        for (i=0; i < numItems; i++) {
                           currentName = listBody.getItem(i);
                           len = currentName.length();
                           if (len >= nameLen &&
                               len != 0 &&
                               nameLen != 0) {
                             for (j=0; j < len - nameLen + 1; j++) {
                             if (currentName.regionMatches(true,
                                                     j,
                                                 nameToFind,
                                                     0,
                                           nameLen) == true) {
                                    listBody.select(i);
                                    return;
                                }
                             }
                           }
                        }

          }
        break;
```

```
      case 3:
        {
List listBody = (List) gui.namesList.getBody();
int selectedIndex = listBody.getSelectedIndex();
listBody.delItem(selectedIndex);
        }
        break;
      default:
        throw new Error("Bad callback index: " + index);
      }
  }


  // methods from lib/visual/gen/methods.java

  /**
   * Converts a string to the specified type.
   */
  private Object convert(String type, String value) {
    return(Converter.getConverter(type).convertFromString(value));
  }
}
```

RoloRoot.java

```java
/**
 * This file was automatically generated.  Do not manually modify this
 * file.
 *
 * Runtime vendor: SunSoft, Inc.
 * Runtime version: 1
 *
 * Visual vendor: SunSoft, Inc.
 * Visual version: 1
 */


import sunsoft.jws.visual.rt.awt.GBConstraints;
import sunsoft.jws.visual.rt.base.*;
import sunsoft.jws.visual.rt.shadow.*;
import sunsoft.jws.visual.rt.shadow.java.awt.*;
import sunsoft.jws.visual.rt.type.*;


public class RoloRoot extends Root {
  public FrameShadow RoloFrame;
  public ButtonShadow addButton;
  public ButtonShadow deleteButton;
  public ButtonShadow findButton;
  public GBPanelShadow gbpanel2;
  public LabelShadow listLabel;
  public LabelShadow nameLabel;
  public TextFieldShadow nameTextfield;
  public ListShadow namesList;
  public LabelShadow phoneLabel;
  public TextFieldShadow phoneTextfield;
  public Root root1;

  public RoloRoot(Group group) {
    setGroup(group);

    RoloFrame = new FrameShadow();
    RoloFrame.set("name", "RoloFrame");
    add(RoloFrame);
    RoloFrame.set("title", "Rolo");
    RoloFrame.set("layoutSize", new java.awt.Dimension(457, 570));
    RoloFrame.set("layoutLocation", new java.awt.Point(55, 174));

    gbpanel2 = new GBPanelShadow();
    gbpanel2.set("name", "gbpanel2");
```

MULTIC.java

```java
/**
 * This is a template.  You can modify this file.³
 *
 * Runtime vendor: SunSoft, Inc.
 * Runtime version: 1
 *
 * Visual vendor: SunSoft, Inc.
 * Visual version: 1
 */


import sunsoft.jws.visual.rt.base.*;
import sunsoft.jws.visual.rt.shadow.java.awt.*;
import java.awt.*;
import sunsoft.jws.visual.rt.awt.ColumnList;


public class MULTIC extends Group {
    private MULTICRoot gui;
    int currentRow;
    int lastRow = -1;

    public void makeButtonInactive(ButtonShadow button) {
        button.set("visible",Boolean.TRUE);
        button.set("enabled",Boolean.FALSE);
    }

    public void makeButtonActive(ButtonShadow button) {
        button.set("visible",Boolean.TRUE);
        button.set("enabled",Boolean.TRUE);
    }

/**
 * Sample method call ordering during a group's lifetime:
 *
 * Constructor
 * initRoot
 * initGroup
 * (setOnGroup and getOnGroup may be called at any time in any
```

3. Many of the frequently asked questions about Java WorkShop concern Multiple Column Lists. MULTIC.java is provided to illustrate one approach to accessing items in a Multiple Column List. It is the only example that is not on the CD-ROM. You can download it from the World Wide Web. See page 205 in Appendix C for more information about the example, including where to find it on the Web.

```
 *    order after initGroup has been called)
 * createGroup
 * showGroup/hideGroup + startGroup/stopGroup
 * destroyGroup
 */

/**
 * All the attributes used by the group must be defined in the
 * constructor.  setOnGroup is called at initialization for all
 * the attributes.  If the attribute has not been set prior to
 * initialization, setOnGroup is called with the default value.
 */
public MULTIC() {
    /**
     * Define the group's custom attributes here.
     *
     * For example:
     *
     * attributes.add("customString", "java.lang.String",
     *       "Default String", 0);
     */

    /**
     * This method defines the attributes that will be forwarded to
     * the main child (either a window or a panel).  All attributes
     * defined by this method are marked with the FORWARD flag.
     */
    addForwardedAttributes();
}

/**
 * initRoot must be overridden in group subclasses to initialize
 * the shadow tree.  The return value must be the root of the
 * newly initialized shadow tree.
 */
protected Root initRoot() {
    /**
     * Initialize the gui components
     */
    gui = new MULTICRoot(this);
    makeButtonInactive(gui.applyButton);
    makeButtonInactive(gui.cancelButton);
    makeButtonInactive(gui.deleteButton);

/**
 * This method registers an attribute manager with the group, such
 * that attributes marked with the FORWARD flag will be sent to
 * this attribute manager.
```

```
    */
  addAttributeForward(gui.getMainChild());

  return gui;
}


/**
 * initGroup is called during initialization.  It is called just after
 * initRoot is called, but before the subgroups are initialized and
 * before the attributes are sent to the setOnGroup method.
 *
 * initGroup is only called once in the lifetime of the Group.
 * This is because groups cannot be uninitialized.  Anything that
 * needs to be cleaned up should be created in createGroup instead
 * of initGroup, and then can be cleaned up in destroyGroup.
 * createGroup and destroyGroup may be called multiple times during
 * the lifetime of a group.
 */
protected void initGroup() { }


/**
 * showGroup may be overridden by group subclasses that want
 * to know when the group becomes visible.  It is called just before
 * the group becomes visible.  The group will already be initialized
 * and created at this point.
 */
protected void showGroup() { }


/**
 * hideGroup may be overridden by group subclasses that want
 * to know when the group becomes nonvisible.  It is called just
 * before the group becomes nonvisible.
 */
protected void hideGroup() { }


/**
 * createGroup is called during group creation.  Groups can be
 * created and destroyed multiple times during their lifetime.
 * Anything that is created in createGroup should be cleaned up
 * in destroyGroup.  createGroup is called just after the group
 * has been created.  Anything that needs to be done before the
 * group is created should be done in initGroup.
 */
protected void createGroup() { }


/**
 * destroyGroup is called during the destroy operation.  Groups can
 * be created and destroyed multiple times during their lifetime.
```

```
 * Anything that has been created in createGroup should be cleaned up
 * in destroyGroup.  destroyGroup is called just before the group
 * is destroyed.
 */
protected void destroyGroup() { }

/**
 * This method may be overridden by group subclasses that want
 * to be informed when the application is starting.  This method is
 * only called after the entire application has been initialized and
 * created.
 *
 * For applets, startGroup is called whenever start is called on the
 * applet.
 */
protected void startGroup() { }

/**
 * This method may be overridden by group subclasses that want
 * to be informed when the application is stopping.  This method
 * will be called before a destroy is done.
 *
 * For applets, stopGroup is called whenever stop is called on the
 * applet.
 */
protected void stopGroup() { }

/**
 * "getOnGroup" may be overridden by subgroups that
 * store attribute values themselves, and do not depend on the
 * group superclass to store them.  This method should be overridden
 * instead of "get".  Any attributes handled in setOnGroup where
 * super.setOnGroup is not called must also be handled in getOnGroup.
 *
 * The default implementation of getOnGroup retrieves the value
 * from the attribute table.
 *
 * The reason that "getOnGroup" should be overridden instead
 * of "get" is that "getOnGroup" is guaranteed not to be called
 * until the group class is initialized.  This means that initRoot
 * will always be called before any calls to getOnGroup are made.
 *
 * Also, this method is only for attributes that are defined in the
 * subgroups.  It is not called for forwarded attributes.
 */
protected Object getOnGroup(String key) {
  return super.getOnGroup(key);
}
```

```
/**
 * "setOnGroup" may be overridden by subgroups that
 * want notification when attributes are changed.  This method
 * should be overridden instead of "set".  Any attributes handled
 * in setOnGroup where super.setOnGroup is not called must also be
 * handled in getOnGroup.
 *
 * The default implementation of setOnGroup puts the value
 * in the attribute table.
 *
 * The reason that "setOnGroup" should be overridden instead
 * of "set" is that "setOnGroup" is guaranteed not to be called
 * until the group class is initialized.  This means that initRoot
 * will always be called before any calls to setOnGroup are made.
 *
 * During initialization, "setOnGroup" will be called for all
 * the group's attributes even if they have not be changed from
 * the default value.  But for attributes that have the DEFAULT
 * flag set, "setOnGroup" will only be called if the value
 * of the attribute has changed from the default.
 *
 * Also, this method is only called when attributes defined in the
 * subgroups are updated.  It is not called for forwarded attributes.
 */
protected void setOnGroup(String key, Object value) {
  super.setOnGroup(key, value);
}


/**
 * handleMessage may be overridden by subclasses that want to act
 * on messages that are sent to the group.  Typically, messages are
 * either AWT events that have been translated to messages, or they
 * are messages that have been sent by other groups.
 * super.handleMessage should be called for any messages that aren't
 * handled.  If super.handleMessage is not called, then handleEvent
 * will not be called.
 *
 * The default implementation of handleMessage returns "true".  This
 * means that no events will be passed up the group tree, unless a
 * subclass overrides this method to return "false".  AWT events are
 * not propagated regardless of the return value from handleEvent.
 *
 * If you want a message to go to the parent group, override
 * handleMessage to return false for that message.
 *
 * If you want an AWT event to go to the parent group, you need to
 * call postMessageToParent() with the event message.
```

```
      */
  public boolean handleMessage(Message msg) {
    return super.handleMessage(msg);
  }

  /**
   * handleEvent may be overridden by subclasses that want to get
   * notified when AWT events that are sent by the gui components.
   * The return value should be true for handled events, and
   * super.handleEvent should be called for unhandled events.
   * If super.handleEvent is not called, then the specific event
   * handling methods will not be called.
   *
   * The message's target is set to the shadow that sent the event.
   * The event's target is set to the AWT component that sent the event.
   *
   *
   * The following specific event handling methods may also be
overridden:
   *
   * public boolean mouseDown(Message msg, Event evt, int x, int y);
   * public boolean mouseDrag(Message msg, Event evt, int x, int y);
   * public boolean mouseUp(Message msg, Event evt, int x, int y);
   * public boolean mouseMove(Message msg, Event evt, int x, int y);
   * public boolean mouseEnter(Message msg, Event evt, int x, int y);
   * public boolean mouseExit(Message msg, Event evt, int x, int y);
   * public boolean keyDown(Message msg, Event evt, int key);
   * public boolean keyUp(Message msg, Event evt, int key);
   * public boolean action(Message msg, Event evt, Object what);
   * public boolean gotFocus(Message msg, Event evt, Object what);
   * public boolean lostFocus(Message msg, Event evt, Object what);
   */
  public boolean handleEvent(Message msg, Event evt) {
    if (msg.target == gui.addressColumnList) {
      if (evt.id == Event.LIST_SELECT) {
        makeButtonActive(gui.applyButton);
        makeButtonActive(gui.deleteButton);
        gui.rowNumber.set("text",evt.arg.toString());
        Integer intObject =  (Integer)evt.arg;
        int row = intObject.intValue();
        currentRow = row;

gui.namefield.set("text",((ColumnList)gui.addressColumnList.getBody())
.getItem(row,0));

gui.addressField.set("text",((ColumnList)gui.addressColumnList.getBody
()).getItem(row,1));
```

```
gui.cityField.set("text",((ColumnList)gui.addressColumnList.getBody())
.getItem(row,2));

gui.stateField.set("text",((ColumnList)gui.addressColumnList.getBody()
).getItem(row,3));

gui.zipField.set("text",((ColumnList)gui.addressColumnList.getBody()).
getItem(row,4));

gui.phoneField.set("text",((ColumnList)gui.addressColumnList.getBody()
).getItem(row,5));
        }

    }
    return super.handleEvent(msg, evt);
  }
  public boolean action(Message msg, Event evt, Object what) {
    boolean handled = false;

    if (msg.target == gui.applyButton) {

        ((ColumnList)
gui.addressColumnList.getBody()).putItem(currentRow,0,gui.namefield.ge
t("text"));
        ((ColumnList)
gui.addressColumnList.getBody()).putItem(currentRow,1,gui.addressField
.get("text"));
        ((ColumnList)
gui.addressColumnList.getBody()).putItem(currentRow,2,gui.cityField.ge
t("text"));
        ((ColumnList)
gui.addressColumnList.getBody()).putItem(currentRow,3,gui.stateField.g
et("text"));
        ((ColumnList)
gui.addressColumnList.getBody()).putItem(currentRow,4,gui.zipField.get
("text"));
        ((ColumnList)
gui.addressColumnList.getBody()).putItem(currentRow,5,gui.phoneField.g
et("text"));
        makeButtonActive(gui.addButton);
        makeButtonInactive(gui.applyButton);
        makeButtonInactive(gui.cancelButton);
        if (lastRow==0) {makeButtonActive(gui.deleteButton);}
        handled=true;
    }
    if (msg.target == gui.addButton) {
        makeButtonActive(gui.applyButton);
```

```
        makeButtonActive(gui.cancelButton);
        gui.namefield.set("text","");
        gui.addressField.set("text","");
        gui.cityField.set("text","");
        gui.stateField.set("text","");
        gui.zipField.set("text","");
        gui.phoneField.set("text","");
        String data[] = {"","","", "","",""};
        ((ColumnList)
gui.addressColumnList.getBody()).addItem(data,true);
        currentRow=lastRow+1;
        lastRow=currentRow;
        ((ColumnList) gui.addressColumnList.getBody()).highlight(-1);
        makeButtonInactive(gui.addButton);
        makeButtonInactive(gui.deleteButton);

        handled=true;
    }
    if (msg.target == gui.cancelButton) {
        makeButtonActive(gui.addButton);
        ((ColumnList)
gui.addressColumnList.getBody()).delItems(currentRow,currentRow);
        ((ColumnList) gui.addressColumnList.getBody()).highlight(-1);
        makeButtonInactive(gui.deleteButton);
        lastRow=lastRow-1;
        makeButtonInactive(gui.applyButton);
        makeButtonInactive(gui.cancelButton);

            handled=true;
    }


    if (msg.target == gui.deleteButton) {
        ((ColumnList)
gui.addressColumnList.getBody()).delItems(currentRow,currentRow);
        ((ColumnList) gui.addressColumnList.getBody()).highlight(-1);
        lastRow=lastRow-1;

        makeButtonInactive(gui.deleteButton);

        handled=true;
    }
    if (msg.target == gui.loadDataButton) {
        String data[][] = {{"Boyer","3567 Benton","Santa Clara",
"CA","95051","555-1212"},
        {"Smith","123 Easy Street","Los Angeles", "CA","80333","555-
2222"},
        {"Miller","7 Main, Apt 4","San Francisco", "CA","91111","555-
3333"}};
```

```
        ((ColumnList)
gui.addressColumnList.getBody()).addItem(data[0],true);
        ((ColumnList)
gui.addressColumnList.getBody()).addItem(data[1],true);
        ((ColumnList)
gui.addressColumnList.getBody()).addItem(data[2],true);
        lastRow = lastRow + 3;
      makeButtonInactive(gui.loadDataButton);

      handled=true;
    }
    return handled;
  }


}
```

Index

DESIGNING VISUAL INTERFACES:
Communication Oriented Techniques

Kevin Mullet and Darrell K. Sano

Useful to anyone responsible for designing, specifying, implementing, documenting, or managing the visual appearance of computer-based information displays, this book applies the fundamentals of graphic design, industrial design, interior design, and architecture to solve the human computer interface problems experienced in commercial software development. It describes basic design principles (the what and why), common errors, and practical techniques (the how). Readers will gain a new perspective on product development as well as an appreciation for the contribution visual design can offer to their products and users. Six major areas: Elegance and Simplicity; Scale, Contrast, and Proportion; Organization and Visual Structure; Module and Programme; Image and Representation; and Style.

1995, 304 pp., Paper,
0-13-303389-9 (30338-8)
(includes 4-color plates)

DEVELOPING VISUAL APPLICATIONS XIL:
An Imaging Foundation Library

William K. Pratt

A practical introduction to imaging into new, innovative applications for desktop computing. For applications in the technical, commercial, and consumer environments, imaging should be considered as basic as putting text or user interface elements into an application. This book breaks down the barriers that developers may have in integrating imaging into their applications. It acquaints developers with the basics of image processing, compression, and algorithm implementation by providing clear, real-world examples of how they can be applied using XIL, a cross-platform imaging foundation library. This book acquaints knowledgeable imaging developers with the architectural features and capabilities of XIL. It can also serve as a primer for new XIL programmers.

1996, 400 pp., Paper,
0-13-461948-X (46194-7)

HTML FOR FUN AND PROFIT, Gold Signature Ed.

Mary E. S. Morris

This book is about writing HTML pages for the World Wide Web. Written in a step-by-step, hands on, tutorial style, it presents all the information needed by an aspiring web page author. Platforms are also discussed. Includes:

- Setting up your server
- Learning HTML formatting basics, including lists and special characters
- Integrating multimedia into web pages
- Formatting tables in HTML
- Creating interactive HTML documents with CGI scripting
- Customizing HTML pages with Server Includes
- Designing effective web page layouts
- Appendices on installing and using Xmosaic, WinMosaic, and Mac-Mosaic browsers are included.
- A CD-ROM containing shareware and extensive examples of sample HTML pages and sample perl scripts is also provided.

This book also includes a chapter on Netscape with HTML examples on the CD-ROM. The CD-ROM includes a web server for Microsoft Windows 3.1, NT, Macintosh and UNIX.

1996, 330 pp., Paper,
0-13-242488-6 (24248-7)
Book/CD-ROM

EXPERT C PROGRAMMING:
Deep C Secrets

Peter van der Linden

Known as "the butt-ugly fish book" because of the coelacanth on the cover, this is a very different book on the C language! In an easy, conversational style, *it* reveals coding techniques used by the best C programmers. It relates C to other languages and includes an introduction to C++ that can be understood by any programmer without weeks of mind-bending study. Covering both the IBM PC and UNIX systems, this book is a *must read* for anyone who wants to learn more about the implementation, practical use, and folk lore of C!

1994, 384 pp., Paper, 0-13-177429-8 (17742-8)

MULTIPROCESSOR SYSTEM ARCHITECTURES:
A Technical Survey of Multiprocessor / Multithreaded Systems Using SPARC, Multi-level Bus Architectures and Solaris (SunOS)
Ben Catanzaro

Written for engineers seeking to understand the problems and solutions of multi-processor system design, this hands-on guide is the first comprehensive description of the elements involved in the design and development of Sun's multiprocessor systems. Topics covered include SPARC processor design and its implementations, an introduction to multilevel bus architectures including MBus and XBus/XDBus, an overview of the Solaris/SunOS™ multithreaded architecture and programming, and an MBus Interface Specification and Design Guide. This book can serve as a reference text for design engineers as well as a hands-on design guide to MP systems for hardware/software engineers.

1994, 528 pp., Paper, 0-13-089137-1 (08913-6)

PANIC! UNIX System Crash Dump Analysis
Chris Drake and Kimberley Brown

PANIC! is the first book to discuss in detail UNIX system panics, crashes and hangs, their causes, what to do when they occur, how to collect information about them, how to analyze that information, and how to get the problem resolved. *PANIC!* presents this highly technical and intricate subject in a friendly, easy style which even the novice UNIX system administrator will find readable, educational and enjoyable. It is written for systems and network administrators and technical support engineers who are responsible for maintaining and supporting UNIX computer systems and networks. Includes a CD-ROM containing several useful analysis tools, such as adb macros and C tags output from the source trees of two different UNIX systems.

1995, 496 pp., Paper, 0-13-149386-8 (14938-5) Book/CD-ROM

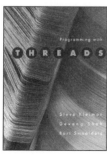

PROGRAMMING WITH THREADS
Steve Kleiman, Devang Shah, and Bart Smaalders

Written by senior threads engineers at Sun Microsystems, Inc., this book is the definitive guide to programming with threads. It is intended for both novice and more sophisticated threads programmers, and for developers multithreading existing programs as well as for those writing new multithreaded programs. The book provides structured techniques for mastering the complexity of threads programming with an emphasis on performance issues. Included are detailed examples using the new POSIX threads (Pthreads) standard interfaces. The book also covers the other UNIX threads interface defined by UNIX International.

1996, 250 pp., Paper, 0-13-172389-8 (17238-9)

RIGHTSIZING THE NEW ENTERPRISE:
The Proof, Not The Hype
Harris Kern and Randy Johnson

A detailed account of how Sun Micro-systems implemented its rightsizing strategy going from a mainframe data center to a heterogeneous client/server distributed environment. This book covers the key infrastructures of an IT organization (the network, data center, and system administration), the rightsizing/management tools, and the training/resource issues involved in transitioning from mainframe to UNIX support. The facts contained in this book provide you with the PROOF that 'rightsizing' can be done.and has been done.

1995, 352 pp., Cloth, 0-13-490384-6 (49038-3)

RIGHTSIZING FOR CORPORATE SURVIVAL:
An IS Manager's Guide
Robert Massoudi, Astrid Julienne, Bob Millradt, and Reed Hornberger

This book provides IS managers with "hands-on" guidance for developing a rightsizing strategy and plan. Based upon research conducted through customer visits with multinational corporations, it details the experiences and insights gained by IS professionals that have implemented systems in distributed, client-server environments. Topics covered include:

- Why rightsize?
- What business results can rightsizing produce?
- Key technologies critical to rightsizing
- Good starting points for rightsizing
- What is the process to rightsize an information system?
- Cost considerations and return on investment (ROI) analysis

• How to manage the transition

Throughout the book, case studies and "lessons learned" reinforce the discussion and document best practices associated with rightsizing.

1995, 272 pp., Paper,
0-13-123126-X (12312-5)

READ ME FIRST!
A Style Guide for the Computer Industry
Sun Technical Publications

A comprehensive look at documenting computer products, from style pointers to legal guidelines, from working with an editor to building a publications department—in both hard copy and electronic copy with an on line viewer, FrameMaker templates for instant page design, and a detailed guide to establishing a documentation department and its processes. Based on an internationally award-winning Sun Microsystems style guide (Award of Excellence in the STC International Technical Publications Competition, 1994)

1996, 300 pp., Paper,
0-13-455347-0 (45534-6)
Book/CD-ROM

SOLARIS IMPLEMENTATION:
A Guide for System Administrators
George Becker, Mary E. S. Morris and Kathy Slattery

Written by three expert Sun system administrators, this book discusses real world, day-to-day Solaris 2 system administration for both new installations and for those migrating an installed Solaris 1 base. It presents tested procedures to help system administrators to improve and customize their networks by eliminating trial-and-error methodologies. Also includes advice for managing heterogeneous Solaris environments and provides autoinstall sample scripts and disk partitioning schemes (with recommended sizes) used at Sun.

1995, 368 pp., Paper,
0-13-353350-6 (35335-9)

CREATING WORLD WIDE WEB SOFTWARE:
SOLARIS, Second Edtion
Bill Tuthill and David Smallberg

Written for software developers and business managers interested in creating global applications for the Solaris environment (SPARC and x86), this second edition expands on the first edition and has updated information on international markets, standards organizations, and writing international documents. New topics in the second edition include CDE/Motif, NEO (formerly project DOE)/ OpenStep, Universal codesets, global internet applications, code examples, and success stories.

1996, 250 pp., Paper,
0-13-494493-3 (49449-2)

SOLARIS PORTING GUIDE,
Second Edition
SunSoft Developer Engineering

Ideal for application programmers and software developers, the *Solaris Porting Guide, Second Edition*, provides a comprehensive technical overview of the Solaris 2.x operating environment and its related migration strategy. The second edition is current through Solaris 2.4 (both the SPARC and x86 platforms) and provides all the information necessary to migrate from Solaris 1 (SunOS 4.x) to Solaris 2 (SunOS 5.x). Other additions include a discussion of emerging technologies such as the Common Desktop Environment (CDE), hints for application performance tuning, and extensive pointers to further information, including Internet sources.

1995, 752 pp., Paper,
0-13-443672-5 (44367-1)

SUN PERFORMANCE AND TUNING:
SPARC and Solaris
Adrian Cockcroft

An indispensable reference for anyone working with Sun workstations running the Solaris environment, this book provides detailed performance and configuration information on all SPARC machines and peripherals, as well as on all operating system releases from SunOS 4.1 through Solaris 2.4. It includes hard-to-find tuning information and offers insights that cannot be found elsewhere. This book is written for developers who want to design for performance and for system administrators who have a system running applications on which they want to improve performance.

1995, 288 pp., Paper,
0-13-149642-5 (14964-1)

THREADS PRIMER:
A Guide to Solaris Multithreaded Programming
Bil Lewis and Daniel J. Berg

Written for developers interested in MT programming, this primer overviews the concepts involved in multithreaded development. Based on the Solaris multithreaded architecture, the primer delivers threading concepts that can be applied to almost any multithreaded platform. The book covers the design and implementation of multithreaded programs as well as the business and technical benefits of threads. Both the Solaris and the POSIX threads API are used as the interface needed to develop applications. Extensive examples highlight the use of threads in real-world applications. This book is a must read for developers interested in MT technology!

1996, 352 pp., Paper,
0-13-443698-9 (44369-7)

WABI 2: Opening Windows
Scott Fordin and Susan Nolin

Wabi™ 2 is here and now you can run Microsoft and Windows 3.1 applications on UNIX-based computers! Written for both users and system administrators of Wabi software, this book covers everything you wanted to know about Wabi 2, including: Wabi technical history, how Wabi works, UNIX for Microsoft Windows users, Microsoft Windows for UNIX users, X Window terminology and interface objects, additional sources of information on Wabi, sample settings in which Wabi is used, and common questions asked by users.

1996, 400 pp., Paper,
0-13-461617-0 (46161-6)

NEW!

VERILOG HDL:
A Guide to Digital Design and Synthesis
Samir Palnitkar

Everything you always wanted to know about Verilog HDL, from fundamentals such as gate, RTL and behavioral modeling to advanced concepts such as timing simulation, switch level modeling, PLI and logic synthesis. This book approaches Verilog HDL from a practical design perspective rather than from a language standpoint. Includes over 300 illustrations, examples, and exercises, and a Verilog Internet reference resource list. Learning objectives and summaries are provided for each chapter. The CD-ROM contains a verilog simulator with a graphical user interface and the source code for the examples in the book. This book is of value to new and experienced Verilog HDL users, both in industry and at universities (logic design courses).

1996, 400 pp., Cloth, 0-13-451675-3 (45167-4) Book/CD-ROM

TOOLTALK AND OPEN PROTOCOLS:
Interapplication Communication
Astrid M. Julienne and Brian Holtz

This book discusses how to design, write, and implement open protocols and includes examples using the ToolTalk™ messaging service. Both procedural and object-oriented protocols are covered in detail. While the ToolTalk service is used as a point of reference throughout, the information provided conforms to the standardization efforts currently in progress for inter-application communication. A valuable resource for the developer writing applications for both the common desktop environment (CDE) and SunSoft's Project DOE system (now known as NEO™).

1994, 384 pp., Paper, 0-13-031055-7 (03105-4)

WEB PAGE DESIGN:
A Different Multimedia
Mary E. S. Morris and Randy J. Hinrichs

Everything you always wanted to know about practical Web page design from the best-selling author of *HTML for Fun and Profit*. Written for Web page authors, this hands on guide covers the key aspects of designing a successful web site including cognitive design, content design, audience consideration, interactivity, organization, navigational pathways, and graphical elements. Includes designing for VRML and Java sites as well as designing with templates, style sheets, and Netscape Frames. Also contains many examples of successful Web pages, including 16 color plates.

1996, 200 pp., Paper, 0-13-239880-X (23988-9)

INSTANT JAVA
Second Edition

John A. Pew

Now anyone can instantly create sizzling Web pages filled with sound, animation and interactivity! All you need is *Instant Java*, your cookbook of more than 75 prefabricated, easy-to-customize Java applets.

The new second edition contains 10 new applets—plus updated, foolproof instructions for adapting them and plugging them into your Web site.

Instant Java includes more than 50 new examples that show how these flexible applets can be used and customized.

You'll find all the applets on CD-ROM—along with HTML sample pages that show you exactly how to embed them in your Web pages.

More than 75 working Java applets—just plug and play!

- Text applets
- Image applets
- Animation applets
- Slide shows
- Tickers
  And much more!

1997, 384 pp., Paper
0-13-272287-9 (27228-6)
Book/CD-ROM

JAVA BY EXAMPLE
Second Edition

Jerry R. Jackson and
Alan L. McClellan

If you're an experienced programmer, *Java by Example* is the quickest way to learn Java. By reviewing example code written by experts, you'll learn the right way to develop Java applets and applications that are elegant, readable, and easy to maintain.

Step-by-step, working from examples, you'll learn valuable techniques for managing memory, I/O, multithreading, exception handling, and interfacing with C programs.

This brand-new second edition adds extensive coverage of remote methods invocation (RMI), networking, and database access using the new Java Database Connectivity (JDBC) API.

Java by Example teaches what you need to know, the way you want to learn: from real, working code.

The accompanying CD-ROM gives you all the book's sample code, plus:

- The complete Java Developer's Kit for Solaris™, Windows 95, Windows NT, and Macintosh
- Java™ Workshop™ from Sun Microsystems
- Symantec's Café Lite, the complete integrated development
- environment for Java

It's the complete resource for working programmers.

1997, 400 pp., Paper
0-13-272295-X (27229-4)
Book/CD-ROM

IMPORTANT—READ CAREFULLY BEFORE OPENING SEALED CD-ROM

This CD-ROM contains the Java Development Kit and sample code from Inside Java WorkShop, as well as other copyrighted software.

SUN MICROSYSTEMS LICENSE AGREEMENT

This is a legal agreement between the purchaser of this book/CD-ROM package ("You") and Sun Microsystems, Inc. By opening the sealed CD-ROM you are agreeing to be bound by the terms of this agreement. If you do not agree to the terms of this agreement, promptly return the unopened book/CD-ROM package to the place you obtained it for a full refund.

SOFTWARE LICENSE FOR SAMPLE CODE

1. Grant of License. Sun Microsystems grants to you ("Licensee") a non-exclusive, non-transferable license to use the software programs (sample code) included on the CD-ROM without fee. The software is in "use" on a computer when it is loaded into the temporary memory (i.e. RAM) or installed into the permanent memory (e.g. hard disk, CD-ROM, or other storage device). You may network the software or otherwise use it on more than one computer or computer terminal at the same time.

2. Copyright. The CD-ROM is copyrighted by Sun Microsystems, Inc. and is protected by United States copyright laws and international treaty provisions. Therefore, you must treat the CD-ROM like any other copyrighted material. Individual software programs on the CD-ROM are copyrighted by their respective owners and may require separate licensing. The Java Development Kit is copyrighted by Sun Microsystems, Inc. and is covered by a separate license agreement provided on the CD-ROM and reprinted below.

3. Inside Java WorkShop Sample Code. Sun Microsystems, Inc. grants you a royalty-free right to reproduce and distribute the sample code or applets provided that you: (a) distribute the sample code or applets only in conjunction with and as a part of your software application; (b) do not use Sun Microsystems, Inc. or its authors' names, logos, or trademarks to market your software product; and (c) agree to indemnify, hold harmless and defend Sun Microsystems, Inc. and its authors and suppliers from and against any claims or lawsuits, including attorneys fees, that arise or result from the use or distribution of your software product.

DISCLAIMER OF WARRANTY

The SOFTWARE (including instructions for its use) is provided "AS IS" WITHOUT WARRANTY OF ANY KIND. SUN MICROSYSTEMS and any distributor of the SOFTWARE FURTHER DISCLAIM ALL IMPLIED WARRANTIES INCLUDING WITHOUT LIMITATION ANY IMPLIED WARRANTIES OF MERCHANTABILITY OR OF FITNESS FOR A PARTICULAR PURPOSE. THE ENTIRE RISK ARISING OUT OF THE USE OR PERFORMANCE OF THE SOFTWARE OR DOCUMENTATION REMAINS WITH YOU.

IN NO EVENT SHALL SUN MICROSYSTEMS, ITS AUTHORS, OR ANY ONE ELSE INVOLVED IN THE CREATION, PRODUCTION, OR DELIVERY OF THE SOFTWARE BE LIABLE FOR ANY DAMAGES WHATSOEVER (INCLUDING, WITHOUT LIMITATION, DAMAGES FOR LOSS OF BUSINESS PROFITS, BUSINESS INTERRUPTION, LOSS OF BUSINESS INFORMATION, OR OTHER PECUNIARY LOSS) ARISING OUT OF THE USE OF OR INABILITY TO USE THE SOFTWARE OR DOCUMENTATION, EVEN IF SUN MICROSYSTEMS HAS BEEN ADVISED OF THE POSSIBILITY OF SUCH DAMAGES, BECAUSE SOME STATES/COUNTRIES DO NOT ALLOW THE EXCLUSION OF LIMITATION OF LIABILITY FOR CONSEQUENTIAL OR INCIDENTAL DAMAGES, THE ABOVE LIMITATION MAY NOT APPLY TO YOU.

U.S. GOVERNMENT RESTRICTED RIGHTS

The SOFTWARE and documentation are provided with RESTRICTED RIGHTS. Use, duplication, or disclosure is subject to restrictions as set forth in subparagraph (c)(1)(ii) of The Rights in Technical Data and Computer Software clause at DFARS 252.227-7013 or subparagraphs (c)(1) and (2) of the Commercial Computer Software—Restricted Rights 48 CFR 52.227-19.

Java Development Kit, Version 1.0.2, Binary Code License

This binary code license ("License") contains rights and restrictions associated with use of the accompanying software and documentation ("Software"). Read the License carefully before installing Software. By installing Software, you agree to the terms and conditions of this License.

1. Limited License Grant. Sun grants to you ("Licensee") a non-exclusive, non-transferable limited license to use Software without fee. Licensee may re-distribute complete and unmodified Software to third parties provided that this License conspicuously appear with all copies of the Software and that Licensee does not charge a fee for such re-distribution of Software.

2. Java Platform Interface. In the event that Licensee creates any Java-related API and distributes such API to others for applet or application development. Licensee must promptly publish an accurate specification for such API for free use by all developers of Java-based software. Licensee may not modify the Java Platform Interface ("JPI," identified as classes contained within the "java" package or any subpackages of the "java" package), by creating additional classes within the JPI or otherwise causing the addition to or modification of the classes in the JPI.

3. Restrictions. Software is confidential copyrighted information of Sun and title to all copies is retained by Sun and/or its licensors. Licensee shall not modify, decompile, disassemble, decrypt, extract, or otherwise reverse engineer Software. Software may not be leased, assigned, or sublicensed, in whole or in part. Software is not designed or intended for use in on-line control of aircraft, air traffic, aircraft navigation or aircraft communications; or in the design, construction, operation or maintenance of any nuclear facility. Licensee warrants that it will not use or redistribute the Software for such purposes.

4. Trademarks and Logos. Licensee acknowledges that Sun owns the Java trademark and all Java-related trademarks, logos, and icons including the Coffee Cup and Duke ("Java Marks") and agrees to: (i) comply with the Java Trademark Guidelines at http://java.com/trademarks.html; (ii) not do anything harmful to or inconsistent with Sun's rights in the Java Marks; and (iii) assist Sun in protecting those rights, including assigning to Sun any rights acquired by Licensee in any Java Mark.

5. Disclaimer of Warranty. Software is provided "AS IS," without a warranty of any kind. ALL EXPRESS OR IMPLIED REPRESENTATIONS AND WARRANTIES, INCLUDING ANY IMPLIED WARRANTY OF MERCHANT-ABILITY, FITNESS FOR A PARTICULAR PURPOSE OR NON-INFRINGEMENT, ARE HEREBY EXCLUDED.

6. Limitation of Liability. SUN AND ITS LICENSORS SHALL NOT BE LIABLE FOR ANY DAMAGES SUF-FERED BY LICENSEE OR ANY THIRD PARTY AS A RESULT OF USING OR DISTRIBUTING SOFTWARE. IN NO EVENT WILL SUN OR ITS LICENSORS BE LIABLE FOR ANY LOST REVENUE, PROFIT OR DATA, OR FOR DIRECT, INDIRECT, SPECIAL, CONSEQUENTIAL, INCIDENTAL OR PUNITIVE DAMAGES, HOWEVER CAUSED AND REGARDLESS OF THE THEORY OF LIABILITY, ARISING OUT OF THE USE OF OR INABILITY TO USE SOFTWARE, EVEN IF SUN HAS BEEN ADVISED OF THE POSSIBILITY OF SUCH DAMAGES.

7. Termination. Licensee may terminate this License at any time by destroying all copies of Software. This License will terminate immediately without notice from Sun if Licensee fails to comply with any provisions of this License. Upon such termination, Licensee must destroy all copies of Software.

8. Export Regulations. Software, including technical data, is subject to U.S. export control laws, including the U.S. Export Administration Act and its associated regulations, and may be subject to export or import regulations in other countries. Licensee agrees to comply strictly with all such regulations and acknowledges that it has the responsibility to obtain licenses to export, re-export, or import Software. Software may not be downloaded, or otherwise exported or re-exported (i) into, or to a national or resident of, Cuba, Iraq, Iran, North Korea, Libya, Sudan, Syria or any country to which the U.S. has embargoed goods; or (ii) to anyone on the U.S. Treasury Department's list of Specially Designated Nations or the U.S. Commerce Department's Table of Denial Orders.

9. Restricted Rights. Use, duplication or disclosure by the United States government is subject to the restrictions as set forth in the Rights in Technical Data and Computer Software Clauses in DFARS 252.227-7013(c) (1) (ii) and FAR 52.227-19(c) (2) as applicable.

10. Governing Law. Any action related to this License will be governed by California law and controlling U.S. federal law. No choice of law rules of any jurisdiction will apply.

11. Severability. If any of the above provisions are held to be in violation of applicable law, void, or unenforceable in any jurisdiction, then such provisions are herewith waived to the extent necessary for the License to be otherwise enforceable in such jurisdiction. However, if in Sun's opinion deletion of any provisions of the License by operation of this paragraph unreasonably compromises the rights or increase the liabilities of Sun or its licensors, Sun reserves the right to terminate the License and refund the fee paid by License, if any, as Licensee's sole and exclusive remedy.

Read before opening CD package!

LICENSE AGREEMENT AND LIMITED WARRANTY

BY OPENING THIS SEALED SOFTWARE CD PACKAGE, YOU ACCEPT AND AGREE TO THE TERMS AND CONDITIONS PRINTED BELOW AND IN THE FULL AGREEMENT PRINTED ON THE PAGES FOLLOWING THE INDEX. IF YOU DO NOT AGREE, DO NOT OPEN THE PACKAGE.

The software is distributed on an "AS IS" basis, without warranty. Neither the authors, the software developers, Sun Microsystems, nor Prentice Hall make any representation, or warranty, either express or implied, with respect to the software programs, their quality, accuracy, or fitness for a specific purpose. Therefore, neither the authors, the software developers, nor Prentice Hall shall have any liability to you or any other person or entity with respect to any liability, loss, or damage caused or alleged to have been caused directly or indirectly by the programs contained on the CD. This includes, but is not limited to, interruption of service, loss of data, loss of classroom time, loss of consulting or anticipatory profits, or consequential damages from the use of these programs. If the CD medium is defective, you may return it for a replacement CD.

Software on this CD-ROM requires Windows 95, Windows NT 3.5.1, or Solaris 2.x.

Windows NT 4.0 IS NOT SUPPORTED

Praise for *White Rabbit*

"Kate Phillips has written a humorous, sometimes sad, unusually astute first novel about old age, love and romance."

—*Detroit Free Press*

"Remarkable....Phillips gets into the head and heart of an old woman and never misses a beat."

—*Boston Herald*

"Phillips has looked outside herself for her characters and her story, and she has treated them forthrightly but kindly. That is no small achievement."

—*Washington Post Book World*

"Kate Phillips first novel is a funny and sophisticated 'day in the life' story of an aging, eccentric and thoroughly independent soul whose memories of events and of people she loved often interrupt her present consciousness.... A moving book."

—*Houston Chronicle*

"Wise and witty....Deftly balancing humor with difficult questions about living and dying, Phillips, an author who, at age 28, is still near the beginning of her own adulthood, has managed to write a perceptive and sophisticated novel about a woman at the end of hers."

—*Publishers Weekly*

"Both a saddening and genuinely funny day-in-the-life of an aging woman, sensitively rendered with vibrant, witty dialogue and zoom-lens glimpses of humanness."

—*Booklist*

"Remarkably, Phillips has created a triumphant portrait of a character who transcends the humiliating debilities of old age."

—*Elle*

"A beautiful first novel. Remember the name Kate Phillips."

—*Charlotte Observer*

"A wonderful first novel, insightful and detail-oriented."

—*Grand Rapids Press*

"This first novel is audacious, funny, and full of the irreverence of a woman who has reached a point in life where she has little left to lose."

—*Arizona Republic*

"A wonderfully wrought, seriocomic stroll through the frailties and nobility of the spirit in the face of that great leveler, Time....*White Rabbit* is engrossing, entertaining and compassionately observant."

—*Los Angeles Rapport*

"*White Rabbit* shows that Phillips knows how to get a laugh. More importantly, she understands the human heart. In Ruth Caster Hubble, she's created a woman who is a real character, in both senses of the word."

—*Hartford Courant*

"*White Rabbit* is a remarkable exploration of the mind of one of society's forgotten elderly. Phillips' portrayals...are insightful—sometimes poignant, sometimes irritating, sometimes baffling—just like real people are."

—*Wichita Eagle*

"Phillips has created a wonderful, multidimensional character in Ruth Caster Armstrong Hubble, one capable of great strength, weakness and humor."

—*Memphis Commercial Appeal*

"Phillips' masterful touches in this microscopic study extend far beyond reasonable expectations for a first novel. She looks like a major talent in the offing."

—*Milwaukee Journal Sentinel*

"Leaving the past behind and knowing it might flash ahead of you anyway—that's the point, and Phillips's loving valentine to the old cranks with pastel hair we might all become makes that point, gracefully and unforgettably."

—*HotWired*

"Phillips has created a character of depth in Ruth. Her maddening mannerisms and opinions juxtaposed against her tenderness and insight make Ruth complex and interesting....This is a novel worth reading, and Kate Phillips is an author to watch."

—*San Antonio Express-News*

"[An] impressive, poetic debut."

—*Boston Phoenix*

"At 88, Ruth is as ornery as they come. *White Rabbit* is an affectionately funny chronicle of a day, perhaps the last, in her eccentric existence....Kate Phillips happens to be roughly sixty years younger than her protagonist, but she understands completely the comedy, absurdity, and poignancy of old age."

—*Buzz* magazine

K A T E   P H I L L I P S

Harper Perennial
A Division of **HarperCollins***Publishers*

XII

XI   I

X   II

W H I T E R A B B I T

. . . .

IX   III

VIII   IV

VII   V

VI

This book was originally published in 1996 by Houghton Mifflin Company. It is here reprinted by arrangement with Houghton Mifflin.

HarperCollins books may be purchased for educational, business, or sales promotional use. For information please write: Special Markets Department, HarperCollins Publishers, Inc., 10 East 53rd Street, New York, NY 10022.

First HarperPerennial edition published 1997.

Designed by Anne Chalmers

ISBN 0-06-097719-1

97 98 99 00 01 RRD 10 9 8 7 6 5 4 3 2 1

For Tim O'Brien, and for
my family, in memory of
Elizabeth Soyster Hammond,
Fred Hammond, and
Eric Phillips

I am grateful for the support and encouragement of my editor Janet Silver, Wendy Holt, and my agent Anne Borchardt. Also, I want to thank Jessica Dorman, Larry Cooper, Lori Glazer, William Lung, Lena Deevy, Jennifer MacFarlane, and Lina Lee.

Facing west from California's shores,
Inquiring, tireless, seeking what is yet unfound,
I, a child, very old, over waves, towards the house of maternity, the
        land of migrations, look afar,
Look off the shores of my Western sea, the circle almost circled;
For starting westward from Hindustan, from the vales of Kashmere,
From Asia, from the north, from the God, the sage, and the hero,
From the south, from the flowery peninsulas and the spice islands,
Long having wander'd since, round the earth having wander'd,
Now I face home again, very pleas'd and joyous,
(But where is what I started for so long ago?
And why is it yet unfound?)

                    —Walt Whitman, *Leaves of Grass*

XII

XI I

X II

P A R T O N E
. . . .

IX III

VIII IV

VII V

VI

5:25 A.M.

RUTH SLEPT on her back, face up, mouth open, eighty-eight years old. When she breathed — and there were times when she did not — she exhaled with a wheeze and a jerk and a long dry hum from the bottom of her lungs. She lay deep in her green sleeping bag.

"Henry, for God's sake!" she mumbled. "Henry!"

Even in her sleep, the old man gave her fits. Thirty-six years they had been married, thirty-six years he'd been upsetting the fragile order Ruth lived to polish and perfect. Now, in her tireless dreams, he stood at the kitchen sink, trying to skin a big yellow grapefruit with the carrot peeler. A great fire raged all around him; flames lapped against his collar, oily black smoke came from the cupboards and drawers, but even so Henry stood there calm and quiet, skinning his grapefruit with the rusty carrot peeler. "Yes, sir," he muttered, "damn thick skin." He blinked stupidly and shook his head and turned the grapefruit in his hands. His shirt was burning. "Boy oh boy," he said, "*too* damn thick."

Ruth grunted and rolled sideways.

"Idiot!" she yelled.

"Texas grapefruit. Got to be."

"My God, man, that's a *carrot* peeler!"

"Texas for sure," Henry said. His ears and nose were burning. "Yes, sir, bet your life, this here's one of them mutant Texas jobbies, I seen 'em before, buggers just don't skin right — never did, never will, and there's a fact."

"Boob!" Ruth yelled.

Her own voice woke her up. She opened her eyes, adjusted her glasses — she wore them even when she slept. For a few seconds, still half asleep, she peered into the shadowy early-morning dark. No fire, no grapefruits. No sound except for her old Emerson radio.

"Texas," she said. "What a boob."

She sighed, reached out, turned up the volume on her radio. It was always on; she hadn't switched it off since the day she and Henry moved to Laguna Beach.

. . . So all you California dreamers, let's look alive! Out of the sack! Touch those toes! Another new day, and you've started it out with FM Ninety-seven, voice of the New Southland, and I'm your breakfast buddy Bruce Gentry . . .

It had been Bruce Gentry for ten years now. Another bone-head.

Ruth turned her head toward the door, yelled, "Henry!" There was no answer. At five-thirty in the morning, the whole state of California seemed deserted. Marooned with a moron, she thought. Trapped three stories high in her Paradise Lagoon condominium.

"Henry! You awake?"

Again, there was no response from the room across the hall. Ruth rolled onto her side, pressed her toes against the zipper at the bottom of her sleeping bag. A light, almost buoyant sense of familiarity came over her; she'd spent every night of the past five years in the bag. Not because she liked the feel of nylon against her skin — she despised it — but because washing sheets struck her as a profligate waste of time and money.

For a while, lying still, Ruth listened to the drone of a half-dozen radio commercials. Saturday, she thought. December the first. A White Rabbit day.

Time to get on with things.

"Henry!" she yelled.

5:35 A.M.

Ruth pushed herself up. She sighed again, released a squeaky little fart, then inhaled to test the efficiency of her lungs. The world seemed oddly different today — the air, maybe, or the fluttery morning shadows, or the scent of her own gas. A new and unwholesome gloominess filled the room. Even the bed beneath her seemed sad and dreary; her yellow candlewick bedspread, folded down around the bedposts, had long ago turned brown with age at the top of each tufted cotton ball. Ruth knew this, didn't need to see it. But it didn't matter — no detergent on earth could remove the residue of all those long, slow years.

She reached for her bedjacket, which hung to her left over the bedpost. The jacket was light pink and embroidered with looping blue flowers, an old lady's design, and Ruth had been wearing it every morning for almost fifteen years. She slipped it over her flannel nightgown. The jacket hung loosely, a bag on bones. When, Ruth wondered, had she become so small? She pushed away the sleeping bag and bent her legs, one knee at a time, slowly shifting her weight to the edge of the bed. Her right knee made a sharp popping sound. Dr. Ash said she'd been born with the bad knee, an inheritance of sorts, and that it certainly wouldn't kill her. Still, the knee had never hurt like this before — maybe it had to do with that cheap safety rail they'd installed above the bathtub.

Two mornings ago, when Ruth reached for the rail, the stupid gizmo had slipped through her hands and sent her sprawling back into the water, her rear end slamming against the tile as the right knee buckled.

Ruth sighed.

Born with it my eye.

She'd always had good legs, pretty legs; like a ballerina, Hale used to tell her. But now the knee had swollen up like an eggplant left to rot in the sun — an ugly, purplish lump — and to make matters worse, Henry hadn't heard a thing when she'd taken the fall, hadn't come to rescue her until she'd called out at least a half-dozen times . . . Yes, gorgeous legs, my little ballerina, Hale would say, and he'd run a hand along the curve of her calf, and sometimes higher, and he'd do sweet tickling things that didn't really tickle, and he'd even lean down and kiss the kneecap . . . Amazing legs.

"Henry! You awake?"

Such a boob.

Probably still snoring away in the room across the hall in that big old double bed of his. Ruth could hear him now, almost smell him.

She slid down from the high mattress. She dropped to the floor with a little gasp, then tottered cautiously toward the foot of the bed. There on the rug was her sit-up pillow, an old white thing that she liked to slip behind her back for support. She leaned against it every morning as she put on her face, and she leaned against it every evening as she took off her face. Fluffs of cotton stuck out where the seams had split; it had served her very nicely for almost forty-two years.

She bent down for the pillow — one click in the knee — then hesitated and told herself to retrieve it later. The disorder irritated her, but it couldn't be helped, she'd have to let the creaky old joints loosen up first.

On the radio, Bruce Gentry was still doling out his greasy

nonsense: *So come on, California, let's get an early start! A beach day in December, how good to be alive!*

"Right," Ruth muttered, "unless you're some platitudinous bonehead."

Good to be alive — how could you argue? — but better yet to be alive and be a Caster. Ruth Caster Armstrong, never mind this second marriage to Henry Hubble; Ruth Caster Armstrong, and that was something she could take pride in forever. "Posture, boys!" she used to tell her two sons. "Stand up, kid!" to her only granddaughter. "Straight and solid, no hunchbacks in the Caster clan."

Ruth pulled her shoulders back and shuffled over to the bedroom door. Bad knee and all, she still had that erect Caster posture. She shut the door with authority and turned her back to it, lining herself up against its flat surface. Heels first, then bottom, shoulders, head. She sucked in her stomach, pressed the small of her back against the door, and held herself there for a count of ten.

"So *there*," she said. "Ha!"

Eighty-eight years old, yes, but nobody could ever claim she didn't have spine. That Caster backbone. Which was the whole secret to making it through all those years. One thing for certain, even the most ordinary, unremarkable life would finally wear a person down — the weight of marriage and children, the funerals and Christmases and Easters, the simple burdens of memory that kept accumulating and growing heavier with each tick of the clock — all that could turn you into jelly, drag you right down into the grave. Yes, it could. Unless you had spine.

"Ha!" she said again, louder. "So *there*."

A little tickle of triumph went through her as she moved away from the door and into the speckled shadows of another morning.

By habit she again glanced down at her wristwatch. Almost five forty-five. She didn't need to see the back of the watch to know what *it* said: "To Ruth, love Hale, 1938." And here it was now,

1995. Approaching the year 2000, and she was almost . . . Dear God, almost a full century on this earth.

The fierce, blurry speed of all those years amazed her. Impossible, she told herself, that she had lived so long without him. Hale had died in January 1944 — murdered by an evil, implacable, utterly invisible virus.

Bugs, Ruth thought. Vicious little bugs.

She pulled a loose thread from the hem of her bedjacket, inspected the stitching in each sleeve.

Just for an instant, a wave of speckly white light seemed to rush in on her, and then, just as quickly, the white speckles faded away. Ruth lifted her glasses and rubbed her eyelids.

Teetering slightly, she moved back to the end of the bed, bending down again for the sit-up pillow. Then past the slippers she'd left out the night before (her toes were freezing) and up to the head of the bed, to push the sit-up pillow against the wall. And then back onto the bed, back into the sleeping bag.

Ruth looked left toward the bedside table and stretched to turn on the table lamp. The little pillbox from Gump's (a gift from her son Carter, before he'd lost all his money — would he ever remake it before she died?) sat on the table, waiting for her.

One Mevacor to lower her cholesterol.

Naprosyn and Tylenol, for the knee and aching joints.

One Cardizem on waking, another at nine or ten, a third in midafternoon, a fourth just before bed. Four a day. Dr. Ash — he took over after Dr. Rhodes retired — Dr. Ash said it didn't matter how high her blood pressure rose. What mattered was blasting the arteries open, four times a day. At bedtime, arteries wide open, Ruth sometimes treated herself to a little pink tranquilizer to help her sleep.

Now, in the morning, it was one Mevacor, one Cardizem, one Naprosyn, one Tylenol. She washed them down with water from the cup she kept beside her pillbox. Again, almost instantly, the bedroom went dimly with that strange white light.

Curious sounds, too. Curious shapes here and there.

Ruth lay very still for a moment, a bit puzzled, then blinked and reached for the phone.

"Oh, my," she murmured.

Stiffly, with a bony index finger, Ruth dialed and cleared her throat and waited, still puzzled, watching the odd white shapes move about the room like the tracks of some living creature — a fat, furry bunny jumping here and there beneath a wizard's magic wand.

5:52 A.M.

"White Rabbit!" Ruth shouted. "Got you!"

"I'm sorry?"

Ruth jumped. The voice sounded peculiar. Too low, too deep — as if its owner had swallowed an avocado pit.

"I *said*, White —"

"Yeah, sure. White Rabbit yourself."

Ruth was startled. For as long as she could remember — and her memory was good — the Caster clan had played this little game on the first of every month. The idea was simple: get up early and place the call and draw in a deep breath and yell "White Rabbit!" into the mouthpiece. Whoever got the words out first became an automatic winner. Victory brought a month's worth of good luck; defeat meant you'd best watch your step. To Ruth, the contest was more than a diversion. In one form or another she had been playing the game since childhood, passing along the rules to friends and family, and over time it had become one of the solid cornerstones in her life, a source of order, a base ritual that somehow supported and justified a great many lesser rituals.

She took the game seriously; she required the same of others.

Ruth rubbed her eyes.

"Who is this?" she said fiercely. "Where's my grandchild?"

"Hey, listen —"

"No, sir, *you* listen. If Karen's harmed — if you so much as looked at her — I'll have the authorities there before you can say . . . Who *is* this?"

There was a muffled whispering on the other end. Ruth ran her fingers through her hair, tried to remain calm. A hundred times she'd told Karen to bolt her windows. Men were men, and L.A. was L.A., and it was getting to the point where a woman had to wear body armor in her own bed.

After a moment, her granddaughter spoke. "White Rabbit!"

Ruth snorted. "Nonsense. I've already said White Rabbit."

"Not to me you didn't," Karen said. "Rules are rules, Grammy. I win, you lose."

"Oh poof, don't be silly, I most definitely said it first. Definitely and absolutely. That rapist who answered, he heard me." Ruth paused, collected herself. "So who is he? And why of all things is he answering your phone?"

"Mike," Karen said gently. "The man I married?"

"*That* one?"

"Right, that one. Do you know what time it is?"

Ruth frowned. "I have no recollection of this individual, whatsoever. Far as I'm concerned, you were never married."

"Oh, come on now. The schoolteacher. *Mike.*"

"Schoolteacher? What's a schoolteacher doing breaking into somebody's —"

"He didn't break in. He's my husband."

"Husband! Breaking and entering?"

Karen released a quick, shallow sigh. "Just stop it," she said. "Hang on a minute — he's on his way out the door."

"And now he's abandoning you. Stays there all night, this sweet Romeo, then skulks away at sunrise."

"Grammy, please. One second."

Karen pressed her hold button, leaving Ruth to listen to a screech of flutes and harmonicas. Ruth shook her head. All that grief, she thought, and the poor girl's just taken the louse right back. It made her blood hot. Ruth had known only two trustworthy men in her entire adult life. Her own father, Walt, and her own first husband, Hale. Both were dead.

After a moment there was a rattling sound on the other end of the line.

"Hi, there," Karen said, "I'm back."

"You and everybody else."

"Well, I know, but this time it's —"

"Always *this* time," Ruth snapped. "I'd just like to know one thing. If you let Mr. Wonderful stay there all night, why's he in such a hurry to run out now?"

"His name's Mike. And he *is* wonderful. He has things to do, is all — had to get going."

Scowling, Ruth drew the bedjacket around her shoulders and considered the situation. Karen seemed tense, a little defensive.

"Well, maybe so," Ruth said, "but it still strikes me as very, very peculiar. This revolving door of his. In and out. A word of advice — don't get too cozy — he may be up to something. Always was, if you remember. Probably a drug addict by now. And you know about these new diseases."

Her granddaughter groaned. "Please drop it, Grammy. It's too early in the morning."

Ruth ignored her. "I'll tell you this much. When I was your age, things were decent. I'd already been married seven whole years, almost eight — no, nine. The first time, that is. My real marriage."

"I know, Grammy. Really, you've explained it all a thousand times. Hale had this car, right? And he drove you the whole way from Los Angeles to the Grand Canyon for your honeymoon, and it rained like crazy, and the car broke down and the roads were terrible, but even so it was this genuine religious experience, perfectly thrilling and sublime and beautiful."

"I never said religious."

"Please," Karen said, "don't get started. I need some sleep."

"I can imagine. Kept you awake, did he?"

"The other way around."

"My God."

"Listen, why don't we talk later?"

Ruth shook her head sadly. Eyes closed, she found herself picturing Karen's face, the sunny brown skin and blond hair and green eyes, and it was a few moments before she realized that the face belonged to a twelve-year-old. Hard to believe that this lovely little girl was now a married woman.

"Well, in any case," Ruth said, "it's considerably more than I'll ever understand. The man runs off on you, who knows where, then one day he busts in again and has his perverted way with you and all you can do is . . . I mean, you *allow* it. One minute it's divorce, the next minute you're letting him . . . Honestly, I don't understand."

"I was only considering divorce," Karen said. Her voice had again gone defensive. "Thinking about it. Barely even that."

"Is that so?"

"Yes, of course."

Ruth sniffed. "Funny that I don't recall it that way. Anyway, when I was first married, divorce was the last thing on *my* mind, God knows. I was so busy just worrying about little things, like would Hale catch me plucking the stray hairs from my chin in the morning. And the two of us were such dodos! We both had the feelings and the urge, but we didn't quite know . . . Have I ever told you what he thought about my legs?"

"Look, not right now, okay?"

"Ballerina legs, that's what my Hale called them, and you should've seen his eyes, the way he'd lean down and put his tongue right up against —"

"Not *now*."

Ruth wagged her head from side to side. A few years with some fancy job, a little time in her apartment without what's-his-name — and now what's-his-name back in the picture — and Karen seemed to think she knew everything. The girl would be sorry soon enough, brushing her grandmother aside this way.

"I'll call you later, Grammy. Maybe even stop over, okay?"

"Fine," Ruth said, "if you want."

"I do want."

"Well fine," Ruth said, and hung up.

For a few seconds she stared down at the phone. The image of twelve-year-old Karen flickered up again, bright and clear, then gradually melted into twenty-nine-year-old Karen. Still blond, still lovely. But the lightheartedness was gone now. Snatched away, as usual, by a burglar dressed up as romance.

Ruth felt a powerful, inexplicable sadness, as if the day itself were somehow infected with the poisons of melancholy. The sun was up now. December the first, a very peculiar White Rabbit day in Southern California.

Ruth leaned back against her sit-up pillow.

"Henry!"

6:08 A.M.

It was Saturday, cleaning day, which meant Luzma would come breezing in just after three o'clock, late as usual. Meanwhile, Ruth had things to do, business to take care of. There was the letter to mail to Douglas, a bus to catch. All the way downtown and back — it might well take the entire morning. And only one bus, too. She'd probably have to wait an eternity while it made its loop and came back to pick her up. Of course that wasn't so bad. She'd wait on the bench by the curb, or in the library (everybody there knew her) if it started to rain. This early sunlight could be deceptive. She'd take her umbrella, just in case. First, though, breakfast.

"Henry! Would you come here, *please!*"

Almost instantly, as if he'd been lurking there, Henry appeared in the doorway, already dressed, wearing his usual brown corduroys and thin white shirt. Ugly, she thought. And the clothes, too. The shirt was always filthy at the neck.

Henry gave her his hopeful morning smile. "What's all the hollering for?"

He was tall, almost six three. His face was pinkish, splattered with tiny brown nubs. (Without a hat, he couldn't tolerate even twenty minutes in the sun — a high risk for skin cancer.) Henry Ho-hum Hubble. Who on God's earth would have thought she'd end up with *him?* Dropped out of school in the tenth grade. And that hair. Back then, in those high school days, the hair had been as red as a vine-ripe tomato and slimy as a clump of seaweed. His brother Bill hadn't been so bad — a good dancer — but Henry, unfortunately, was the one who'd finally worn her down. It was Henry's house that had lured her in the end; and now this, for almost four decades. The thought gave her cramps. She'd been married to him twice as long as she'd ever spent with Hale.

"About time," Ruth said. "I almost thought you'd stopped breathing, the way you don't hear a single blessed thing." She frowned at him. "I believe it's breakfast time."

"Right now?"

"Certainly now. When else?"

"Well, sure, but I was thinking —"

"Now," Ruth said.

It was Henry's responsibility to serve her breakfast in bed each morning, to carry it up from the tiny second-floor kitchen on her special red plastic tray. A simple enough job, really. Everything was always prearranged according to a strict set of rules; even an old goat like Henry could understand the basic system. Each evening, just before bed, Ruth would pour Shredded Wheat cakes — the small kind, the bran kind — into her blue porcelain cereal bowl: one-half cup exactly. Next she'd add a quarter cup of All-Bran pellets. (They *did* look like rat turds.) Then, with a practiced eye, concentrating, she'd place a medium-sized banana on the tray, three inches from the side of the bowl, to be peeled and cut on top of her cereal in the morning. Finally, she'd position a knife and an eight-ounce box of prunes beside the banana. Henry, of course, had his own variation on this procedure, preferring to pour his milk on at night so that by breakfast time each little wheat biscuit had dissolved into sodden nothingness.

Now, standing in the doorway, he reached into his mouth to straighten a tooth. "Seeing as how you're in such a hurry," he said, "maybe you ought to try my method. Saves all that milk-pouring time. Barely got to chew at all."

Ruth rolled her eyes. "Just bring up my carton of nonfat, like always."

"Sure, okay by me," Henry said. He tapped the tooth and shrugged. "But my way's quicker. Gentle on the gums, too."

Henry had ten teeth left in his head. Several of these were loose, and he lived in fear of swallowing one of them, of losing another precious tooth forever. Now and then Ruth would catch him standing at the bathroom mirror, squinting into his open mouth as he made a careful count. Since his gums were too soft for dentures, he was constantly forced to readjust the teeth he had. The canine at the top right side of his mouth dropped out at least twice a week, and turned one or two complete revolutions every day. In Ruth's opinion, the whole business was disgusting. *She* had all but one of her original teeth, and went for checkups at least twice a year.

"Forget your gums," she said. "I'm not worried about gums. Just bring me the milk carton. And please, please, please don't forget my cup of decaf."

"You're the boss," Henry said, stuffing his hands into his pockets and shuffling off toward the stairs.

Ruth rearranged her sit-up pillow and spread out a small towel across her lap to catch crumbs. For her, breakfast in bed was both comforting and essential, the only decent way to begin a day. Henry, thank God, kept his distance at mealtimes. He ate breakfast — as he ate every meal now — in his own room, at his desk by the window. From the desk he'd look out over the tennis court to a narrow strip of green grass, then to the iron fence surrounding Paradise Lagoon, then beyond to Coast Highway. He'd watch the passing cars, or the early-morning tennis players, or the Rain Bird lawn sprinklers going round and round. Most often, though, he just sat there.

It truly amazed her. How the man could stay utterly motionless for hours on end. If it was baseball season, he waited for the pregame show; if it wasn't baseball season, he waited for opening day.

He could wait for months.

"Don't matter none to me," he'd say. "One thing about baseball, Ruthie, you got to have patience to burn."

Sometimes he wore his Dodgers cap while he waited. Sometimes he took it off to scratch his head.

6:23 A.M.

The radio was still babbling, though Bruce Gentry had signed off with the rising sun.

The main order of business today was to mail that letter to Douglas, Ruth's eldest son, the retired cardiologist. It was a matter of financial urgency, right up his alley. Douglas had a knack for money matters: every April, he prepared her tax papers; during the year, as necessary, he handled her health insurance and Medicare and all the silly forms and documents that came crushing down through the mail. These days, Ruth thought, they didn't bury a person under dirt, they just held you below the mail slot and piled on the paper. Anyway, Douglas would know how to fix those idiots at the Blockbuster Book Club. Talk about paper — they were swamping her.

"I need action," she'd written her son last week, "and I need it now."

She'd been a club member for more than two decades, but a year ago, when her eyes could no longer tolerate the strain, she'd reluctantly informed the Blockbuster people that her membership was now null and void. A murderous phrase: null and void. Except the books kept coming. Sometimes two a month, sometimes three or four. Books she hadn't chosen, the worst sort of books: horticultural dictionaries and Italian sex manuals and low-fat Tex-Mex cookbooks. Rapidly, over the course of a few months, she'd acquired a large and expensive library, to which the club kept adding — volume after volume — thanking her profusely with each new shipment. "Our favorite Blockbusting customer," they'd declared at one point. "We remain confident that literature will bloom forever in the fertile gardens of Mrs. Henry Hubble." Ruth was not amused. Block*heads*, she'd thought. She'd taken to leaving the books in their cardboard mailing envelopes, stacking them unopened on the big oak dining table.

It was a nightmare, obviously, but somehow Douglas would get her out of it. Along with the letter, she'd enclosed her latest bill. Four hundred and fifteen dollars, for God's sake.

"I mean it," she'd written to her son, "these people have to be dealt with firmly. Make them do something. Number one: cart away their junk. Number two: a personal apology. Number three: ample compensation. I've suffered, haven't I? Yes, I have. And if those Blockbusters start to hem and haw — if they so much as make a peep — you have my authorization to drag the swindlers into court. Like that old Perry Mason show on television. A big trial, all the trappings." The idea made her smile. She could see it. How she'd wear a shabby dress to the courtroom — maybe that rose-colored jumper with the little mauve flowers she'd bought for Karen's baptism. Smear spit under her eyes and hobble up to the witness stand, give her bad knee a nice loud crack, take out a Kleenex and make a few old-lady moaning sounds as the bailiff used a wheelbarrow to haul in pile after pile of unopened books. Yes, and then she'd start reading aloud. Make the jury listen to all the claptrap these Blockbuster people were inflicting on her. She'd drone on for hours and hours — maybe weeks. Batter them with excerpts from *Cooking for the Single Parent Child*. Give them a good long sample from *Life Cycles of the African Violet* or *Dirty Mouths* or *Pagan Prayer for Pagan Protestants*.

And if all *that* didn't earn some pity, well then, she'd just throw an old-fashioned fit. The jury wouldn't have a choice.

Guilty.

Guilty as sin. Mr. Big-Bucks Blockbuster would end up paying through the nose.

Ruth peered around the bedroom, imagining how she'd spend the riches. A new wide-screen television, luxurious damask curtains, maybe an original Van Gogh. Those Blockbuster creeps had money to burn — a million dollars would do just fine, especially when she'd been getting by on those paltry Social Security payments. Yes, a flat million.

She grinned a thin little grin.

Two million.

Towel in her lap, eyes fixed on the sleeping bag, Ruth raised first her left foot, then her right, shaping the green nylon into an expanse of gently rolling hills where she might one day discover a world better than this one. A world where people got what they deserved, and where making ends meet was never a problem. A daydream, maybe, but why not? A safe, happy place where she could stop clipping coupons and stop cutting corners and stop nagging old Henry and stop dipping into Hale's veteran's pension, which she kept downtown at the Security Pacific.

She closed her eyes.

Yes, those gentle green hills, and a shadowy forest beyond, and a waterfall and a river and puffy white clouds. It made a pretty picture, which calmed her, but even then the morning's curious shades of melancholy did not quite vanish.

6:35 A.M.

"Hey, Ruthie, I said here's your breakfast. What are you, asleep?"

Ruth looked up and there was Henry, his nubby-red face hovering six inches above her chest.

Reality was irksome.

"No, I'm not asleep, I've been up forever. Just put the tray here on my towel."

Henry set down the tray and watched as Ruth poured milk on the cereal, peeled her banana and expertly cut it over her bowl. She took a swallow of decaf, scooped up a spoonful of Shredded Wheat and All-Bran. Henry waited. Ruth ate several bites in silence.

"Ready with the grocery list?" Henry said. "Ten minutes, I better slap pavement."

"I'm eating."

"Well, sure, but —"

"Oh, all *right*. Go get your little pencil."

Each day, after breakfast, Henry walked the six blocks to the Alpha Beta for their groceries, trudging out the Lagoon gates and straight across the highway, stopping traffic with a battered wooden cane he'd painted white. Though he'd been walking with more difficulty lately (too cramped to move at all on days he was constipated), his trips were by and large successful. Of course, there were times when he picked out the wrong label — Cherry Coke for Diet, white Wonder Bread for Farmer's Wheat — but the checkout girls gave him a hand with most major problems. And he carried home bags that Ruth could hardly lift.

"Back in a jiff," Henry said, and left to select a pencil from among those he kept neatly sharpened in his top desk drawer. Ruth took a few more bites of cereal, drank some decaf, chewed two prunes. Boring, she thought, and pushed the tray away. She closed her eyes, sliding down against her sit-up pillow. How in God's name could her life have turned out like this? A pile of shriveled-up prunes.

Nineteen twenty-nine, Washington, D.C., and she awoke with a start. A red mist had been swallowing her. Eating her alive: a hungry red mist.

She pushed herself up.

Hale was still there, buttoning the pants of his best wool suit, bags packed and ready to go at the foot of the bed. Saturday morning. Just like all the other mornings, really, except he was going away, and somehow the bedroom was already registering his absence — darker than usual, all those deep, shadowy holes; she could actually feel him leaving her.

There was still that red mist at the margins of her vision when Hale looked up and winked.

"So you're back among the living," he said.

"I suppose. Everything's ready?"

"Sure, just about. One more minute."

Ruth made herself smile. "Well good, but you'd better hurry," she said, barely managing it, then lay back and watched him insert gold cufflinks into his crisply starched white sleeves.

A heavy silence pressed up against her ears. More than a year of marriage, she thought, and not a single night apart, and here he was going away for weeks and weeks and weeks, and she loved him so much, and she didn't know how she could say goodbye or keep herself from crying or get through the rest of the day. It wasn't forever, of course; she knew that. And this was his job — the Geological Survey needed him out in Oklahoma — but even so, God, she *loved* him.

Right then she almost said it.

"Hale?" she started, then stopped.

He slipped a tie around his neck, knotted it with his usual precision, moved to examine himself in the mirror above the dressing table. He looked elegant and dignified. "One second, baby, and we'll talk about whatever you want," he said, glancing at his wristwatch. "Plenty of time still."

"Not enough."

"Sorry?"

"We can't even —" Then she was crying. Not loud, but it was crying.

And then Hale was there beside her, close. "Hey, you," he said, "stop it."

Ruth made a meaningless gesture with her hand. It wasn't just the leaving, it was something else, too. Like a pebble lodged somewhere in the deep folds of her brain, something half forgotten, something never completely known. "It's stupid," she said, "but I can't make myself feel right. Really, it *is* stupid." She pressed her whole body against him: toes, stomach, breasts. "Just this stupid, stupid dream."

"A bad one?"

"I'm not sure." She kept pressing against him. "Ridiculous, isn't it? I'm like some silly little girl, I shouldn't be acting . . . This *red* stuff, Hale. It was *eating* us."

"Ruth, come on now."

A red mist, she told him.

Bright red. Not a gas exactly — something alive, something wet and red and hungry — and it was chasing them across a huge red desert. Red dunes and red tumbleweed and that voracious red mist. They were running hard. Hale's feet were gone. He was hopping and laughing, and the mist was eating his ankles, and then suddenly they came up on a boiling red river — red water and red spray and frothy red waterfalls — and Hale laughed and hopped into the river and made a sound she couldn't hear. His face had turned deep red, and his skin, too, and he was hopping across the river on big red stones. The mist was eating his knee-caps. So she chased after him. She put her head down and closed her eyes and moved fast, stone to stone, except the mist was eating her own lungs — she couldn't breathe, couldn't keep her balance — and then things suddenly went upside down and she was tumbling into the hot red river. She was swimming now. Thick red water, like raspberry cement, and she couldn't keep her head up, so she let herself go down deep, to the bottom, where Hale sat calmly waiting for her on a red bench at a train station — red trains and red tracks and a small red depot. Hale's ears were gone. His skull was going. He laughed and pointed up at a giant red clock. "Easy!" he yelled. "Hold your breath, Ruthie! Watch that clock!" So, yes, she did it — she took a deep breath and watched the clock spin. It told time in years. One tick and it was 1930. Then 1930 ticked to 1931. The clock chimed on 1944. "Easy," Hale kept saying, "so easy!" Then the train was pulling out. Red steam and red noise. And Hale jumped aboard and laughed and reached up high and seized the giant clock and squeezed it to the size of a softball and threw it to her and yelled, "Easy! See there? Just keep watching, Ruthie." He waved at her. The mist was eating his hands, so he waved with his wrists, then later with his elbows, and all the while he kept laughing and yelling, "Easy!"

Henry prodded Ruth on the forearm. "All set," he said. "Let's get that list made."

The sound of his voice was uncommonly reassuring.

Ruth opened her eyes and wiggled to sit up straight. Just some silly old dream, she told herself, but the day was clearly getting off to a bizarre start. Her skin was damp with sweat.

"All right, take this down correctly," she said, and drew the bedjacket tight around her shoulders. "No mistakes for a change. One bran muffin — oat bran, like usual. One carton coleslaw, small. Put 'small' in parentheses. Two bananas, medium. Make sure they're not green this time, or mushy, either. Four TV dinners, turkey. Don't forget to use the coupons. And remember Luzma and Luis will be here for dinner, so get *four*."

"Four," said Henry. "Check."

They would have their customary Saturday night guests for dinner. Luzma was coming at three, with her son Luis, and at six-fifteen, when the laundry was done, they would all sit down for a meal of cottage cheese and turkey.

Henry stood working on the list, his nubbed face three inches from his little memo pad, tongue poking out from the space between his front teeth.

"Did you get all that?" Ruth asked. "Turkey, I said."

Henry grunted, held the list out at arm's length, and blinked several times. He made a few painstaking corrections, dotting *i*'s and crossing *t*'s, then tucked the pencil behind his ear and turned toward the door.

"Turkey! Did you write that down?" Ruth called after him.

Ruth wore two watches.

One was studded with diamonds — a gift from Hale. It lost several minutes a day, sometimes hesitating at the half hour, sometimes even clicking backward a notch or two, but Ruth worked hard to keep it running on time. She never took it off — never. Even before bathing, she was careful to wrap a plastic sandwich baggie around it, securing the bag with a pair of thick rubber bands. It was this old diamond watch she consulted for the purpose of telling time. The other, from Save-On across the highway, had cost her five dollars. She wore it under her sleeve, out of sight, using it only as a gauge by which to adjust the precious watch from Hale. The cheapie meant nothing to her: a nuisance more than anything, the first item she removed before retiring each night. It was one of those new digital gadgets with lots of fancy displays and buttons, like some silly computer game, the numbers blinking and flashing and zipping around as if they had their own crazy agenda. Ruth lived in vague but relentless terror that she would accidentally hit the wrong button, making it stick forever on Date or Second.

Now, according to both watches, it was five minutes past seven. She had to hurry — the Postal Connection would close at noon.

Each morning, Ruth put on her makeup in bed, a soothing ritual she'd carefully attended to for nearly fifty years, with only one brief period of interruption. But it was a period she'd never forget: those horrid newlywed days with Henry.

Even now she got a chill when she remembered it.

"If I marry you," she'd warned him when he proposed, "there's one thing you can't ever forget. Separate bedrooms. And I'm afraid that's final. Let's face it, we've both been through this marriage business before, we've both had enough poking around to last us a couple of eternities." She gave him a cool, frank stare. "I've been a widow fifteen years now, almost exactly, and I'll never get sexy again, not with anyone." She smiled charmingly. "That includes you."

Henry shrugged. "What the heck. Okay by me."

They were married two days later.

Bam, he was all over her, a sex boob, and for weeks he kept slinking into her room just after breakfast — slithered, actually, like a sex snake — wiggling his way under the covers and making those vulgar sizzling sounds in her ear. "I need you in the mornings," he'd hiss, one clumsy hand on his own private parts, the other reaching out to paw at hers. He'd fondle her ankles and knees, pry at her thighs; he'd slobber on her face and drool into her mouth and then finally shoot all his slimy sperms across her stomach.

One morning as Ruth sat in bed, toiletry kit in her lap, mirror in hand, applying lipstick, Henry crept in with that same perverted grin on his face.

"Out!" she yelled. "You promised!"

"I did?"

Ruth glared at him. "'Okay by me' — your exact words. Loud and clear. A promise."

"Well yeah. But Jeez, Ruthie, I'm in love."

"Love?" Ruth said, almost startled. "What does *that* matter?"

Henry took a slithery half-step to the side. He blinked, moved to the foot of the bed, ran a thin forefinger up and down the bedpost.

His shoulders slumped.

"But see, you're my cutie pie, Ruthie, you're my own little doll, especially when you rub on all that juicy lipstick. Makes a guy's heart go pitty-pat." He straightened his shoulders, reached out, pinched her toes through the covers. "It's like I told Bill yesterday. We're on the phone, my brother and me, and Billy Boy says, 'How's that wife of yours?' So I tell him point blank, I says, 'Big brother, I roped me one high-class woman. Woman knows how to do herself up right. Lips like red apples.' That's what I tells him.

'Big red apples,' I say, 'but not them crunchy kind. Ripe and juicy.'"

Ruth felt her stomach flop over. "I believe I'm about to be ill."

"Well, sure, except we're talking pie-type apples."

Ruth blotted her mouth with a tissue. "Henry, forget apples," she said. "And while you're at it, you can forget this sex nonsense, too." She pulled out her jar of liquid base and applied the ointment to her forehead and cheeks, smoothing it out with the tips of her fingers.

Henry kept circling the bed like some ravenous hyena.

"And that face potion, Ruthie, that's the killer. Awful artistic. Awful creative-like." He touched the bedspread, fingered the blankets. "Like I always explain to my barber. 'Jimmy,' I always tell him, 'Jimmy, what you need is an artistic-type wife, like mine. Wife knows how to decorate herself.'" Henry moved toward the head of the bed. His fingers skimmed along the sheets, circling in tighter.

Ruth flinched and closed her eyes. A moment later, when she glanced into her hand mirror, Henry loomed directly behind her, hand on his crotch.

"So I'm in the chair, getting my two-buck shave, and I'm telling old Jimbo how he ain't ever seen the likes of my Ruthie, all fresh in the morning, just putting on that nifty paint job of hers." He was smiling, unbuckling his belt. " 'Pretty as a picture,' I says, 'or like one of them Greek statues, except plenty of ointment all smeared — ' "

"Stop!"

Ruth hurled her makeup bottle at the ceiling. "No more '*ointment*'! No more nothing!"

Henry was fumbling to hold his pants up. "Hey now, Ruthie, you're my lawful wedded wife."

"Laws get repealed."

"Like how?"

"Like this instant."

Henry's eyes wandered off on a brief journey. "But I'm happy. I mean — God, Ruthie — I *need* you."

"Well, fine, you've got me."

"But you said —"

"Just keep your word. No more bedroom antics."

Henry bent down for the makeup bottle. A viscous brown liquid oozed from a crack in the glass. He wiped the bottle on his pants, used the palm of his hand to press the spilled makeup into the carpet, then stood up cautiously and placed the bottle on the bedside table. He murmured something to himself — something that sounded like surrender — then folded his hands and sat down gently beside her.

"Well," he said, "I can *look*, can't I?"

7:07 A.M.

Ruth moved her breakfast tray to the bottom of the bed and reached for her toiletry kit, which she kept on the bedside table near her lamp and pills. She pulled out a jar of facial cleansing cream and rubbed the cream on and off with Kleenex tissue; she hadn't washed with soap and water in more than fifty years. She held up a small, round mirror and tweezed the stragglers from her chin, then used a piece of black emery paper to smooth out the skin. Meticulously, with a piece of cotton, she spread on a brown base — "Indian Face," she called it — which gave her a deeply tanned look even in December. As a final touch, she applied a layer of bright red lipstick. The face took eighteen minutes.

According to Hale's diamond watch, it was now almost seven-thirty.

She swung her knees to the side of the bed, careful not to knock off the tray. With a quick, puffing gasp, she plopped to the floor, one hundred and eight pounds, stepping into her slippers and heading — one hand on the bed for balance — toward her walk-in closet.

No, she thought, the bathroom first. And just in time. She sighed and settled down on the toilet.

Ruth kept her nitroglycerine in a tiny silver locket (souvenir from one of her son Carter's trips to Asia — would he ever have money to travel again?) that hung at the end of a blue silk cord. At night she left the locket in the bathroom, on a small table in front of and almost blocking access to the toilet. She stored the locket there as a reminder to put it on first thing after her morning b.m., and to take it off last thing just before bed. Of course, she also kept a few nitroglycerine pills in the top drawer of her bedside table, in case of nighttime emergency.

Leaning forward, Ruth picked up the locket and gingerly lowered its cord over her head; the pills made a sharp rattling noise that gave her the jitters. She hesitated for a moment, running a finger up and down the long cord, then closed her eyes and arranged the locket on her chest.

Surrender, she thought.

Head of the conservation branch of the U.S. Geological Survey, director of the Oil and Gas Leasing Division, Hale was at the height of his career when the Naval Reserve Board called him out to the Pacific. Nothing grand, not war or diplomacy or the exploding of nuclear bombs, just some ridiculous fossil-fuel study. He'd received his immunization shots and begun making his farewells when he was snatched up by a murderous disease.

Almost instantaneously, as if under the power of some evil spell, he fell apart. He couldn't keep his meals down. In the space of fourteen days he lost twenty pounds and all of his strength, his skin shriveling up like an old man's, downy clumps of hair falling from his head and body. "Something's missing," he kept saying, again and again, as he moved through the house, unable to remember why he'd entered a particular room or where he'd placed his car keys or whether he even owned a car. Soon he stopped trying to remember. He went to bed and simply lay there, dying. Even the best doctors weren't sure what it was. A virus, probably.

Maybe something he'd picked up from the immunization shots; maybe something hereditary.

The day after New Year's, his skin began to burn — he couldn't bear to have Ruth touch his hands or legs — and finally, when his breathing faltered, Ruth drove him to the hospital. The doctors hooked him up to a monstrous-looking machine, administered painkillers, then left the two of them alone in a small, brightly lit room. Ruth sat on the edge of the bed, a hand on Hale's chest as if to help him breathe. He kept asking her to take off his socks, then to put them on again: a man who had always known everything, he no longer even knew if he was hot or cold.

Every so often he pointed vaguely toward the blank white wall in front of him and said, "Something's wrong. Can you move it, please?"

"Move what?"

He waved at the wall. "It's wrong."

"The wall? Honey, I can't move walls."

"Not the *wall*," he said, and seemed to doze off. Then suddenly he tried to sit up. "Move it. Please, there's too much."

"Hale, I don't know what —"

"There," he said, "*look* at it."

"At what?"

"Time! Right there!"

Later he took her hand. She could tell it was hurting him, the touching itself, but he summoned up a weak smile. After a moment he shook his head. "God, all that *time*, Ruthie. I never *saw* such a mess."

"Yes, yes," she said.

"Just time and time."

An hour later his eyelids fluttered.

He breathed once or twice, waved at the wall, then did not breathe again.

Ruth remembered walking into their bedroom that evening. She remembered going to his dresser and pulling out a tie. She remembered wrapping the tie around her neck. She remembered lying face-up on the floor and kissing the tie and pressing it against her face and talking to it and smelling it and examining the incredible vastness of their white bedroom ceiling.

Once, turning her head, she almost strangled herself. Somehow that helped.

Death, she thought, was a baffling adversary. A capricious trickster. Like sorrow or disappointment or betrayal, its advance could not be checked by any ordinary means; sorcery was required. The ability to change the past, perhaps, or to endure the unendurable, or to conjure up a whole new life.

With a cluck of her tongue, Ruth released her grasp on the nitroglycerine locket, finished on the toilet, stood up to wipe herself from front to back, dropped her nightgown over her bare bottom, and told herself to stop dawdling. At her age, if you weren't careful, you could most definitely poop the rest of your life away.

7:59 A.M.

Moving briskly, Ruth went into her closet and picked out one of the several outfits she kept on separate hangers. She liked to prepare entire combinations in advance — pants, blouse, sweater, and belt, for example — an orderly bit of forethought that saved her time and exasperation. Today she chose her white-pants ensemble, the white pants with the seams down the front, which went so nicely with the pink lace-collared blouse and the blue pullover vest. The outfit would be ideal for dinner with Luzma, she thought. Plenty of color. Perfect for the Spanish eye.

She lay the clothes over the back of the big chair next to the TV, pulled her nightgown off over her head — the cord of the silver locket twisting uncomfortably around the folds of her neck for an instant — and then put on her camisole, panty girdle, garters, and nylons, which she'd left on the cushion of the chair the night before. Balancing in her underclothes, left hand on the back of the chair, Ruth looked down at Hale's watch.

Five past eight. In a hurry now, she fumbled with the hanger of clothes and managed to struggle into the pants, blouse, and blue knit vest in just under ten minutes. She fetched her best pair of white sandals (they'd lasted ten years) from their place on the closet floor, sat in the chair to strap them on, headed back into the bathroom.

She glanced at herself in the mirror on the medicine cabinet, took her comb and bobby pins from the top left drawer beneath the sink, and started in on her curls. In years past she'd pulled them straight back with a barrette to show off a strong forehead, but the new hairdresser had given her these shorter ringlets, and she struggled with the bobby pins now, to clamp them into place.

Her hair was so white it almost glistened.

"Sure to be a beauty when you grow up, honey, a real heart-breaker," Auntie Elizabeth had said on one of their innumerable shopping excursions — 1914, was it? — as Ruth stood in the corner of a dressing room at Hinkley's, watching her aunt try on a series of outlandish hats. "You'll find yourself some wonderful fellow, that's a sure deal, too. Just make sure he's got class, like my man."

Ruth frowned into the mirror. "What'd you say his name was?"

"Chahhl-ton," Elizabeth said, in the funny voice she used when she talked about her fiancé. "Chahhl-ton P. Hahhll, and your ahhn-tie is going to marry him and move to Los Ahhn-geles." Elizabeth placed an exotic silk bonnet on her head, stuck her nose high into the air, curtsied for the mirror. Then she fluffed her pink taffeta skirt and spun around in a graceful circle, sequins glittering from her neck and sleeves. To Ruth, at seven years old, Aunt Elizabeth seemed the most glamorous creature on earth.

Ruth slumped. Without her aunt, she thought, life would be so boring. No more trips to the opera house to hear Elizabeth rehearse; no more late nights in Elizabeth's room, listening to gossip; no more of these weekend shopping excursions or walks down to the marina for ice cream, just the two of them.

For a few seconds Ruth felt herself drifting, just bobbing along, carried like a cork on the flow of memory. Then she began to brush her teeth. "But if you marry him," she said, voice garbled by toothpaste, "you won't live with us anymore."

Elizabeth stopped spinning and turned to face her. "I certainly will *not*," she said, lapsing into her normal voice. "I'm not about to sit around that dark, flat old ranch house all my life, your grandpa telling me what to do all the time. Honestly, if I have to spend one more day looking at his stupid sawed-off arm, I'll go absolutely insane." She hung the bonnet on a hook, pulled on a small satin cap, looked into the mirror. "Anyway, please don't start pouting. You're supposed to be happy for me."

"Naturally," Ruth said, almost to herself. She peered straight into the mirror and tried to force a smile. Few other girls her age had such beautiful teeth.

Elizabeth straightened the cap, frowned, and shook her head. Then she grinned. "Now watch me," she said, her eyes glowing. "Who am I?" She tucked one arm behind her back, so it looked like it was missing, and brought her free hand to her forehead in a stiff salute. "Always remember your origins, young lady, and be prudent," she said in a low, growling voice. "Gettysburg. Massachusetts Second. Two days lying on the battlefield, arm shot up and not a soul around to give aid or succor . . ."

Ruth swallowed hard, frightened but in love with her aunt's daring — *nobody* was supposed to make fun of her grandfather.

"Not a soul around to dress my wound, young lady, and no one to weep for me." Elizabeth puffed up her chest and strutted back and forth, pounding her heels into the carpet. "The vultures were circling and I was wailing and praying and sure I was a goner —"

"Until you fainted and those bugs ate out the poison," Ruth said, beginning to giggle.

"Maggots, child," Elizabeth said in her deep voice. "Those

were maggots, and don't forget it. Maggots saved your grandpa's life, maggots let him keep fighting to save this great country of ours, maggots made possible your very presence on this earth."

Ruth laughed and took a step toward her aunt. She'd heard those same words a thousand times.

Elizabeth dropped her arms and became herself again. "The way he talks, you'd think those damn bugs were God's own hand-maidens. So self-righteous! And treats your mother just like a slave, ever since your grandma died — expecting her to do every little thing for him *and* your daddy. Which is another matter, why your mother ever got married so young in the first place. Right after we moved out here. Who would've guessed it back in Massachusetts, precious little Lydia married to that hardscrabble bore?" Elizabeth coughed and glanced away for a moment, as if she'd realized her words were scandalous.

Ruth studied the carpet, digging at it with the toe of her patent leather shoe, embarrassed but intrigued, aware that her aunt was being wicked, hoping she would go on.

"All I mean is, your mother's always so sensible and thrifty, always so *perfect*, but she never even gave herself a chance to really live." Elizabeth pulled off the satin cap and lay a handkerchief on her head so it hung down over her eyes. She folded her hands and bent her head. "And I made this hat with my very own pin money," she said in a soft, self-deprecating voice, Lydia's voice.

Ruth remained still.

"And your daddy, he's even worse." Elizabeth slid the handkerchief off her head and tucked it into her collar like a tie. "All his talk about respectable life and a person's duties. But I'll tell you a secret. He himself deserted his poor mother and sister back in St. Paul, Minnesota, and that's a fact." She put a hand on her chest and, pretending to wheeze and cough, turned to face herself in the mirror. "Rode the train out here all by myself," she said in her husky Daddy voice. "Only fourteen years old and full of tuberculosis, but found myself a steady job. Hardest work there is, being a teamster. But I scrimped and sweated and nearly broke my back until I'd saved enough money to deserve sweet little Lydia here."

Curtsying for the mirror and batting her eyelashes, Elizabeth pulled the handkerchief from her collar and held it above her head, becoming Ruth's mother again. "Oh, Walter," she said in her soft voice, "it truly wasn't your money that won me. It was your charm! Why, from the very first time you spoke to me, I knew you were the acceptable family type."

Elizabeth dropped her arm and began folding the handkerchief into a neat square. "You ask me, your daddy looks like some scrawny chicken. No different from all these other fellows with tuberculosis — you know the ones — filling up the whole city like it's a giant sanatorium."

Elizabeth straightened her dress, checked her makeup, reached for the silk bonnet and positioned it on her head. "Come along," she said. "I'll buy this one."

Ruth wasn't sure *what* to think. She'd never heard anybody criticize her parents like this, not even Elizabeth. She asked the only question she could think of. "You think Daddy's a *chicken?*"

Elizabeth rolled her eyes and, taking Ruth's hand, led her out of the dressing rooms. "I suppose I shouldn't have talked that way about your mother and father," she said. "All I mean is, for me it's got to be the real thing. I need excitement. You know, *passion*. Spotlights! Orchestras! Romance with a capital R. Extravagance and undying love and all that. Not this boring, comfortable, workaday-type thing. My God, I'd rather have nothing."

Worse than nothing, she'd gotten in the end. The affair with Charlton had ended in disaster.

Ruth shook her head gravely.

It was her sober parents, of course, and not her reckless aunt and the sophisticated Mr. Hall, who had made it to the end of their days together.

Pensively, even somberly, Ruth replaced her toothbrush in its cup and began to examine herself from head to toe, a preening habit she'd inherited from Auntie Elizabeth. She turned her back to the medicine cabinet and held up a hand mirror to see how she must appear to others from behind; she studied her bottom in the mirrors — sagging but not fat; she plucked off a few gray hairs that had fallen to her shoulders. Then she turned for a profile, lifting her nose high into the air and glancing to her left, into the mirror. What she saw was a bit of mucus, firm and greeny gray, dangling there like a filthy old barnacle.

The human body, she thought. Always ready with a disgusting little surprise.

Glad she was alone, Ruth reached for a Kleenex.

8:19 A.M.

Ruth had practiced the piano almost every day, sometimes twice a day, since the year she turned eight. Now she hurried to complete her morning agenda so as to get in at least a few minutes of practice before the next Laguna bus came, at ten past nine.

She went to the bed and rolled up her sleeping bag, tight as she could. She stuffed the sleeping bag into a plastic sack, tied the sack with a piece of yellowed yarn, and carefully balanced the finished bundle on the space heater next to her TV. She returned the sit-up pillow to its place on the floor and pulled up the bedspread. Then, humming quietly to herself, she started down to the second floor. She used the stairs, not the elevator; she almost always climbed from floor to floor by foot, and believed this policy to be in part responsible for that string of eighty-eight birthdays.

The piano was positioned diagonally across from the couch in the room adjacent to the kitchen and dining area, just three feet from the sliding door that led out to the balcony. It was the same parlor grand that had been in Ruth's family for well over a hundred years, the same piano upon which her mother had improvised dramatic background for those marvelous magic-lantern shows. Ruth sat down on the bench, brought her hands to the keyboard, and began to play. She played loudly. Good, hard, straightforward technique. Though she made mistakes here and there, the trick was to keep banging away and not waste energy fretting about things that couldn't be changed. Like life itself. Mistakes were part of the music.

For some time Ruth lost herself in the Sonata Pathétique, eyes closed, lips tight, and it wasn't until she'd entered the second movement that she became aware of a loud, rhythmic knocking against the wall.

Her glasses slipped down her nose, then dropped to the left of the piano bench; a ribbon of dazzling white specks floated across the room.

"Too early, Ruth! The weekend!"

The voice came echoing through the wall she shared with 23. The knocking sounds continued.

Oh brother, Ruth thought. Hassan didn't intend to be rude, she knew; the man liked to hear her play and he didn't mind mistakes. But she wished he would just listen quietly. His pounding was distracting, and had now made her very dizzy.

She groped for her glasses, pushed them up onto her nose, then sat still for a moment, collecting herself. Those bright specks were still twinkling around the room like a million tiny lamps.

The knocking on the wall of 23 was always loudest when she played especially well. It had started long before Hassan moved in, when the previous owner of the place — who had died mysteriously — decided to haunt her.

In life he had been a friendly man, if somewhat reserved, in his mid-fifties with three cats and an ugly German shepherd that he walked four times a day. Ruth had thought him quite a gentleman. He kept his dog under strict control when he walked it, never letting it off the leash no matter how much it yapped and bucked, and only allowing it to defecate in Doggie Canyon — a sandy, bush-surrounded area just behind the community trash dump. In any case, one evening the poor man in 23 led his shepherd down to the Canyon and never came back. The next morning, just after sunrise, a neighbor came across him in one of the bushes along the edge of the Canyon, shot in the head. The dog had vanished. No weapon was ever found, no suspects apprehended.

Ruth secretly suspected the White Rabbit, as the incident had occurred on or very near the first day of October. Or had it been September?

Whatever the truth, it was almost immediately after this incident that the knocking began in Ruth's wall. It happened only during her sessions at the piano, and it became loudest when she played well. For a long while no one wanted to move into number 23. Which made Ruth uneasy — no one living next door and the wall knocking like that.

Finally, in the twentieth year of marriage to Henry, her sixth year with him at the Lagoon, Hassan had arrived. He was new to the country from Iran, and had come to Paradise Lagoon in search of a beachfront property. But in the end he chose number 23, even though it was two blocks up the hill from the ocean, mainly because the unit came with a custom elevator. It was, in fact, the only place aside from Ruth's that had one.

Hassan paid cash for 23. He was not superstitious. Maybe in Iran, Ruth sometimes mused, *all* the houses were filled with mysterious knockings.

Ruth sat still, hands folded in her lap, gazing at the keyboard. All those separate little notes, black and white, interlacing and blending to make up eight octaves. Or was it fewer than eight? She squinted down, counting. And then suddenly, as if struck by a hammer, Ruth again felt the hard, abrupt shock of sadness, almost overwhelming this time. Eighty-eight years old.

"Don't," she murmured. Then she shook her head. "Keep playing, just don't give in. Fight the bad with the good." But her quavering voice belied all clichés of positive thinking.

She lifted her hands into position, her right thumb above middle C. Slowly, she began to play. The white skin on the back of her hands looked like wrinkled tissue paper. Beneath the skin, thick cords of blue vein seemed to strangle the tiny bones. Her fingers felt dull and dry, like little twigs: however hard they might work, they could never reproduce the sweet sounds of her youth.

Still, there was that peculiar, almost audible sadness all around her, but a moment later it was broken by the sound of the door-bell.

Irritated, interrupted for the second time in one session, Ruth slammed down the fallboard. Why, she wondered, were people forever intruding on her peace? Impossible to finish even fifteen minutes of serious practice. She pushed herself up and marched downstairs to what she called The Room. The Room, which had to be traversed in order to get to the front door, or even to the small bathroom beside the front door, held a tattered guest bed and couch, a TV, a washing machine and dryer, and several old wall calendars. Ruth passed through all of this to the front door, which she opened. She blinked against the sun — the morning was already bright.

Kaji stood before her in a white bathrobe. The robe was tied loosely, and patches of the woman's bikini poked out.

"Nice sexy swim?" Ruth asked.

Kaji blushed. "My husband sent me," she said. Kaji was only recently arrived, new to the liberated ways of the West. Small clots of mascara clung to the tips of her eyelashes; her dark eyes glittered with a moist concern. Her long black hair was tousled. "Hassan says if Mrs. Ruth so awake and noisy, does she want to come decorate the Christmas tree?"

Ruth crossed her arms. Like hell, she thought. She knew Kaji had really come over to make sure she was still alive. No doubt Kaji and Hassan had become worried when the music stopped so abruptly.

"And does Mr. Henry want to come?" Kaji asked. "Children want Maman Bozorg to help put on the tinsel. We got the rain kind."

("Maman Bozorg" meant Grandmother. It was supposed to be flattering, Ruth knew, never mind that it sounded God-awful.)

Ruth shook her head. "I'm afraid Henry's over at the Alpha Beta," she said, "and I have to go downtown. Life isn't all tinsel and sex swims, you know." She took hold of the girl's bathrobe belt. "Come in here a minute, I'll show you something."

Ruth led the girl into the bathroom. "Since you're all dressed up for the nudist colony," she said, "you might be interested in what the beach looked like when I was your age, even younger than you." She pointed to the photographs that covered every wall of the bathroom and surrounded the toilet down to its base.

Kaji blinked at the arrangement.

"Now, you see, we used to summer at the beach in San Diego," Ruth went on. "Of course my first husband —"

"Yes? I summer at beach, too." Kaji tested a short smile. "I winter at pool."

Indeed. Ruth had seen her there, lying for hours on a tinfoil mat, with little plastic cups over her eyes and cotton balls between her toes. The pool lay only a hundred yards from the window above Ruth's dining table. It was surrounded by glass panels and approached by way of an iron gate, which Ruth passed on her daily afternoon walks. Sometimes, feeling curious, she'd stop and peer in through the gate, but she rarely entered for fear she might end up locked inside.

"You like to go to the pool in December?" Ruth asked.

"Yes."

"And you don't find it a bit . . . a bit chilly?"

"No. Very nice."

Well fine.

Ruth nodded and adjusted her glasses. "Suit yourself," she said. "But look, dear, these pictures were taken ages ago, before you were even born in Iran, before you ever saw a pool in your life." Ruth gestured at a photographic collage above the toilet.

Kaji blinked several times, slowly. "We had good pool in Iran," she said. "Good big pool."

"Yes, but look closely. Things used to be so splendid, so civilized here in California. We lived in houses with names, not numbers. There were still cesspools, but there wasn't any smog. We had gas meters for the lights, not electricity, and we used to have to put quarters in them. And look here — I'll show you a secret."

Ruth took down one of the more recent photographs, less than fifty years old, that hung above the sink. "A picture of good old Frank Deeds," she said. "And look at this." She turned the frame and slid out the cardboard mounting. She stripped away a piece of tape from the back of Frank's picture.

Kaji tightened and retied her bathrobe belt. "What you have there, Mrs. Ruthie?"

"Just wait a minute."

"It looks like —"

"Patience, young lady. Keep your pants on."

Ruth peeled off a pocket-sized snapshot, which the tape had been holding to the back of Frank's portrait. She handed it to Kaji. It was a picture of Ruth, sitting on a rock by the ocean, her toes buried in white sand. "I was forty-five then," Ruth explained. "Hale had died, you know, and I was visiting my aunt in San Diego. Frank took this picture. He'd moved there long before I ever returned, after he was divorced. Read the back."

Kaji turned the picture over, squinting to read the faded writing. "'You will — always be close — to my dart,'" she read.

"No, that says *heart*. 'You will always be close to my heart.'"

"No, it says 'dart.'"

"It most definitely does *not*," Ruth insisted. "Look here, I should know, it's addressed to me."

"Oh. But that man is not Henry."

"He certainly isn't! This is a man who loved me, and wanted to marry me after Hale died. He used to carry this picture in the pocket of his shirt — so I'd always be close to his heart, understand? That's what he'd always say, those exact words."

Kaji looked confused. "But that man is not Henry."

"That's what I'm *telling* you. This man is *Frank*, and he was very well known, very successful, and he was in love with me. For a while I thought I might love him, too." Ruth cleared her throat, handed Kaji the portrait of Frank. "But then I realized it would never work."

"Oh, Mrs. Ruth," Kaji said, gazing sadly at Frank's face. "I feel so sorry. He was old? He was sick or something?"

"Not that. *That* worked just fine. Too fine, in fact, which is exactly the point."

"The point?"

"I couldn't trust him. The man had this very — you know — this terrible squirmy wormy."

"Wormy?"

"*You* know."

Kaji still seemed confused. She studied both sides of Frank's portrait, then held it up to the light and looked at it from every angle.

Exasperated, Ruth put her hands on her hips. "I didn't think I could *count* on him."

"Oh!" Kaji said, smiling and nodding.

Ruth suddenly felt exhausted. "I'll explain it to you another day," she said. "Maybe when Hassan's not waiting. He probably thinks I've kidnapped you. Anyway, you need to go put that rain on your tree. And *I* need to go to the bathroom."

"Sure, Mrs. Ruthie," Kaji said. "Maybe I see you later, at the pool? You're okay — you feel okay?"

"Just wonderful," said Ruth. "Hardly a day over eighty."

Kaji nodded again, began to turn away, then stopped and turned back. Her bathrobe had come undone to expose a pair of slim brown legs, tufts of crinkly black hair poking out from under the elastic of her bikini bottom.

"That man Frank, he your big love-love?"

"I should say not."

"Mr. Henry then?"

"Now you're getting ridiculous," Ruth said. "I've told you several times, my first husband, Hale —"

"But I thought he was very dead? A long time dead."

"What possible difference should that make?"

Kaji made a motion with her shoulders. "Well, big difference. No love, a woman shrink like dust and blow away. Hassan tells me that many, many times. Woman needs always a big love-love. A live one, Mrs. Ruthie."

"Hale was *extremely* alive."

"Not now. He is extremely not alive now."

There was a pause before Ruth's tongue caught up with her thoughts.

"My dear Kaji," she said crisply, "Hale gave me all the 'love-love' I shall ever require. Now, please, tuck in your hairs."

8:51 A.M.

Alone in the bathroom, Ruth smiled to herself: at her age, with a weak bladder, the call of nature always made a good excuse to slip away from people. The truth, of course, was that she simply wanted a little quiet time and privacy, and this tiny bathroom was her favorite refuge. She stepped over to the sink. Carefully, her hand shaking slightly, she secured the snapshot of herself to the back of Frank's portrait, returned them both to their proper position on the wall. Then she gazed at the surrounding gallery of photographs, running her finger across the top of each frame, as if to make physical contact with those early years in Southern California. Los Angeles had been *the* place then. She and her parents had moved there from San Diego, her mother shipping their things on the *Santa Maria*, to escape public embarrassment after Aunt Elizabeth's misfortune.

They moved into the Wilshire District, though there was not yet a Wilshire Boulevard, and they saw Hollywood people —

Charlie Chaplin, Mary Pickford — though there was not yet a Hollywood. It was only a neighborhood then, and the famed Hollywood sign was merely the marker for an enormous real estate development, Hollywoodland.

They cut out the "land" a few years later.

Ruth finished eighth grade at Virgil Intermediate, then entered the new Los Angeles High; hers would be among the first classes to graduate from that school, in 1924.

Now Ruth glanced at her finger. It was covered with dust. She sighed and bent over the sink and began to soap up her hands. *Some* people, she remembered, had not graduated. Certain incompetents. Certain mental indigents. It was at Los Angeles High that she'd first put eyes on Henry Hubble.

Chemistry class, sophomore year: even without a picture on the wall, she could still see it clearly. The whole class standing at their lab tables as Mr. Purdick outlined the day's experiment on the blackboard. "Nothing to it," he was saying, "but if there's a question, just raise your hand. And be careful with those burners." Right then, Ruth heard a curious whimpering behind her. A skinny red-headed boy was hopping up and down, hand in the air, a light, squeaky voice yelling, "Teacher!"

Mr. Purdick did not seem to hear.

"Teacher, sir! Question — over here!" The boy's fingers were wiggling. He was hopping from one foot to the other. "Mr. Teacher!"

Mr. Purdick still took no notice. He kept his back turned, erasing the blackboard.

"Right here, sir!" The boy was squealing and hopping and waving a hand. "Question! A nice one!" He dropped his arm and lit a match and turned his burner up high as it would go. "A pretty good question! Teacher! A real good smart one!"

Mr. Purdick turned slowly. "Any questions?"

"Me!" the boy screamed.

"Henry?"

The boy's face went blank. He looked at the ceiling and

moaned and then, with an angry, fumbling gesture, swept his test tubes to the floor.

"Crap," he muttered, "I *forgot*."

Ruth stared down at the shattered glass. She examined the boy's yellow socks, his scuffed-up shoes, his brown corduroys. The trousers were cinched above his navel, held tight by a worn leather belt; his shirt was filthy; his face was pale and damp and freckled.

Genuinely pitiful.

"Well, it *was* good," he said. "It was a *real* good question."

A week later Henry Hubble dropped out of school. His excuse was Spanish influenza, but in truth the disease was much grander: colossal stupidity. Now and then, over the next two years, Ruth bumped into him in peculiar places — a tomato stand, a horse auction — but after she started college, they did not meet again for some thirty-five years.

Shaking a few drops of water from her fingers, Ruth turned to dry her hands. There she was at her high school graduation, in the photograph above the towel rack. She stood in the middle of the second row. She was impossibly young, and pretty, and smiling.

9:00 A.M.

It was exactly nine o'clock when she stepped out the front door.

Another fickle Laguna morning. Still hazy — the fog had not quite lifted — but bright enough to make you squint. Ruth reached into her purse, pulled out her clip-on sun lenses, and snapped them into place over her glasses.

She paused for a moment on the front steps. Then she lifted the tip of her cane, took aim at a yellow fire hydrant across the cement courtyard, and set off with a determined stride. She felt solid. Eighty-eight years old, yet still independent, still taking care of her own daily business. She moved her cane forward and back, forward and back, her umbrella swinging gently from its strap on her left wrist. When she reached the fire hydrant, she again lifted the tip of her cane and, squinting ahead toward a sprinkler at the start of the path between the tennis court and pool, marched off fiercely.

Her lungs were aching by the time she reached the Lagoon gates, at the top of a short hill. She took a quick breather, stooping to examine a small bush that Rodrigo had molded into the shape of a dog. Rodrigo was the groundskeeper, and this was his hobby: like a gardener at Disneyland, he was steadily transforming all the bushes in Paradise Lagoon into animals of different types and sizes. This particular dog, standing guard just inside the gates, had perked-up ears and a full green tail. Its body was mostly bare wire — the bush was young and hadn't yet filled out — and as she studied it this morning, leaning on the cane, Ruth felt rather queasy. Like some weird doggie autopsy. That exposed chest cavity, the various organs and blood vessels. Quickly, eyes averted, she walked past the dog to the Pedestrian Passage.

No sooner had she stuck her Auto-Mate gate card into its slot, opened the Passage, and walked outside the Lagoon, than the bus pulled up. She flashed her senior card, climbed on board, and glanced around for a seat.

9:11 A.M.

The bus was almost full. Most of the passengers had hair as gray as her own, except for a young, pleasant-looking man sitting toward the back, wearing a Stetson. There was a space beside him, and Ruth moved down the aisle to fill it.

The driver started up and they were on their way downtown, past row upon row of Lego houses in the hills. Ruth took careful stock of her surroundings. The hills, which were usually brown, had a touch of green on them now, as sometimes happened with even a little winter rain. Most of the trees along the highway still had their leaves. The bus rolled past four Italian restaurants, two video rental outlets, three or four frozen-yogurt shops, a good half-dozen real estate offices. Ruth flipped up her sunglass lenses and turned toward the gentleman beside her.

"Well, good morning," she said. "Pleased to meet you."

The man spat on the floor of the bus and smiled. A brown plug of tobacco pressed up against his lower lip.

"Enchanted," Ruth said.

She moved her feet out toward the aisle, protecting her good white sandals, then lifted her gaze to the window. Something terrible had happened here in Southern California. In her childhood, and during the Washington years when she'd returned with Hale for summer vacations, and even later when she'd first moved back, alone, to stay, people did not spit at your shoes. Things were civilized then. No pizza joints, no trash in the streets. And not all of these tract houses, every fifth one alike.

The man hacked a few times and spat again. The woman to Ruth's right, across the aisle, at least as old as she, was busy fishing through her shopping bags. The bags seemed to contain all of the lady's worldly possessions, from an evening gown to kitchen supplies to a giant Random House dictionary. The woman was dressed for subzero temperatures, in frayed woolen pants and a long tweed coat.

Ruth smiled at her. "Moving here to Laguna, dear?" she asked. "A little overcrowded, I'm afraid, but I think you might find it interesting."

The woman looked up from the orange she was peeling, her eyes blank, and smiled without opening her lips. Her fingernails were yellow — from the orange, maybe, or from some mysterious illness — and her fingers were red and chapped. She looked back down at her orange.

"Well," Ruth said, "enjoy your stay."

She pulled a strawberry Twizzler from her purse. She thought of her own great-grandfather, her father Walt's grandfather, who had lived in the same house in Geneva, Illinois, for one hundred and two years, dying in the same bed in which he'd been born. This poor old lady moves around too much, Ruth thought. She sent a smile in the woman's direction, tried to shape her face into a welcome.

Her jaw popped audibly, as it did so often now, which was maddening. She opened and closed her mouth, listening to the pops. It didn't hurt, but it was annoying. She wondered if anyone else could hear it.

For a time the bus rolled along Coast Highway. Things were quiet except for the drunk man up front, who rode the little Laguna bus all day, every day. Ruth had seen him at least a dozen times over the past month. Today he was complaining about someone who had apparently cheated him, swearing violently, gesturing at the air. The man beside Ruth rustled his morning paper; Ruth turned to see what he was reading.

CANYON KILLER APPREHENDED, read the headline in bold black. From beneath the bold print, a pale man with small, pointed ears stared out at Ruth. The face looked strangely familiar. She'd heard talk of him before, how he'd gone on a rampage through Canyon Homes, in the hills outside Laguna. He'd killed four men, the *Sun Times* said, with a sawed-off shotgun. She peered closely at the picture until her neighbor cleared his throat.

"Terrible," he said.

Ruth pointed at the photograph. "That maniac — he reminds me of a man I used to know."

The man laughed. "Yeah, well. Don't we all."

Ruth ignored him. "My Uncle Stephen, I mean. The same pointy ears. Of course, Stephen committed only *one* murder."

The man gave her an odd look. "What a pity."

"But not with a shotgun, of course."

"Of course not."

"A revolver."

"Revolver. Right, what else."

Turning uncomfortably, the man shifted his weight away from Ruth. For a half block they rode along in silence.

"Anyway," Ruth said, "in Uncle Stephen's case it wasn't really murder, if you know what I mean. Nothing in cold blood, like our friend here."

"Lady, listen —"

"Certainly *not* murder," Ruth said firmly. "They *called* it that, but . . . I suppose now you'll want to hear the whole unfortunate story."

The man sighed and folded his newspaper. "I suppose so," he said dismally. "But start at the start. Who the hell's this Uncle Stephen?"

Ruth rearranged herself in the seat. People sometimes baffled her. The way they kept intruding on her privacy.

In a crisp, no-nonsense voice, sticking to the essential facts, she explained that Stephen had been the second important gentleman in Auntie Elizabeth's life. "What you have to understand," she said, "is that Elizabeth was a talented, gorgeous young woman. A voice like a bird. Back when we all lived with my grandfather in San Diego — Jonathan Huntley, that was his name — back then, Elizabeth was singing with the San Carlos Opera. I used to go and listen to her rehearse. A soprano, you know."

"Yeah," the man said. "Really."

"Yes, *really*. Do I give the appearance of a common liar?"

The man yawned.

"So it should go without saying," Ruth said, "that Elizabeth had the whole world at her command. That beautiful, beautiful voice. And a lovely figure, too — elegant legs — I suppose that part runs in our family." Ruth glanced at the man. "Her prospects, as we used to say, were unlimited. But then she met her *first* man, Mr. Charlton P. Hall, which started the whole terrible downfall."

Beside her, the man pulled his Stetson down over his eyes. Ruth nudged him with her elbow, hard, but he seemed to have lapsed into a coma.

No matter, she thought.

With a cluck of her tongue, she continued with the story, talking past her neighbor to the bus window and the passing storefronts and the vast Pacific Ocean.

Charlton P. Hall. Dapper and handsome, one of San Diego's leading lawyers. A typical sweet-talking attorney-at-law. Yes, and poor Aunt Elizabeth was doomed from the instant they glanced at each other across the aisle of the First Presbyterian Church. A short, familiar tale: after the service they had iced tea together, and that same night he kissed her on the lips, not to mention elsewhere. (Lots of elsewheres, Ruth knew, but this part of the story she did not feel it proper to tell.) For weeks afterward, Elizabeth and Charlton were seen together at the theater and at parties and on the sidewalks of San Diego, strolling arm in arm, in a rapture so sublime that passing strangers stopped to smile. In the evenings, as they walked along the marina, they played a little game called What If.

"What if I told you I wanted to sing in Vienna?" Elizabeth would start.

"Well, yes, but what if I could not afford to send you?"

Elizabeth would think for a moment. "In that case, what if I found a magic lamp that turned grass into money?"

"But what if I could not use the magic, because . . ."

The possibilities were inexhaustible and the game could go on forever. So Charlton invented a rule by which the process always had to lead to the same final question: "What if I asked you to marry me?" he'd ask.

"And what if I said yes?" she'd answer.

When the wedding was only a month off, Charlton moved his practice north to Los Angeles. All the up-and-comers were headed there, and it seemed just the place to raise a family. Elizabeth stayed on in San Diego, making wedding plans, bragging to everyone, preparing for the happy life that was to be hers.

Then a telegram arrived: "What if I told you we could not be married?"

Ruth made a sharp snuffling noise.

"Boob," she muttered.

Handsome or not, men were hopeless. Hale excepted, all they ever wanted was to get their paws on all the elsewheres.

The bus had entered traffic. Ruth settled back with a heavy sigh. "Well, naturally," she said, "poor Elizabeth was crushed."

Crushed, yes, because with that telegram Mr. Charlton P. Hall simply vanished. Elizabeth stopped singing, stopped sleeping, stopped eating. For many weeks there were serious questions about her sanity. But then a piece of fortune intervened — an accident, really. A small advertisement in the *San Diego Telegraph*: SINGERS WANTED FOR REVIVAL GROUP. YOU BRING THE VOICE, WE HAVE THE STAGE. The next morning, as eight-year-old Ruth watched, Elizabeth packed her suitcases.

Of course Ruth's grandfather, old Jonathan Huntley, raised all sorts of objections — even made a few outright threats — but twelve days later Elizabeth was in Clayville, Rhode Island, decked out in a black robe and a yellow sash, singing "Rock of Ages" and "The Old Rugged Cross" for a traveling religion show. She'd found the Lord. She'd also found Uncle Stephen.

Stephen MacLeod: King of the Boobs.

A preacher, of all things. A fire-and-brimstone bozo. With his squeaky voice and pointy little ears, but with an eloquence far beyond his twenty-three years, Stephen was already famous on the tent circuit for his frenzied two-hour sermons. Women had visions. Men actually prayed. Elizabeth fell in love.

Clearly, the man was mad, or on the edge of madness, but it was partly this that intrigued her. She loved the way Stephen waved his arms before the big crowds, the way he sometimes stiffened and jerked up and down and shrieked at the sky, the way he'd collapse after his spasms of boil-in-hell sermonizing. Over the course of that summer, as the show traveled up and down the eastern seaboard, Stephen's behavior turned increasingly peculiar. On stage he'd sometimes fall dead silent, peering off into space as if transported to some other world. Other times he'd be struck by quick, violent seizures. In the middle of a homily, for example, he might suddenly throw back his arms and begin howling — loud animal howling — then he'd lurch forward and whisper "Dear Jesus!" and savagely thump his head against the pulpit. Acute dipsomania, a couple of the singers warned her; once, just before a camp meeting, they'd found him skulking behind the outhouse, stealing furtive swallows from a thin silver flask. Brain-damaged, others claimed; as a child, they hypothesized, he must have suffered a terrible kick to the head. All of which only piqued Elizabeth's interest: she believed she could win power over him, that she could save him, that under her tender care he would soon recover his senses.

One hot afternoon in Trenton, New Jersey, she saw her chance and instantly grabbed it. Another on-stage seizure. More howling and dribbling and sputtering. But this time, without a second thought, Elizabeth took Stephen firmly by the arm, led him to his tent, clamped an icebag to his forehead, knelt down beside him, and ran a finger across his frothy lips.

Years later, Ruth would hear the intimate details from Elizabeth herself. How Uncle Stephen gazed straight ahead like a blind man. How Elizabeth placed one hand over his eyes and the other upon her own belly, which was round and swollen with the child of Charlton P. Hall.

How she was silent for a time, planning her strategy.

"What if I were to tell you," she said, "that I can end this suffering in an instant? That I can save you, bring you serenity and joy and lasting peace? That I can make miracles happen?"

Stephen squirmed. "You're a witch?"

Elizabeth smiled at this. "Oh, yes."

"You mean —"

"First, a child. A successor, to carry on your work and great name. I do believe, Stephen" — she paused for just an instant — "I believe, in fact, that I'm destined to bring you some prodigious delight."

Lifting a weak arm, Stephen grasped Elizabeth's buttocks.

"You have to *believe*, though," she said, submitting to the pressure of his fingers, even gyrating slightly at the waist. "Keep them closed, now," she said, removing her hand from his eyes, untying her yellow sash. "Don't peek."

"Like this?"

"Tighter. You're peeking."

So Stephen shut his eyes, tight, and Elizabeth wound her sash around his wrists, binding them together above his head. "After the child," she whispered, "nothing but rest and endless pleasure." She lifted her black robe. "Holy pleasure, you understand, nothing crass or unlawful. I'd be a mother, after all." She hesitated and said, "Your wife."

Stephen was quiet for a moment. He mumbled a few prayers and then grunted. "Yes, a wife, go ahead."

"A legally binding marriage," she said, to make sure he'd understood.

"Of course," he said. "On with your magic."

9:29 A.M.

Ruth snorted. Witch, for crying out loud. Pure trickery, nothing else, but Uncle Stephen remained a believer for years to come. Right up until the day of the murder.

The bus made a sudden stop, then turned onto Glenneyre Avenue. The man in the Stetson was still comatose beside her, lips ajar, snoring away. She had a good mind to shove a cork down his throat.

For several minutes Ruth sat rocking amid her memories. "Witch!" she muttered, then a block later she chuckled and said, "On the other hand, though, it landed her a father for the child. But not for long." Elizabeth and Stephen were married immediately. They gave up the revivals and moved back to San Diego, to live with Ruth and her parents and old Jonathan Huntley.

Elizabeth was no longer so arrogant and carefree as she'd been in her younger days, but she claimed she was happy — glad to have found a good man of God, she said. Within little over two years, Stephen's seizures seemed to disappear and he took on a small local ministry. Elizabeth had two lovely babies, Margaret and McGregor.

"So, yes," Ruth explained to the bus window, "they made a fine, respectable couple, and for all I know Elizabeth *was* in fact a witch — who really understands these things? — but eventually her spell was shattered in the most terrible way." Ruth wagged her head sadly. "That's how it happens. Spells come, spells go."

Leaning toward the man beside her, rocking with the movement of the bus, Ruth found herself slipping back to that disastrous evening in the winter of 1918. A quiet evening, actually, until Uncle Stephen came crashing through the front door, grunting like an animal and shouting hysterically. Ruth was in her bedroom at the time, getting ready for sleep, yet even now, all these years later, she could hear the sudden commotion in the kitchen — things slamming, Stephen's voice bouncing against the walls and floorboards. The words were mostly indistinct. Something about betrayal, something about trickery and revenge. "I'll *show* her," he'd yelled, then again his voice went blurry, and then a moment later he shouted, "Don't tell *me* to be calm! I am not drunk! And I'm not imagining *anything!* I'll show her what the Lord has in store for people who . . ." And then came a thumping noise, as if a brick had fallen, and then the measured sound of Jonathan Huntley's voice as he tried to calm the man down. Again, most of it was lost now; just bits and pieces — "Yes, but the child is still yours in all the ways that matter" — "Of course it is" — "Been drinking!" — "Don't be an idiot, that musket's been around since Gettysburg." A high laugh echoed down the hall. There was a muffled shout, then the clatter of dishes breaking. Ruth remembered hurrying from her room; she'd almost reached the kitchen when a single shot rang out. She paused, frightened and confused, then pushed open the door. Jonathan Huntley lay curled on the kitchen floor, blood gushing from his mouth and from his one good arm — the only arm he'd carried off the field at Gettysburg. Stephen sat slumped beside him, crying and praying, whispering, "Lord, our Lord."

Ruth remembered standing very still in the doorway. It seemed an eternity before her mother and father and Elizabeth came up behind her. Lydia screamed when she entered the kitchen, and dropped to Jonathan Huntley's side. For a while, no one moved. Then Walt left to call an ambulance, and Lydia stood up and hurried down the hall to the nursery, to quiet Elizabeth's two crying babies.

Staring down at Stephen, Elizabeth slipped her hands into the pocket of her apron and was silent for a long time. She didn't blink, didn't move, didn't even seem to breathe. When she finally turned to Ruth, her face was oddly serene.

"Never trust a smooth-talking man," she said. "And never think you can change a fellow's ways."

Ruth brought a hand to her neck, cleared her throat, and nodded at the bus window. "Then the police arrived and carted Uncle Stephen away. My grandfather was dead, you see. And five days later, my parents and I moved to Los Angeles."

Shifting in her seat, she glanced at the man beside her. He was still snoring, his head bobbing up and down. So why should she expect the sympathy of strangers?

She sighed and let her own head drop, to rest on his shoulder, beneath his broad-brimmed hat.

"Excuse me, ma'am, here's my stop." The man patted her on the shoulder — slapped, really — then pushed past her to the aisle, crushing her bad knee. "You take good care now, you hear?" she heard him say.

Disoriented, knee throbbing, Ruth opened her eyes. The bus had pulled up to her stop by the library, midpoint in its circular route, which took an hour to complete. Quickly, she glanced down at Hale's diamond watch. It was past nine-forty. Time for her heart pill, and she'd almost forgotten!

Furtively looking around her, she tossed her chewed Twizzler on the floor. She pulled her daytime pillbox from her purse and picked out a Cardizem. She didn't need water; she could swallow it right there by simply gathering enough saliva in her mouth. She'd learned long ago how to do without, in situations more difficult than this.

The drunk man up front was yelling now — he went purple in the face, punched his fist into his palm; he drooled and stamped his feet and swore at his invisible enemy.

Sick, Ruth thought. Sick and very peculiar. She swallowed the pill.

She stood and gathered her things and moved toward the door at the back of the bus. "Rear door, please," she called to the driver. Her voice came out weak and raspy. "Rear, please," she called again, but the door remained tightly shut. "Excuse me!" she called. "This is my stop!" She reached over to push the yellow signal tape, but tumbled forward as the bus lurched into gear. "Stop!" she shouted, reaching up toward a safety loop that dangled high out of her reach. Eventually, she caught hold of the back of a seat and steadied herself.

Somewhere in the bus, someone laughed.

The door sprang open.

Ruth took a few deep breaths. Then she hobbled over, planted her cane firmly on the first step, and eased her way down to the sidewalk.

Three kids knocked up against her. They were dressed entirely in black; they had headsets over their ears and large silver hoops through their lips and eyebrows and noses. Ruth couldn't tell if they were boys or girls. They pushed past her and into the bus, shouting, singing, laughing uproariously.

9:49 A.M.

Ocean Avenue was crowded. As always, Ruth paused to survey the people strolling by: lean young men in white pants and deep tans, fat middle-aged women in tent-shaped tropical muumuus, senior citizens in bright leisure wear with crooked limbs and pastel hair. Ruth blinked several times; the world had become a strange and difficult place. After a moment she slung her purse over her right shoulder. She grasped the cane in her left hand, letting the umbrella dangle from her wrist, and peered down the sidewalk toward the Postal Connection, two blocks ahead. The sooner this letter was safely on its way, she told herself, the better. She pointed with the tip of her cane, drew a bead on the mobile newsstand at the corner, and set out.

An airplane flew by slow and very low, trailing a banner over the water, parallel to Main Beach. Ruth watched it pass, squinting to make out its message: "Party All Weekend with Oldies 92 FM!" Why not? she thought, as she lowered her eyes; people flew around the moon now, and advertised in the sky. What a world.

She arrived at the newsstand and paused to catch her breath. From shelf upon shelf of glossy magazine covers, half-naked girls gaped at her, their pouting mouths wide open. Ruth stared back at them in disgust. The girls were very young, even younger than her granddaughter. "Lose Weight While You Sleep," read the cap-tions. "Eat Enough for Two and Still Keep Your Man." Ruth wondered if Karen read this kind of trash. The girl was certainly a pouter. She'd seemed awfully tense on the phone that morning, and she *was* very skinny. What's more, she was letting that Romeo sleep in her bed. How could she? Ruth wondered. It didn't make sense. That so-called husband of hers was not like any schoolteacher *she* had ever known.

With a cluck of her tongue, Ruth lifted her cane and took aim at the Connection. The day was becoming warm and much brighter; she flipped her sunglass lenses down. Walking fast, she soon arrived at the edge of a fiberglass planter, brim full of wilted succulent plants, next to the Postal Connection's front door. The Connection was housed in a concrete building, circa 1950, newly refurbished with false wood siding and a roof of asphalt tile. A sign hung above the door: "Your Connection to the World: Swift, Safe, Sufficient."

Ruth stopped to set her purse on the edge of the planter, struggling to undo the purse's zipper with her right hand without losing her left-hand grip on the cane. Slowly, she worked the zipper open, right thumb and index finger pinching the tag, the remaining three fingers pulling from behind. She found the letter to Douglas, took it out and set it beside a succulent, and proceeded to close the bag as she had opened it, but with the three fingers pushing from behind this time. It was no easy thing. Exhausting, in fact. Ruth took a deep breath, removed the letter from the planter, brushed off some specks of soil, headed into the Connection.

The lobby was cool and shady. Potted palms and rubber plants stood in every corner; lush ferns and philodendrons hung in baskets from the ceiling. Rising onto her toes, Ruth reached up to touch a fern frond and discovered it was plastic.

"Naturally," she said. "And next it'll be plastic food. Then plastic people."

She stepped in line behind a barefoot girl wearing a beaded gypsy dress. The girl was staring up into the eyes of a much older man beside her — mostly bald, except for a stringy gray ponytail at the back of his head. At his feet sat a package addressed to the North Pole. Every few seconds the couple kissed, or he pulled on her beads, or she tugged his ponytail. Ruth watched them as she would a movie, waiting to see what might happen next. As she looked on, she absently opened and shut her mouth, cracking her jaw. What if strangers could hear the every move of her mouth, she wondered, without her even knowing? Ruth grew concerned, peering at the couple in front of her. She leaned in close, opening and closing her mouth several times in quick succession.

The girl glanced at Ruth, then looked back into the eyes of her lover. They kissed. A long one, tongues and closed eyes.

Ruth held a finger to her jaw, opening and closing her mouth, waiting patiently for them to finish.

The man began licking the girl's face. Hands on her shoulders, eyes closed, he enveloped her nose with his lips and sucked on her nostrils. Ruth gaped. She opened and shut her mouth with feeling, popping hard, and after several moments the man finally turned and glared at her with a beady right eye.

Ruth stared back at him. "May I ask what you're *doing* to that young lady?"

The man released the girl's nose, but continued to glare. "Hey look, Grandma," he said with two flicks of his ponytail, "what I'm doing is none of your beeswax. And about what *you're* doing, it's not like it's a pleasant sound or something, if that's what you want to know. Nasty as hell, actually."

The girl beside him smiled. Her tiny nose glistened like a wet pebble. Apparently, she'd been enjoying the sucking business.

Ruth stood silent. They were almost at the counter.

"Comprendes, Mendez?" the man said. "I mean, it's not like the end of the world or something. Just respect our space, is all. We're occupied."

"Oh, shit on you," said Ruth. "Just wait till *she's* almost a hundred, *then* see how you like sucking noses!" Ruth folded her arms tightly across her chest. Just then, as if ignited, a couple of flickering images sparked up: Hale dipping his nose into her hair, running a hand along her leg; Hale smiling down at her after they made love. "And besides, since you're obviously so nosy, it's not like I didn't have plenty of men eager to attack me back when . . ."

"What?"

"Hale," she said, then hesitated, her voice snagging. She looked hard at the man in front of her. "None of your beeswax. And go find a barber."

The man shrugged and turned away.

Beeswax, Ruth thought. The word had a nice solid ring to it. The next time someone started prying into her feelings, she'd just click her tongue and say, "None of your beeswax," and then she'd give a brisk nod and wait for . . .

Out of nowhere, a sudden chill swept through her. It made her gasp — a quick, icy freeze, cold like she'd never felt it before. With her free hand Ruth pulled down her sweater vest, half clutching herself, blinking, and then a moment later something white and furry seemed to bolt across the Postal Connection's tile floor. Ridiculous, she told herself. Impossible and silly. Except there it was, right now, a furry white creature that paused and studied her for a second before hopping toward the door.

"You?" Ruth murmured.

Then she said, "What *is* it?"

She squeezed her cane, shook her head from side to side. The couple in front of her were staring. The ponytailed man rolled his eyes. The gypsy girl started to reach out but then decided against it.

"Hey, listen," the man said, "you all right?"

Ruth nodded. "Perfectly. For a moment there I thought I recognized someone."

"Yeah? I don't see any —"

"Oh, just a face. Gone now." Ruth tapped her cane against the floor and straightened up her shoulders. "It *is* chilly in here, don't you think?"

"Sure," the man said. "Real chilly. Down to seventy-five, easy."

He turned away and took the girl's arm and moved up to the window. Ruth stood waiting for another four or five minutes, now and then glancing behind her, scanning the floor, but everything seemed back to normal. An extraordinary day, she thought. One thing after another. In a way, almost, it was as if all her routines were under attack by some insidious force of nature.

Enough was enough.

When the couple had finished at the window, Ruth marched forward and placed her letter firmly on the counter.

"Nice permanent, Root," the clerk said. "Brand-new one, I betcha."

At least that much was familiar. It was the Chinese clerk today, the one who worked there every Saturday, the one who had so much trouble with his grammar.

"Yes, well," Ruth said, "I do try to keep up repairs. Thanks for noticing. Many chi-chis, sir."

"Sorry, Root?"

"Chi-chi," Ruth said. "It *is* your language, I believe."

The clerk frowned, then broke out in a luxuriant grin. "Ah, I see, you mean thank you. And you are welcome! But you should say 'xie, xie' — like that. Where you learn speak Chinese? Pretty darn good, Root. And how about Henry? How he's doing?"

"Same old thing." She handed him the letter. "It's to my son, Douglas. The doctor."

"Yes, I know."

"You do?"

The man was still beaming at her. "Oh, sure, you talk about this son always. I know address by heart, and granddaughter, and other son, too." He weighed the letter, stamped it, placed it in a box beside him. "Fifty cent," he said.

"Fifty?" Ruth frowned at the man. "I was under the impression that a letter, just a regular old letter, costs exactly thirty-two cents."

The man pointed to a list of prices on the wall. "Not at Connection, Root. You want quality, you got to pay for it. Otherwise, you go to regular government post office."

Ruth felt her heart begin to palpitate. "But I can't make it over there. There's no bus."

The man nodded. "Okay now, Root, no worry. Fifty cent. He get it for sure by Tuesday."

"Well, I should certainly hope so."

Ruth passed a dollar bill across the counter.

"No problem. Okeydokey."

"Now what you may not realize," she said sternly, waiting for her change, "is that Douglas is an extremely busy man. Not rich, of course, not like his brother, Carter — you know, Karen's father, the one who's traveled all over the world. But that Douglas of mine, well, he was always the eager beaver. Very clever, too. Even when he was a boy, all those years ago, even then you'd never find him loafing or wasting time or . . . Just like his father, you could say. Have I ever mentioned my first husband, Hale?"

"Sure, Root. I guess maybe two thousand, three thousand times maybe."

Ruth blushed. "As he well deserves."

"A good man, you tell me. That Mr. Hale."

"Exceptional," said Ruth.

She put her change into her purse, thanked him, and moved off to the door. When she stepped outside, the ponytailed man was giving a long farewell suck to his girlfriend. Repulsive, Ruth thought. And Karen was probably subjected to the very same thing: that maniac husband wrapping his lips around her granddaughter's nose, clogging her breathing apparatus and spraying God knows what sort of germs right up into her head. Ruth clucked her tongue. Maybe that was why the girl had become so nervous and short-tempered — bugs crawling around her pretty little brain.

Pausing on the sidewalk, Ruth calculated the time that remained. She'd stepped off the bus at nine forty-two. With a half-hour trip back to the Lagoon, and then a half-hour trip from there back here, and the loss today of approximately two minutes for traffic in both directions, the bus should arrive at exactly ten forty-six. She could still do her math, all right.

It wasn't raining, so she would wait on the bench. She wanted to be early, just in case, so she started right away, lifting her cane and taking aim at a green mulberry bush and walking briskly down the sidewalk.

Almost immediately, from a bay window off to her right, a large red banner caught her eye: "Anytime Is Teddy Time at Intime!" Two mannequins in their mid-thirties, wearing red contraptions with black straps and black lace, posed provocatively beneath the banner. The brunette straddled a mutilated briefcase, its contents spilling everywhere, as she leather-whipped a half-open file cabinet while eyeing her next victim, a personal computer. The blonde looked calmly out the window past the fury of her friend, nursing a baby through the hole in her brassiere.

Intime was owned by Ruth's most Francophile acquaintance, Nora Gretts, and was managed by Nora's two assistants. Since 1924, when Nora and Ruth were freshmen together at UCLA, Nora had dreamed of owning just such a boutique. She had always been thin and high-strung, and wild in those days — always game to smoke in the bell tower or serve laxative-laced brownies for dessert or take the forbidden trip to Balboa Island. In their sophomore year, Nora and Ruth became sisters in Kappa Kappa Gamma. In their senior year, Nora was elected homecoming queen, and was the sorority's most-dated young woman. After graduation, she went off on a tour of Europe, and for many years afterward none of the sisters heard another word.

No one knew why Nora returned to California in 1953, looking a great deal worse for wear. Among those Kappa sisters still in the area, bizarre rumors began circulating. Some said it was syphilis, others that she'd lost a child. Whatever the case, in a matter of months Nora had opened Intime and was back in form — asking to be called Lady Soirée and boasting that she was the "première source of the latest modes, importées de France." Over the years, Nora's thinness turned to frailty, her wild exuberance to the realization — all the more bitter for its delayed arrival — that time passes and beauty fades. As her breasts and cheeks began to sag, she took to staying home, smoking and drinking coffee in bed, reliving her glory days in a scrapbook of yellowed clippings from the *Daily Bruin*. Except for holidays and weekends, when her assistants demanded time off, Nora ignored her duties at the shop. She kept careless records, avoided bill collectors, ordered shoddy goods from Korean catalogues. And when she did go to work, her behavior was more than a little erratic, and extremely bad for business. She would kowtow to customers, fawning over them as if they'd been friends for years; she'd sing and dance, twirling through the aisles and pinning discount tags on every item that had even a tinge of pink; she'd try on various new articles — an edible negligee, a high-tech chrome leotard — appraising her puffy flesh in the full-length mirrors; she'd stroll through the shop in a garter belt and bra, "soliciting customer opinions." But then, perhaps only an hour later, Nora's mood would suddenly turn critical. Grumbling that the stock was in a mess, she'd tear through the Korean nighties, spraying them with perfume, soiling them with her newsprint-stained fingers. Shocked at her own prices and scandalized by the merchandise she sold, she would shout, "There ought to be a law!" before stalking out in a huff.

Ruth hesitated for a moment outside the red-curtained door. Today was Saturday, one of those rare occasions when Nora would actually be here. Ruth straightened her hair and glanced at Hale's wristwatch — just enough time for a quick hello. She looked both ways, then slipped inside.

The room was stuffy, almost unbearable, and the overhead lights were dimmed. A scratchy recording of *Bolero* was playing, the volume turned high, but there was no one behind the counter.

Ruth moved up and down the short aisles, past fur-topped camisoles and gowns of imitation tiger skin. Twice she called out for Nora, with no luck, now and then stopping to peer through shelves of slippers and racks of bras. "Nora, yoo-hoo," she yelled. "I know you're here."

A squeal shot out from the back of the shop. Then a shuffling noise, then another squeal. "Don't you dare! What do you take me for?" It was Nora's voice — Ruth would have known it anywhere. And it was coming from the john, at the end of the panties aisle.

Ruth paused. "Hey, it's me, Ruthie." No answer. "Look, Nora, I don't have a lot of time here."

Nora squealed again: "Watch those hands!"

"Pardon me?" Ruth said.

"Your hands!"

Ruth gripped her cane tightly. "Listen, have you lost your mind? I'm not touching a thing."

Instantly, Nora let out a quick, shrill giggle.

Well fine. Ruth lifted her cane, drew a bead on the bathroom door, and advanced with determination down the aisle. She knocked twice, noticing that the lock was on her side of the doorknob. "I've had it, Nora, no more games. I'll give you a count of ten, then I'm afraid I'll have to make a forcible entry."

The laughter stopped. Ruth detected a rustling behind the door.

"One, two, three . . ."

"Now just a *minute*," Nora yelped.

"Oh, for God's sake, it's just me," said Ruth, and skipped the next several numbers. "Nine, ten! Here I come." She pushed the door open.

Nora stood on the toilet seat in a white peignoir and long lace gloves. A young man — very young, Ruth noticed, considerably younger than either of her own sons — stood facing Nora, with a camera. He turned toward Ruth as the door opened.

"My lucky day," he said. "A double feature."

"I'm sick," said Ruth.

Nora winked at her. "Well, that's your privilege," she said. "Just don't do it here." She lifted the hem of her gown, extended a gloved hand toward her companion, and descended daintily to the floor. Two circles of cherry-red rouge swung like gleaming Christmas ornaments from the tips of her pointed cheekbones. "Ruthie, darling, I should've known it was you. Always popping up to ruin someone else's good time."

"Good time?" Ruth stepped back, her cane extended in front of her like a rifle. "If you call this a good . . . Well, you obviously do, but this pervert's young enough to —" Ruth stopped as the boy crouched down to snap a picture.

"Great!" he said.

Nora smiled at the boy and threw out her chest. With one hand she hiked up the skirt of her gown, far above the top of her knee-highs; with the other she reached toward the sink and splashed water on her face and hair. "We'll go for that seaside look."

"You're eighty-seven years *old*," Ruth said. "I refuse to participate in this ridiculous spectacle."

"*Seventy*-seven," Nora said quickly. She glanced at the boy and cleared her throat. "One *is* as old as one *feels*."

"In that case," Ruth said, "I'm God's mother."

Nora made a huffing noise and let her gown drop back to her ankles. Then she pushed past Ruth and closed the bathroom door on the boy, locking him inside. "The lad's harmless," she said, and sniffed. "Like to try on a little something?" She glided over to a circular rack, plucked off a pair of bikini panties. "Maybe one of these gorgeous new garments? Except with the way you've let your midriff go, Lord knows if you'll fit a decent size."

Ruth held the panties out in front of her, pinched between her index finger and thumb, scowling at the foul smell she imagined they emitted. "Decent," she muttered. "What's decent about no crotch? Or about those goings-on in your bathroom?"

"Once the prude, always the prude."

"Prude my eye." Ruth dropped the panties to the floor. "I came in here to pay my compliments, such as they are, but it appears you're getting along just fine without me. Too fine, if you ask my opinion." She lifted her cane. The tip snagged on the panties, scraping them off the carpet.

Nora laid both hands upon her breast and said, "Dieu!"

Flushed, eager to escape, Ruth turned and hurried down the aisle toward the front door, nudging it open with her left shoulder. She paused at the threshold, blinded by the bright sun. "And you can tell that young man in there to go" — she searched for a proper phrase — "to go soak his pathetic apparatus."

10:36 A.M.

Her mind in a whirl, Ruth made it to the bus stop and collapsed heavily on the bench. She had to go to the bathroom. Badly, in fact — upsetting events almost always brought on the urge. Across the street was a Mobil station, but she didn't dare risk it. Only a single bus traveled the circular Laguna route — the same bus that had brought her downtown — and with the inevitable struggle to adjust her girdle, Ruth feared she might still be stooped over the toilet when the bus pulled up for its only stop that hour.

She felt a warm dribble against her thigh. Leaks everywhere, she thought. Fluids and words and ancient history, it all came spilling out willy-nilly, no control at all. She tensed herself, straining, holding on for dear life. It occurred to her that Nora might sell rubber panties. Probably with obscene little leopard-skin flaps.

When the bus pulled up at ten forty-one, five minutes ahead of her estimation, Ruth congratulated herself on the prudence and discipline she'd shown in not leaving the bench. She climbed on board, showed her card, and looked for a seat near the front. The purple-faced drunkard was still there, settled down now, asleep against a window. He burped as Ruth passed, and the smell — bourbon and bologna — reminded her of Henry.

She sighed and sank into an empty seat.

Henry had first been seduced by the promises of alcohol shortly after realizing that his marriage would be bone dry. For a time, at least, the booze seemed to offer comfort: a couple of martinis at lunch, a few more before dinner, then he was prepared to face another night alone. But after retirement and the move to Paradise Lagoon, boredom drove Henry to the bottle with a ferocious new thirst, something close to desperation. Part of the problem, Ruth assured herself, was purely physical. Henry was legally blind (though Ruth knew he could see just fine when he truly wanted to), and as a result he was hard put to find diversions of any kind. Listening to the radio, earplug tucked in tight, he'd spend hours staring blankly at the Lucky Strike thermometer above his desk, or he'd play long silent games of solitaire, or he'd just yawn and scratch himself and fiddle with his pencils. Some days, as second climbed over second, slow and empty, Ruth would overhear him counting aloud the minutes before he mixed his first drink.

One summer morning just before eight o'clock, she'd found him passed out on the floor beside his desk. He lay with his arms bent beneath him, his nubby-red cheeks crusted with dribble, sunlight washing over him in pale waves. His cereal bowl had fallen to the floor; dozens of mushy, swollen Shredded Wheats were pasted to the rug.

At that instant, Ruth recalled, something gave way inside her. The sting of a new affliction, perhaps; the pang of old disappointments that were best left unremembered.

She bent down, sniffed his collar. Whiskey, for sure. It was odd, though. She hadn't heard him open the liquor cabinet when he went down to fetch their breakfast trays that morning, and she hadn't heard him leave his room since then. For a while she looked him over, from the white socks to the floodwater corduroys to the dirty cuffs on his baby blue windbreaker. She frowned. Presently, she took note of a queer bulge near his left armpit.

In truth, she'd first noticed it long ago. For a month, at least, Henry had been wearing the same blue windbreaker day and night, elbows pressed against his ribs, hands entwined at the navel as if to cradle some private pain; more than once she'd found herself wondering about it all. The bulge seemed to move each time she looked. Not much, just an inch or two, like some sort of slow migration. What it was, however, she had not really hoped to discover. Maybe something he'd swallowed years and years ago, a giant artichoke or an undigested hamburger. Or perhaps benign cancer — a restless, wandering tumor.

She could no longer ignore it. She drew in a breath, lifted her chin, tore open his jacket. There, nestled inside the inner pocket, was a glass mouthwash bottle. "Well, so," she said.

Henry opened his eyes and grinned.

"Didn't know you was in here," he said.

Ruth snatched the bottle from his pocket. She held it up to the light, unscrewed the cap, and put it to her nose.

"Right," she said. "Jimmy Walker."

"That's Johnnie, hon."

Ruth narrowed her eyes. "*Degenerate.*"

Sighing, pushing up to his hands and knees, Henry looked at her like a mangy pup begging for dinner. "Hey, just kidding, sweetie. I'm off to the bathroom, get the old teeth scrubbed up."

"Whiskey," Ruth said.

"The old breath potion, it keeps the kisser in order. My brother told me that. 'Lots of mouthwash,' Billy always says."

"*Whiskey*," Ruth said again, lowering her voice. "Not in this house. And certainly not at this hour."

Still on his hands and knees, Henry reached up for the glass bottle. "Well, you're right. Maybe one last splash, okay?" He scrambled forward. "That's class-A stuff, Ruth. Damn tasty over Shredded Wheat."

Ruth gave him a hard, level stare. Quietly, she put the bottle on the floor in front of him, straightened up, and turned to leave the room.

"Okay, okay!" he yipped. "Bad breath ain't the only problem!"

He panted and wagged his bottom, gazing up at her with huge moist eyes. For an instant Ruth had to fight back an impulse to scratch his ears.

Henry picked up the bottle.

"Listen, Ruthie, I ain't no saint." He burped. He shook his head. Slowly then, he hoisted himself up and stood wobbling in the sunlight, still gripping the bottle with both hands. "A man gets dull as dirt in his bedroom all alone, miserable lonely. No offense, naturally. Anyhows, I see the drift, so to speak. Won't do it no more — drinking on the sly, I mean — and that's for sure. Swear to God in heaven. Apostles, too, and all the martyrs."

He wobbled sideways again, and winked.

"Watch this."

He made his way to the window, pulled off the screen, licked his lips, and tossed out the bottle. There was a sharp shattering sound.

"Amen," he said.

Ruth walked over to his side. She gripped his elbow and made an effort to steady him. She peered out the window, down into the public courtyard below. "Go fetch the broom," she said, "before someone steps on all that glass."

11:12 A.M.

Dazed, blinking herself awake, Ruth looked out the bus window and took stock of her surroundings: more Italian restaurants and frozen-yogurt shops, more video rentals and real estate offices. Fast-breeding Salmon Estates covered the hills, smothering open spaces beneath their smiling pink façades. "Coming Soon! Seven New Neighborhoods!" said the billboards at the side of Coast Highway.

The bus pulled over briefly at a stop near Treasure Island. Ruth peered ahead, past the few remaining passengers and out the front window, looking for her palm tree. It was an advance warning sign that her own stop was approaching.

"I spy!" she whispered as the tree came into view, over sixty feet tall on the highway's ocean side.

The skinny palm stood on Paradise Lagoon's greenbelt. When Ruth and Henry were first moving in, bringing down carloads of things from Los Angeles each day, they had held competitions to "spy" the palm tree first. The earlier you saw it, the better your luck for the day. Driving south down Coast Highway, behind the wheel of her trusty Studebaker, Ruth sometimes had to let Henry win, his eyes were so much worse than hers.

Over twenty years had passed since then. Originally there had been three palms; the one that remained had been the runt of the three. Alone and badly weathered now, stripped bare except for a tuft of leaves at the very top, it held on stubbornly, proud to be the tallest living thing around.

To Ruth, the first sight of the tree brought on a warm, cozy sensation, like coming home was supposed to feel.

Behind the tree, the giant condominiums loomed. Slick and self-assured, almost pompous behind their half-million-dollar price tags, they stood row upon row on a slope facing the ocean. They were not worth their price, but unabashed they stood in ranks of muted green, one identical to the next. Had they always looked so frightening? Ruth wondered.

Number 24, behind the tennis court, was hers.

She gathered her cane, umbrella, and purse, and when the bus doors snapped back, she stepped down to the sidewalk.

She walked briskly over to the iron fence that guarded Paradise Lagoon. Today for some reason a snarl of six or seven cars was backed up behind the Lagoon gates. The new California, Ruth thought. Traffic jams in your own driveway — blaring horns and red faces — cars jerking forward as the twin gates slowly opened and closed like a pair of heavy steel curtains. Some of the drivers had Auto-Opens, which they aimed at the gates from behind their steering wheels; others were forced to lower their windows and reach out toward a black iron stand, to insert their Auto-Mate cards into a narrow slot. Several of the cars made false starts as Ruth looked on, and there seemed to be more than the usual confusion. Probably the gates were broken again.

"Cadillac quality" my eye, thought Ruth. Installing this fence had been just another ploy of the management to raise her monthly Association dues.

The Pedestrian Passage, which swung out to open like a regular door, was tightly closed. It had its own card mechanism; the slot sneered at Ruth now like some defiant hoodlum. She was the only pedestrian around, so she'd have to use her own card. Usually she kept it rubber-banded to the outside of her wallet, inside her purse, but today it wasn't there — she must not have put it away properly at the Postal Connection, after paying for her letter. Using her left hand both to balance on her cane and to hold her purse, she fumbled through the purse's contents with her right hand.

By now she desperately needed to pee. The gate, however, could not have cared less if she was stuck there all day.

Finally she dug out the card, hidden in a corner beneath a sticky wad of Kleenex. Bending down, reaching out toward the slot, she was about to slide the card in when the gate sprang open of its own volition.

She jumped, almost dropped her cane. But there was no time to consider the matter; right now, the whole world had condensed into a single hard pressure in her kidneys. She hurried past the sculpted dog, with only one glance at his perked-up ears; she hurried down the hill as fast as she'd ever walked in her life, then down the path between the tennis court and pool. Once at her door, she rang the front bell.

She glanced at Hale's wristwatch — almost eleven-thirty.

The pressure was intense now, almost unbearable. "Henry!" she cried. She rang twice more, but there was no answer. With a weak yelp, she opened up her purse and began digging again. This time she knew to go for the corners, and after what seemed an eternity she found the keys hidden exactly where her card had been. She unlocked the door with a shaking hand, hustled into the tiny bathroom.

"Thank the Lord," she said.

It was a lovely moment. The fine, warm spray reached out for her thighs, but she could relax now, no damage done. All the photographs looked down, proud of her. Not a single drop in her underpants.

When she was finished, she called again for Henry.

Asleep, no doubt. Or maybe still at the Alpha Beta. She started for the second floor. She was more fatigued than usual, and feeling a little dizzy, but she would still use the stairs, not the elevator.

"Henry!" she called.

Slowly, a bit wobbly, she climbed to the third floor. Her knee popped audibly all the way. They had always been so good, her legs. She moved into Henry's open doorway.

There he was — deaf as a stone.

Back turned, standing straight up at his window, he cackled to himself and looked out toward the condo gates, left hand on the windowsill for balance. In his right hand he gripped an Auto-Open, which he aimed in the general direction of the gates. He pushed the button randomly, absorbed in his game, obviously taking great pleasure in all the chaos down below.

Ruth watched as Henry refused assistance to a red Honda Accord. Next in line was a blue hatchback. The driver rolled down her window and began to reach out toward the slot with her card when Henry leaned forward and pushed his Auto-Open button and laughed as the gates rolled apart. The blue hatchback hesitated. Then it drove through fast, hitting the speed bump much harder than could have done the car good. Next was an old black convertible — pausing just long enough for Henry to beep the gates closed. The driver braked hard and reached out with his card, and Henry beeped the gates open; there was another short hesitation; the convertible edged forward and Henry beeped the gates shut. His skinny shoulders were shaking. He giggled and waited for a line to form behind the trapped convertible and then hit the button four times in rapid succession — open-close, open-close.

Henry's eyes were bad, it was true, but he clearly sensed the confusion he was causing. With each push of the button, he'd snort and slap his leg and do a little dance in his size-thirteen loafers.

A child, Ruth thought. Married to a twelve-year-old.

He jumped when she poked him in the back.

"Hey, you made it," he said. "Long time no see. I've been worried."

"Is that so?"

"Bet your booties." He slipped the Auto-Mate behind his back. "Just keeping my eyes peeled."

"Well, here I am," Ruth said, "but I could've drowned in my own urine out there. Don't think I'm not on to your foolish games."

"Games?"

"The gate," she said. "You let me in yourself."

"I did?"

She glared at him. For the second time in less than an hour, she remembered the day he'd thrown his booze bottle out this very bedroom window.

She sighed. "So where's the change from my groceries?"

11:45 A.M.

It was part of Henry's job, when he went to the Alpha Beta every morning, to pay for their food separately and return Ruth's share of the change, down to the penny. Each day before he headed out, he took ten dollars from Ruth's grocery money, which she kept in a pickle jar on the kitchen counter. When he got home, having made it one more time across the highway with no accident, he handed Ruth her own receipt and change, which she carefully counted before preparing her lunch.

Like the morning routine at 24 Paradise Lagoon, the midday rituals never changed.

At eleven o'clock sharp, without exception, Henry made himself a bologna sandwich. Or rather, two open-faced bologna sandwiches. He would toast two slices of wheat bread, spread them both with butter (lots of butter; so much, in fact, it made Ruth queasy to watch), and then pile on alternating layers of bologna and Chef Tooley's Famous Peanut Sauce. He would place the sandwiches on a flowered paper plate. He would drape a napkin over the sandwiches, pour himself a Diet Coke, position everything on his tray, and carry the tray up to the desk in his bedroom. Screwing in his radio earplug, he'd finally sit down to eat. As he munched the atrocious sandwiches, he liked to watch Rodrigo hose down the tennis court and then sweep off the water with his big push broom. Some days Rodrigo made elaborate and beautiful patterns in the water, which Henry would admire from the window. Huge spirals, for instance. And flowers. Once Rodrigo drew the wavy figure of a woman. Once he drew a flag. The patterns were clear from above — clearer than they could have been to Rodrigo himself — and Henry took special pleasure in staring down at the unfolding pictures as he ate his daily bologna.

Ruth, too, had her own rigorous lunch procedure. The same sandwich, without variation, each day: coleslaw and salami on wheat. And two bites of oat bran muffin. The muffins cost seventy-nine cents apiece, and they were huge; Ruth almost never finished an entire muffin in one day. She'd have precisely two bites at lunch and then, depending on what she was doing, nibble at the leftovers throughout the afternoon.

These habits were important to Ruth in ways she could never entirely explain, not even to herself.

All those years maybe. All the accumulated tastes and sensations that pile up over a lifetime — they could be overwhelming — they had to be sorted out and labeled and filed away in their proper mental folders. No choice really. If you lasted long enough, as she had, you could end up choking on the debris of your own life.

Not that she gave it much thought. What was necessary was necessary, it was that simple.

Ruth looked at Hale's watch. Almost noon. She was starving.

She made her way down to the kitchen, went to the counter, and pulled today's muffin from its crisp new bag. She took the first bite, holding her left hand beneath her chin to catch any crumbs. Inevitably, she missed a few — four little specks on the counter. She licked her index finger, pressed down on a crumb, brought it to her mouth. She called it The Index Test. If a scrap adhered to the index finger of her left hand, it was obviously safe to eat. Anything small enough to stick, she reasoned, could not possibly carry sufficient germs to poison her. She did not hesitate to perform The Test on the counter at the bank, for example, or even on the bench downtown, where she waited for the bus. Any crumb that did not adhere to her finger was to be picked up and saved until it could be properly thrown away.

In this case she knew the exact nature of the crumbs, and she finished them off: two, three, four. Then she took her second bite from the top of the muffin and replaced the leftovers in the bag, which would be dealt with according to another specific procedure later in the afternoon.

Next, she made her sandwich. She did not toast the bread, nor spread butter on it. She preferred cream cheese — light cream cheese, with half the calories. Methodically, concentrating on each step, Ruth dropped on three slices of salami from the processed roll that lasted her two weeks, then added a few spoonfuls of coleslaw. She cut the sandwich in half and arranged it on her tray with a glass of buttermilk. Then she carried the tray to her place at the dining table, to the one small space that she kept cleared of papers.

She slid into her chair and took a few deep breaths. At last, she thought. Life was exhausting.

12:20 P.M.

After lunch, Ruth began to sort through the day's mail, which Henry had carried up to the table when he got back from the supermarket. Today it was mostly catalogues. Buried among the catalogues was a slim cardboard mailing envelope addressed to Mrs. Henry Hubble. It was marked with red lettering: "Holiday Blessings from Your Buddies at Blockbuster." Scowling, Ruth grabbed the envelope and shook it from side to side; an unpleasant, fetid odor wafted up through the air. Probably some scratch-and-sniff guide to the animal kingdom, she thought. She leaned forward and placed the envelope atop a stack of similar envelopes piled high in the center of the table.

She sighed and looked about.

Normally, after sorting her mail, she also paged through the newspaper, but unless a sensational story jumped out at her, she never read much but the horoscope and the obituaries. She liked to check the astrological predictions for her two sons and her granddaughter, and she liked to search for death notices of people she had known. In the event she found one, she would cut it out. She kept her pile of obituaries in a tidy zip-lock bag, the most recent notice on top, in the drawer of her bedside table. She'd been doing this for years, and had a substantial collection. Lately, though, she hadn't found much: more people died in their seventies than in their eighties, she'd learned.

Her second clipping project was the television listings. Except for *Wheel of Fortune* and *Jeopardy*, between seven and eight in the evenings, she rarely watched television; still, it was good to have the listings, just in case. She would cut out "Tonight on TV" and "Tonight on Cable," and paper-clip them to the appropriate day in the TV guide that came in Sunday's paper. She had to fold the clippings twice to make them fit inside the booklet; though she struggled to do it right, they always stuck out the edges in a mess.

Today, though, Ruth skipped her entire clipping routine. Those peculiar white specks were back again, flickering here and there like some sort of television static, and she decided it might be best to lie down for a few minutes. She picked up her tray, carried it to the kitchen, added her plate and glass to the morning's dishes in the sink. On her way out she bent down to drop her napkin in the trash and stopped in her tracks.

"My God," she said. The plastic sandwich baggie, clothespinned inside a corner of the brown paper bag, was completely full. Overflowing, in fact.

Ruth stooped down for a closer look. This would not do, with Luzma coming to clean. If there was one thing Ruth could not tolerate — and there were many such things — it was a stinky, overstuffed garbage bag. Embarrassing, too. A maid should never have access to one's private leavings.

She left the kitchen, moved to the bottom of the stairs, and yelled up to Henry. It was a few moments before she heard his slow, lumbering steps on the landing.

"Henry!" she yelled again. "Garbage time!"

He stood looking down at her, frowning, then pulled out his radio earplug. "Cribbage time?" he said.

"No, I said *gar*bage."

Henry shook his head. "Well, it's your call," he said, "but I never even knew you *liked* cribbage. Live an' learn, I guess."

Ruth wondered if they electrocuted old ladies for murder. "Garbage!" she yelled. "You know perfectly well I despise cribbage. I *despise* little games." There was a tinge of real disgust in her voice, which startled her.

Henry blinked, glanced at the ceiling, then shrugged. "You're right. Must've thrown it away."

"Thrown *what* away?"

"The cribbage board, sweetie."

Ruth was having trouble breathing. "Listen, Henry — the

trash. Take out the trash. Just leave me my View and Calendar sections, and take the rest of today's paper, too."

Henry shook his head as if perplexed and started down the stairs. "A mysterious lady," he said. When he reached the bottom of the stairs, he gave Ruth a sly, knowing look.

"*What?*" she said.

"Full of surprises, aren't you, cutie?"

"What?"

He flicked his eyebrows.

Suddenly, despite herself, Ruth released a quick snort of laughter. It was the first time she had laughed in days.

Henry did a little dance step, then turned and headed out to the kitchen.

Ruth stood there for a moment, quite still, looking after him. Remarkable, she thought. For a silly man, he could be singularly shrewd.

Though the Lagoon regulations did not require it, Ruth separated her trash in a most particular way. She called it The Arrangement. The process began with an ordinary brown grocery bag, with which she lined her plastic garbage bin. Before insertion, the paper bag had to be folded down one or two inches along its upper edge, so that it would remain upright even under the weight of some substantial piece of trash. Next, she would carefully attach a plastic sandwich baggie to one of the paper bag's corners, by means of three clothespins. The clothespins stretched the plastic baggie and held it taut, forming a triangular-shaped compartment for small bits of refuse. Finally, she would place a coffee can at the bottom of the brown bag as a third receptacle.

The question of what went where was complicated. If Kaji brought over some foreign dish in unusual wrappings, things could get confusing in the extreme. For the most part, however, Ruth and Henry ate the same meals every day, which made it possible for Ruth to establish certain rules. Most items went straight into the brown bag. Cottage cheese containers, TV dinner boxes and their plastic dishes, various aluminum cans, cereal and prune boxes — all these were deposited into the big brown bag. Peanut butter jars and yogurt cartons also went into the brown paper bag, but *not* the tinfoil yogurt tops. Certain bits of refuse required special treatment. Soiled wrappers of all sorts were to be placed inside the crinkled bags that Ruth pulled out of cereal boxes whenever she or Henry finished off their Shredded Wheat or All-Bran: these included greasy wrappers from Ruth's salami rolls, her cream cheese wrappers and muffin papers, and Henry's plastic bologna cases and coffee filters. Banana peels had to be stuck inside cardboard toilet-paper tubes. With two people in the house, a roll of toilet paper was normally finished off every three days; if constipation happened to set in, reducing the use of paper, it was permissible to stuff several banana peels into a single cardboard tube.

The triangular plastic baggie was reserved for chewed strawberry Twizzlers, hair balls, wadded-up Kleenexes, and little bits of rotten cheese. Also prune pits, lids from Diet Coke bottles, tinfoil yogurt tops, and candy wrappers.

The coffee can, finally, was exclusively for crumbs — those that had not passed Ruth's Index Test, and were thus not pure enough for consumption. Ruth would carry crumbs home inside her purse from the various places around town where they had failed The Test, then she'd use a pair of rubber gloves to transfer them into the can. It was among her favorite procedures. An act of environmental consciousness. And good fun, too. She liked to contemplate each crumb that found its way into her collection, and she liked to imagine the lives of the people who had dropped them.

For years Ruth had encouraged Henry to follow her system. She tried to teach by example, calling out to him from the kitchen each time she used the trash, letting him know which receptacle was about to receive which piece of trash. She watched over Henry like a hawk whenever he dumped in his own wastes, pointing out errors, scolding and cajoling and sometimes even begging.

At times, Ruth thought, the man seemed to be suffering from a learning disability. He simply couldn't catch on, tossing things indiscriminately, especially when Ruth wasn't watching, and as a consequence she was constantly having to rearrange his refuse. It was a wearisome and frustrating task.

In the end she did what she should have done from the start, writing down a complete list of rules and posting it on a cabinet above the trash. Even then Henry had trouble. "Greek to me," he'd say, and though Ruth explained and reexplained the rules, trying to persuade him of their simplicity and obvious merit, it eventually became clear that the man had absolutely no ability to recognize subtle distinctions. After Ruth realized this, her frustra- tion — which had begun to manifest itself indirectly, in argu- ments over matters completely unrelated — settled into a steady, suspicious, resigned malaise. Though it piqued her, she lowered her expectations of Henry and handled the matter herself. She did insist, however, upon his correctly *distributing* the garbage among the various dumpsters down at the community trash yard, which Ruth called The Pig Pen.

He was to carry the whole Arrangement across the cement courtyard just as it was; the contents of the three receptacles were not to be mixed together. Once he'd arrived safely inside the fenced-off grounds of The Pig Pen, he was to remove the clothes- pins from the little baggie, seal it up tight, and place it inside one of the community dumpsters. Next he was to put the coffee can aside and deposit the brown paper bag inside a second dumpster. Then, as a concluding embellishment, he was to retrieve the coffee can and sprinkle its assortment of crumbs over each dump- ster in The Pen.

It was, Ruth thought, an elegant ceremony. Logical and ef- ficient. Of course, things did not always come off according to plan — but what in her life ever had?

Ruth stood at the kitchen counter, watching as Henry stooped to pick up the garbage. For him, she knew, the distribution process was humiliating. He grumbled about it constantly. He hated the clothespins. He hated the plastic baggie. He hated the coffee can and the brown paper bag and the toilet paper tubes stuffed with banana peels. It was demeaning, he kept telling her, to walk across the courtyard carrying it all, and he felt plain foolish standing there in The Pig Pen, separating his trash and scattering little crumbs around.

Right now, in fact, he was obviously stalling.

Drumming her fingers lightly on the countertop, Ruth spoke in her most commanding voice. "Now be careful. Let's not get things all jumbled up."

Henry lifted the plastic bin to his hip. "Right," he said skeptically. "Think I got the hang of it." He clamped his baseball cap securely on his head, lumbered past her, and started down the stairs.

When the front door banged shut, Ruth hurried over to the window. There he was, directly below her in the courtyard. Except he wasn't moving. He'd set down the plastic bin and was hovering above it, hand in his mouth, playing with the revolving tooth. He stood transfixed like that for several minutes. Then he lifted a hand and crossed himself. There was a short hesitation — knees bent, shoulders arched — then he swooped down over the bin. In three quick pinches, he released the plastic baggie from its clothespins and spilled it open into the paper bag. He pulled the coffee can from the paper bag and, turning the can sideways, scattered the crumbs as if from a giant salt shaker: some floated through the air like dandelion puffs; others fell to the ground, where Henry danced on them.

12:54 P.M.

Sabotage, Ruth thought.

To think — thirty-six years with a man like that. She turned from the window, shuffled over to the couch, and lay down. A clear case of sabotage. And if Henry was capable of one deception, he was certainly capable of a thousand. She fluffed and stacked two thin toss pillows and slipped them under her head.

With Hale, of course, life had been different.

Senior year at UCLA. The first night of spring vacation, a sorority party, honeysuckles and orange blossoms and streamers twisting from the ceiling and people dancing and flirting and full of the future.

Ruth stood at the hors d'oeuvres table, alone, trying to hide. She felt ugly. God, she *was* ugly. That afternoon she'd gone in for the first professional permanent wave of her life, but to say the least, the results were not what she'd expected. When they'd removed the clips, down at that fancy new salon on Seventh Street, her whole head was in need of salvation: a loathsome mass of waves and curls and tangled knots. Later, she wet down her hair a dozen times, used an iron on it, combed it and brushed it and soaked it in salt water. Nothing, though. Ugly wasn't quite the word. Freakish — that was closer. Especially with all the other girls in their impeccable bobs and fancy braids and perky ponytails.

Ruth glanced around the room, sighed to herself, and poured a glass of grapefruit punch. That damned hairdresser. In the morning she'd march downtown and give the woman a good —

"Well, darling," someone said behind her, "how incredibly pretty."

Ruth froze. It was Nora, of course. Ruth winced and swallowed hard.

"So *very* pretty," Nora said, coming to her side, plucking an asparagus spear from the table. She took a dainty bite and rolled her eyes. "So special-looking. So *interesting*. Just so absolutely and perfectly *you*."

Ruth pulled back her shoulders, ran a hand through her electric spirals. "Thirty cents a curl," she said bravely.

"Oh, it shows, and you clearly got your money's worth, every penny." Nora's lips settled into a smirk; her own hair had been sculpted into a rock-hard bob. "Hear about my Easter plans?"

"A date?"

"Be gone for three weeks — invited out to Atlantic City."

"Wonderful," Ruth said. Her heart sank as she pictured Nora gliding down the boardwalk along the sand, fancied-up in fringe and sequins, swarms of hungry men nipping at her heels.

Nora smiled. "Oh, and listen to this. Judy Snyder and Edith Tumay just got themselves suspended — stayed overnight at Balboa Island last weekend. Not alone, either. With the boys from Alpha Delt."

"Really," Ruth said.

Christ, what next? All she needed was one more success story, somebody else's grand adventure. Again, despite herself, she ran a hand through her hair. What she should do, maybe, was just disappear. Run away to the Philippines. Albania, maybe, or China or New Guinea or some other exotic spot. A place where the natives wore bones in their hair.

"Well, Nora," she said, "I guess I'd better wander over —"

And then he tapped her shoulder.

A crooked nose. Flecks of brown in the hazel-green eyes. A pinstriped seersucker suit. Far too young for the balding head. But even that — especially that — was beautiful. The way the yellow light glanced off his forehead.

Ruth smiled as a streamer blew across his cheek. Suddenly, ridiculously, she felt an urgent need to put a hand on that fine shiny head.

"Dance?" he asked.

Nora leaned over to whisper in her ear. "Petroleum engineer. Nine hundred a month."

Ruth would have no memory of walking to the dance floor.

She *would* remember glancing up at the man, positioning her feet, sliding her hand into his. Then they were moving — a windy kind of moving. Her legs felt like wheat. There was a dampness under her arms, warm and clammy; she hoped it didn't show through her silk dress. She could feel the man staring at her, a kind of ticklish heat, but she kept her eyes fixed on the knot in his tie.

"Beautiful hair," he said. "Adorable."

She wasn't sure she'd heard him correctly. She was sure she *hadn't*, the music was so loud.

"Your hair," he said, "it's gorgeous."

"Oh, don't."

"Perfect."

She glanced up at him — he didn't seem to be joking. She lifted her chin. "Well," she said, "that's a generous thought, but it's a wreck."

"No, I love how it fluffs up that way. All these women here, they look like peas out of the same boring pod. I bet they're all jealous of you." He smiled at her. "And now every man's jealous of me."

"Well, I like yours too. The hair, I mean."

He laughed. "Not much to like."

"But I mean . . . You know, how the light sparkles off your forehead."

"Mr. Mirror?"

"Just like my father," she said. "Sometimes his whole head starts to —" She sucked in a breath. Idiot, she thought. "I meant — you know — bald isn't *old*."

He was smiling at her in a funny way. She could smell his shirt and skin. They were barely moving, ignoring the music. Briefly, as Ruth closed her eyes, it occurred to her that maybe the new permanent wasn't so terrible after all. At one point he seemed to dip his nose into her hair — like a honeybee, almost — and a moment later, when he stroked the curls at her neck, Ruth tried to recall whether she'd left a decent tip for the hairdresser.

Chunks of blurry time went by. Music and party sounds, and awkward silences too, and after four dances Ruth found herself searching for something to say. Work, she thought, then blurted it out. "What about work?"

"I'm sorry?"

It was hard to make her tongue move. "Do you work here? In town?"

"For an oil company. Graduated from Berkeley two years ago. My name's Hale."

"Dale?"

"*Hale*. With an H."

"H," she said. "H is nice. I'm Ruth Caster."

"Yes, I know."

"I'm a senior here, I'm about to —"

"I know."

"You know?"

"Oh, sure," he said. "Lots."

When the band stopped for a break, people began drifting off the dance floor; someone turned up the lights. Ruth stared at the knot in Hale's tie. She hoped they'd keep talking — his eyes were so pretty to watch — but again she had trouble coordinating tongue and brain. Nothing came to her. She glanced over at the hors d'oeuvres table. Nora looked up and waved and blew a kiss.

"Hungry?" Hale said.

"Oh, no."

"What about air?"

"The air's perfectly fine, thank you."

"No, I mean do you *want* some? Outside."

She nodded stupidly.

And what now — reach for his arm? Yes. Grip it hard? Be brave? Yes, just this once. And she did it: she even smiled. She raised her eyes, kept her spine straight, allowed him to lead her out to the back porch.

Again, there was that blank, blurry feeling. A cool, windy night. A bright half-moon. Many stars. The physical universe seemed to press against her skin.

"So," he was saying, "when's graduation day?"

"Soon enough. Two more months."

"Plans?"

"Yes, well —" She let herself look up at him. "Not yet."

At ten o'clock he offered her a drink from his flask. At ten-fifteen the moon slipped under clouds. At ten-twenty he was explaining the oil business, his voice slow and deliberate, and Ruth smiled and nodded and watched the flecks in his eyes; she studied his hands and lips; she felt a peculiar calm. Not much later, he kissed her. Then he kissed her again. Around eleven, when they returned to the dance floor, he took her by the hand.

His expression was almost somber.

"Well?" he said. "How do we firm up those plans of yours?"

They saw each other every night.

Hale had his own car, which was rare back then, and in the evenings he'd drive over and pick her up and take her back to his place on Heliotrope Drive. Of course there wasn't any real hanky-panky — Ruth remembered her Aunt Elizabeth's misfortunes, and was careful to look behind Hale's flattering words, to get to know him before doing anything she might regret. Almost immediately, though, she realized there would be no trip to the Philippines after all.

And then one evening, when Hale proposed, she also gave up on the idea of graduation itself.

They were married, in a chapel with loud brass bells, just six weeks after they had met. Ruth vowed to take the name of Armstrong and she kept that vow; and after their honeymoon trip to the Grand Canyon they moved into a house on Santa Barbara Avenue, out by Exposition Boulevard.

Ruth remembered the first months well, as if they were only yesterday. She and Hale painting the walls of their very first bedroom, and ending up painting each other. Driving out by the ocean, stopping along the road, climbing up into a tree to watch the sunset. The day a bird got trapped in the kitchen and Hale rushed home from work to perform a rescue operation. How at night they shared secrets in bed, and how Hale murmured "Yes, I know" to everything she said, and how he really *did* know. The morning they had their first fight. The night they made up. The tuneless tunes he used to whistle as he washed dishes, which at times almost drove her crazy, but which now ran through her head whenever she was lonely.

She remembered Hale's laugh, his bushy eyebrows, the smell of his undershirts. The funny faces he made to cheer her up before he got out of bed in the morning. The strange searching smile he gave her as they made love. The big vein that ran back along his bare, broad forehead, and how very soft his skin felt for a man so strong.

After fourteen months in the house on Santa Barbara Avenue, Hale took the job with the U.S. Geological Survey and they moved to Washington, D.C. That winter, Ruth became pregnant with Douglas, the future doctor, and Hale took his first trip out to the new oil fields in Oklahoma, leaving her behind. Ruth missed him desperately, but it helped a little that his letters were loving and indulgent. "My Darling Girlie," they'd always start, and he wrote her almost every day, even when nothing at all had happened.

Years passed. Carter was born, a child with a rhythmical bounce who would one day become an artist. Hale's responsibilities increased, and he received regular promotions; soon he was staying in Oklahoma for months at a time. He continued to write regularly, and his letters were consistently kind: they described Ponca City, where he had a little house, and the men and women at the Indian reservation, where he did his work.

Once, for Hale's thirtieth birthday, she visited him at the little house in Ponca City.

It was a big surprise.

For over a month, back in Washington, she'd made secret arrangements for the trip: the children were to stay with the Deedses, and she taught them to behave as proper guests; her parents wired money for the train ticket, despite believing her plans too extravagant. And then one evening, exactly a week after Hale boarded the train for Ponca City, Ruth herself boarded the same train, and followed him. June 16, 1935: she had never before traveled by herself.

The journey lasted two days and three nights — three hot, exhausting, unnerving nights. At one point, rather late in the course of the final night, just as she was drifting toward sleep, Ruth was roused by the sound of a woman's loud pleadings and protestations in the neighboring berth. She heard a drunk man's steady, insistent drone, then a woman's — it hardly sounded like the same woman — muffled shriek and giggle and groan and a strange, quick thumping noise that sounded like somebody bouncing a ball. There was passionate talk — "That's right, honey, now, yes, that's right!" "Please, honey!" "Yes!" — then, suddenly, quiet. An imploring, drawn-out sort of quiet. Intrigued, filled with a vague but real desire to be nearer the disturbance, Ruth slipped from her bed, pulled a robe over her nightgown and, stepping out into the corridor, almost bumped into a very young, diminutive girl — she couldn't have been older than sixteen — dressed in an expensive, silky black cocktail dress, with lace sleeves and a low-cut neck. Her chest, Ruth noticed, was almost as flat as a child's. Her hair was reddish, long and curly and damp, several matted clumps slicked flat against her neck; her eyes were dark and tired; her tiny face was glowing. She was, Ruth thought, disarmingly beautiful. The girl leaned against the wall with the languid, complacent grace of a creature immune to love.

She twisted her red lips into a serpentine grin. "Silent suffering," she said, gesturing toward the closed door of her berth. "Don't *we* do enough of it?"

"We?"

"You know, *we*," the girl said, moving forward and dropping a hand on Ruth's forearm. "We women."

Speechless, Ruth stared down at the hand: an immense white stone sparkled from the wedding-ring finger. Ruth wondered if it was real, the stone, and if it was really a *marriage* stone. More likely, she thought, it was just some ruse devised by the girl's desperate lover: the shimmering, immodest jewel seemed to wink at all conventional notions of propriety. Ruth looked into the girl's face. The lips were too red, she thought; wet and smudged with excessive kissing, probably, or red wine, or fruit punch; they both fascinated and unnerved Ruth, as if they might swallow all her secrets in one giant gulp, then spit them back out into the mocking night.

Ruth said, "I'm not sure I understand."

"*You* know." The girl rearranged her posture. "A woman needs to take charge once in a while, don't you think? Make him pay attention."

Ruth said nothing. Briefly, she was reminded of her Aunt Elizabeth. The same immodesty, the same sexual flippancy. Ruth felt a familiar mix of admiration and envy and fear.

"Well?" the girl said. "Cat got your tongue, lady?"

"My what?"

"Your tongue," the girl said. "You got one?"

Ruth hesitated, stepping backward into the threshold of her little sleeping chamber. It wasn't that she didn't want to talk. She did, but she was unaccustomed to discussing personal matters with anyone, let alone a half-naked stranger. In the Caster and Armstrong clans, public mention, indeed any mention, of private emotions was considered unacceptable, a sign of bad breeding and bad taste. Still, there was something alluring about the girl, something unfettered and innocent, and Ruth could not quite bring her usual judgments to bear. She felt an intense curiosity.

"Well, I," she stammered, "I heard some noises. But so long as you're okay —"

The girl hooted and gave Ruth's arm a squeeze. "Marvelous," she said. "Even better." She glanced into Ruth's berth, looked her over from head to toe. "And you?"

Abruptly, rather painfully, Ruth was struck by the prudery of her own neat comportment, her thick green robe and cool skin and tight curlers and delicately scented ointments and upright, honorable behavior. She forced herself to make the conventional response.

"Fine," she said.

"*Fine*," the girl repeated. The expression on her face was irreverently reverent.

"You see, Hale —" Ruth's voice was strained. "He's in Oklahoma, you see. Working there."

"*Oklahoma.*"

The girl released her grip on Ruth's arm and began to twist a strand of wet red hair around and around her finger. "Well, Oklahoma." Was she laughing? She was certainly smiling an unsettling smile. "Well, now, lots of time before Oklahoma. Must be ten stops before then." Her red lips puckered with compassion. "Ask me, you're liable to get a trifle bored all alone in there by yourself, Miss . . ."

"Mrs. Hale Armstrong," Ruth said.

There was an awkward silence. A question was on the tip of Ruth's tongue, and she finally asked it.

"What about you?" she said.

"Me?"

"Yes. Well, your name. And your . . ."

Her voice sounded nervous, she realized — she wasn't used to being nosy — and she struggled to appear more composed.

"Your destination."

The girl only stared.

"I mean, well, as for myself, it's my husband's birthday, his thirtieth, so I'm going out to Oklahoma. A surprise."

Still no answer.

Ruth took a step forward. "And you?"

"No destination," the girl said at last. "Wherever the train takes us." She laughed. "Wherever I want."

Suddenly, a kind of growl came from the girl's berth. They both turned as the door opened and a man stepped out — middle-aged, for sure, though his sand-colored hair and puckish, delicate features gave him an oddly boyish air. He wore a black satin robe;

he had fine pale skin and dark, exhausted eyes. Absently, he nodded at Ruth. Then he put one hand on the girl's waist and, squeezing her there, pulled her back toward their chamber.

"See?" the girl said, slowly closing her eyes. "Isn't it nice?" She reached for the man's hand. With a faint moan, she pressed his fingers into the flesh of her tiny left breast.

Ruth glanced away. Countless thoughts — a vast tidewater — flowed through her brain. At one point it occurred to her to wonder about the status of her own marriage. But she dismissed the question: she was in love.

Then the girl spoke.

"Sorry, Oklahoma." She made a little curtsy, closed the door in front of Ruth's face.

Alone in her little bed again, Ruth lay face-up, sleepless, gazing at the images that danced before her eyes: red lips and tired eyes; her breast, his fingers. She was filled with a new kind of wonder. What *were* the ingredients of physical intimacy? How could they be measured and combined? Spontaneity and unabashed attention-grabbing were required, that much seemed clear, and she vowed that she would be more demonstrative with Hale. More daring, more expressive.

Her love for her husband would never diminish. It would grow with the years, become more fervent, more sensual, more alive. Yes, she would make sure of it.

She twisted on her side, all desire and anticipation, desperate to arrive in Ponca City. "Oh Hale," she whispered, "I love you, I —"

"Hey, no sweat," a voice said.

He touched her.

"We're shipshape on the garbage front. Everything in its right place, just like the doctor ordered."

"Yes?" Ruth blinked and looked up from the corner of an eye. She lay curled on her side, warm and sticky, clutching a toss pillow tight against her stomach.

"Trashwise, I'd have to say we're —" Henry gave her a worried look. "Hey, you okay?"

"Yes, fine," she said, lying. "What else?"

"All right, but you seem a little — what's the word? — kind of worn out. Kind of daydreamy." Tenderly, with palpable concern, his hand found a resting place on top of Ruth's head. "Guess I'll just go on up to my desk now." He hesitated for a moment. "Course, you need anything, just holler."

Ruth reached up and pushed his hand away. She ran her fingers through her hair: it was cut very short, the curls neat and tame.

"Yes, go on then," she said, "I've got things to accomplish here."

"Righto," he said.

"So many things."

"Absolutely."

Henry was still gazing down at her, his eyes troubled, hand in his mouth now, twirling the loose tooth.

"*Well?*" she said.

"Right as rain. I'm on my way."

He turned and shuffled toward the stairs. After a few steps, though, he stopped and grinned back at her like a little boy.

"Didn't mean you aren't cute," he said. "Just tuckered out."

"*Henry.*"

"Holler loud, I'm always there."

Ruth watched him trudge up the steps.

Cute, she thought. An utterly preposterous notion, of course, but somehow the sound of it gave her a moment of quiet, almost indecent pleasure.

She looked at Hale's diamond watch: already past one-fifteen. Normally, on the afternoon of a White Rabbit day, she'd spend at least an hour calling relatives and friends, never mind the cost. But this was cleaning day, and Luzma was due in less than two hours. Ruth yawned. The thing to do, she decided, was to get in some exercise right away. Once the girl left, it would be too dark to venture outdoors.

Sometimes the days seemed very full.

"Cute." She sighed, and pushed herself up.

Ruth stood on the steps outside her front door, sunglass lenses clipped into place, umbrella swinging from her wrist. It was becoming warm now: silvery waves of heat seemed to snake up from the cement. She lifted her cane, aiming across the courtyard toward the yellow fire hydrant, then lowered her cane and struck out, moving fast. At the hydrant, she took a short breather before aiming the tip of her cane again, drawing a bead on a lemon tree at the end of the path between the tennis court and pool, and continuing on her way. It usually took Ruth forty-five minutes, propelling herself in this cane-pointing fashion, to complete her daily exercise.

Destination Zigzag, she called her walking game. The object was to move from point to point like a boat tacking across the wind, changing course every fifty yards or so, stopping to catch her breath at each Destination along the way. The word "Destination" seemed essential to her; it implied purpose and meaning and maybe even adventure; a simple exercise walk became a daring little voyage. Though Ruth played the game often in the course of each day, the Destination Game had special meaning on her afternoon walks, because these walks began and ended without interruption at her own front door. If, as she stood at her penultimate Destination, Ruth spotted number 24 in her exact line of vision, approximately fifty yards across the courtyard, she could point to her door with relief and resignation, knowing that it was the proper Final Destination.

She almost always followed a route around the same two rows of condominiums, which jutted out from the pool yard like a skinny thumb and index finger rising from a knotted fist.

Alongside the first row, on a strip of land between the condominiums and the visitors' parking lot, was a garden. The garden was done in mixed Spanish Revival and Oriental styles. At its center stood a plaster mission church, about five feet high, surrounded by bamboo fronds. Rodrigo watered the garden twice a day, which kept it a nice lush green; there were a few small palms, a few small bush-animals — elephants, giraffes, flamingos. Rodrigo had been training the animals on molded wires. Like the dog at the front gate, they were flimsy and full of holes, so that as Ruth walked by she could look not only through their bodies, but also straight through their heads.

Swinging her cane with a nice rhythm, feeling jaunty, she made her way past eight front doors to the end of the first row and circled around the last condominium. The road on this back side was a mess. That whole week, men from the gas company had been digging it up, leaving chunks of asphalt and pieces of pipe scattered all over the place. Ruth picked her way cautiously through the debris. Another waste of monthly Association dues — she'd have to help pay for this unsightly and unnecessary project, one she'd never wanted undertaken in the first place. Sighing to herself and shaking her head, she lifted her cane to skirt a deep hole, then walked around an orange plastic warning cone.

Three steps later, she came across a snail in her path. She stooped to examine it for a moment, then squashed it with the end of her cane. Brown and green and slimy, the crushed slug oozed out from its broken shell. It gurgled and frothed, shimmering as it expired in the afternoon sun.

Death: the aftermath was never pleasant.

Ruth winced and resumed her walk.

Only a few months after Hale was buried, she began making preparations to return to California. It was nothing like her dreams of moving home with Hale and the boys. Douglas had already started at a private high school and wanted to stay there, and Carter, a precociously artistic youth with the temper to match, demanded that he be allowed to join his older brother.

"You should leave the boys right here in Washington with me," Mr. Squib, Douglas's headmaster, told Ruth; he added something about talent and stability and decent father figures. And so, one August morning, Ruth said goodbye to her two sons.

She packed all of her things into a trailer, the Mullen's Red Gap luggage trailer that Hale had bought for summer vacations, and set out across the country, alone. She hadn't shed a tear since the day of Hale's funeral. Already she'd discovered both the power and the solace of routine — death had its own relentless requirements — and the journey west was one more bit of business that had to be transacted. So don't think, she told herself. Just drive. Pick out a target on the map and point the car and then later pick out another target farther down the road. In any case, the driving was all she could handle. The heavy trailer terrified her, always swinging wide on turns, and there was no choice but to concentrate on the physics of velocity and mass. She locked both hands on the wheel; she took her time, resting every two or three hours, buying meals in roadside diners and staying in cheap motels at night, where the bath water came out brown. Mile after mile, it was all routine. The tires beneath her, the horizon ahead. Don't think, she'd remind herself, but now and then she'd find herself thinking. Hale lighting the barbecue. Hale talking on the telephone. Hale coming out of the bathroom with a towel around his waist. Hale playing catch with Douglas and Carter on the beach at San Diego. Hale running his fingers through her hair, kissing her on the neck; Hale lifting up her skirt and pulling off her stockings and saying, "Pretty legs, pretty legs." Hale dancing and Hale dying.

One afternoon, somewhere in the flats of New Mexico, she felt a sharp jolt at the back of the car. In the rearview mirror she could see the trailer wobbling back and forth like an untracked roller coaster. Ruth squeezed the steering wheel and tried to brake gently, but after a second the car jerked hard to the left. Almost instantly there was a loud pop, then a grating sound, then something snapped and the trailer went careening into a ravine at the side of the road.

Somehow, struggling, she brought the car to a stop. For a moment she sat perfectly still. There was no traffic at all. No houses or restaurants or gas stations — no one to know whether she lived or died.

All alone, she thought.

No Hale, no God. Just an expansive white nothingness.

The desolation was startling. Sand and mountains and empty road. Sweat dripped from her curls; her blouse stuck to her skin like a piece of damp plastic. Slowly, not quite conscious of her own movements, she reached into her purse for her sunglasses, slipped them on, blotted her face and neck with a tissue. She told herself to stay calm. Sooner or later help had to come — a public highway after all, and things could be worse, and all she had to do was be patient and wait for . . . Right then something seemed to spring open inside her. Partly sorrow, partly rage. It all came out at once: a loud howling sound from the bottom of her lungs. She dropped her forehead against the horn and let it blare.

For the rest of her life it would lurk on the edge of her dreams. A blaring horn. The sound of her own ferocious howling.

"You *idiot*," she wailed, "I *loved* you."

It was her greatest secret: the hurt and horror.

Actively, with startling self-discipline, she purged this anger from her thoughts. She would not remember it again.

She would remember a stretch of empty time passing by, a bland void. Later, when she sat up, absolute silence filled the car. Permanent silence, pure and thick and mortifying.

"Well," she murmured, "now what?"

But still only silence.

"Hale?" she said.

She opened the door, stepped out, walked around to the front of the car, and lifted the hood. A plume of steam curled up, licked at her nose and eyes. She leaned back, fanning the air with her hand, then studied the maze of machinery parts: little red wires and little blue wires and several black caps that sizzled when she touched them. For a moment she stood sucking at the tips of her fingers. Then she scowled, pushed the dirty curls from her forehead, backed away from the car, and sat down in the middle of the road.

She didn't budge. Legs crossed, hands folded, she stared willfully at the endless white stripes unfolding toward the mountains.

Ruth would not remember how long she sat there. Maybe two hours, maybe longer. All she would remember with any certainty was the scorching sun, the asphalt burning through her skirt, the long empty desert road. Later, probably much later, a car appeared on the horizon like a tiny sailboat on the waves of a great white ocean. Ruth sat still as it approached. Only when the car had come to a stop did she stand up, straighten her blouse and skirt, and walk over. A man and a woman and three children and a dog were crowded together inside, as cozy and secure as anything Ruth had ever seen in her life.

The man smiled at her. "You okay?"

Abruptly, for the very first time since Hale's death, Ruth permitted herself the great luxury of sarcasm.

"A widow," she said. "I'm just *fine*."

1:51 P.M.

A plane flew overhead, dragging a banner: "Rock Around the Clock with AM 660!"

Ruth had completed her first loop. She was feeling lightheaded, much more tired than usual, so she paused to catch her breath. Her current choice of a Destination had landed her on the second of three steps that led up to the pool.

The pool yard was surrounded by large glass panels draped with vines of hanging ivy. Fiery red bougainvillea bushes grew just inside the glass; quite often, the midafternoon sunlight reflected off the glass at an angle, casting the red from the bougainvillea up into Ruth's eyes.

Though anybody could look through the glass as into a giant

fishbowl, to see who was swimming or lying by the pool, the area could be entered only through a black iron gate at the top of the three stairs where Ruth now stood. The gate opened with the usual Auto-Mate card. When the management had campaigned for increased monthly Association dues, they'd promised that this gate, like the fence that surrounded the whole Lagoon, would offer "Cadillac quality" protection. It would keep unwanted lechers from the pool, they said, just as the fence at the highway kept out unwanted vehicles.

Now a hand-printed sign hung from the gate: "Members! We don't Swim in our Toilets. Let's not Pee in our Pool!"

Ruth climbed to the top stair to see if Kaji was inside. She raised a hand to her eyes, shading them from the bright sun, and peered through the iron bars. She saw the figures of several women — hips and halters — but couldn't quite make out who they were. She would not enter to take a closer look, however, since she lived in dread of somehow ending up locked inside. For not only did you have to insert a card to get in, but you had to insert one to get back out — and what if she dropped hers in the water as she walked beside the pool, or what if someone took it from her by mistake as she sat watching the people swim? She worried about this constantly: locked up in her own pool yard, dying of sunstroke or starvation.

Behind her, a horn suddenly blared. Ruth cringed, thrown off balance. For an instant she was transported back to that empty desert highway. "Help," she said quietly, to nobody but herself, "I'm a widow."

"Hey, Grammy!" someone yelled.

Ruth teetered slightly, pressing her nose between two of the iron bars and looking slowly from one sunbathing figure to the next. Then the voice came louder:

"Grammy! Over *here*, in the parking lot. Hang on a minute, I'll drive over."

It was Karen. Ruth's heart leapt.

The girl was driving a white convertible; as she pulled up alongside the curb, Ruth noticed that her hair was a mess, as usual, and still that terrible silver-blond color: she'd taken to dye since turning twenty-nine. She was wearing bright red shorts and a green tank top, which reminded Ruth, in a flash, that it was almost Christmas.

Ruth walked down to the bottom step, leaned into the car to offer her cheek, then tapped at the white door with the tip of her cane. "Where'd you get *this* contraption?"

Karen reached out for Ruth's hand. "Bought it myself, just last week. Mike helped, of course."

"Mike?"

"Oh, stop that. Mike-the-husband — you talked to him on the phone this morning."

"Well, yes, of course," Ruth said. "Him." She saw no point in pursuing the subject. "I guess you're sorry about this morning."

"Sorry?"

"You know, Karen."

"What? I was a little sleepy, that's all." She tucked her hair behind her ears, pulled a long strand of neon-green gum from her mouth. "I mean, really, it was barely sunrise, for Pete's sake. What do you expect? Anyway, I tried to reach you later but nobody answered."

"Tried when?"

"Around ten."

Ruth thought it over. She'd been downtown then. And Henry, no doubt, had been asleep — he wouldn't have heard a siren, let alone the phone.

"Well, I accept the apology," she said. "But in the future, you might try to remember an old lady like me needs all the good luck she can get. I would have won, you know, if you'd answered the phone yourself."

"Won?"

"You know."

"What? Oh, right." Karen laughed. "White Rabbit."

Ruth cringed as if the blow had been physical. "Fine," she said. "A repeat offense." She stared into the space behind Karen's head. Then she tapped the car door with her cane three times. "Go ahead and park, and come walk with me. I've got one more loop."

Karen bit off the strand of gum, rolled it into a little ball, flicked it over the windshield. "Can't stay," she said. "I'm meeting Mike down at Five Crowns. Just wanted to let you know I'll be stopping over later — be back as soon as we're done with lunch."

Ruth raised her eyebrows. "Five Crowns? Just how does the maniac make a living these days?"

"A schoolteacher, Grammy."

"Schoolteacher? At Five Crowns?"

Karen laughed and rolled her eyes. "He's been saving it up or something, Grammy, I don't know. The point is, I'll be back in a couple of hours. Can you remember *that*?"

Ruth clucked her tongue. The girl had always been wiry and nervous, but today she seemed particularly tense. "Just asking, sweetheart, no need to get excited." She gave her right knee a pop, squared up her shoulders. "Anyway, why meet him way down here? Aren't there enough overpriced restaurants in Los Angeles?"

"We'll talk about it later, okay? I have to run — supposed to be there at two, he'll be furious if I'm late."

"Furious?" Ruth said.

"Well, I didn't mean —"

Ruth snorted. "What is it with this man? After all that nonsense he's been up to lately, running away on you like that, you're awfully eager to accommodate his schedule, not to mention his other requirements. If you want my opinion, you should just —"

"Not now," Karen said. "I already promised you, I'll be right back."

Ruth shrugged and adjusted her glasses. "Fine then, it's your life," she said, "but I've had some experience with men myself. Remember what I told you about old Frank Deeds? Used to work myself into quite a tizzy, trying to be all gussied up and punctual for those shabby weekend trysts of ours. And you know what good it did me."

"Frank Deeds was an ass."

"I beg your pardon?"

"You heard me."

Ruth forced a small, threadbare smile. She stared down at the curb, tapping the cement with her cane. What was the point in talking if the girl was so closed-minded? Frank had *not* been an ass. Thirteen years older than Hale, a man full of worldly news and advice, he was one of the best-known lawyers in Washington, D.C. Ruth and Hale had met him their first year there, when they had their place on Nevada Avenue and Frank and his wife were living up the hill on Oliver Street.

Still gazing at the curb, Ruth shook her head. "Hardly an ass, dear. Quite a catch, in fact."

"Oh, right," Karen said.

Ruth ignored her. "Very debonair and quick-witted, if you follow my meaning. Not to mention expensive suits. He used to come over, bottle of Scotch in hand, and he and Hale would be up half the night, trading silly stories from work or chortling about the latest antics of Frank's wife, Myrna. I used to overhear them, you understand, I never got involved directly —" Ruth felt herself slip away for a moment. Like switching TV channels, like plucking ancient reruns from some swirling electric time-air — *Time!* Hale had cried. *Right there! So much time!* — and the time-screen lighted up with ghostly speckled static, then shapes and voices, then grainy episodes of a sad old comedy that kept spinning itself out forever — Frank stealing glances at her ballerina legs, Frank opening doors for her with a gentlemanly flourish. The night she'd accidentally overheard him discussing his thoughts on love, and how he'd given her a wink and a wide rakish smirk that made her turn away. And then of course the time when he tried to put his tongue in her hair, and the time he almost . . .

"Grammy, are you *there?*"

"Pardon me?"

"Welcome back."

Ruth pretended not to hear. "In any event," she said, "the man did have his faults. Too many hormones. But he was earnest in his own way — and he saved my life the winter your grandfather died." She tapped the car door. "Which, I do believe, is more than we can say about this flashy man of yours, who almost kills you himself, deserts you, runs off in the middle of a marriage, and then thinks he can make it all up with a fast car or two."

Karen laughed. "Volkswagens aren't exactly hot rods, Grammy." She started the engine.

Ruth stepped back and rearranged her shoulders. She didn't want to make the girl angry or press her too hard — she might not return at all. The thought terrified her.

"All right, sweetheart," she sniffed, lifting the tip of her cane and turning to pick out a Destination near the row she was about to circle. "I do miss you."

It hadn't been necessary for Frank to confess his marital problems a great many times before Ruth began to feel awkward when she met Myrna at the market, or when the four of them went out for dinner together. "How lucky we are," Ruth would whisper to Hale, nudging him under the table with her foot while Frank and Myrna argued over what wine they'd order or who would drive home at the end of the evening.

Later, predictably, Frank and Myrna ended up in divorce court, and Frank left his firm and moved out to San Diego. He went on Ruth's recommendation, or so he'd said when he left. He never wrote. At one point, Hale heard word that the man's life had gone downhill a bit — too many women, too much gambling, too many drunken jaunts down to Mexico.

In any case, Frank returned to Washington the winter Hale died. The day after the funeral, feeling like wood inside, barely able to function, Ruth had phoned him on impulse: she remembered picking up Hale's address book and reaching out to dial the number in San Diego. "I'll be there," he'd said. "Day after tomorrow, I'll be there."

Day after tomorrow.

That was Frank.

To his credit, of course, he did eventually take charge of things. Escorted her to dinner. Made her eat and talked reassuring talk and encouraged her to wash her hair and change her clothes and pluck the stray hairs from her chin. That first evening he helped her draw up a budget, went over Hale's investments and property holdings.

For nearly three weeks Frank stayed on in Washington just to keep her company. Or so he claimed. Motives aside, Ruth couldn't have made do without him. It was touching, really, the way he sat comforting Carter and counseling him about school; he began looking into prospects for selling the house; he spent whole afternoons listening to Ruth's worries, sipping coffee and nodding thoughtfully and coming up with crisp, lawyerly suggestions. At the same time there was a funny feeling to it all. If, as he often did, he took her hand as he tried to console her, he would squeeze her fingers a fraction too hard. He seemed overly eager for her return to California. And once or twice, in the middle of the night, she'd opened her eyes to find him standing above her, mumbling to himself and gesticulating.

Finally, one rainy afternoon, Frank made his position clear. The roof above Hale's old office had begun to leak, and water was streaming across the cracked ceiling, dripping off at various places to form puddles all over the floor. Ruth scurried about the room, strategically positioning buckets and bowls. She gathered together some sponges and rags and was just bending to mop the hardwood paneling when she felt Frank's fingers on her back.

The skin seemed to curl around her bones. "I thought you were spreading that tarp on the roof —"

"My love," he said, "my great dear love —"

" — cleaning leaves out of the rain gutter —"

"It's been love, Ruthie, from the moment I first put eyes on you. Knock-down hammer-hold love."

Ruth knelt there on the floor, her bottom in the air, drips of water splashing against her forehead. "Me and fifteen other women," she said, and tried to laugh. "Maybe *fifty* others."

Frank shrugged his shoulders. "Very true," he said. "I've had my share, that's for sure, but now it's different. I mean, I've never felt like this before, not even close. It's love, Ruthie. The kind that wakes a tired man up."

Ruth turned to look at him, startled but also half amused. Carter was due home from school at any minute.

"Frank, be serious," she said. "I have two grown children. And you're practically old enough to be their grandfather." What she did not say, of course, was that he'd been her husband's good friend — maybe best friend — and that Hale had been in the grave barely a month.

"You're right," Frank said, "except I've felt this forever. Known this forever. I was born knowing it, and I'll always know it. Can't you even . . . Can't you feel that?"

Ruth could not even *guess* what she felt, let alone know it forever. Beyond a certain point she simply wasn't capable of thought. Frank was a good man, no doubt, and if he really meant any of this, he'd wait for her. She stood up and pulled away from him, moving to another puddle across the room.

"Back to work," she said.

She was panting as she passed a diamond-shaped orange construction sign next to number 39, the last condominium in the row. She felt terribly lightheaded — her vision had gone fuzzy at the edges — and for a time she could not recall how she had arrived at this particular spot on the planet. Her internal compass seemed out of whack. No true north. She put one foot in front of the other, watching her sandals trudge along like a pair of separate creatures; they no longer seemed attached to her feet, and as she rounded the corner of number 39 there was the queer sensation that she'd lost authority over her entire body — everything. The past seemed to steer her. She walked slowly, trying to regain control, wondering if it was even worth the effort, until suddenly, inexplicably, a white chalk circle appeared on the asphalt before her. She took a half-step forward. Inside the circle, at its very center, was a soupy pile of dog feces. Ruth stared for a moment, surprised. The management had *finally* done something useful with her monthly dues. A brilliant idea, actually, to send someone out to draw a warning circle around this mess. She smiled to herself, making a mental note to congratulate the managers, then she lifted her cane and gingerly navigated around the circled-in poop.

In a way this incident reassured her. There were real things in the world, things you could touch, things the imagination could never distort. Things that demanded attention, even action. Things that — whoever saw them, from whatever angle — always looked the same.

Ruth took another breather after arriving at the rear of number 39, placing her hand on the condo's wall, swinging her right knee in and out, loosening it up. She blinked several times to be sure her vision had cleared. Then stiffly, feeling the heat, she pulled back her shoulders, aimed fifty yards ahead toward the bumper of a silver BMW, and continued down the smooth black asphalt.

Arriving in Los Angeles, that summer after Hale's death, Ruth moved in with her mother and father, into the same upstairs bedroom she'd used as a girl. Nothing at all had changed. The same quilted bedspread, the same white dresser with pink knobs, the same wooden trunk below the window. Fresh poppies and marigolds peeked up from a vase on the windowsill. Something about the flowers, and the unchanging sameness of things, made Ruth cry.

At dinner that night she was still crying. It went on through the main course and into dessert — she couldn't stop — and then her mother began crying too, sniffling and dabbing at her eyes with a napkin.

Ruth's father tapped a plate with his fork. "What *is* this?" He looked at Lydia, then at Ruth. "All right, of course, I know it's an awful time," he said. "Hale's death and all. And I'm not opposed to regular sadness. Except it's been five months now. Almost six. Sooner or later people have to pull themselves together. The truth is — don't take this wrong — the truth is, you've got certain obligations. Responsibilities like everybody else. Your two boys, Douglas and Carter, sometimes I think you've completely forgotten them."

Ruth stared at her strawberry shortcake. "They're in school. They don't need me. *Nobody* does."

"Don't be ridiculous."

"But it's true, I'm just a —"

Across the table, Lydia released a loud, breathy sob. Ruth handed over a fresh napkin. Oddly, her mother's crying made Ruth feel firmer inside, almost hard, as if someone else had stepped forward to take up the exhausting burden of emotion.

"So right now," her father was saying, "right now you should try rejoining the world. Find things to do. A hobby, maybe, or a good job." He gave her a short, hopeful smile. "Think about it. Isn't there some — how do I phrase this? — some *interest* you've always wanted to pursue?"

Lydia blew her nose and looked up. "The piano," she said. "That's a possibility. More piano lessons."

"Great," Ruth said, "I'll play my own funeral march."

Tears bubbled up in Lydia's eyes again. "Don't even suggest such things. What about art? Watercolors? Ballet? Or maybe — maybe give gardening a try. That little patch out back where it's all weeds, I'll bet you could grow some absolutely spectacular tulips there."

"Or I could chop off my head."

"Darling."

"Eat steak knives."

Her father reached across the table and took Lydia's hand. "Ruthie, please. No need to take this out on your mother and me. We just want what's best."

"Water torture. Join a convent."

"Nonsense," her mother said. "You aren't Catholic."

Ruth looked down at her shortcake. What did they know? Her parents still had each other. More than anything now, Ruth was simply and crushingly lonely — that wild howling desert loneliness — loneliness that made her skin dry up and her bones go brittle.

Besides, a widowed woman in her late thirties should not be living in her father's house. She should die.

The idea tempted her.

In bed that night she tried to make it happen. Not one more breath — never. Her face went hot, her lungs itched, her throat seemed to clog up with a substance like thick wet tar. Don't breathe, she told herself. *Never*. A few seconds later, when the dizziness came, she found herself imagining her own pale corpse. Buried in Hale's coffin. Wrapped around him, snuggled tight, cozy and peaceful and happy and dead.

She woke up early the next morning. Alive, of course, which she took as an omen.

That same afternoon she enrolled at the Sawyer School, where for three months she studied shorthand and typing. In late October she secured a secretarial position at a doctor's office over on Figueroa Street. It was a godsend. To her surprise, she actually enjoyed the work, enjoyed fussing over patients, enjoyed the way so many people suddenly needed her — like that pregnant girl who came out of the examination room crying, like the poor vagabond who panicked when he saw his bill.

For half a year, Ruth was content.

Then Frank Deeds showed up again, with his absurd notion that happiness was always possible.

It was a pleasant time, for the most part. Like a convalescence. At least twice a month, Frank would come up on the train from

San Diego and take her out to lunch or a show. They laughed together, they talked, they had fun. Ruth could almost feel herself mending. The man was a little too smooth, maybe, but he was urbane and well mannered and handsome, even charming. A man who had once rescued her, who had literally led her by the hand out of that paralyzing depression.

Other things, too. Those wonderfully expensive suits. The way he used words. "The Lord's honest truth," he'd tell her, "you're like an aged French wine, perfect tannins, perfect nose, more exquisite with every passing day."

Talk like this made Ruth's stomach flutter — she couldn't help herself — but at the same time it bothered her when Frank issued his standard pleas before boarding the train to go back. Always the same lopsided grin, the same artful pitch: "Hop on, Ruthie, San Diego or bust, we'll have ourselves a ball." She'd laugh a little, and come up with an excuse, then go home to hide. The man scared her. He pushed too hard — too certain, too passionate. Now and then, though, she was frightened by her own late-night stirrings, certain needs and desires. She'd stare into the dark, feeling a vague guilt, remembering all the promises she'd made to Hale, things like faithfulness, and devotion, and how she'd love him forever.

There was also the problem of Frank's reputation.

"Don't fool yourself," her father warned her one evening. "I know the type. Sneaking down to Mexico. Drunken binges and dice tables. Probably dilly-dallying with every female in San Diego."

"Well, I suppose," Ruth said quietly. "But he loves *me*."

And that was something.

Yes, it was.

Her father huffed. "Then why doesn't the man act like it? Straighten out and stop splashing money around like toilet water? Because he's an ass, that's what. He's Frank Deeds."

"Listen, Daddy, you don't even —"

"A donkey. A downtown dandy."

Ruth inserted some stiffness into her voice. "You're not even listening. I'm the one who's stalling. I'm the one who can't agree to a serious commitment. If you want the truth, the real truth, he's crazy about me. Wants me to visit him in San Diego."

She hesitated.

"And if you want more truth, I'm going."

2:07 P.M.

Ruth leaned heavily on her cane, feeling faint. She'd made it around the second row of condominiums and was back at the pool. Yet something wasn't quite right — her heart was pounding, filaments of sparkly white light moved in ribbons across her field of vision. For a few seconds she wondered if she might pass out, or something worse, but then, just as suddenly, she felt perfectly fine again. Her pulse slowed, the waves of light were gone. Never mind, she thought. She could walk farther than people seemed to realize. Despite prevailing attitudes, especially here in California, old age did not necessarily equate with infirmity. Even Henry still managed to cross and recross the highway each morning — with an armful of groceries, for God's sake. And she could certainly outwalk *that* fumblebum. She'd do an extra loop, this time on the path that circled the pool. She raised her cane, squinted at a lamppost near the far end of the pool, set off with a clipped, determined stride.

Her whole life was about to explode.

July 26, 1947. Like riding dynamite — bang, a new Ruth — and the train wheels had the hot fizzling sound of a lighted fuse. Ruth watched the ocean and houses and thirsty brown hills roll by, picturing Frank's face, imagining a weekend of dancing and dinners and, if things went well, almost certainly a proposal of marriage. It was a life pivot, she told herself, one of those either-or moments that can turn things around forever. It was also a declaration of her own serious intent.

To keep things proper, and to protect herself, she'd be staying with her Aunt Elizabeth. Not the ideal situation, but at least the blast would be cushioned a bit: somebody to talk with, somebody she trusted and treasured. How long since they'd last seen each other? Three years? Probably closer to four. No matter, though, because they were like sisters, and time couldn't change a thing like that. In ten minutes they'd have their shoes kicked off; they'd be talking about their children and old times and the latest radio shows and the men in their lives. Mostly men. Mostly Frank. How she cared for him, maybe even loved him, but how in a funny way she was also apprehensive. How his words were always so beautiful and convincing, but how his behavior sometimes wasn't. How he'd sworn to be faithful to her, but how in the end she couldn't quite trust him.

Men.

She took several deep breaths, thinking, *Men*. They could blow you to pieces.

At four o'clock, when the train pulled in, Elizabeth was there on the platform, dressed in a red leather jacket and skirt, waving a feathered green hat. Same as ever, Ruth thought happily. The woman was sixty-seven years old but still lively, still slim and smooth-skinned and bristling with sharp arrowlike angles. Still eccentric, too.

"A drink!" Elizabeth yelled. "First a drink, then down to basics. Sex talk! Sex, sex, sex — nothing else!"

An hour later they were sitting at Elizabeth's kitchen table. A box of crackers, a bottle of sherry.

"Sexwise," Elizabeth said grimly, "it's chronic drought."

She pulled on a pair of long black gloves. Drinking gloves, she called them. With a grunt, sighing heavily, she folded her legs beneath her and spent a few minutes recapping her last several years in San Diego, the ups and downs. Almost entirely downs, she said. Maybe it was a function of age: after sixty, things drooped. In any case, up until recently her days had been massively and ferociously boring, pure drudgery. "The usual old-lady crud," she said. "Shopping, farting, teaching voice to little boys without penises."

Elizabeth burped and flashed a smile.

"Until *recently*, mind you." She winked. "Right now, just maybe, things might be looking up. Glorious things. Big hot ripe manly things, if you catch the innuendo."

"I do."

"Oh, I'm quite *sure* you do. Another drink?"

"Certainly."

"To manliness," said Elizabeth. "To firmness and solidity in all its enticing variety."

Ruth couldn't help smoothing down her skirt, grinning. "Immensity, too," she said. "Immense and exploding things, to be precise."

It was the sherry, no doubt — Ruth was shocked by her own tongue. She glanced down at Hale's wristwatch.

"Speaking of which," she said, "I'll be meeting someone over at the marina this evening...and I'll need time to get myself...It's important."

"A *sex* appointment!"

"Not quite, but it's still —"

Elizabeth grinned and thumped the table with her fist. "No spice, no dice. Just cancel. Let the man squirm."

Ruth began to protest, then felt a smile come on. A postponement might give Frank a few things to ponder. "Right back," she said. She stood up, moved to the telephone, dialed quickly and left a short message with his secretary. It took only a moment.

As she sat down again, Elizabeth giggled. "Beautifully done. Elegant. You've got the worm wiggling."

"Not this one," Ruth said. "Anyhow, I'm free until tomorrow." She smiled at her aunt, uneasy, slightly tipsy. Her throat ached. "May I suggest one more round?"

"Indeed!" said Elizabeth. "Tiny nip, great big zip!"

By dusk they were feeling fine. Later, when full dark settled in, they found sweaters and moved to the porch and rambled on like a pair of teenagers. They'd forgotten about dinner. Old times, Ruth thought, that same togetherness. She raised her glass.

"Auntie," she said, "what if I told you I've been lonely?"

"Well, of course you have. And me too — more than you know." Elizabeth paused. "But what if I told you it can end?"

"And what if I asked how?"

Elizabeth smiled. It was a tender, wistful smile. "What if you did? And what if I were to say, 'Ruthie, there's something I've been dying to tell you, something beautiful'?"

"What if I guessed?" Ruth said. "What if I guessed love?"

"Ah, well. Then you'd win."

Elizabeth topped off their glasses and leaned back and explained that for several years a certain gentleman had been her constant companion, though till now she'd never mentioned it to a soul. Because the gentleman was somewhat younger than she. And because, frankly, there was still a great deal to be learned about him. At first they'd met only for lunch, or to go out to a show, but for some time now — was it appropriate to say this? yes, of course, they were both adults, weren't they? — for the past few months this certain gentleman had been calling on her most evenings, at home, and not always leaving before sunrise. Even so, it wasn't at all the way it sounded. Granted, the man had something of a reputation, and people might find his intentions with an older woman suspect, but in fact it was she who'd been avoiding any formal commitment. Especially after those horrendous experiences with Charlton and Stephen. Twice burned, forever shy, yes? So as a matter of course she was leery, to say the least, and always would be, but in recent weeks and months her opinion of men in general had been raised substantially. Ridiculous, she knew, but she was in love. Floating. Just like the happy young woman she'd been back in the early days. "Maybe it's old-fashioned prudishness," she said, "but the fact is, I've been too embarrassed to talk about it."

"Embarrassed?" said Ruth.

"Well, naturally. Your mother, for instance — who knows what she'd think?"

Ruth shrugged. "She'd be thrilled for you. Excited and thrilled." She gave her aunt's arm a squeeze. "So tell me. What if I asked his name?"

"Oh, I wouldn't dare say."

"What if I insisted?"

"What if?" said Elizabeth, and her eyes seemed to fill with something soft and youthful. "In that event, perhaps, I might be forced to confide in you. Mr. Deeds, I might say. Mr. Franklin Marshall Deeds."

Ruth's ears warmed.

"Frank?"

"Well, yes, exactly."

"Frank Deeds?"

"As in reeds and beads."

Ruth missed a breath. For a second her eyes blurred; her heart thumped so rapidly she feared she was having some sort of attack. She dug her fingernails into the palm of her left hand until it hurt.

"Whatever's wrong, dear?" Eyes narrowed, Elizabeth bent forward. "I hope you're not offended. Really, I was so sure you'd understand. And I *do* know you'd like him. Absolutely positive."

Ruth nodded. "You said Frank?"

"Precisely correct. Rhymes with sank."

Ruth attempted a smile, pushed herself up. "The sherry, it's making my head spin. To be honest, I'm reeling. I'd better lie down awhile."

Elizabeth stood and took her by the arm. "No problem, dear, just too much zip, I'm sure."

"Franklin Marshall Deeds?"

"You'll adore him."

It was a bad night. Odd dreams, odd shapes and colors. At one point she jerked up in the dark and found herself praying a laugh-aloud kind of prayer. She giggled and folded her hands. She said, "Oh, God." She giggled again. It occurred to her, almost surely for the first time, that even the most banal of human lives was ripe with the ingredients for some ongoing cosmic soap opera, coincidence teetering upon coincidence, absurdity upon absurdity, all the ludicrous episodes unfolding for the midafternoon delectation of a worn-out and dull-witted Housewife God.

Early the next morning, when Ruth arrived at the marina, the maggot named Frank Deeds was leaning against a wooden railing, back to the water, facing her. He grinned and reached for her arm. "I was worried," he said. "My God, when I got your message . . . I mean, hell, I thought you'd lost your nerve." He adjusted the sleeves of his blue worsted suit. "But hey, you look wonderful, better than ever. Which is lucky, because I've brought my camera."

"It wasn't nerves," Ruth said, "it was integrity."

"I don't follow," said Frank.

"Integrity. Exactly how the dictionary defines it, not that you'd know or care, not that you'd have the slightest little moral inkling." She almost laughed but didn't. When the absurdities were your own, humor was hard to locate. "Frank as in stank, Deeds as in weeds."

"Yes? I don't quite get it."

Ruth rebuffed that with her shoulders. She could not immediately say anything more — in fact, did not know what *could* be said — and so after a long vacuumed-out second, when Frank suggested they go for a stroll on the beach, she simply nodded and followed along. For several minutes they moved in silence. The beach was deserted, waves and rocks and white sand.

"A fact," she finally said. "I know about Elizabeth."

Frank smiled and reached for her hand, but she jerked away.

"Elizabeth. Remember her?"

"Well, listen, do you mean —"

"My *aunt*," Ruth said. "You're dating her."

"Dating?" Frank turned and grasped her by both shoulders, hard. "Now, come on, let's be reasonable here. There's a problem, I admit. I do admit that. You see? But then at the same time . . . Put it this way. Where there's a problem, there's a way around. An old lawyer's saw. Got a guilty client, you plead his ass, you try to settle, you do some bargaining and reduce the charges and try to . . . God, Ruthie, you're gorgeous when you're upset. You know that? Like a poor little kitten that's lost its ball of string." He chuckled and made a light purring sound. "Well, okay. Fair's fair — you know. But I wouldn't exactly call it dating. Plenty of other words."

Ruth stared at him. "My aunt, for God's sake. She's in love with you. And I thought —"

"There, you *see?* Reduced charges. It wasn't pure sex, nothing seamy."

"No," Ruth said, "it was sick."

"An improvement. Better than seamy, I'd say." He gave her earlobe a tug. "And like you said, she is *your* aunt. A wonderful family."

"Sick and disgusting — especially me. I almost believed in you, I almost did, and that's the sickest thing of all . . . I thought just maybe you loved me or cared about me or *some*thing." Ruth looked at him for an instant, then turned and walked over to a large black rock, where she sat down and dropped her face into her hands. The absurdities were multiplying. How could her instincts be so out of whack? She imagined that Housewife God looking on from her heavenly La-Z-Boy recliner — teary-eyed, no doubt — a purple housedress and curlers and a small midafternoon Scotch.

Right away, Frank hurried after her. "Don't be ridiculous, Ruthie, I do love you. Honest to God. A million times I told you that, maybe two million, but hell, let's face it, you've kept me waiting over two years. See the point? I've got — you know — I've got needs."

"Deeds, needs," Ruth muttered. "*Seeds.*"

"Right," he said, and grinned. "I guess that's the plain truth of it." He kneeled down in the sand. "Look, I'm too old for games. If you can forgive me, we'll put an end to all this silly waiting. Right now."

Ruth closed her eyes. She felt something move in her stomach, something moist and slippery. "How do you mean that?"

"You know."

"I don't. I don't know anything."

"There's this institution called marriage." He smiled a charming Frank Deeds smile. "First things first, though."

"That's my breast!"

"For sure," he said.

Later, when Ruth was sitting on the rock again, Frank took out his camera and snapped a picture. Gently then, he kissed her. "This is a solemn promise. I'll carry that photo right here in my pocket — right next to my heart — until you marry me."

2:24 P.M.

She was back at the entrance to the pool.

Her lungs ached, she couldn't catch her breath, then a pair of hammers seemed to crack against her temples. Damn, she thought, pushed too far, too long. Countless fingers seemed to seize her by the throat — they wouldn't let go. Her cane slipped away. A flood of white specks came down on her, like that TV static, and then she was falling. No chance to yell. Her right knee buckled and she toppled to her side and the sky went to a lovely shade of red.

Her eyes — open or shut?

There was still that gorgeous red in the sky, a shimmering spilt-paint red, and now it swirled into an animal shape. Like a rabbit, she thought, yes indeed, a rabbit in the sky, a giant red rabbit spouting up bright red foam. Where was everybody? Couldn't anyone see her from the pool yard? What about Kaji — wouldn't she notice and come running? Or had those goddamn gates locked them all inside? Suddenly, out of the red light, she heard a tremendous bang. And then a dog came racing at her, a wild red dog. It came storming out of Doggie Canyon, ears drawn back, and there were more bangs and more dogs and more rabbits and everything was blending with everything else.

She had loved to dance, and they were dancing *ladadada* . . .

and God! how she loved him

and she had never felt like this before, and she could not catch her breath, and her hands jumped all around . . .

Hale! she said

so full of love and yearning.

But then with Frank she had felt like that again

and who was this man anyway? and he most certainly was not to be trusted

but all the same

it was so much the same and Jesus! she thought this might just keep happening, and who knew where she'd end up.

But anyway he said he loved her

a widow alone and forty years old

while her hands twitched and waved

like one hand did not know what the other hand was doing

like one hand could not hold the other hand still.

The sky went blue, the swirling stopped. Her hands steadied, and she was able to open the silver locket at her neck, dumping out her pills onto the asphalt. One came to rest near her nose. She licked her index finger, pressed it down on top of the tiny white pill. It passed The Test.

She put it under her tongue. Her insides dissolved.

Some time passed — how much, she didn't know — and she was able to crawl to the steps that led up to the pool. She sat on the bottom step for a while, listened to the seagulls screaming from the ocean.

When her pulse slowed, she pulled back her shoulders and stood up.

She pointed the tip of her cane in the direction of number 24. Which was what she needed now, a Destination that mattered.

XII

XI   I

X   II

P A R T   T W O
~~~~~~~~~~~~~~~~~~~~~~~~~~~

IX   III

VIII   IV

VII   V

VI

3:10 P.M.

"Well, I *did* it," Ruth was telling herself, "I overexerted myself, just walked too far." She sucked in a breath and eased herself down on the toilet. Her panty girdle and slacks lay in two wads on the bathroom floor, soaking wet. "Yes, yes, obviously," she muttered, "just too much for one day."

It occurred to her then that she had forgotten to take her third Cardizem. And here was the consequence. A horrible attack, which she'd survived, only to wet her pants the minute she walked through her own bathroom door.

For a moment she had the curious sensation of being watched. All those photographs on the walls, all those faces from her cluttered past. Quietly, breathing cautiously, she lifted her head and looked from one set of eyes to the next. Her high school graduating class. The entire Oil and Gas Leasing Division of the U.S. Geological Survey. Douglas's medical school class and her granddaughter's third-grade class. Walt and Lydia on the front lawn of their house in the Wilshire District; her own little Carter on a cliff above Woods Cove, flying a kite; Frank Deeds winking at her above his button-down collar; Hale grinning happily, decked out in Navy blues. And all the others. Nora at a sorority picnic. Cousins Margaret and McGregor building castles in a sandbox — Ruth herself standing to the side, face half averted, watching the children to be sure they wouldn't swallow sand.

A ghost gallery, she thought.

Hundreds of eyes looking on with dour pity at her wet pants and humiliation.

In a way, too, as Ruth squatted there, it almost seemed as if the eyes were regarding her with a kind of expectation: of mutual sympathy, perhaps; of a generosity far greater than any she was accustomed to feeling.

She studied the photograph directly in front of her, the one of her high school class. Lips pursed, head tilted back, she peered down her nose at row upon row of children standing quietly with folded hands, until, beneath her scrutiny, all their tiny white fingers began to pucker up and ooze and melt away like hot wax, the wrists liquefying, and then the arms, and then — Ruth was jittery now, breathing in quick gasps — and then the entire photograph began to bubble and go frothy like milk on a too-hot burner, each small head dissolving before her, each little chin and mouth, and the ears too, and then whole sheets of flesh curdling and peeling back, until at last Ruth could no longer recognize a single face, not even her own. When she squinted, the figures in the front row went to fluid and dripped away altogether. Ruth removed her glasses. She rubbed her eyes, sniffed the air. A musty scent of smoke and wet soil and molten leaves filled her nostrils.

A warm breeze swished through the tiny bathroom.

What's this? a voice thought at her.

Ruth's glasses slipped from her hand and fell between her legs into the toilet bowl.

She spread her thighs and peered down into the water.

You, thought the voice, which was high and chuckly, *who are you?*

The chuckly voice then in fact chuckled.

"Why, it's me. It's Ruthie Caster."

Looking down, she recognized the liquid warp of her own reflection in the bluish water of the toilet bowl. She pushed up her right sleeve, pulled her legs farther apart, and reached deep down into the bowl, grunting as she stirred the water, until her arm was wet halfway up to the elbow.

You!

Ruth's heart did an acrobatic tumble.

"Well, of course it's me. Mrs. Ruth Caster Armstrong. Ruth Caster Armstrong Hubble." Her fingers brushed up against the glasses, which were down at the very bottom of the bowl, near the mouth of that mysterious black tunnel leading to the sea.

Ah, the little voice thought at her. *A mistake, then.*

Ruth grabbed the glasses, straightened up, and slid back on the toilet seat, telling herself to ignore this preposterous voice which she both recognized and did not recognize, which she had never asked to hear in the first place. One more intrusion. And in her own private sanctuary. She shook the water from her fingers, slipped the glasses back onto her nose.

Mistake, mistake, the voice thought at her again. *We're late, we're late! Important date!*

Ruth glanced furtively around the bathroom: every photograph was blurry and jumbled. Somewhere, somebody sniggered.

A bad fall, but falls ain't all.

"What the hell is this?"

She put her right hand into her hair, rubbed her scalp. Amazingly, her skin was warm and wet, as if she had a fever. When she lowered her hand to examine it, her fingertips were bright red. She blinked several times, unnerved, and rolled down her sleeve.

A chippery laugh filled the room.

Without thinking, Ruth again put her hand into her hair. She

withdrew it immediately: an enormous blister, the size of a quarter, spread out across her palm.

Clock goes tick, just a nick.

Ruth felt a surge of real panic. "Excuse me. Please quit singing
like that, I can't understand a word. Please just leave me alone."

The voice thought a little chuckle at her.

The voice thought, *Sorry to say, no luck today.*

"What?"

Hippity-hop!

"Now, sir, I'm not about to —"

The chuckly voice chortled. It thought, *That's the game! Hippity-hop! Time, Ruthie. Watch it. Zip ziiiip, zip ziiiip, zip zip ziiiip!*
Another chuckle.

Ruth squirmed on the toilet seat. Briefly, it crossed her mind
that she was engaged in a dialogue with some secret part of herself, the secret howling part, the blank empty desert part, the part
that understood things that should not be understood.

She addressed this possibility.

"What do you mean, zip zip? What is this zip? What time is it,
anyway?"

She raised her arm, glanced at the face of Hale's wristwatch.
The numbers were so blurry she couldn't see a thing. "Now how
am I supposed to read that?" she asked herself. She began to fiddle
with the winding device, worried that some kind of damage had
been done. Just then the image of Hale's face bobbed up before
her. God, how she loved him! The joy of her life. She would put
aside all other obligations, all routine endeavors, and devote herself to him; the universe, and time itself, would stand still in
celebration.

Ruth pulled down her sleeve, fingers trembling.

Itty-bitty! Ruth's self-pity!

Getting late!

Surf's up!

The voice thought these things at her. A distinctly rabbity voice,
for that matter.

Ruth once again directed her gaze to the photograph in front of her, which was blurrier than ever.

The voice thought at her, *Time goes ticky, don't be picky!* And then, *Nubby-hubby Henry! Compassion's the fashion! Karen, too, she's feeling blue!*

Ruth stole another glance around the tiny bathroom. Nothing at all except for that warm summer-seeming breeze. With a sigh she looked back down into the toilet bowl, where her own reflection gently swayed and stirred. "For God's sake," she muttered. "Almost a hundred years old."

An enormous guffaw came rolling at her from somewhere both close and far away.

Surf's up!

Ziiippp! Oh, where have you gone, charming Ruthie? A tisket, a tasket! Hippity-hop!

People steeple!

People here, people now!

Hear that chime? Now's the time!

Don't be cruel, off that stool!

Ruth put a hand to her forehead. When she drew it away, the palm and fingertips were still a bright blistered red.

"Well fine," she murmured.

There was a crackly, snapping sound like a telephone disconnecting.

Can't stop, gotta hop!

"Whiiiite Rabbit," called Luzma, "Whiiiite Rabbit!" and she swung the door open and stepped into the bathroom.

"Dios mío," she said, "poor Ruthie."

The girl used a foot to stir the wad of wet clothing on the floor.

"Little accident, I guess."

Ruth looked up blankly. "Not at all," she said. "A damn big accident, obviously."

Luzma reached down and gave Ruth's shoulder a reassuring squeeze. The girl had on a bright yellow blouse, tight black jeans, spike-heeled sandals. She always wore the same jeans with that fancy designer label, which pulled up in little white lines from the zipper to her hips. The same red sandals, too, though Ruth could never understand why anyone would clean a house in heels. The yellow blouse was new. It was embroidered all over with small blue stars and topped off at the neck with sequined psychedelic flowers — some bright purple, some deep green, others a glowing sunset orange with shiny pieces of black plastic at their centers.

Latins, Ruth thought. Colorblindness seemed to be locked into their DNA. "Lovely, lovely blouse," she said. "Something new?"

A belt of red cotton snaked through the loops of Luzma's jeans, twisting over and over upon itself so that it barely reached around her waist. She'd tied it in a very small knot, secured with two safety pins. A yellow ribbon held back her long brown hair; her eyebrows were two upside-down V's.

Ruth shifted back on the toilet seat. "Dazzling, as always," she said, not quite snidely, but snootily enough to bring to mind the business about compassion. She tried to follow up with a generous smile. "And complex, too, I should add. The whole outfit today, it's dazzling and *very* complex." Ruth nodded to herself. That should be more than sufficient. "Now may I ask why you made that little comment?"

"Which little comment?" Luzma said.

"Just now, when you walked in here. 'White Rabbit,' you said. I heard it most distinctly. Maybe you noticed a . . . I mean, did you *see* something?"

"Dios mío," Luzma said again. "You sick, Ruthie?"

"I certainly am not."

"Well, I didn't see nothing. What's to see?"

Ruth smiled politely from the toilet, relieved. No doubt the whole episode *was* just a conversation with herself. Some peculiar symptom of fatigue. But that rabbity voice . . . the swirling animal visions just before her fall . . . She gazed down at her fingertips: they were red and bleeding.

"Hey, look!" Luzma said, bending over Ruth, grabbing hold of her hand. She reached for a piece of toilet paper, wet it on her tongue, and began to dab at Ruth's fingers. "What happened? You fall somewhere?"

"No pity required," Ruth said, dropping her hands to her sides. "That new doctor — Dr. Ash — he says I was born with my problems." Feeling embarrassed, she turned her eyes up at Luzma. The girl had probably seen much stranger things, what with all the old ladies' places that she cleaned, but Ruth thought of herself as different from those others — not better necessarily, just slightly elevated — and she treasured the notion that Luzma thought so, too. "Well, anyway, I'm perfectly spry, thank you," she said, her voice a bit wobbly. "I might've walked one loop too many, that's all. Let's just get on with things." Ruth nodded at the wet slacks, keeping her eyes averted from the watchful photographs all around her. "I'd picked those out because they match my blouse — a nice dinner outfit, I thought."

Luzma reached out toward Ruth's face and slid her glasses from her nose. "Soaking wet!" she said, as she wiped them on her own blouse. "I guess maybe you get caught in the sprinkler too?" She raised her eyebrows and looked at Ruth, but Ruth remained silent. Shaking her head, Luzma replaced Ruth's glasses, stepped back from the puddle on the floor, and leaned down for the wet pants. The girl made a grunting noise as she bent forward, and Ruth couldn't help noticing that Luzma had gained some weight in recent months.

"Don't you worry, I can rinse them out nice and fresh," Luzma said. "So what happened? Another dizzy thing?"

"Well, to be frank, I don't exactly know," Ruth said. For a second she tried to reconstruct the chronology of recent events, but the effort only made her more confused. Her left shoulder was tingling. "I did take a spill out there," she said, "but it's not worth talking about. An accident. No sense dwelling on spilt old bones." She leaned against the lid of the toilet and watched the girl fill the sink with water. After a moment it struck her that the faces in the old photographs were peering at Luzma, too.

"Stand up straight, dear. The walls have eyes."

"What?"

"The photographs. Haven't I shown you?"

"Oh, those. Yes, for sure, you showed me a thousand times." Luzma scrubbed at the pants with a bar of soap.

"Well, there's always an audience," Ruth said. "That's one thing I've definitely learned. Just a few minutes ago I was speaking with —"

Ruth's shoulder tingled again.

"Speaking with who, Ruthie?"

"Whom, dear."

"Yeah, whom?"

"Whom doesn't matter. Certain parties, let's just say. Enough said."

Ruth was frowning at her left arm, bending it in and out, monitoring the tingles that were now creeping down toward her elbow. It was a prickly, teasing sensation, an electric current that kept turning itself on and off, and Ruth worried that the problem might keep on spreading. When she clenched her hand into a tight fist — not a sissy fist, but with thumb bent across her index and third fingers, as her sons had taught her — her fingers did not feel quite right.

"Well, I guess those certain parties made you pretty mad," Luzma said. "Maybe you want to beat them up?"

"Of course not. I'm testing something."

"Oh, yes?"

"Yes. And I'm *fine*."

"Okay then. Okay, good. But you still seem awful funny-acting."

Under normal conditions, Ruth would've had a snappy response ready, something to divert the girl's attention, but right now her reflexes were out of order. All her efforts seemed vaguely ridiculous. Still, she thought, it would be best to continue with her regular routine.

"Just a bit tired," she said. "Can you help me up? I want to go get the laundry while you finish in here."

"Sure, all right," Luzma said. The girl stood thoughtfully for a second, appraising Ruth's face, then turned from the sink and took a towel off the rack. "We'll wrap this around you till your pants are dry."

3:23 P.M.

With a towel of green terry cloth wrapped around her waist, Ruth opened the bathroom door and walked slowly across The Room. She was stiff from her fall. Luzma followed behind, a hand against Ruth's back.

"You don't have to do that, you know," Ruth said. "I'm no invalid, for crying out loud."

"Course not," said Luzma. "Just ignore me."

Luis, Luzma's son, was leaning against the stair railing with his head down, arms crossed, one ankle locked around the other. His black hair was matted, a few wispy tufts sticking up high in the back. The boy was in his usual foul mood, upset that he had to ride around on the bus with his mother on Saturdays while all his friends were out playing.

As Ruth approached, Luis uncrossed his arms and jammed his thumb into his mouth without looking up. Luzma reached down and pulled it out.

"Luis, Luis, such a grump," she cooed. "And too old for thumb-sucking." She scuffed up his hair with her fingers. "Come on, now, say hello to Ruth." She tried to pull up his chin. "Say hello to Abuelita."

"Hola!" Ruth said. She liked using the Spanish she'd studied at UCLA.

Luis said nothing.

"He'll feel better after a nap," Luzma said, and smiled at the boy. "Right, Luis? For now, you be a nice boy and stay with Ruth while I work. If something happens, something wrong, you come tell me."

"What on earth could happen?" Ruth said. "I'll just help with the laundry like I always do. Seriously, dear, let's not be making mountains out of molehills."

"Holehills what?"

"*Mole*hills."

"Yes?"

"An expression," Ruth said. "It's one of those idioms that refer to . . . Oh, forget it. Holehills — that'll do fine."

Each week Luzma did two loads of laundry, which Ruth and Henry collected and set aside in a yellow plastic basket. Now the loaded basket was waiting upstairs, on the landing of the third floor, between the two bedrooms.

Though Ruth still felt a bit strange, she was determined to walk up the stairs, retrieve the basket, and carry it down to The Room. There was no reason to disrupt the proper order of things. After Luzma returned to the bathroom, Ruth took several deep breaths and walked around Luis, who stood sulking, slouched against the stair railing — "Stand up straight, kid!" she said. "No hunchbacks allowed!" — and made her way up the first two stairs. Her right knee popped audibly. And now her entire left arm seemed to sizzle with electricity. She reached for the railing, pulled herself up another step. But once again she felt that sudden dizziness — so dizzy, in fact, she thought she might fall. She shut her eyes. Wavering slightly, she wondered if a doctor might be needed, but then shook her head. No doctors. She raised her left foot and struggled to pull herself up to the fourth step.

The walls began to close in. All at once the ceiling spun and everything went silver-white. Ruth felt herself teetering backward; she yelped and squeezed the rail with both hands. Marooned, she thought — she didn't dare turn back.

"Hey, Mamá!" Luis shouted. "Something's sick with Ruth!"

Luzma ran out from the bathroom. "You were supposed to stay with her!" she snapped, and grabbed Ruth around the waist, dragging her back down to the bottom of the stairs. "Better sit down, rest awhile," she said.

Annoyed, more with herself than with the girl who was trying to help her, Ruth pushed Luzma's hands away. "There's laundry to do, for Pete's sake. I can't just *sit* for the rest of my life."

Luzma reached out to straighten Ruth's towel, made a tsking sound with her tongue, and nodded. "Then take the elevator. Luis can go along, make sure you're okay." She nudged the boy, who had buried his chin again and was staring down at his feet. "Right, Luis? You go help Ruth bring the laundry to Mamá."

The boy raised his head slowly, rubbing his eyes with his fists. He looked from Ruth's sandals to the green towel wrapped around her waist. "I see those little blue worms under your skin," he said.

Ruth pulled back her shoulders. "Varicose vessels."

"Worms."

"*Veins*. You get them when you have babies. Just ask your mother. She probably has them, too."

"Yuck," said Luis. "You got no blood left."

Oddly flustered, insulted even, Ruth looked at the boy's mother. "What's this he says?"

Luis was poking Ruth's leg.

"Okay now," Luzma said, swatting him on the shoulder. "Enough." She smiled apologetically at Ruth. "One of his new ideas. His friend Tony told him . . . Anyway, it's nonsense. Sorry, Ruth. He's mad at everybody." She looked at the boy, shaking her head from side to side. "Another fight yesterday, some boy beating him up, and then his father yelling and —"

"White skin, no blood," said Luis. "Like a ghost." The thought seemed to please the boy, and he giggled and poked Ruth's leg again.

Drawing in a breath, Ruth decided to drop it. The child obviously had his father's temperament, which was not good, and how could she complain to Luzma about *that*? Anyway, Ruth knew that of all the old ladies Luis saw on Saturday, he liked her best.

They were longtime friends — he'd been coming with Luzma since he was just a baby — and the sullen moods didn't really matter. Ruth liked him, even loved him. Those huge, unblinking brown eyes; the way he could be so sweet sometimes; how he reminded Ruth of her own two sons when they were little boys.

"All right, white blood," she said, "no blood, whatever you want. I'm an old lady." She reached out and gripped Luis's shoulder, forcing him to straighten his spine. "Come on now, straight and solid. Elevator time."

She did *not* love the elevator. She hated it. The walls were lined with artificial cedar paneling and the space inside was cramped and tiny, like an old wooden coffin. It gave her a creepy, claustrophobic sensation to be shut up in a space so small and without windows. Today, though, she'd have to endure the ride. She smiled down at Luis.

"Come help your old abuela."

Luis glanced at his mother, who stood with her hands on her hips, tapping her toes. He frowned indecisively, nibbled at his lip, then nodded and grabbed on to a fold in Ruth's towel. Without a word, he pulled her toward the elevator, pushing open the flimsy, accordion-style door.

Luzma shut them in and they were off, jerky and slow. The overhead cables made a harsh jiggling noise; the lights flickered; Ruth blinked several times and tried to orient herself. For a second she couldn't tell if the confusion was located inside her body or outside or somewhere in between. It *was* a creepy experience. "Just another minute or so," she said, mostly to herself. "Fun, isn't it?" As they passed the second floor, the elevator made several sharp rumbling sounds and the lights flicked off again. Ruth gasped. She reached out for the safety rail on the door, only to find the wall much closer than she'd thought: her knuckles scraped up against something sharp. The darkness collapsed in on her. Suddenly, as if injected with poison, Ruth felt a rush of true terror.

"Fun!" she said.

Her voice, she realized, was pitched a bit too high. Images from recent nightmares popped up: gaping black tunnels, snake people wrapping themselves around her ankles, blood-red lips on the walls, unspeakable creatures with see-through bodies and revolving heads. An insistent gurgling rose from her chest. She began to feel along the walls for the emergency alarm, but then Luis took her hand in his own and wrapped his fingers around her thumb.

Ruth coughed. "Nice ride so far?"

Luis giggled and gave her thumb a squeeze. "Don't be such a scaredy cat."

"Nonsense. Who's scared? I thought *you* might be." She made a defensive throat-clearing sound. "What about worms, for instance?"

"Worms?" the boy said, his voice suspicious. "Why?"

"No reason. It's just that we all have our little bugaboos, if you see my point. Fat greasy worms wiggling out your eyeballs."

The boy didn't move.

With a final jolt the elevator began running smoothly again, and Ruth resolved not to mention her visions to anyone. What good could come of it? Henry would just gape at her, Nora would make a federal case of it, Karen would start in with all that new psychology mumbo-jumbo, analyzing Ruth's whole damned existence. God knows, you had to be careful talking with people about your private thoughts. They might declare you incompetent, like they'd done to poor Edith Tumay last year, or maybe even shut you up inside a hospital.

Gently, she pulled her thumb from Luis's grasp and reached for the safety rail. "Don't worry," she said, "it's just the dark."

Luis let out a nervous giggle. "Who cares?" he said. "I don't believe in bogeymen and all that stuff. They aren't even real, I bet."

"I wouldn't be so sure," Ruth said. "Sometimes I sense things. You know, like ESP and voices and so on. This old neighbor of mine, for instance —"

There was a quick sparking noise, and the lights came on. Luis was staring at her with his mouth open.

Ridiculous, she thought. Trying to prove her courage to a seven-year-old. When the elevator stopped at the third floor, she stepped out and shuffled over to her bed, then climbed onto her high mattress. She extended her arms behind her and leaned back for a minute, legs dangling.

A strange confusion had come over her. She didn't understand what had been happening lately — the dizzy spells, the visions and voices — and now, after her incapacity on the stairs and in the elevator, she felt awfully shaken. How would she keep up with the daily chores if she couldn't stand on her own two feet? Right now, for instance: Henry would have to take care of the laundry. No doubt he'd mess it all up, but there was no way on earth she could manage it herself, not feeling like this.

She pictured the old man hunched over his desk, caught up in one of those endless solitaire games.

"Henry!" she yelled.

She waited a moment, then tried again, more politely: "Henry?"

There was a dense silence. If he wasn't at his desk, Ruth wondered, where was he? She pushed herself upright at the edge of her bed, ran her fingers through her curls: they were stiff and oddly warm. Bizarre new thoughts filled Ruth's mind. What if something actually had happened to the old man? Who'd be there if anything went wrong while she was setting up her breakfast tray or getting undressed at night? Who'd bring home the groceries? Or carry up the mail and newspaper? But it was more than just that, Ruth realized, and she slumped. Henry had been there every day, no matter what, for thirty-six years. And day after day, month after month, he'd hardly ever complained. He'd never left her. He'd never died.

And that was something, wasn't it?

Yes, it was. A boob-something, but still . . .

Nervously, Ruth pushed the bobby pins around in her curls. Then she dropped her hands and pulled back her shoulders — she mustn't let herself be so foolish. She looked over at Luis, who was standing by the elevator door, kicking at the carpet. His silences, when he was tired like this, were more frustrating than his wildest bouts of mischief. "Luis," she said, "go find Henry for me. Tell him — ask him — to come in here."

Without a word, the boy nodded and walked out.

Ruth sat still a moment. The whole house suddenly had a hollowed-out feel. Barren and expectant, like an empty garbage bag. No doubt Henry was just asleep, dozing inside his closet with that silly radio earplug in his ear, blocking out the world. She waited, straightening the towel in her lap. Everything was going awry today, and the man had slept right through it all. In his *closet,* for God's sake.

Henry could sleep anywhere, anytime. In the middle of the day he preferred his overstuffed chair, the big blue one that was shredding at the arms. For years he'd kept the chair positioned next to his bed, until the day he'd resolved never to drink again. That very afternoon, after sweeping up the glass from his shattered booze bottle, he'd moved the chair into his walk-in closet. "It's more comfortable in here," he'd told Ruth. "A little nest — real cozy, you know?" He'd covered the worn-out seat cushion with a blue-and-red-striped beach towel. Then, sitting down, he'd screwed the radio earplug into his ear. "Cooler and darker," he'd said, leaning forward to fold the closet doors shut like a fan in front of her face.

3:53 P.M.

Ruth heard Henry holler "Leave go of me!" and a moment later she heard his feet, those deliberate, lumbering steps mixing with the boy's soft padding. She took a breath and exhaled slowly. In that instant, which seemed prolonged and significant, she felt a surge of enormous relief, even gratitude. Then Luis ran into the room, past her bed, and into the elevator, and Henry appeared in the doorway.

"Kid's a troublemaker," he muttered. He shook his head and looked at Ruth. He paused, his pale eyes flooding with concern. "Hey, you look kind of rotten. No offense."

Ruth's breath caught.

Nubby-hubby! Compassion's the fashion!

It was difficult, but she resisted the urge to retaliate. Instead, she frowned and watched Henry tug at the collar of his filthy shirt, which was bunched up like a brace around his neck, three or four buttons stuck into holes a slot too high. Finally, though, she couldn't stop herself. "Oh, right," she broke out. "You're no great beauty yourself."

"That's a fact," Henry said.

Ruth sighed. "Would you kindly bring the laundry in here?"

"Okay by me."

In a moment he returned with the basket, his mouth hanging open.

"Go ahead, put it in there," Ruth said firmly, gesturing at the elevator.

Henry nodded and turned like a big genial robot and placed the basket on the floor of the elevator. He ignored Luis, who stood quietly sucking his thumb.

"Now," Ruth said, "I'll need help getting into that contraption myself."

"What sort of help?"

"Well, you know, just like with the laundry basket. Put me inside."

"Body contact?"

The thought made her hesitate. "How else?"

"Righto," Henry said.

He reached up to play with his loose tooth, his eyes locked on the towel at Ruth's waist. It had been more than thirty-three years since he'd approached her bed with even the possibility of anything vaguely physical.

"But don't try —" Ruth paused again. The man was gaping. "Henry, don't *think* about it."

He grinned and opened up his arms. "Like old times," he said, and slapped his big hands against her hips.

"Not *there*," Ruth said. "My God!"

His hands slid up past her waist, almost dislodging the towel, and then settled into the flesh at her ribs.

"And not there!"

Henry took her under the armpits. He was wheezing slightly.

"Any complaints?"

"Well, I don't know," Ruth said. "Just don't wrinkle my blouse. And no more squeezie business."

With a low grunt Henry lifted her off the bed. He rested a moment, hoisted her up again, then trundled her over to the elevator and gently put her down. His face had become flushed; he stood panting, grinning like a schoolboy. "Felt pretty darn satisfying," he said. "You too?"

The man was deliberately provoking her.

"I didn't notice," Ruth said.

"No?"

"Don't be ridiculous."

The only way to be pleasant, she realized, was to ignore his absurdities. She took hold of his shirt sleeve, tried not to wobble as she stepped into the elevator. Once inside, she pulled away and clamped her arms across her chest. She looked down at Luis. "Still having fun, dear?"

Henry stood at the door. "Lots," he said.

"The boy. Not you."

"Him too?"

Henry flicked his eyebrows, made a kissing sound, then pressed the button to send them on their way.

"All these years," he said, "you're still my cutie pie."

4:02 P.M.

Ruth and Luis got out on the second floor, sending the laundry on to The Room by itself. "Coming down," Ruth yelled, though she did not know if Luzma would hear. She reached for the boy's hand and led him past the dining table and into the kitchen. If she moved slowly, she discovered, she could manage fairly well.

"Come on, amigo. How about a couple galletas?"

She opened the pantry and pulled out the foil-lined bag of Sweet Spot chocolate chip cookies.

"Now listen, I'll tell you a secret," she said. "If you put a match to one of these cookies, it'll burn like gasoline. Pure chemicals. Karen told me that — my granddaughter."

Luis eyed the sack of cookies. "My mom says not to eat sugar."

"Sugar? I told you, kid, these are *chemicals*. They'll scrub your teeth right up." She grinned at the boy. "Besides, they taste great."

Ruth dug around in the bag until she found two whole cookies for Luis — most had a bite or two taken out of them — and while Luis ate, she took a second bite from an already-bitten cookie. Delicious, if a little stale, she thought; everything was always turning soft from the moisture in the air. She ran her tongue along the chewed-off edge of the cookie, licking up the dark brown goo that oozed from the broken chips. Then she tossed the rest of it back into the bag, for later.

"Muy bien, hey?"

"I guess," said Luis, nibbling on his second cookie, one ankle locked around the other. He glanced up at her from the corner of his eye and said, "You're a weirdo."

Ruth grinned down at him, a smudge of chocolate on her bottom lip. "You too," she said.

When they'd finished their snack, Ruth led the boy out to the coffee table by the couch. She kept his crayons, paper, and scissors on top of the black-and-white TV at the far end of the table.

She got him set up, then walked over to her piano bench. It was the same thing each week. He'd sit on the floor at the coffee table, coloring and cutting things out while she played Beethoven or Bach or Chopin. The boy didn't mind the background music, and, for her part, Ruth took pleasure in performing for a live audience.

"So, Luis," she said, "what's for today's concert?"

Ruth opened her book of Chopin preludes and chose one at random, the Fourth Prelude in E Minor. Her left hand was still a bit cramped, so she played slowly and quietly, careful to keep her breathing steady. Except for one or two passages, she had the piece committed to memory, and now and then she glanced over at Luis, who was busy drawing figures with his crayons. Like her son Carter, the boy had a creative bent, a real imagination. He'd always begin by drawing the same three characters: Mr. Blue, Mr. Red, and Little Greenie. Mr. Blue was a fat, lumpy circle with a squiggle of a face on top. No arms or legs, but the kind of person you'd listen to anyway. Rather stern, Ruth thought, almost pompous-looking, but he could make you laugh. Mr. Red was tall (he did have arms and legs) and looked mean — the type who rolled his own cigarettes and pushed up his sleeves, a schoolyard bully, the guy who stole your lunch money and made you say thanks. Little Greenie had all his appendages, like Mr. Red, but he was tiny and very short, almost dwarfish.

As she played, Ruth watched the boy cut out the figures and begin stationing them here and there in his coffee-table kingdom. He was mumbling under his breath — "Now you go right up there, Mr. Blue" — he lay the cutout on a pile of magazines, where Mr. Blue could be in charge of things. "And you be good and stay in there, Little Greenie" — he wedged the figure upright into a dish of ivy. "And you, Mr. Red, you're stuck *there*" — he shoved the poor man into an ashtray, left over from Ruth's smoking days.

For five minutes or so everyone in the make-believe kingdom played his proper role, communicating peaceably as neighbors sometimes do. Little Greenie minded his own business in the bushes, a nice ordinary guy; Mr. Blue turned out to be something of a power-monger, greedily thrilled with the position he'd been given atop Magazine Mountain, which he knew he deserved; and Mr. Red was a bad seed through and through, who would've run amuck if he hadn't been ground into the ashes from the very start.

It was a small community, rather provincial, but Luis seemed to take joy in governing its affairs, like some all-powerful god.

For a time Ruth turned back to the piano. Eyes closed, she rocked with the music, feeling warm and calm, but as she neared the final triplet, all hell broke loose on the coffee table to her right. Someone was shouting at the top of his lungs.

"Get out, get out!" the voice shrieked. "Right now, before I burn this bush and everyone around it! Get away from here, you creepos. I mean it, scram!"

A tremor ran through Ruth's chest, bouncing down from her shoulder to her navel. Her left arm throbbed. She jerked back, looked over at Luis.

It would not have surprised her if Mr. Blue, the authority in the region, had raised his voice to settle a dispute. Or if Mr. Red had gone on a rampage, leaping from the ashtray, a mass murderer. But this was very strange. For it was Little Greenie who was crazed — the goody-goody mama's boy. "Asshole!" Greenie yelled, and when Mr. Blue tried to restrain him, he only shouted louder, "I mean it, buddy, scram!" His voice seemed tense and strained as he vented his anger on everyone around him. "Bueno, Blue, you asshole," he said. "Say hello to Abuelita. Say, 'Hello, Abuelita, scaredy cat in your stupid green towel. How are you on this shitty day today?'"

"Darling," Ruth said, "I wish you wouldn't —"

"You too!" Little Greenie screamed. "Scram!"

Ruth told herself to ignore it. Obviously, the boy was staging this demonstration for attention, still in his foul mood; just like her son Carter, his artistic expressions of identity were sometimes rather flamboyant. Anyway, Ruth mused, the boy had reasons enough to be frustrated — fierce poverty, to begin with, and an even fiercer father — and a little indulgence might do him some good. She turned to the piano again, though her arm and fingers ached. She pumped the pedals, banged hard on the keys. If it was a competition between Chopin and Little Greenie, Ruth was determined that real artistry, not mere self-assertion, should carry the day.

"Shit!" Little Greenie yelled.

Ruth played louder and hummed along.

A moment later, when the knocking began on the wall of 23, Ruth knew that Chopin had the edge: Hassan liked to compliment fine music, not nasty language. As she finished the prelude, there was a tremendous thundering of knocks.

"Super!" Hassan called through the wall. "Extra nice, Ruthie! You make that music super!"

Luis looked up from his game. "Hey," he said, "who is that? You'd tell *me* to shut up if I made all that noise."

"Otro amigo," Ruth said. "Hassan." She stood up from the bench and turned in triumph toward the boy.

Luis slouched at the coffee table. He closed his fingers around the cutout characters, tossed them all into a wrinkled heap in the ashtray, and scowled down at the wrecked kingdom. "I'm not playing anymore," he said, and he climbed onto the couch to curl up.

4:21 P.M.

Ruth picked up the little boy's feet and sat down with them in her lap. She removed his shoes, rubbed his toes and arches. In a few minutes he was fast asleep.

"Well, there," she murmured, "Little Greenie's better now."

Again, the house took on that scooped-out feel: a vast and enduring silence. She wondered what to do with herself. An unusual weariness had entered her bones, like a weight of some sort, or the utter absence of weight. Usually she'd follow Luzma as she cleaned, making sure things were done properly and thoroughly, seizing every opportunity to issue instructions in Spanish so as to practice vocabulary. But now her entire left side, from her index finger down to her toes, had begun to tingle. Her whole life, she'd never felt this way. Maybe this was how the man from 23 felt the day he walked down to Doggie Canyon and never came back.

She closed her eyes, tired and old.

"Hey there, White Rabbit," Karen said. "Thought you didn't believe in sleep."

Then a smacking sound.

Even with her eyes shut, Ruth recognized that wad of chewing gum. She wiggled to sit up straight.

"Quit that chomping," she said sternly. "Anyway, I'm not asleep. I'm trying to regulate my breathing."

Karen stood above her, bobbing up and down on the worn-out toes of her tennis shoes. Her legs were long and thin, the knees nicely formed. A good-looking girl, Ruth thought — took after her father, thank God, and not that mediocre mother of hers. The girl's thick blond hair, though, was still a mess. Too long and bushy. The roots, Ruth noticed, had gone to an amber shade of brown.

She pursed her lips and twisted sideways so Karen could kiss her cheek.

"I'm awfully glad you've —" Ruth hesitated. This compassion business was considerably more difficult than Chuckly Voice had let on. "I mean, thanks for taking some time out from your love life. It's so important —" She stopped again. Sympathy was one thing, syrup was something else. No need to overdo it. "So how was lunch with Count Dracula? Worth all the hurry, I hope?"

Karen pulled a strand of gum from her lips, bit it off, began rolling it into a ball. She was still bouncing. "Lunch was fine. I talked to Luzma, she says you're not doing too great."

"No worse than you, from the look of things," Ruth said. "Just what did Luzma tell you?"

Karen plopped down on the couch and rested a hand on Ruth's knee. "Didn't sound so good. How she found you in the bathroom, how you couldn't make it upstairs. Grammy, listen, you should've told me something was wrong. I would've stayed." She slid a fresh stick of gum into her mouth, rolled the used-up glob into the wrapper. Embarrassed, she cleared her throat and said, "Still trying to give up the smokes."

Ruth smiled an I-told-you-so smile.

"Well, kiddo," she said, "I did ask you to stay, as I recall. And, by the way, when I stopped smoking, after almost fifty-nine years, I managed it in one single day. Bam. Just like that. I remember vividly, in fact, how your Uncle Douglas explained what it was doing to my lungs, a very graphic description, so I just —"

"Have you taken a pain pill? I know you're supposed to."

"I most assuredly did *not* take a pain pill." Ruth adjusted her shoulders, straightened her spine. "And I don't plan to. I took a little spill on my walk — so what? — I made it back all by myself." Absently, she wrapped the fingers of her right hand around her silver locket.

Karen started. "Hey, what happened?"

She reached for Ruth's injured hand, but Ruth gripped the locket even tighter. The blister tingled on her palm. "Nothing," she said. She would keep up appearances, as she always had.

"Well, suit yourself. But let me take Luis upstairs. That way you can spread out here."

"No, dear, I do not *want* you to take Luis upstairs." Ruth looked down on the sleeping boy. "I like him to be with me. And I don't want to take a nap. I want to put on my pants, the ones I picked out to wear for dinner, and —" *People-steeple! Surf's up!* Perhaps she was being self-centered. "I don't suppose you'd like to stay and eat with us. Luzma and Luis always do."

Karen slumped back. "Can't, Grammy. Mike's waiting."

"I see. Love before blood."

"Come on, Grammy. Always making me feel so guilty. I'm twenty-nine — a grown married woman." She popped a bubble. Suddenly her eyes moistened. "Oh, Christ."

"Karen?"

"Forget it. Nothing."

Ruth leaned forward, pushing Luis's feet from her lap, and tried to stand up. She paused for a second, arms held out as if she were about to take a dive, then lost her balance and flopped down again. She glanced over at Karen.

"A Prince Charming problem?"

"I guess. Sort of."

Ruth took Luis's feet back into her lap, squeezed his toes one after the other. The boy could sleep and sleep.

"If you want my opinion, the problem's obvious," Ruth said. "This full-grown adult — a man who's supposed to be your husband — he leaves you for almost a year, then just happens to show up on your doorstep. You throw the doors open, he stays all night, God knows what else. Then he sneaks away again. He's a louse. Problem solved."

"It's not his fault, Grammy. Not now, I mean." She looked down at her hands. "And he's sorry."

"Sorry-schmorry," Ruth said. "Boob."

Karen released a quick laugh. "A pretty old-fashioned word, Grammy."

"And rude," Ruth continued. "He was rude with me on the phone. I suppose he's sorry for that, too?"

"But he's changed now, much more . . . more serious."

Ruth looked up at the ceiling. "Serious, she says."

"You know, settled down. It's hard to describe, sort of, but he's full of energy and new ideas and . . . I can really feel the difference."

"I'll bet you can," Ruth said. She moved Luis's feet down to her knees. She tugged at the towel in her lap, trying to close up the gap that ran between her legs. "Just how did you happen to cross paths with this creature again?"

"Does it matter?"

"Maybe so, maybe not."

Karen rubbed her eyes. "Well, a couple weeks ago I was out on assignment, this story about a third-stage smog alert — pretty awful. Went out to shoot the pictures, do the usual reaction stuff. Senior citizens, asthmatics, that sort of shit."

"Karen."

"Right. So anyway, I end up at this elementary school. Kids stuck inside, no recess, the red smog flags. That's when Mike trotted over."

"*Hot,* no doubt."

Karen only shrugged.

"Wonder of wonders," Ruth said. "And I suppose you were wearing the skimpy little outfit you've got on now? I swear, I've seen more cotton at the top of aspirin bottles."

Karen laughed and rolled her eyes. "No, just work clothes. You're not exactly interested in the emotional side of all this, are you?" The girl pulled another strand of gum from her mouth and chomped it off. "Anyway, Mike says he started teaching there last September — permanently, I mean, no more substituting — and he's doing pretty well. We got to talking. He likes teaching math best."

"X equals the unknown. The only thing I remember about math."

Sighing, Karen rolled the chewed gum into a ball, took out a fresh piece, and slid it between her lips. Each time she carried out this procedure, Ruth noticed, the wad in her mouth grew conspicuously larger.

"Not to interrupt," Ruth said, "but that's a very unattractive habit. Maybe gum's your problem. Maybe Prince Charming doesn't appreciate —"

The phone rang.

Karen threw her hands up as if electrocuted. "Don't let Henry answer it!" she shouted. "Or Luis!" She raced toward the phone table at the foot of the stairs, almost slipping on a small piece of yellow paper. There were dozens of them scattered about — little yellow scraps on the rug and floor. "God, what *is* all this?" she yelled, then snatched up the receiver. Her face had gone bright red. There was a pause before she sighed and lowered the phone.

"For you, Grammy. Nora Somebody. Calling to say White Rabbit."

"Well, for crying out loud," Ruth muttered.

Slowly, gloomily, it dawned on her that she had forgotten to White Rabbit Nora at the shop that morning, and now it was too late. The old bird had got her. So had Karen, for that matter, and Luzma. She could not remember a month when she'd been so unsuccessful with the game.

She squinted at Karen. "Who did you *think* would be calling?"

Karen shrugged. She was still holding the receiver in her hand. "I thought — Mike, I guess, maybe." She bent her lips into a weak smile. "I didn't want a man to answer."

"Mike? You just got here."

"Well, he's sort of — he's a little —"

There was a loud squawking sound. Even from across the room, Ruth could hear Nora's high voice through the receiver.

"Jealous," Karen said.

"*Jealous?*"

"Right! Jealous!" Nora shrieked over the phone. "You always were jealous, Ruth Caster, and you still are! But I win today, you hear? *White Rabbit!*"

Karen dropped the receiver back into its cradle. She seemed dazed, like a sleepwalker, the eyes not quite in register, and for a moment Ruth felt a mixture of indignation and pity.

"Excuse me, sweetheart," she said, "I believe that was a human being you hung up on. Not even a goodbye."

The girl didn't seem to hear. "Thing is, I have to be extra careful just now. We've been through a lot, you know."

Ruth snorted. "For Pete's sake, girl. What's happened to your dignity?"

Karen waved a hand in the air, as if the question were completely irrelevant. "He's waiting down at the beach for me this very second."

"At the beach?"

"Sure, right here."

"Here? At Paradise Lagoon?" Ruth's indignation grew as she realized he had not even stopped to say hello.

"So what he says," Karen went on, "Mike says he's ready to spend the rest of his life with me. Again. Do it right this time. Never be apart forever and forever and forever." Karen crossed the room and stood with her hands dangling at her sides, as if exhausted, as if she'd just dropped an enormous burden.

Ruth lifted her eyebrows. "And that's what *you* want?"

"I don't know."

"If it was, you'd know," Ruth said with authority, sounding much more confident than she had ever felt about such problems in her own life. "Kiddo, I hate to repeat myself, but Mike is exactly like Frank Deeds. Another smoothie. Always saying how happy you're going to be, how wonderfully and perfectly and beautifully happy. In the meantime, though, he's off God knows where, you've got headaches and diarrhea, you're jumping for the phone every time it rings — it's not healthy."

Karen sat down stiffly. She was silent for a few moments.

"God," she finally said, "what am I supposed to do?" She brought a hand to her throat. "All this time missing him, wanting him, feeling miserable without him, and now that he's back, none of it seems real. Like I've been dreaming about him for a year, and then now — I mean, just one *day* after he comes back, it's already . . . But I still love him, Grammy. God, I really do."

Ruth grimaced.

"Don't be ridiculous," a voice said.

It was Hale's voice.

Ponca City, 1935. She was twenty-eight at the time, even younger than Karen.

He hadn't been home the morning she arrived at his one-room house — already out at work in the oil fields — so, exhausted after the long train ride, she crawled into his bed to wait for him. How thrilled he would be to see her. God, how she loved him! She drifted off to sleep thinking strange, excited thoughts, picturing the young couple she'd met on the train: the tired eyes and tousled hair; her breast, his fingers; the impulse, the passion, the intense physical togetherness. *She* could be passionate too. She, too, could be impulsive. This visit to Hale proved it.

Yes, it did.

And in her dream, Auntie Elizabeth came to her, proffering advice about ice bags and yellow sashes and convenient magical powers; and Ruth smiled and lifted Hale's hands above his head; she removed his tie and wound it tight around his wrists; she unbuttoned his shirt and ran an ice cube over his chest.

Passion.

It rose into her throat. It was suffocating her.

When she awoke, the room was hot and stuffy and full of the dusty Oklahoma summer sun; her nightgown was damp with sweat. Hale sat on the edge of the bed eating a sandwich, staring down at her.

"Well?" he said.

His voice was uncommonly stern.

"Happy birthday!" she said, "Oh, Hale!"

She rolled over, lifted herself up, flung her arms around his neck. "Surprise!" she said, trying to pull him down on top of her.

He pushed her away and frowned. "Don't be ridiculous," he said. He took three bites of his sandwich, finishing it. Then he stood up, lifted his hat from a chair beside the bed, and moved to the door. "I have to get back to work." He turned to look at her. "And I always get home late."

"But Hale," she said, jumping to her feet and moving across the room to him, "I just arrived, I just —"

"I'm here to work, Ruthie. Not to honeymoon."

"But aren't you surprised? Aren't you even happy I'm —"

"Surprised?" His eyes widened. At other moments, better moments, those eyes had made her promises of faithfulness and love. "I'll say I'm surprised. Fellow works out at the fields spots you in the station this morning, asking total strangers for directions to my house." He glared at her. "Like a regular boxcar tramp." He placed his hat on his head with precision. "You should have warned me."

"*Warned* you? But Hale —"

"I don't like surprises, Ruth."

"But your birthday — I wanted — I — God, I *love* you."

"Don't be ridiculous." He opened the door. "I don't know what this is all about. I don't like irrationality. And I detest little games."

4:41 P.M.

Karen stood holding a messy handful of yellow paper scraps. She was saying something, her lips moving, but Ruth couldn't quite follow — she must have drifted off. It took a moment before sounds began to register.

"So it's all taken care of," Karen was saying. "Now you can lie back and —"

"What's taken care of?"

The girl squinted at her. "I just *told* you. I took Luis upstairs to Henry's bed. He's all tucked in, safe and sound. You can go ahead and stretch out."

"Thank you, I'll just sit."

"But you really *are* tired, Grammy — I mean, you blanked out or something. Right in the middle of our conversation." Karen shuffled through the wad of papers. "By the way, what are all these messages doing on the floor?"

"Mine," Ruth said. "They're private."

Karen rolled her shoulders. "Well, sure, but —" Then she read aloud from a few scraps:

"Henry — Bill about baseball game — 7/20/90.

"Henry — hearing aid ready — 10/23/92.

"Henry — Happy Hardware, radio fixed, pick up — 2/19/89.

"Henry — do you want hearing aid or *not?* — 2/1/93.

"Henry — Bill says Happy Seventy-ninth — 11/18/86."

Ruth held up a hand. "All right, you've made your point," she said. "You can just put those back where they belong."

"All over the floor?"

"Obviously. If that's where you found them."

Karen shook her head. "Well, I suppose, but poor Henry doesn't seem to *get* these messages. On the floor, I mean. He doesn't even seem to look there."

"Is that my fault?"

"But if —"

Ruth huffed. "Near the phone is certainly a proper place to deposit any such messages. They're doing just fine where they are." She stretched her numb hand out toward Karen. "Sit back down here next to me, please, dear."

The truth — not that it was Karen's business — was actually quite simple: Henry's hearing was bad, therefore Ruth took all phone calls. This in itself was no problem. After all, she was a trained receptionist, graduate of the Sawyer Secretarial School, and it was only natural that the phone should be her responsibility. Whenever calls came in for Henry, she was careful to write down the important details, names and dates and subject matter, and over time she'd developed an equally meticulous four-part Delivery System: (1) If Henry was nearby, she'd jot down the message and hand it to him in person. (2) If he was within shouting distance, she'd yell at him to come fetch it. (3) If he was out of range — on another floor, for example, or on his way to The Pig Pen — she'd leave his message beside the second-floor phone, on the table at the foot of the stairs. Henry was to check the table occasionally to see if anyone had been trying to reach him.

Almost always, in fact, the System functioned without flaw. There was only one exception: when she took calls in her bedroom upstairs. On those occasions, delivery became difficult. She'd first try System Parts 1 and 2. But if Henry was beyond shouting range — at the grocery store, perhaps, or preparing their coffee in the kitchen — the System threatened to break down under the weight of serendipity. She was not about to roam through the place in her nightgown, walking downstairs with God knew who peeping at her through the windows. Instead, she'd slip on her bedjacket and step into her slippers and walk to the landing above the stairs. There she'd pause, taking aim at the table below, then flip the message over the banister. This was Delivery System Part 4.

The Scrap Pile, she called it. If Henry chose not to pick up the messages, well, that was his problem.

4:53 P.M.

"Earth to Grandmother, Earth to Grandmother," Karen said, waving her hand in front of Ruth's eyes. A hunk of moist gum went flying from the girl's fingers and dropped through a gap in the towel that covered Ruth's lap.

"Well fine," Ruth muttered. She lifted the towel and began searching between her legs. "My God, girl, what if I'm gummed *shut?*"

Karen prodded Ruth in the arm, gently. "Stop daydreaming! No kidding, I'm beginning to think you're on your own private planet — someplace like Mars, not enough oxygen in your tanks. And you say *I'm* not healthy."

A loud cry filled Ruth's ears, like the shriek of some ravenous animal, and a pain shot through her chest. She bolted up straight.

This time it hurt. Not a little — a lot.

"You okay?" Karen said.

For a moment Ruth was dead silent. Then she said, "Of course I am. Mars, I was thinking about Mars."

Karen took Ruth's arm and slid a toss pillow behind her back. "Look, you better take one of those pain pills. And probably a tranquilizer, too. Let me run up and get them."

"Never mind."

"But you can't just wait for —"

"No," Ruth said.

She wanted to say more, but the words wouldn't come. Her popping knee and jaw, her infrequent headaches, even her bad eyesight — these were problems she could discuss and analyze; they had a solid, well-defined quality, they were things a doctor might diagnose. But she couldn't find language for the discomfort she was suffering today, the dizzy spells and tinglings, the quick stabbing pains in her chest, the bizarre voices and visions, the vague sense of dread. Especially the dread. Besides, to articulate all this would only overwhelm Karen, shattering the girl's own fragile fears. Better just to leave it alone.

She leaned forward a little, continued to dig between her legs for the gum. "Mars, Mars, Mars," she said. Then, "This man of yours, Mike. We were talking about Mike."

"And?"

"You tell me."

"I don't know," Karen said. "It's complicated."

"Complicated." Ruth located the wad of chewed gum, began rolling it between her fingers. "And since when is desertion so complicated? Or an extramarital affair?"

Karen glanced away. "There was never any proof of that. No real evidence. Just a thought I had, for a while."

"Yes, you were once capable of it."

"Excuse me?"

"Thought."

"Stop it, Grammy. That's cruel. Really, you can be so insensitive."

Ruth frowned.

"Anyway," Karen said, "there were lots of reasons for the separation."

"Separation!" Ruth snorted. "Since when was it a separation? The man walked out on you, for God's sake. Don't start pretending you had any say in it."

For a time Karen sat motionless. Then she snatched the chewed gum from Ruth's fingers, dropped it in the ashtray on top of Luis's cutouts, slid a fresh stick into her mouth. "Look, let's drop it. I'm married, remember? I'm twenty-nine years old. The biological clock. Enough said?" Karen pulled her feet up on the couch and sat leaning forward, arms cradled around her knees. "Anyway, Mike was . . . I mean, he was terribly depressed."

"Oh, I see, depression. Funny how in my day, depression was no excuse for —" Ruth put her hands into her hair; she removed them immediately, fingertips burning. *Surf's up! Time goes ticky! Don't be picky!*

There was some silence. Ruth took the occasion to clear her throat. "Well, okay, depression."

"Down on himself. You remember those big dreams of his, all those ambitions, how he wanted to be a spy."

"An actor, last I heard. A movie star."

"No, the last you heard, he wanted to be a spy. I told you all about it."

"Nonsense."

"I *did*."

"A spy?"

"Close enough," Karen said, and laughed without humor. "You know, join the Secret Service or the FBI or something. Jump on presidents. Save their lives. He even wrote away for application forms — I *told* you all this, remember? Those stupid night classes over at USC. Forensic Science. Apprehending the Criminal Mind. It got to the point where he . . . I mean, all of a sudden he seemed so caught up in it, always daydreaming and stuff . . ."

A thin coat of moisture had formed on Karen's forehead. Her eyes, too, seemed a little damp.

"Honey?" Ruth said.

"Huh?"

"Are you so sure depression's the real issue here?"

"What are you trying to say?" The girl's voice went tight. "That Mike and I don't really love each other? That you're the only person on earth who ever really loved someone?"

Ruth blinked at her, perplexed.

"No, no," she said, "not at all."

In truth, Ruth had no idea what she was trying to say. "But I *love* you," she told Hale on that day in Ponca City, lifting his hand to her breast and squeezing it. She stared at him, dumb with romance and desire, struggling to think of the right words: "Honey," she tried, but the word stuck on her tongue; "Darling," she said, and "Dear," but they did not sound quite right either. "Silly girl," he said, moving his hand to her head and patting her like a child, "don't be ridiculous. You *know* I don't like little games." With Frank Deeds, of course, the dynamics had been very different — "That's my breast!" she said, as she slumped back against a rock, her toes curled in white beach sand; "For sure," he said, squeezing until it hurt — but the results had been nearly the same. All her painful deliberation, her desire, her love or lack of love . . . finally these things had mattered only to herself. Mere details. They had not affected circumstances.

"Grammy, what are you *saying?*"

Ruth blinked at her granddaughter.

There was a slight tremor about the girl's lips, and for an instant Ruth felt worried. Had she revealed something shameful? She was relieved when Karen made an angry, jerking motion with her shoulder.

"You don't listen. You don't hear a word I say."

Ruth took a deep breath. "Not true," she said. "Mike. I've heard every word — been hearing it for years." She readjusted the towel at her lap. "Now, what I want to know is, how much time have you spent with him lately? How well do you really know him?"

Karen blew a bubble. "Well, last Tuesday I went along on a field trip out to the La Brea tar pits — you know, where they have all those preserved fossils. His whole fourth-grade class was there. Not exactly romantic, I guess, but it was fun. Mike's good with kids, I never would have —"

"Fossils!" Ruth said. "Listen, I can't stand it. This whole business, this *change* business, it's the oldest story in the world. You *can't* change a fellow in one afternoon. And even if Mike has transformed himself, which I very much doubt, he certainly can't turn into a completely different person. You sound just like your Great-Aunt Elizabeth on her second time around, with that big religious boob Stephen MacLeod. *He* was supposedly transformed too. And look how it ended up."

"This is different," Karen said. "Elizabeth was stupid."

"Hardly. You think she was so stupid to fall in love with Stephen? Everyone did — you should have just seen him! They started out very hot and passionate, just like you and your dreamboat. So she marries him. Has two children by him." Ruth paused for a moment. That was not strictly accurate. "In any case, two fine children and then disaster. He gets some crazy, jealous notion in his head and blows her father's brains out."

"Oh, brother," Karen mumbled. "Not this again."

"*Father.* Jonathan was Elizabeth's father. *My* grandfather."

Downstairs, the washing machine made a loud thumping sound, then clicked into the rinse cycle. As the machine swished and whirred, the sound of Luzma's voice drifted up the stairs — a happy song about bumblebees and summer afternoons. Ruth and Karen sat still for a while, listening. Then Karen made a sudden, violent motion with her arm.

"Mike isn't Stephen," she said fiercely, "and he's not Frank. Really, Grammy, you're so stuck on these old stories. You make everything seem so horrible and hopeless. I mean it. You've practically given up living."

Ruth pulled the towel tight around her legs as if to protect herself. "I *am* a full century old," she said.

"You're not. You're eighty-eight."

"Quibble, quibble."

"No, it's not."

Ruth hesitated. She felt frail and hurt. "Well, I'm very sorry if you don't enjoy my stories. I was trying to help."

Karen sighed. "I didn't mean it that way — stories are fine. All I'm saying is, people have to care about the present, too. And the future. The world's full of *new* stories."

Ruth nodded. The girl seemed very, very young.

"The future," Ruth said. "I'll keep it in mind." Down inside, though, she felt a familiar hardness in her stomach, as if it were full of wet sand, thick and solid, and there was simply no room for anything new. It wasn't a question of right or wrong. She recognized Karen's meaning; she even approved of it. She'd felt the same way a long time ago, when there was still space inside her, still openness and hunger, back when newness was truly new.

Karen sat up quickly, as if jolted awake. "My God, what am I doing here? On and on about myself, when you're feeling sick." She shook her head. "Anyway, about Mike and me, it's not so bad. Not really." She nudged Ruth. "One thing's for sure — we've still got chemistry."

Ruth nodded.

"Chemically speaking —" Karen giggled. "Scientifically, I'd have to say we're . . ."

Ruth lifted the edges of her mouth into a smile.

Chemistry. Like the time she and Edith Tumay went skinny-dipping in Santa Monica, the summer before their junior year in high school. A warm, moonlit night, and Little Boy Mackelroy was there, the one who drowned in a riptide later that summer; his older brother Chester was there too, with a friend of his from college; and Tom Snelson and Ricky Gwynn and Henry's brother Bill. Henry might have been there, she supposed, but that part she couldn't remember. So, yes, a warm summer night, and she and Edith had been so modest, crouching behind that big white boulder, waiting for the boys to dive under a wave before they stripped off their clothes. They kept their naked shoulders beneath the water at all times, and didn't splash, and later, when Little Boy Mackelroy stole their skirts, they stayed in that freezing ocean for almost half an hour, maybe longer, waiting for the coast to clear. Finally, almost numb with cold, she and Edith made a wild naked dash for the shore, shrieking and hugging their own shoulders and snatching their clothes back from Little Boy Mackelroy. The memory made Ruth smile. So many years ago. And what stuck with her most vividly — more than the cold water, more than the ensuing pneumonia and those weeks she'd spent recuperating in bed — was Little Boy standing there buck naked on the beach, big and bold, waving two skirts at the moon, and how, in one glimpse, she'd understood where he got his foolish name. "I think I'm in love," Edith had said as they dressed in the dark, "I really do, I think Little Boy's my big, big man." A month later Little Boy drowned in the riptide off Seal Beach. Chemistry: it was not reliable.

Upstairs, there was a loud clattering noise.

"Help!" Henry yelled. "Save me!"

5:16 P.M.

They stepped out of the elevator, hurrying through Ruth's bedroom and across the landing to Henry's door. Just inside the doorway, Karen jerked to a stop.

"Wow," she said, "what *happened?*"

Ruth was panting, rushing to catch up. She nudged Karen aside and entered the room.

Henry's top desk drawer was wide open, and empty; the contents lay scattered across the rug — pencils, paper clips, a Scotch tape dispenser, a pencil sharpener, memo pads, a broken pair of scissors. And strings, too. Dozens of long white strings. Like fishing lines, Ruth thought, each attached to an item from the desk. The strings snaked across the floor and disappeared into Henry's walk-in closet.

"Mother of virgins!" he was yelling. "Help!"

Tentatively, Ruth picked her way through the debris and peered into the closet, waiting for her eyes to adjust.

"Judas Priest!" Henry squealed. "Get me loose!"

It took some time for Ruth to make sense of it all. The man sat wiggling in his overstuffed chair; a band of strings was wrapped around his forehead like a pauper's crown. Struggling, he yanked his neck back, which set off a chain reaction: the strings went taut, there was a clattering sound, and a procession of desk items came scooting across the rug. A small plastic ruler slithered up to his left foot.

Henry's eyeballs made a long, wide revolution in their sockets.

He sat tied firmly to the chair, yards of string winding around his wrists and chest and knees and ankles. The King of Trinkets, Ruth thought, strapped to his throne. She stepped into the closet and switched on the overhead light.

Luis peeked out from behind an old overcoat, a ball of string in his hand.

"Help!" Henry yelped. "One minute I'm sleeping like a baby, next minute I lift my head, I'm hog-tied. And every damn thing in my desk comes flying out." He tried to blow a string off his nose. "Kid's nothing but trouble."

"He was snoring," Luis said. "I can't sleep when he snores."

Ruth nodded grimly. "*That* I can understand."

With a quick laugh, Karen moved into the closet and began to undo the maze of strings.

"Angel of mercy!" Henry said, and grinned stupidly. "Karen — darling — God bless you!"

Ruth watched for a second, then shook her head. "If I were you, Karen, I'd just leave him be. Let Mr. Solitaire figure his own way out." She put a hand on Luis's shoulder. "Go on, amigo, run on into my room and I'll come tuck you in." She smiled at the boy as he left, then turned to Henry. "Hurry up, now," she said. "We're going down to the beach."

Karen looked at her grandmother, astonished, then continued to disentangle Henry.

"What?" the man hollered.

"The beach," Ruth repeated. "Mike's waiting."

"For Chrissakes," said Henry. "I got this damned plug in my ear, can't hear a friggin' word."

"The beach!" Ruth yelled.

A bright, almost playful glow of pleasure came into Henry's face. "Swimsuit time!" he said.

He began to struggle against the strings with renewed vigor.

Ruth leaned over, yanked out the radio earplug, and said, "Good luck. We leave in fifteen minutes."

Back in her own room, Ruth shuffled over to the space heater next to the TV. She picked up her sleeping bag and, when Karen arrived, handed it to the girl. Luis lay at the foot of Ruth's bed, sound asleep.

"If you're done helping the old geezer," Ruth said, voice slightly bitter, "you can do a favor for youth and zip this boy in for a proper nap."

Karen pulled the sleeping bag from its plastic sack and sniffed at the nylon. "Thing's filthy," she said. "You should let Luzma wash it or else sleep between the sheets like a regular person. And, by the way, if you'd ever turn that radio off," she said, nodding toward Ruth's bedside table, "you'd be able to hear the ocean from your bed."

Ignoring the girl, Ruth bent down for her sit-up pillow. A sharp, painful jolt shot down her spine. She grabbed on to the TV antennas for balance, squeezing with both hands, but even then she couldn't steady herself. The makeshift rabbit ears had been molded from strips of tinfoil — like holding on to air — and after a second she teetered backward, scattering the pile of catalogues at the foot of her bed.

Karen dropped the sleeping bag and reached out to catch her. "Jesus, Grammy, I'm really worried. No kidding, I think we'd better call the doctor. Right now."

"Don't *touch* that phone," Ruth said.

With effort she pushed herself upright, stood with her feet widely separated. Even so, she felt like a cattail in a brisk wind.

"When I talked to Dr. Ash about my knee two days ago, he said I was born with my problems. Some genetic nonsense. So if I've made it this far, I'll be just fine today."

"But you can't —"

Ruth covered her ears with her hands. She smoothed her hair, brought her arms to her sides, and walked around the TV to her chair. "Well, I'll rest here for just a minute, if you can handle that sleeping bag properly." She tugged on the towel at her waist, moving the flap to her left side, then tucked in her blouse and sat down. "But I won't be idle for long."

Karen groaned. "You're impossible," she said, and lifted the sleeping bag, carrying it over to Ruth's bed. She paused at the nightstand, turned the radio down low. Then for several seconds she stood very still, as if distracted, or as if contemplating some hidden internal puzzle. "And this old pillbox, too — you've had it as long as I can remember. How about if I get you a new one for Christmas?"

The box *was* a sad thing, Ruth knew, chipped and dirty, like everything else in the bedroom. But still, it seemed odd how the girl kept poking through the pills, sliding a hand down toward the pocket of her shorts.

"I hope you realize," Ruth said, "that those drugs are prescription. People can't just swallow them willy-nilly."

"Swallow what?" Karen said.

"Whatever's in that pocket."

"Oh, that's —"

"Listen, I know you're upset, dear — this Mike business — but if you need to calm your nerves, I'd recommend a nice cup of hot milk. Not tranquilizers."

Karen seemed relieved. She smiled and said, "Well, thanks, but I'm afraid you're seeing things."

"Perhaps so," Ruth said. She adjusted her glasses. "Lately I've been . . . Just remember, though, you can't medicate your life."

As Karen spread the sleeping bag over Luis, he grumbled in his sleep and said, "Shit!"

Karen looked at her grandmother. "What's with him?"

"Oh, nothing new — fighting at school, that ferocious father of his, you get the picture."

Karen looked personally wounded. "Really, Grammy. The things you say sometimes."

Ruth let out a small snort and looked down at her stiff bony fingers, folding them in and out. "We all have our troubles, Karen, but I certainly don't go constantly complaining or chewing on pills every time a little predicament pops up. Just stick to my routine and hold my head high and keep marching on, no matter what."

She looked up.

Karen was gone. A soft purring sound drifted through the bedroom, and for an instant it seemed the girl had been sucked away by an invisible vacuum cleaner. Then Ruth noticed the tip of a tennis shoe bobbing on the floor near the bedside table. Partly hidden, her back against the bed, Karen had sunk down to the carpet. She was holding her head in her hands, weeping.

Ruth felt quite helpless. "Come on now," she finally said, shuffling over to the side of the bed. "Self-control, Karen. Keep yourself together."

The girl's sobs only thickened. "I'm *trying*. Except it feels like my whole stupid goddamned life is . . . Don't you realize these things are hard for some people? Maybe not for you — it doesn't even seem like anybody matters very much to you."

Ruth stared. How could Karen, of all people, say that? It didn't make sense. Just like that Mr. Chuckly Voice with his flippant reprimands. Briefly then, as she looked down on the weeping girl, she felt a bizarre heat radiate up through her body, a kind of visceral comprehension. Her granddaughter, for all her complex rationalizations, was terribly frightened. This boy Mike had set her head spinning; she'd lost her internal compass. Her hair dyeing and gum chomping and fast car and glamorous job — these were mere breakwaters, bulwarks against the shifting demands of ordinary human uncertainty. Ruth recognized herself in her granddaughter. And down inside, where the sand was, she felt the same shifting ambiguities, the same terror.

She waited for a moment, one hand grasping the bedpost, then lowered herself to the floor. Her knee popped; her entire left side tingled. "There," she murmured, "there now." Hesitant, she reached out toward the girl. "I'm sorry."

Karen bent her head against her grandmother's chest. "Mike and me — I mean, *me*, I guess — I was so in *love* with him. I thought we were so absolutely, perfectly *made* for each other." Her shoulders heaved. "God, it's like —" She pulled a wad of gum from her mouth, wrapped it up, and tossed it feebly in front of her. "I don't know — I guess you're right, Grammy. I guess he *doesn't* really love me." Her voice wavered. She pulled in a heavy breath.

Awkwardly then, aware of the tension in her own body, Ruth reached out and put an arm around her granddaughter's shoulders. For a long time she simply cradled her. "Sweetheart, sweetheart," she said, but then her breath caught. A sudden thought struck her. Not a thought, exactly: a picture. Karen as an eight-year-old, Carter dropping her off to spend a weekend in Laguna, the first of many weekends she was to spend at Paradise Lagoon during her parents' bitter divorce. Despite all the sorrows at home, Karen was a happy child. Always talking a mile a minute. Always laughing. Ruth remembered how at night they'd sleep in the same bed, how they'd build blanket-forts and make things snug and lie there telling each other bedtime stories. Yes, and how they'd play that game called Lost Spider. "Where's my web, where's my web?" Ruth used to whisper, and she'd run a finger along Karen's tiny ear, tickling, then pulling away. "Where's my web?" she'd keep saying, and she'd bring the finger closer to the ear's opening, hovering there, making spirals, maybe retreating for a moment — "Where am I?" — and then slipping the finger down Karen's arm with a touch so light that the skin would turn to gooseflesh — "Hurry up, Grammy! Hurry, hurry!" — and then, at the last instant, Ruth would plunge the finger deep into Karen's little belly-button — "I'm home!" Now, cradling the girl, Ruth could still see all this. She could hear it, too, and feel it, how Karen kept squealing and giggling, and how later they'd curl up together, side by side, dreaming.

"There now," Ruth said. She paused for a moment: one's options in life were so horridly limited. "I didn't mean to imply he doesn't love you." She thought of Mr. Chuckly Voice and tried to insert some cheer into her words. "All I'm saying is, he needs to get his priorities in order. You know, his people steeple." She nudged the girl. "And you need to remember your dignity."

She waited for a reply.

"Isn't that right?"

Karen made an effort to straighten up, toyed with the laces on her tennis shoes. "I'm just so tired," she whispered.

"I know, honey. I know *exactly* how you feel."

And then for a long while they sat together on the floor, feeling the closeness.

The distant sound of shrieking gulls came through the open window. A cool breeze filled the room as the late-afternoon shadows moved like spilled oil across the dirty white carpet.

Ruth brushed a wisp of hair from her granddaughter's cheek. "Aren't we a pair?" she said. "Two lost spiders."

5:42 P.M.

They walked hand in hand to the elevator. Ruth pushed the button to bring it up, and a minute later, when the door slid open, Luzma stepped out with Ruth's slacks and panty girdle. She was eating a chocolate candy.

"Here's your things, Ruthie, good as new." Luzma wiped her mouth on the back of her hand, tossed her hair behind her shoulders. "I mopped the bathroom floor and put in the second load of laundry. Nothing more to do, really, till it's ready for the dryer."

"What about the dusting?"

"Already done," Luzma said. "Last week, remember?" Her eyes twinkled. "Mike's here, out on the balcony. Says he waited over an hour at the beach." She beamed at Karen. "Muy guapo, as usual."

Ruth looked at Karen, pulled her into the elevator. "I'll dress on the way down," she said.

The elevator was cramped with three passengers, barely enough space to move, and it was a struggle for Ruth to slip the panty girdle over her sandaled feet. She bent down, nudging Karen sideways, then cautiously straightened up again. The girdle still dangled at her knees.

"You want help?" Luzma asked.

"No," Ruth said, "I do not."

"Just turn around, I'll yank it up real fast."

"*Please*. I'm fine."

The elevator cables jiggled. Ruth lunged forward, and then backward, and then waited a moment before reaching down again.

"Perfectly fine," she muttered. Discreetly, one elbow clamping the towel to her waist, she wrestled the girdle over her hips and up to her stomach. Her breath was coming hard. Bad air, she thought — like getting dressed in a casket. She pulled on her slacks, hooked them shut, and draped the green towel over the safety rail.

"Eighty-eight years old," she said to no one in particular, "but I can certainly find the wherewithal to dress myself." She felt strangely loose inside. Her thoughts were rattling around like coins in a large dark piggy bank, and it took effort to focus on the simplest practical details. "You finished everything?" she asked Luzma. "Polished all the silver?"

"Sure, Ruthie, six times in the last two months."

"Good. One more won't hurt."

Luzma glanced at Karen as if to inquire about something, then reached out to tuck Ruth's blouse into her slacks. "What about this dizzy problem?"

Ruth pushed Luzma's hands away. "Never mind. You're still planning to stay for dinner, aren't you?"

Luzma looked at Karen again, raising her painted eyebrows,

and Karen nodded. Luzma patted Ruth on the back. "Sure," she said, "I'm staying."

"I'll stay too," Karen said. "Mike too."

With a jolt, the elevator landed at the second floor. Luzma gave Ruth one more comforting pat, then pushed her way out and lifted the silver tea set from the phone table and headed straight toward the kitchen, whistling. Ruth shuffled to keep up with her. Briefly, she thought of Mike waiting out on the balcony; at the same time, however, she pictured Karen's teary eyes, and decided the boy could use a lesson in patience. "Henry bought some nice frozen turkey dinners for tonight," she said to Luzma. "And I'll make salads. Of course, with Karen staying, and Mike, we won't have enough to eat."

Karen reached out for Ruth's elbow. "Hold on, Grammy," she said. "Please quit rushing, you're not up to it. Anyway, those dinners take thirty minutes to cook." She pointed across the sitting room, past the piano, to a spot where tightly closed drapes hid the sliding glass doors that gave access to the balcony. "Go on out and talk with Mike for a minute while I pop the dinners into the oven."

Ruth looked suspiciously at her granddaughter. "Why on earth would I greet him alone?"

"Come on, he's *waiting* out there."

"Splendid," Ruth said. "Waiting's tonic for the soul." She gave her granddaughter a sly little smile and sat down in her place at the dining table, the only spot that was cleared of old knickknacks and mail. Karen hesitated, glancing toward the balcony. "Well, I guess," she said. "Rest up a minute while I take care of things in the kitchen, then we'll go out and greet him together."

The kitchen, Ruth knew, was a mess. There were piles of used napkins on top of and behind the toaster oven, greasy paper plates stashed between the bread box and spice rack. Grime in every crack, dirty dishes in the sink and drainer. Five or six burnt-out light bulbs — which Ruth had inscribed in permanent black ink with the dates they had ceased to function—were lined up along the kitchen windowsill. Several boxes of chocolates, which Ruth had wrapped in plastic freezer bags, were stashed away in half-open drawers, some of the boxes years old.

As Ruth watched, Karen took one of the freezer bags from a drawer and pulled out a heart-shaped candy box. She peeked inside and selected a candy.

"Well, help yourself," Ruth mumbled.

But just as Karen put the chocolate to her lips, she paused. She held the candy up and examined its bottom, which was gone, the cream center entirely scooped out.

Luzma laughed. "Join the club," she said. "Some days it takes me hours to find a whole one. Our little Ruthie, she's got some weird habits."

Ruth smiled to herself. "They *are* my candies," she said. She looked down at her hands. The palm of her right hand was still blistered; her left hand was still cramped and numb. Damn, she thought. Painfully, she clenched and unclenched her fists. With a sigh, she shut her eyes to rest. She could hear the girls chatting in the kitchen. Luzma, as usual, was complaining about how she had to ride the bus to work six days a week, and how every Saturday for the past five years, since her husband got a job at Margarita Haven, she'd had to bring Luis with her. Together they rode the bus, Luzma said, and together they visited every kind of house California had to offer, like a cheap version of those mansion tours in Hollywood.

"One thing for sure," Luzma was saying, "I'm tired of all this driving around to other people's places. I got my plans. Go to classes, learn real estate. Start *selling* houses."

Ruth opened her eyes and peered out toward the kitchen. Karen was standing beside Luzma, one hand gripping a salt shaker, the other crammed into the pocket of her shorts.

"Well, great idea," Karen was saying. "Lots of women and young people in the business. I hear we're in a down market, but there's only so much California. Things are bound to turn up." She pulled her hand from her pocket, glanced over the counter toward Ruth. "Luzma, could you help me with something? You know how . . ." Karen's voice became curiously quiet, and though Ruth strained to hear, the words seemed to fade in and out. "When those dinners are done, make sure that . . . and plenty of salt so she won't . . ."

"What are you doing in there?" Ruth called. People didn't seem to realize she knew what went on in her own house. That very morning, for God's sake, she'd twice caught Henry red-handed, right in the act.

Karen turned to face her. "Oh, nothing, Grammy," she said. "Discussing real estate."

"Well, don't go rearranging things. You may think I'm old and crazy, but I can still spot a conspiracy when I see one." She felt too tired to say anything else. And, though she'd already rested so many times today, she was having trouble keeping her eyes open. She stretched her arms out on the table in front of her.

"I can *hear* you, too," she mumbled.

5:55 P.M.

"You awake?" Karen asked. "Dinner's in the oven." She lifted a ring of keys from the table; when she jostled the pieces of metal in her palm, they made a light tinkling sound, like sleigh bells. "Mike's still waiting out there."

Hesitating, Ruth lifted her head. The world seemed to have gone blurry during her snooze, a fluid melting at the edges of things; she felt the need to reestablish some solidity. Slowly, with real effort, she stood up and moved to the foot of the stairs. She gathered some oxygen into her lungs.

"Henry!" she yelled. "Come on, man. Visitors!"

Karen took an indecisive half-step toward Ruth. "Look, I'm sorry you're not comfortable with this. I mean, I know you're under the weather."

"Don't be silly, dear. I was willing to go the whole way down to the beach to greet the man, wasn't I?" She kept her eyes fixed on the landing of the stairs. She wanted very much to talk to her granddaughter, but what of any real significance could be said? She glanced over at the girl, who was bobbing up and down, sliding a new stick of gum into her mouth.

"Does it hurt much?" Karen asked.

"Oh, probably."

"Probably where?"

Just then Henry appeared at the landing, bits of string trailing behind his shoes as he lumbered down the steps. Ruth's eyes wandered across his shirt, which was still not buttoned properly. His wispy white hair was matted into strange shapes. With a thump, he came to rest at the bottom of the stairs. "Beach time," he said, and grabbed Ruth's hand.

Ruth allowed her hand to remain in Henry's. To her own surprise she even shuffled toward him, leaning forward a little. "No, Henry, the beach is off. Mike's *here*, out on the balcony. You remember Mike — Karen's alleged husband."

"Oh, yeah, the spy. Good fellow."

"You're entitled to that opinion," Ruth said. "Anyway, he's here for dinner." She lowered her voice to a whisper. "I don't know what he'll eat, though, because we only bought the four turkeys." And she started across the room, pulling Henry along after her like a fishing line heavy with bait.

6:00 P.M.

Henry reached into his back pocket, pulled out his baseball cap, placed it squarely on his head. After a second he sank down into a wicker chair opposite Mike.

"So look here," he said earnestly, "how's the spy business?"

Ruth couldn't help snorting. She took a seat beside Henry and crossed her legs.

Off to the west, beyond a row of pointed condominium roofs, the sky shone with a purplish blue glow like the inside of an abalone shell. A cool, salty breeze swept across the balcony.

"Spy business?" Mike said slowly. A narrow crease formed between his eyes as he slung his feet up on Ruth's glass-topped coffee table. "I'm not sure I follow."

"Hey, mum's the word," Henry said. "State secrets and all that."

Mike shot a quick, accusatory glance at Karen, who stood beside him, leaning against the wooden balcony railing. "Afraid you've been misinformed. I'm no spy."

"Course you ain't."

"Seriously, I'm a teacher."

Henry snapped off a crisp military salute. "Cat's got my tongue. Couldn't even torture it out of me, no sir. Call me Silent Sam."

"Well, thanks," Mike said.

"You guys still use them fingernail-yanker things?"

Ruth waved a hand at the air. "Henry, *listen* to him, he's a schoolteacher."

"I'd just like to take a little look-see if he's got —"

"Fourth grade," Karen said.

"Gotcha." Henry lowered his voice. "Maximum deep cover."

Again Mike glanced at Karen, who found an excuse to fix her gaze elsewhere. The girl's fingers flitted along the railing like nervous butterflies.

Ruth opted for mercy. "Look, I don't know where this spy stuff came from," she said, "but I recommend we change the subject. Nice evening. Typical California December."

"Very," Karen said.

Mike gave her a last sharp look, which promised future discussion, then turned to Ruth and summoned up a pleasant smile. He had excellent teeth, large and very white. A good-looking specimen, all in all. Almost handsome, in a boyish sort of way: freckled and sandy-haired and playful around the eyes. He was wearing one of those fuzzy outdoorsman's jackets, with faded jeans and tennis shoes like Karen's.

There was an uncomfortable silence before Mike smiled again and said, "So here we are."

Then came a longer, denser quiet.

Ruth eased back in her chair, eyes fixed guardedly on Karen, listening with half an ear as Henry began filling up the silence with a spray of baseball chatter. In his own way, she thought, the old man knew what he was doing. Even that relentless spy talk, it was a method of deflection, using his own buffoonery to cut through the awkwardness and tension among them. He was annoying, true, but he also had a generous, well-intentioned manner that she couldn't quite deny.

After a time Karen visibly relaxed, and Mike too. The sun was low on its journey toward Japan.

"Don't get me wrong," Henry was explaining, "I ain't against progress, but these new feminine-style uniforms, they strike me like something you'd see on a bunch of ballet dancers over at the . . ."

Ruth tuned out again as the old man soared off into soliloquy. The descending sun caught her eye, fierce and bloody as it moved below the balcony railing, highlighting her granddaughter's thin figure, and for an instant she found herself overwhelmed by a powerful sense of her own aliveness. She thought of Frank Deeds on that morning forty-some years ago when he leaned cockily against an almost identical wooden railing at the San Diego marina; she thought of Hale, too, how hot his skin had been on the night he died — the way he'd called out that word "Time!" — and how his death, when it came, had seemed an act of pure and ferocious desire.

For a few minutes she sat quite still, hearing nothing, trying to gather up her emotions. She almost felt like crying.

Various obscure thoughts revolved inside her: the notions of youth and age, the fragilities and resiliences of the ordinary human spirit. At one point she lifted up her aching leg. So pretty, she thought. Her mother's legs, too, and her granddaughter's. The promise of happiness was always so rich and infinite, the reality so abridged.

Quickly then, with a jerking motion, she stood up. "I've got to fix the salads," she said. "You coming, Karen?" And she exited the balcony.

6:23 P.M.

Ruth trudged through the sliding glass door, humming to herself, trying to ignore the shifting sensations in her stomach. All this commotion — it was overwhelming.

In the kitchen, Luzma had set the TV dinners on top of the stove and was peeling back their plastic wrappers.

"I hope those things don't cool too quickly, I still need to make our salads," Ruth said. This was a matter of vital importance, she told herself. After all, there was still living to be done; you couldn't eat an old lady's musings. "Of course, we don't have enough turkeys," she said. "I guess Henry and Luis can have bologna." She reached for the refrigerator handle, bending slightly, and suddenly lost her balance. She grabbed Luzma's arm.

"Okay?" Luzma asked.

"Yes, fine."

"You're sure?" Karen asked, coming up from behind.

"Perfectly," Ruth said, but a great black exhaustion seemed to fill her body. Maybe these girls were right, she shouldn't be moving around so much.

"Look," Karen said, helping to open the refrigerator, "I'm not hungry, Grammy. Just salad for me. Henry can have his turkey; I'll make a bologna sandwich for Luis."

Ruth peered straight ahead into the refrigerator. "That's fine. If you want to be anorexic, refusing to eat, sucking noses, I certainly won't stand in your way."

"Sucking noses?"

"Oh, you know." Ruth inserted a healthy dose of authority into her voice. "You know exactly what I mean. I get around. I've seen all the kids doing it. Go ahead, join them if you like. Just don't ever forget it was germs that killed your grandfather."

Karen sighed. "I have no idea what you're talking about." She pulled the packet of bologna from the meat drawer and moved over to the counter.

Ruth continued to gaze straight ahead. Five open quarts of milk — three nonfat and two whole — took up most of the space on the middle shelf; each carton was wrapped in a plastic bag and clothespinned at the top. Tidbits of chicken and other leftovers were sealed in zip-lock sandwich baggies and crammed onto the top shelf between yogurt cartons and margarine tubs. A glass coffeepot, the automatic-drip-machine type, and an old percolator stood side by side on the bottom shelf.

Ruth pushed the percolator aside and reached in for her salad makings.

"Well, well," she said. "Something's amiss."

Luzma laughed. "The famous Refrigerator Rules."

"Don't be smart with me."

"No chance, Ruthie. Rules are rules."

Ruth let the girl's sarcasm pass. Right now there was the problem of getting to her cottage cheese and pineapple: her wax-coated muffin bags were blocking the way. And the bags had clearly been tampered with — Henry's doing, almost for sure. Ruth groaned and shook her head. Muttering to herself, she passed several waxed bags over to Luzma, then reached down for her salad makings on the bottom shelf. When she turned around, Luzma was leaning over the garbage bin, about to throw the muffin bags away.

"Hey, I'm saving those!" Ruth snapped.

"Por qué?" Luzma looked startled. "You kid me, right?"

"I am not a kidder. Those are valuable." Ruth straightened up quickly, arms bent sharply at the elbows, a cottage cheese tub in one hand and a pineapple tin in the other.

Luzma held the bags out in front of her, looking with disgust at the refrigerator. "But why so much old crud in there? It's too hard to get at things."

"Don't say 'get at,' Luzma. Just say 'get.'"

"Yeah, okay, but all these stinky old bags, you catch yourself a disease or something."

Ruth sighed. "Listen, dear, I sincerely believe if you'd been around in 1930, back when the Depression began —"

"Filthy," Luzma said, her voice tight. "Unhealthy. Health hazard."

"Not in the least. They're waxed."

"So what?"

"Moisture resistant, I might add. Extremely sanitary. No germ on earth could wiggle through, not even those evil little villains that took my Hale away. I don't believe I've ever told you how he came down with that terrible —"

"You told her, Grammy." Karen was buttering a piece of bread.

"I wasn't talking to you," Ruth said. She looked at Luzma. "Did I tell you?"

"Dios mío. A lot of times. Remember?" Instantly, Luzma's eyes went soft with compassion.

"Yes, well. To be sure." Ruth nodded at the counter. "Clear me a space next to Karen there, please."

6:32 P.M.

Ruth lumped two tablespoons of cottage cheese into each of six tea saucers, which she always used for salads. She placed four pineapple chunks on each cheese mound, and a spoonful of coleslaw at the side, for roughage. When these operations were completed, she asked Luzma to clear the table — "Keep my papers in their separate stacks," she warned, "and be gentle with those cardboard envelopes, they happen to contain my fortune" — and then she carefully transported the salads to the table, one by one.

As Ruth placed a salad at what was always Luzma's place, at the end of the table beneath the window, a sudden shower of sparks crackled along her neck and spine. Like a lightning bolt, almost, and it sprayed out from the back of her skull and across her forehead and down toward her left shoulder, where it paused to gather new voltage, dividing into two halves and sizzling down her left arm and left leg. The world went null-white. She lost touch with her own whereabouts; consciousness was just a distant tapping amid the electric buzz.

For a few twinkling seconds she felt utterly powerless. Like loving someone too much, or losing him, or waking in the middle of a dream.

When her vision cleared, she was surprised to find herself still standing there, clutching the back of Luzma's chair.

She felt a vaguely familiar pang.

"So *that's* it," she murmured. She stretched her arms, took a few hesitant steps away from the table. Half smiling, calmed by a sense of recognition, she adjusted her glasses and watched with a kind of prideful curiosity as her pretty old legs carried her back to the kitchen. "Yes, of course," she said. "What else?"

Surf's up!

Time chime!

Ruth nodded to herself. She watched Karen carry the last salad dish to the table and arrange the silverware and water glasses. They would all drink ice water, except Luis, who'd have milk.

When things had been orchestrated to her satisfaction, Ruth moved to the stairs and called up to Luis: "Come get it, amigo! Dinner's on." In a moment the boy came tripping down, barefoot and still groggy with sleep, and plunked himself into his assigned chair at the table, between Ruth and his mother. Ruth tucked a napkin under his collar, smoothed it down, then moved out into the sitting room and shouted toward the balcony. "Come on, Henry! Right now, man, dinner's ready!"

Luzma giggled from the kitchen. "Sounds like you're calling a dog," she said. "Here boy! Here boy!"

"Perhaps so," Ruth said crisply, "except most dogs are trained to obey." She shouted again, "Henry!"

Karen drifted past and opened the sliding glass doors. "Okay, boys," Ruth heard her say, "soup's on."

Ruth returned to the table and slipped into her place. She watched Luzma carry the TV dinners out two at a time, placing them on paper plates to catch spills, the way Ruth liked. "This one's yours," the girl said to Ruth.

Across the table, Mike and Karen sat down beside each other. Henry slumped into the chair to Ruth's left, at the head of the table. He pulled over his dinner. "Jeez," he said, "what a day. Trussed up like a damn Thanksgiving turkey." He gave Luis a suspicious, almost fearful stare. "Kid's a bundle of laughs." He tugged on the visor of his baseball cap.

Luzma took her seat. "You're a good sport, Henry. And it's nice to have you down here for a change, not eating all alone up at your desk."

Henry beamed. He'd had a crush on Luzma for years, sneaking peeks at her bottom whenever she happened to bend over. "Well, it ain't often we got guests. I figure it's my job to keep things on the up-and-up." He tucked his napkin into his collar. "Looks like you've prepared a pretty good feast here, Lucy."

"*Luzma*," Luzma said, and laughed. She undid the top button of her jeans to make room for dinner.

Henry's eyes bulged. He tugged at his baseball cap and forced himself to turn toward Ruth. "So how'd business go this morning? See anybody downtown?"

"Just Nora," said Ruth. "She has a new boyfriend. It appears there's no rest for the weary."

Beneath the table, one of Mike's feet nudged up against Ruth's ankle. He didn't apologize. In fact, Ruth noticed, he was conspicuously quiet, prodding at his meal with his knife. Men, Ruth thought. Masters and enforcers of silence. She felt furious. She *would* hear this boy explain himself. "You know," she said to Karen, anger rising in her voice, "for all your lectures about new stories —"

"Dinnertime!" Henry cried.

Ruth sighed and directed her attention toward the man as he grasped his fork and scooped up a mound of mashed potatoes. She wagged her head: his habits were so ridiculously predictable. He wouldn't go for the turkey immediately; it might be too stringy for his gums. He'd avoid the dressing altogether — too crunchy. First the mashed potatoes, then the cranberry sauce, then the peas. Finally he'd screw in his loose tooth and chew as many bites of meat as he could manage, until Ruth came to pick up his plate. Pitiful, Ruth thought. In some ways the man was more helpless than a baby.

"Delicious entrée," Henry said. "I'd have to rate it a genuine gourmet delight."

He drooled a little as he forked the mashed potatoes into his mouth. Then he noticed Luzma sitting across from him with her head bowed; he drew back his fork, staring at her wide-eyed for a moment. Ruth couldn't help smiling. The girl was simply scraping some excess salt off her turkey, Ruth knew, but Henry obviously thought she was in prayer. Henry's first wife, Eleanor, had been Catholic, and he still loved all the rituals and Hail Marys and elaborate hand actions. It made him feel "cleanly," he used to say.

Now, hands folded, he began to mumble a prayer of his own. Luzma blinked and glanced over at Ruth; Ruth blinked too, and stared at Henry. It went on for almost a full minute, then Henry crossed himself and raised up his water glass. "We have a lot to be thankful for," he said. "À la salud."

"Oh, Jesus," Ruth said.

Beside her, Luis made little farting sounds.

Mike continued eating, his movements stiff and deliberate, but Karen giggled.

Luzma said, "Amen."

Ruth studied her TV dinner. Turkey was by far her favorite, much better than the enchiladas or the meat loaf. Diligently, making sure she hadn't been cheated, she took stock of the items in each plastic compartment. All the old-fashioned trimmings were there. Gravy and home-style dressing and peas in seasoned sauce. Cranberry with . . . She leaned forward for a closer look. Instead of deep red cranberry sauce, this stuff had strange pale hunks in it.

She made a sour face and looked around the table. "Is this someone's idea of a joke?"

Luzma shook her head. "Apple-cranberry. So what?"

"Okay by me," Henry said.

"Puke," said Luis, and began to dissect his bologna sandwich.

Ruth frowned, lifted her fork, dipped it skeptically into the sauce. Well fine, she thought. Always fiddling with basics. She tasted it. "Unusual," she muttered, and continued to take inventory. God knows what they'd done to the mashed potatoes: probably laced with tofu. And no dessert at all, not even a piece of apple crisp. Here she was, eighty-eight years old, looking forward to just a little something sweet at the end of her meal, and what did these cheapskates give her? Not a thing. Back when the dinners had been covered with foil — and even more recently, since they'd started using that plastic wrapping you had to peel off or poke holes in — back then, the dinners had *always* come with apple crisp. This new development struck her as positively sinful.

"Karen, Mike," she said, "why do you think —"

And what was *that* on her turkey?

She closed one eye and bent forward over the dinner. A white powdery substance, almost like chalk, had been sprinkled over her entire entrée. For a second she wondered if it might be a defect in her vision, another wave of those blurry white speckles. She poked at the stuff with her fork. And then the truth came to her: cheese. Parmesan cheese — nothing else could look like that.

She turned to Luzma. "Dear," she said crossly, "you *know* I don't like Parmesan."

"Parmesan?"

"Here! See here?" She was raising her voice. "Right here on top of my turkey!"

Henry leaned over. "What's that you say?"

"Parmesan!"

"What?"

"Take your nose out of my dish," Ruth said. "What I *say* is, there's cheese on my turkey."

"Sounds gourmet to me," Henry said, and beamed at Luzma. "Never tried it, now, but Eleanor used to fix turkey with yams and marshmallows on top, and sometimes peaches, and I liked all that pretty fine."

"Yuck-a-doo," said Luis. "Pooh-pooh, too."

"I'm quite sure Eleanor was a fine cook," Ruth said, "but I don't believe that's the issue right now. Luzma, I *despise* Parmesan."

The girl seemed nervous. "Just salt, Ruthie."

"Calm down, Grammy," Karen said, "it's on everybody's dinners. See, look at Henry's."

At that very moment Henry was sprinkling salt all over his apple-cranberry serving.

"Salt my eye," said Ruth, her voice loud. "This is what I call cheese. What do you all think we're eating here? It's supposed to be turkey, just basic regular-style turkey!" She licked her index finger, preparing to Test the tiny white flakes, except she couldn't quite get her fingers to separate. Oddly, this complication had a calming effect on her temper. Never mind, she thought. Maybe the cheese nonsense was some ancient Mexican custom; she certainly didn't want to hurt Luzma's feelings. With a sigh, Ruth gave the girl a sidelong glance, looked down at the dinner, and sliced off a small piece of white meat. There was a first time for everything. She lifted the meat to her mouth and started to chew.

"Not so bad," she said. "Not bad at all. Very Latin." Strange, though, it didn't taste like cheese. Surely not Parmesan. "Very interesting. South of the border, so to speak."

"There's this kid," said Luis. "This black kid named Tony — he's my friend — and he used to scare me all the time on purpose. Like, whenever I walked to school in the morning, he hided himself at that liquor store on the highway. Right behind that big trash can there, and then —"

"That's a dumpster," said Henry. "Next to the Spigot. Used to know the place pretty well myself."

Luis nodded. "Yeah. So this kid Tony, he always hided there, and every time I walked by, he jumped out and yelled bad stuff. 'You're so white,' he goes. 'You're as white as a whale's behind.'"

"Luis, please," Luzma said, "let's everybody just enjoy eating, before it gets cold."

Across the table, Karen sat observing the boy. She looked worried.

"Yeah, but he kept doing it all the time," Luis said. "So I decided to kick his ass."

Henry's mouth hung open; a pale hunk of apple dropped to the table. "Atta boy," he said. "And you let him have it?"

"Henry!" Karen said. "Don't encourage him. Kids are violent enough."

"That's right," Ruth said. "All those knives and guns and gang murders." She patted Luis on the head. "Revenge is never proper, dear. Don't take out your frustrations on others. Just keep a stiff spine. You know, backbone!"

Luzma rapped the table with her knuckles. "That's enough, everybody. I have something important to talk about." She placed her fork beside her plate and turned to Ruth. "Something I want to tell you about. I got this plan. Make a future for myself — right? — don't want Luis riding around on the bus his whole life. Anyway, now that things are going good for Enrique, settled down a little, I want to get my own profession. Like I was telling Karen —

go into the realty business. I read all about it in these brochures, and I . . . Are you listening?"

Ruth was in no mood to answer. As she was stabbing the last bite of her meat, she'd noticed something else on top of it, something pink.

"Just one question," she said grimly. "What kind of salt comes in pink?"

"No kind," Henry said, "and that's a fact. Which reminds me, today I went up to the bakery section —"

"What reminds you, Henry? Pink salt?"

"No, the thing Luzma said a minute ago, about the bus."

Ruth made a growling noise. What was it with this man's selective hearing? He made strategic use of his ears, to be sure — just like his legal blindness and sporadic buffoonery. She put a hand to her stomach. Patience.

Henry smiled affably. "So today I go up to the bakery section for Ruthie's muffin, right? And there's this young kid working there who says, 'I know, one oat bran muffin,' and I says, 'Who the devil are you?' and the kid says, 'We've known each other for two years, Mr. Hubble,' and I say, 'Hey, I know all the girls who work here. I never seen you before in my whole life.' So the kid says, 'I'm no girl, Mr. Hubble' — it's a guy, see — so he says, 'I'm Steve, and I've been giving you muffins here every weekend for the past two years.' And I says, 'Weekend? What day is today?' and he says, 'Saturday,' and I says . . .'"

"Jesus," Ruth said.

Karen giggled.

"Just listen a minute," Henry said. "My little story gets pretty dang interesting."

"*Your* story?" Ruth looked around the table. "What I want to know is, what culture on earth eats pink cheese?"

Henry coughed suddenly and spat a wad of turkey onto his plate. Eyes watering, he ran his tongue across his gums, muttering to himself, then picked up the meat and began pawing at it with his fingers. He plucked a yellow tooth from the meat, said "Bingo!" and dropped the tooth into his water glass.

Ruth nearly gagged. "Henry, I'm warning you, there'd better be some point to this. You interrupted Luzma, you know."

Henry dipped his spoon into his water glass and scooped up the yellow tooth. He spun it between his fingers, getting the angle right, and jammed it back into the opening in his gums.

"I didn't interrupt the lady," Henry said. "You did it first, all your harping about green cheese. Anyways, if you don't mind, I think the señora wants to hear the end of this one, even if you don't." He smiled at Luzma. "So I says, 'Saturday? My God!' And the bakery kid says, 'Hey, Mr. Hubble, come on out back and see how I revamped my old van.' And he takes me out to the parking lot — you know, the one for the employees — and he shows me this big van he's got. Honest to God, he has that thing decked out sweet as can be, wall-to-wall carpeting, indoor plumbing, the works. So I check it out. I look at how the faucet's got hot water, how the bed folds out, and this kid says, 'I bet an old guy like you's got a billion stories to tell,' and I says, 'My God, how old you think I am?' and this bakery punk says —"

"Pink!" Ruth yelled. "I want to know who at this table has ever *once* ingested pink cheese!"

Luzma and Karen were both giggling now, and even Mike had a smile on his face. Luis said, "Asshole, Tony, *you're* white."

Mike turned angrily to the boy and spoke. "Excuse me, young man," he said in a schoolteacher's voice, "I *resent* your racist comments."

A white streak ricocheted across Ruth's field of vision, bouncing from object to object, off the table, up to the hanging lamp, over to the window; when it bounced back onto the table, Ruth recognized the very same creature she'd seen in the Postal Connection that morning. Yes indeed, a furry little white rabbit. She blinked several times. She felt a pain in her head and put her hands up to her temples and said, "Just stop!"

"Hey, qué pasa?" Luzma said.

Ruth straightened up in her chair and looked around the table: nothing out of the ordinary. So fast, she thought. She drew in a breath to settle herself. "Never mind. Go ahead now, Luzma, your plans."

"Ruthie, you look kind of —"

"Please. Let's hear it."

Luzma squinted at her for a moment. Then she looked around the table and cleared her throat. "Well, you know, I just want to improve myself. Real estate's the classy profession these days, especially around here, and you don't need college or anything to get a license. Just go to this class, or even do it by mail. A correspondence course, that sounds good to me."

Ruth put down her fork. Maybe it was Henry's story, or the pink cheese, or Mike's stubborn attitude, but she'd totally lost her appetite.

"So you'll quit cleaning, just like that? Do this correspondence business, then leave?" Ruth stared down at the napkin in her lap.

"Well, I'm thinking it's cheaper that way, by mail, but I could always take night classes."

"No," Ruth said. "What I mean is, it appears you're about to abandon us."

She lifted her head. Across the table, a furry white rabbit was rooting through Karen's salad, snorting and sniffling and thumping its paws. It glanced up at Ruth. It wrinkled its little pink nose. It wiggled its ears. Then, quick and sprightly, it hopped down from the table and out of sight.

"Please —" Ruth's breath caught. Was she going completely insane?

Turning in her chair, her guests momentarily unseen, she gazed past Luzma and out the dining room window. The sky was black. Her head was throbbing. The entire cosmos seemed to press against her temples.

What was this rabbity vision?

The creature of her habits come to life?

Something buried beneath those habits suddenly surfacing?

Something half forgotten, something never completely known, like a pebble lodged somewhere in the deep folds of her brain.

She could feel her heart beating.

All the hope and longing and regret in the world. All the expressions of love, and all the things that passed for love.

She shook her head. Enough.

But she continued to stare out the window, past the lighted tennis court and belt of green grass. Life, she thought, was so incredibly temporary. Nothing ever lasted, nobody ever stayed. But then she pictured Henry bumbling home across the highway with her groceries in his arms, so small from the vantage of this dining room window.

"You know, it's remarkable," she heard herself saying. "How we come to need each other. How we *become* each other."

The others looked up at her — Henry and Luzma and Karen and Mike — but also Hale and Elizabeth and Stephen and Frank and all the others, their faces uniting into a palpable human thereness.

A people steeple: *these* faces, her faces.

"It's hard to explain," Ruth said. "All of us here — we're not just ourselves, we're everyone. All the people we've known." Her eyes came into focus on the young couple across from her. "Like Karen. It's not just that she's my flesh and blood — my daughter in all the ways that matter — she actually helped to make me who I am."

Karen smiled.

"Very profound, Mrs. Hubble," Mike said. "Truly profound and amazing."

"Mike, please," Karen said beseechingly. She looked nervous again.

Ruth cleared her throat. "A teacher, young man. You must know the importance of respect for elders."

Mike rolled his eyes.

"God knows it's never simple," Ruth said, determined to continue. Her dinner was stone cold. "Marriages can be like zoos, I know that. Always that wildness inside the cage." She turned to fix her eyes on Henry. She felt oddly calm and articulate. "This old man and I — we have our ways of doing things, you know, ways of getting along. But it's more than that. He's *part* of me. I'm *part* of him. The things we remember, the things we've done — just circumstance and coincidence and habit, you might say, but —" She broke off abruptly.

"Anyway," she said, "one of life's little ironies, I suppose." She reached over and touched Henry's bony elbow. Then, beneath the table, she brought a foot down on top of Mike's toes — not hard, but not soft, either. "So what about you?"

"Yeah, what *about* me," Mike said, placing his napkin on the table. "Look, I don't know what you're trying to get at. All I know is, we're here to visit you. Doing you a favor. I don't want the third degree."

Henry nodded. "Hey, mum's the word!"

Mike struggled to free his toes. "Anyway, Mrs. Hubble, we agree about Karen. We both care about her. Personally, though, I don't need your approval for my actions."

"But I do," Karen said.

"Right," Luzma said, chiming in. "Me too."

Ruth felt confused. "Yes, yes, approval's fine," she said, staring intently across the table at Mike. "But I'm talking about something else. About faithfulness. Respect for human intimacy. We're not only responsible for our own lives. Sometimes we lead other lives, too."

Mike stared at her blankly.

"Understood?"

He frowned. "Whatever."

"That's it? That's all you have to say?"

Mike sighed. "Look, think what you want, I was never trying to . . . Could I have my toe back?"

"In a moment," Ruth said. "What *were* you doing?"

"Look, I don't know — that *hurts*."

Henry nodded soberly. "Real fingernail yankers."

"Go on, young man," Ruth said, her voice stern. She released his foot and leaned back, crossing her arms in front of her chest.

"Okay, right, we've had our problems, just like everybody else. But we're working things out." For a fleeting moment, the boy looked truly pained. "God, I don't know . . ." He winced. "Sometimes I just feel like screaming."

Ruth turned her eyes toward the dark window. "And that justifies desertion? Abandonment? You feel like screaming, so you just . . ." But the rest of the thought drifted away.

Somewhere in her mind it was 1945 and she was driving down an empty desert highway, alone, towing along all her own dead dreams in a Mullen's Red Gap trailer. Innocence and hope and romance: all of it packed away in cardboard boxes. And then that long savage howl from the bottom of her lungs. Maybe at the center of every human being, she thought, there was some sort of unique and enduring noise — like a fingerprint — the secret wailing sound of the soul.

When she looked up, Mike was leaning forward, his freckled face very close to her own. She felt something approaching affection for the boy.

She turned to Karen. "A man's feelings, dear. You can't predict them. That's one thing I've definitely learned." She cleared her throat. "Maybe the problems start when you love a person too much. I guess if you're too enthusiastic, they just —" Abruptly, she thought of her experience in the downstairs bathroom that afternoon, all those people in the photographs melting and oozing away. "They just disappear, maybe, burning up like fire, melting away into nothing . . ."

"Not me, Ruthie," Henry said, reaching out for her hand. His voice was agitated. "Not me and you."

Ruth gave him a weak smile. Gently, she pulled her hand free.

Mike glanced at Karen, apprehension in his eyes. He was still leaning forward. "Listen, Mrs. Hubble, please don't get all worked up. I'm sorry, I really am. I made a few mistakes, agreed, but I've also made some progress since then. It's all in the past now. Really. I'm back for good."

"Except for parachute missions," Henry said.

Mike nodded. "Right, except for that."

Ruth stared at her granddaughter. Almost imperceptibly, a small fold of skin twitched beneath the girl's right eye as she leaned over to kiss the back of her husband's neck. "So there we are," Karen said. "It'll just take some time."

"Time," Ruth said quietly. "I suppose."

"That's a blessing?"

"No, dear. It's complicity."

For a few moments no one spoke. Then Henry gave a decisive tug to his baseball hat. "Well, hey," he said, "I guess we got things pretty well figured out here. Men and women speaking, it's always a tussle. Like today, for example. Ruthie and me, we barely say a word to each other all these years, then bingo, right out of nowhere she up and wants to play cribbage. And then bingo again, this afternoon she lets me pick her up and waltz her over to the elevator. Right by the armpits. The whole nine yards. Crazy. I'll tell you something, though. I don't complain. Just count the miracles."

Ruth blushed and turned away.

"God," she sighed, "what a hammerhead."

After a few minutes Mike and Karen both stood up. "Take care of yourself, Grammy," Karen said. "I'll call you in the morning." The girl started to say something else but then stopped and gave Ruth a coded look that went woman to woman, partly thanks, partly the collusion of survival. "Better run," she said.

"Yes," Ruth said, "and don't stop."

When Henry and Luis had excused themselves, Ruth turned to Luzma. "Well, we'd better do the dishes," she said. Then she looked down and began to tug at the hairs on her left arm. "Correspondence," she said softly. "With complete strangers."

"Oh, come on, it's not like I'm gonna leave, Ruthie. No way. You do the correspondence stuff at home. I could even study right here."

Ruth didn't respond. From the corner of her eye, she watched the girl stand and gather the silverware and carry it out to the kitchen. Watching, in fact, was all she could manage. She watched Luzma fill the sink with water. She watched her return to the table for the glasses and trays and plates, her face hazy at the edges, everything unwinding in a jerky slow motion.

After a moment Ruth forced herself to speak up. "Now listen, don't throw away those paper plates, they're perfectly fine. Just put them there next to the breadbox, on the counter, in between the —"

She stopped because her eyes had filled with tears. She certainly didn't mean to cry, hadn't realized it was coming, but somehow it seemed the right thing. It felt good, in fact. She hadn't cried in years, maybe decades. With Luzma leaving, whom would she talk to on Saturdays? And who would accompany her to her dental appointments? The doctor's office was nearby on the Laguna bus line, but not the dentist, and how in the world could she ride alone to *that* part of town? She put a hand to her eyes. The crying wasn't loud at all, just a soft spilling sound.

"Right, I know," Luzma was saying, "five inches from the sink. I'm not some crummy amateur, Ruthie." She rinsed the silverware, cheeks glowing with happiness. "So what I'm thinking, Ruth, I try to hook on with the Perpetual Prestige Agency. They hire minority types like me. There's this Vietnamese guy I heard about, could hardly speak English, but he walks right in there out of the gutter, says his family's starving to death, says he needs money bad. So Prestige hires him. That same year, he's top sales-man for March and May. Two years later, he's taking in more than a hundred thousand. A true story, Ruth. I saw him once from the bus — guy's driving a Mercedes."

Ruth wiped her eyes. She didn't say anything.

"Well, he's rich now. Prestige gives their agents this six-week training program, free. Lots of possibilities, too — they got escrow companies, mortgage companies, all kinds of things."

The girl sounded so different, Ruth thought. Where had she learned to talk like this? Again, Ruth pulled at the hairs on her arm. In a dim way, of course, she was pleased for Luzma, going off to follow her dreams. But she couldn't help feeling that strange emptiness inside.

"Well fine," she finally said. "I guess maybe I'll just go to the dentist all by myself. You'll probably be too busy. Probably too famous."

One tear, which her eye-wiping had not erased, slipped down her cheek and dangled at the edge of her jaw. She waited for it to fall. She counted to five, slowly, then to fifteen. She resolved to let it drop of its own power.

Luzma walked out from the kitchen and sat down beside Ruth. "Now, come on, don't be a silly goose," she said. "You won't go all by yourself to the dentist. We'll still be friends, won't we? It's not like I'm moving to Alaska — I'll still always go with you. And I'll come over on the first day every month, no matter what. Fair enough?"

She bent to look into Ruth's face.

"Come on, Ruthie. I know you're glad deep down."

Five minutes, Ruth thought, and that tear was still stuck there on her jaw, like an icicle. Maybe the laws of gravity weren't what they used to be.

Luzma made a tsking noise with her tongue. "You should be happy for me, it's like a happy story. You're the one always telling stories. Always sharing the same old stories, right? Like the one about your father coming to California, remember? And like my dad in Mexico, too, working hard so he could raise a family right. Nothing to be scared about."

"Sure," Ruth said, "okay."

Luzma persisted. "Only thing new is, girls have careers now. Not like when you were young. We're more ambitious. You know, be your own boss. Take charge of things."

"I *was* a professional secretary, if you care to remember," Ruth said. "Anyway, you and Karen — your big careers — I mean, when Hale died . . ."

She fell silent. Her attention was now entirely on that mutant tear. It seemed immune to the stern laws of science — like Henry, who refused to understand the rules of the house — and Ruth was determined to teach it a lesson. She wouldn't wipe it off, or shake it off, or anything. Just wear it down. Make it hang there and suffer until it *had* to drop.

"And for me," Luzma was saying, "it'll be lots of fun, I bet. Especially in Beverly Hills, where I wanna work. I got connections there. Girls who clean houses, you know? They find out first when a place is up for sale, they keep their eyes open, they see if the husband's been in bed with the wife or if he sleeps on the couch or if he's not in the house at all. You follow my thinking, Ruth? They can tell me if it looks like a divorce is coming. Lots of divorces in Beverly Hills, lots of bucks for somebody like me."

Ruth started to raise her head, cautiously, so as not to disturb the adhesive tear.

"One or two sales, I'm rich," Luzma said. "Those places in the Hills, they cost a bundle. The commissions must be amazing. No joke, I could buy a new BMW and drive you to your appointments. No more bus trips for *us*."

"Well, yes, it sounds splendid," Ruth said. She gazed directly into the girl's eyes. "Listen, dear, do you know anything about gravity?"

"Sorry?"

"Gravity," Ruth said. "Like why apples fall, that sort of thing."

Luzma shook her head. "Houses, Ruthie. I'm selling *houses*. It'll take a while to start, though — I don't got all the information yet." She stood up. "You sit there awhile, let me finish with the dishes."

Ruth reached for Luzma's hand. "No, that's all right. Just leave them. You and Luis were my guests tonight. The least I can do is finish tidying up. Enrique will be home soon and he'll wonder what's keeping you."

"Well, I guess. You feel okay?"

In fact, Ruth realized, she felt considerably better: the tingling had died down and the pains were entirely gone. She opened and closed the fingers of her left hand. "Much better," she said. "All I needed was your dinner company, Karen's nice little visit — that's all, not Dr. Ash and his pain pills. I did get the whole way back here from the pool by myself, you know."

Smiling, Luzma tucked in her sequined blouse and buttoned up her jeans. "I'll just put the laundry into the dryer."

"No, leave the laundry too," Ruth said. "Don't worry about anything."

"You sure?"

"Completely."

"Well, if you say so. And it was nice for us, too. Mike back and everything — really super." She called her son in from the living room. "Give Ruthie a kiss goodbye, Luis."

The boy looked up into Ruth's eyes. "So long, Abuelita," he said, and pecked her on the edge of the jaw, taking the tear away.

"Now here's somebody who knows physics," Ruth said, reaching out to straighten his shoulders. "Don't forget, kid. No hunchbacks in *this* clan."

When she heard the front door close, Ruth pushed herself up from the table. Luzma was so optimistic, she thought — just like Karen, just like she herself had once been.

She piled the glasses into the kitchen sink, leaving them for morning, then moved heavily out to the living room. Luis had left the TV on, and *Wheel of Fortune* was just now coming to a close. Absurd, she thought. All these poor souls cheering a half-naked hostess, everyone wild-eyed and gluttonous and ripe for disappointment. Ruth sat down on the couch and pulled off her sandals.

Spin the wheel: there was Frank Deeds.

So many fine shining promises.

True love, he kept saying. He'd be faithful to her always. But though she knew Frank cared for her in his own unique way, which was a careless caring, Ruth couldn't shake off the suspicion — the intuition — that the man would remain a philanderer forever.

It was not passion and anxiety she wanted for her middle years. It was peace. Not surprises, pleasant or otherwise, but certainty.

Romance had died with Hale. Simplicity and practicality, these were the fallout, and so one day she composed a short note to Frank, explaining that she never wanted to see him again. They could exchange letters if he liked, but nothing else. She signed the note "Yours truthfully, Mrs. Ruth Caster Armstrong."

So lose a turn.

Spin again.

She cut her hair short, stopped wearing perfume. She worked long hours at the doctor's office in Los Angeles, filling up her days like a leaky bucket, often staying late into the evenings until everyone else in the building had gone home. For fun, she resumed piano lessons. She grew vegetables and flowers. With her savings from work she bought herself a car, a sleek yellow Studebaker, and on Saturdays she drove herself down to the beach at Laguna, to lie in the sun.

On one of those empty afternoons at the beach — it must have been in the late summer of 1956 — she happened to run across Nora Gretts, who had just recently returned from Europe. Predictably, the two of them had little in common anymore, except for heartbreak and their days at UCLA, but there was enough to get them through an hour or two of conversation under a merciless California sun. In the end, they agreed to meet for lunch the next day, which led to more lunches, and eventually to something not far removed from friendship.

Nora worked regular hours at Intime in those days, and when fall came, and it became too cold to go to the beach, Ruth began spending her Saturdays down at the shop. Just a way of passing time, refilling the leaky bucket that had become her life. Still, there were pleasant moments. Nora's idea of fun, Ruth came to realize, was more than a little odd; in fact, Ruth would've thought the woman a perfect floozy if she hadn't been a longtime witness to Nora's ostentatious declarations of identity. Even then, though, the woman was sometimes hard to stomach. But Ruth needed to distract herself, needed to occupy the hours, so on those Saturday afternoons she'd talk and laugh with Nora, for old times' sake, and together they'd page through tattered back issues of the *Daily Bruin* and sing sorority songs. When no customers came in, they'd smoke cigarettes and eat brownies for lunch behind the counter. And after lunch Nora would model a new camisole or negligee, dancing down the aisles while Ruth hummed Perry Como tunes.

Ruth stretched and yawned and reached for a toss pillow.

She blinked in surprise: her arm didn't hurt. She lifted her left leg, and that too was feeling better: numb, as if she'd been shot full of novocaine.

She pulled both legs onto the couch and curled up.

. . .

And so, yes, it was one of those Saturdays — March 1958, almost for sure — and Nora was strolling through the shop in a purple strapless bra and a pair of beaded blue underpants, and Ruth was doing her best to affect an air of amused indifference — "It's definitely *you*," she was saying, "a match made in heaven" — and at that instant the door swung open and a tall, skinny, vaguely familiar man sauntered in off the street. Nora fled for the bathroom; Ruth turned and stepped behind the cash register.

The thing to do was to behave normally. A salesperson, polite and efficient. She pushed her glasses up on her nose and watched closely as the man moved about the store, sometimes muttering to himself, sometimes pausing to finger an article of clothing. Again, she felt that inexact sense of recognition. For five or ten minutes the man roamed up and down the aisles with a heavy step, the top of his gray-streaked head bobbing above the racks.

Ruth finally summoned up a crisp clerical voice, calling out to ask if he needed help.

"Help how?" he said.

"Well, the usual. Advice or whatever."

"Guess not, cutie." The man was behind a rack of half-slips. "No thanks for now. Just having a general all-around look-see."

It was the voice that seized her memory. A Hubble voice. Bill or Henry — she prayed it was Bill — but she hadn't seen either of them since high school. She leaned over the register. "Billy Hubble?" she said. "It's *me*, Ruth Armstrong. I mean Ruth *Caster*, to you."

The man peeked around the half-slips. It was Henry.

"Well, holy-moly, I'll be hanged and danged," he said, and he walked over to the register. "Ruthie Caster. What's you doing in a joint like this?"

Ruth flushed. Something in his manner, maybe the awkward way of talking, made her conscious of the enduring singularity and unity of a human life. All that Hubbleness. All those years. In the standard ways, of course, he'd undergone the changes that come with age, yet at the center of the man there was something stone-hard and permanent that made her warm inside, that made her touch her curls and smile and explain with a slight nervousness that she was simply helping out an acquaintance for the day.

"I mean, I have my own job during the week," she said. "In a doctor's office."

Henry nodded. "Hey, I'll bet you do. Always the sophisticated lady. Just like the song."

"I was?"

"Right as rain."

Ruth felt herself blushing again. "And you're still a stockboy over at Simpson-Ashby?"

Henry slapped his leg and laughed. "Oh, hell no, I haven't been in produce since I was eighteen. I'm at Bullocks now, moved into housewares. Head buyer."

"Splendid."

"Yeah, I guess I'd have to agree with that."

He took a step forward, sliding a hand across the counter toward her. Ruth removed her glasses. It was an involuntary gesture, utterly unwilled; nor could she wipe off her nervous smile, nor stop herself from reaching up to freshen her curls again.

"Well, good for you," she said. "I always suspected you'd do fine, even if you did drop out of school during that nasty influenza epidemic. Back when so many of my friends were *really* dying."

Just then Nora came out, more or less clothed. It was a relief for Ruth to step back and make the introductions. "Pleased as punch," said Nora, and offered her hand. "Call me Lady Soirée, please do. Mind if I call you Hank?"

"Mind if you don't," he said.

"Well, there we are, Hank. And what brings you here to Intime? Looking for anything special?"

"Not exactly, Lady Sorry. Sort of browsing."

"*Browsing?*" Ruth said. "Aren't there some hardware stores in town?"

Henry lifted his eyebrows, sliding his hand toward Ruth again.

"Hardware's just hardware, Ruthie. I figure to myself, I figure like this, a man's got to expand the old horizons. You know, learn about things that please the ladies. Anyways, I'm passing by this fine establishment here, I spot them artistic dry goods in the window and I say to myself, I say clear as a bell, 'Henry' — Hank, I mean — 'Hank, you best step inside and see what's what with the ladies these days.' All in the line of duty, eh? Customer taste."

He rocked back on his heels, then forward. The hand came to rest a few inches from Ruth's right breast.

She took a step sideways.

The hand followed.

"But aren't you awfully far from home?" she asked. "Why, I heard you somehow managed . . . That is, I hear you have a lovely place in San Marino."

"Well, hey, I don't live here in Laguna, if that's your drift, but I like to come down on Saturdays, to get away. My wife passed a few years back, see, and I have an awful time knowing what to do with my weekends."

"Isn't *that* the coincidence!" said Nora, throwing out her chest, dropping a hand on Henry's arm. "Ruth here, she lives up in Los Angeles, not too far from yourself, Hank, and comes down to visit me on Saturdays. And her own dear spouse also died recently. Well, not so recently, actually, but you know how some women are. She's still in mourning, Hank. Note the clothes. She certainly doesn't follow the latest fashions."

Ruth couldn't help glancing down. Her gray shirtwaist dress *was* a bit dated — she'd seen no reason for fancy clothing since Hale died. Still, she thought, Nora was off base on this one. Out of bounds, too. Ruth clenched her jaw and dragged her finger across her throat like a saw.

Nora took no notice.

"I guess our darling Ruthie just has difficulty getting on with things. Needs to take her own sweet time. But look, Hank, that's a mighty interesting tie you've got on — are those by any chance trombones? — I'll bet a guy like you could show our sad friend here a swell time."

"Nora, for God's sake."

For an instant, a familiar image filled the air in front of Ruth's eyes: Hale slipping a tie around his neck, knotting it with elegant precision, moving to examine himself in a mirror. Handsome and graceful and dignified, the image of perfection. Ruth stared at the man before her. Why, he couldn't even make a proper knot — the tie was pinched into place with a shiny safety pin — and the trombones were positively shameful. Quite unexpectedly, Ruth felt a measure of compassion for this unkempt, uncouth widower, this Henry Ho-hum Hubble.

He winked at her. "The idea suits me fine. Might just show this cutie a trick or two." A flash of yellow teeth appeared in his bright pink face, and he reached into his breast pocket, passing a business card across the counter. His hand brushed up against the front of Ruth's blouse. "Give me a call this week. We'll plan ourselves a jaunt down here together next Saturday. I'd be proud as a plum to make the ride with you. Course, I don't drive or nothing." He flashed his teeth again. "In the prime of life, you bet, but already blind as a bat."

Nora patted him on the shoulder. "Don't you worry about that, Hank. Ruth here has her own Studebaker. She'll just pick you right up, won't you, darling?"

Ruth did not answer.

Henry shrugged. "Well, can't miss my bus," he said, setting his card on the counter. "See you next week, sweetheart. I'm pleased as can be."

"At least you could've offered him a ride home," Nora said when he was gone.

Ruth was furious. "What the hell did you do that for? I haven't even laid eyes on the man in thirty-five years. Walks in here like some pervert — snooping through cheap lingerie, for God's sake

—and now we're supposed to have a date? And I drive? No thanks."

Nora picked up Henry's business card and slipped it into Ruth's handbag. "Cheap lingerie, you say?"

"Well, I wouldn't call it —"

"Who here knows about quality, me or you? Lady Soirée, who spent her entire prime in France, or you, who's been sitting around at her parents' house, crying her life away for years? Anyway, Hank's a splendid male specimen. Lonely, that's obvious, but you can't beat the male part." Nora studied her long red fingernails for a moment. "Look, honey, take it from me, a gal who's been around and back. You won't do better. No great shakes, I'll admit, but at least he's a gentleman."

"Oh, for God's sake," Ruth said, and she took the card from her purse and dropped it in the trash.

That Monday, when Ruth was back at her desk in Los Angeles, busy helping a blind patient fill out a medical history form, Henry telephoned her.

"Hear you're free on Friday," he said, "and I'd sure like to take you out for dinner."

"Free?" Ruth said. *Kill* Nora, she thought. Strangle her with that purple bra. "I am not free," she said. "I will not be."

Henry laughed. "Haven't changed a bit, have you Ruthie?" He made a loud phlegmy sound in his throat. "Listen, I've been pretty lonely these days." He made the sound again. "Real lonely."

"Well. I don't think it's possible."

"Miserable lonely."

"Oh, for Pete's sake, where's your dignity?"

"Too darn lonely for dignity. Lonely like to bust."

Now what could she do? She sighed and glanced up at the blind patient. The man was grinning, head cocked, enjoying this end of the conversation.

"All right," she said at last. "But I'll tell you something. It's pure charity."

"Okay by me," Henry said cheerfully.

Ruth dreaded it. All week, in fact, she tried to think up excuses. Polio maybe. Trapped in an iron lung. But when they walked into the restaurant that Friday evening — a noisy steak house Henry had picked out — she was pleasantly surprised. His posture, for example, was erect and confident. Of course his skin had gone a bit nubby, but she liked the way he moved. Very slowly, with a measured gait that conveyed — she sincerely believed at the time — a firm and manly self-possession. Later, less charitably, she would come to refer to this walk as "lumbering."

Once at the table, she placed her napkin in her lap and asked about his parents.

"Oh, they passed a few years back," he said. He tried to smile at her. "Hear yours are still with us."

"Oh yes, they're just fine," Ruth said. "Well, you know, tuberculosis. But other than that."

Henry shifted in his seat.

"Hale, that was your husband's name, I hear."

Ruth froze. "You hear quite a lot, Henry, don't you?"

He frowned and licked his lips. "I guess that's right. Maybe when the eyes start to go, the ears . . . Anyways, I know he was sick, Hale, before he died." He tried again to smile. "One thing I understand," he went on, "it's sickness. You see, my own Eleanor was sick a long time, too, before she passed. Well, ten years, just about."

"Ten *years?*" Ruth stared.

"About that, I'd say."

"My God. I'm sorry, Henry."

"Well hey, look now. Never did have any kids, that's the killer. But all in all I've been pretty lucky." He smiled weakly. "She was a Catholic, did I tell you? An honest-to-God living saint. I swear. I was so proud of that woman." His lips quivered. Like waves, Ruth thought, forever gathering themselves up into frothy smiles, forever crashing down again, defeated.

"Sure do miss her."

Ruth sat in silence, looking down at the napkin in her lap, thinking. She felt sorry for the man. He was kind — Nora was right about that. He was sensitive. And at times he could even be charming. Really, she was not at all ashamed to be seen with him. He looked a lot better than he had as a boy, now that his tomato-red hair had turned gray, and he seemed much more self-assured. On top of all that, he had that beautiful house in San Marino. An elegant Victorian house, she'd been told; nothing like her parents' little bungalow or the flat old Caster ranch house out in San Diego. To an extent, Ruth felt guilty thinking such thoughts, but it occurred to her that she wouldn't mind living in San Marino, she wouldn't mind at all. It was near her parents' place, and near the first house she'd shared with Hale, and San Marino was one of those ritzy areas she'd always had an eye on. All in all, not a bad bargain.

"How's your ribs?" Henry asked.

"My ribs?"

"Your dinner, cutie pie, how is it?"

Cutie pie! Clearly, Ruth thought, the man would require some extensive training. But there was something in his voice that struck her as dependable, something firm and unchanging, something that promised she would never again have to worry about being alone. The object, after all, was no longer perfection. Certainly not joy. And there was much to be said for that singular and enduring Hubbleness now gazing across the table at her. In a way, like a kind of cement foundation, it seemed to offer support to her own fragile Ruthness.

"Well, as ribs go," she said, "they're not bad. Quite the barbecue, in fact."

7:37 P.M.

Jeopardy! had started. Ruth blinked once — a contestant was explaining how his career as a butcher had been "born" on his father's farm in northern Idaho. She blinked again. Her eyes fell on those paper characters that Luis had cut out — a spirit world full of spirit people — all of them heaped into the ashtray. Little Greenie seemed to be at rest.

Valentine's Day, 1959, and Ruth Caster married Henry Hubble.

"Hale, I'm sorry," she'd said the night before. "I loved you. I loved and loved you. Hale?"

They were married at the courthouse in Pasadena, and that evening there was a small reception at Henry's house — which was now *her* house — in San Marino. By and large it was a fairly pleasant gathering. Except she couldn't stop whispering things to herself: "God, I'm sorry, I *loved* you, Hale."

At one point, she recalled, Henry found her standing alone in the kitchen.

"Hale," she was whispering, "I'm sorry."

"My new bride," he said, slapping her bottom. "Helluva day, but the name's Hank."

"Fine," she said.

Just then Douglas and Carter arrived, both late. Douglas had been performing emergency surgery, and Ruth smiled with pride as he came into the kitchen to meet Henry. Not yet thirty and already a successful doctor, the boy had made quite a name for himself in Hollywood and Bel-Air. Carter was late because of thunderstorms in Caracas, Venezuela, where his plane had been delayed. In this case, too, Ruth felt the stir of pride. Barely twenty-six, president of his own commercial-design firm, traveling all over the world. His expensive and conceited new wife, Melinda — who would later be Karen's mother, and later still, the obese and conniving financial ruin of Carter — pressed herself against him like a case of chronic hives.

Ruth cast a cheerless smile on her boys and said, "Don't Mr. Hubble and I have a beautiful house here?" She glanced at Henry. "My boys," she said. "Hale's boys."

Henry said, "Righto." He clicked his teeth and held out an unsteady hand.

Right then, Ruth felt a rare surge of anger. At herself, partly, and at this bargain-basement marriage, and at the man standing before her, this husband who now reminded her of a soda jerk in some tacky Hollywood drugstore. His jacket was white and his shirt was white, and his pants and belt and shoes and socks. His face, and the wilted carnation in his buttonhole, were a ghastly shade of red. Like a drunken ghost, Ruth thought.

She couldn't stop the rage from bubbling up. "What in God's name," she whispered, "were you thinking? Meeting my sons for the first time, dressed like that, like a giant maggot!" She made a fist, trying to control herself. Then, by chance, she noticed his tie. It was a tie she had given him just two weeks before — an elegant Brooks Brothers red-and-blue-striped silk tie, a beautiful tie. She reached up to Henry's neck and adjusted the knot; a quiver of tenderness passed through her fingers. For a moment, she stood just smiling up at him.

Then Henry tossed back a shot of tequila. It was easily his sixth or seventh of the evening.

"Sons," he said, "I've worked long, hard hours all my life. Saw my share of success, carved out a niche for myself in housewares, clobbered the competition. But even though it looked like I had everything, I was always asking myself, 'Hubble,' I asked, 'what's it all for?' Well, now I know." He threw an arm around Ruth's shoulders, almost knocking her down. "Your little mother here suits me just right, and I know I'm gonna make her happy as a clam."

Henry kissed Ruth's cheek, then Douglas's, then Carter's and Melinda's. "Call me Hank," he said.

Later that evening Ruth shut herself in her bedroom to write a final letter to Frank Deeds.

Valentine's Day, 1959

Dear Mr. Deeds,

I regret to inform you that I have been married.

I am quite content. I have a perfect house. I have every

convenience a woman might desire, and am only a forty-five-minute drive away from my parents. Things are very, very, *very* fine. The sun comes up peacefully; the sun goes down peacefully. And every night, when I go to bed, I know what will happen the next day.

I hope you will be happy. Please never write to me, and try never to think of me again.

Cordially and Even Fondly,
Mrs. Ruth Caster Armstrong Hubble

A week later, Frank sent Ruth the snapshot he'd taken of her at the San Diego marina, inscribed on the back with the words "You will always be close to my heart." He also sent a large, flattering portrait of himself and a letter declaring his lasting love.

She stashed the photographs in a drawer of her roll-top desk.

She disposed of Frank's letter.

She never spoke to him again, never saw him again, never regretted it.

On occasion, though, especially in the hours before bedtime, it came to her that she had been offered the risk of a second chance, which was something in itself, and that by declining she had willfully and freely chosen to become the Ruth she was, the Ruth she would now always be.

7:48 P.M.

She rolled onto her side. Curious white shapes were drifting through the air again, moving slowly from place to place: they seemed distant now, almost unearthly. A kind of laziness trickled through Ruth's body, like sweet warm milk, or like one of Dr. Ash's no-need-to-suffer medications.

Surf's up!

. . .

Ruth and Henry passed many years together in the San Marino house. Then, in the summer of 1973, shortly after Henry's retirement (Ruth had long since quit her own job), the inland heat and the demands of caring for such a large house began to wear on Ruth's health. Both of her parents were dead, and her own life batteries were weakening. No more spark: her skin had dried up, her curls began to flatten and thin out. Idly at first, then with resolution, she and Henry visited several condominium sites along the coast, and after long discussions (with Douglas offering frequent counsel) they eventually reached the decision to move to Paradise Lagoon. They made a down payment on number 24 and contracted to take up residency that winter.

Over the next several weeks, Ruth spent countless hours sorting through her belongings, discarding much, packing up only the essentials in cardboard boxes and plastic trash bags. The compelling notion of ruthlessness had taken hold of her. Partly literal, partly a pun: less and less Ruth. One morning, only a day or so before the move, she had just begun to sort through a shoebox full of trinkets when she heard the mailman at the front door. She rose from her spot in the back corner of the living room, where she was sitting Indian style on the shag rug, and squeezed her way through the boxes and bags to the door. The mailman handed her a letter from Margaret, Aunt Elizabeth's girl, whom Ruth had often taken care of as a child down at San Diego, and who was now a waitress in Las Vegas.

The mailman tipped his hat and hurried down the sidewalk. Ruth opened the letter.

"Dear Cuz," it said, "I am sorry to be the one to tell you that my mother has died. I know you were close to her in the past, and I'm sure the news will come as a great blow to you, as it did to me. Mr. Deeds is also deceased. They were found at the table in Mother's kitchen. Heart attacks in both cases — pure coincidence, I'm told, though no official investigation was done."

Oddly, Ruth felt no great emotion. She stood for a while in the doorway, aware of her own breathing. What eventually impressed itself upon her was not sorrow, but rather a wide and shallow melancholy.

Ruthless, she thought. Just less and less.

She had been prudent. She had risked little. She had lost little. She had chosen correctly — sound judgment, sound instincts — and here was the validation. Sadness without sorrow.

"Well now," she said.

Back in the living room, Ruth stared absently at her boxes and bags. At one point she almost cried, but did not permit it. She concentrated instead on the reward of unfelt pain. All those untold lies. All the foreclosed misery. The frustration and broken promises and suspicion and excuses and betrayal — none of this was hers. It would've ended exactly as it ended: Elizabeth and Frank at a breakfast table. A bad wager from the start. She had known this all along, even while hoping otherwise, and what she felt now was the dull ache of her own good sense.

"Poor us," she murmured. "*All* of us."

For a few seconds the tears were very close by.

Then she shook her head. She crossed the floor to her roll-top desk and pulled open the drawer full of old photographs. There was Frank in his bow tie and con-man smile, making an attempt to look earnest. And there was Ruth herself — a younger Ruth, an almost happy Ruth — blushing at the camera with what now seemed the last faint glow of passion.

Yes, a bad risk.

She sat down at the desk. With two pieces of Scotch tape, she carefully attached the snapshot of herself to the back of the larger portrait. "Ha!" she said. Then she took a frame down from the wall, removed the photograph of Carter deep-sea fishing in the Bahamas, and inserted the pictures of Frank and herself, Frank's facing out.

A souvenir of sorts. A tribute to good sense.

She put the frame into one of the boxes destined for Paradise Lagoon.

"Ha," she said again. "There."

When she and Henry had settled into number 24, after unpacking and arranging the furniture, Ruth devoted herself to the problems of household decoration. Paradise Lagoon: this far and no farther. Except to the cemetery, there would be no more moves. She displayed her paintings and Oriental scrolls in the third-story bedrooms and second-story sitting room; she repapered the living room walls, installed new linoleum in the kitchen, purchased lawn furniture for the balcony. As a final act, with something like devotion in her heart, she spent a long and quiet afternoon arranging her gallery of photographs in the tiny bathroom by the front door. An old lady's monument, she thought. Her own little people steeple.

The last picture to go up was Frank's. She placed it above the sink, at eye level, where visitors might take notice as they glanced up from washing their hands. And behind Frank's face, hidden there, was the shadow of her own.

As she stepped back, something seemed to swing shut inside her.

Just an old friend, she'd tell Henry if he asked. An old, old acquaintance.

But Henry never did ask.

8:00 P.M.

Ruth opened her eyes and sat up straight, holding her shoulders back. She felt tired. Enough of Frank, she thought. Enough of Elizabeth. Just a stew of worn-out memories, and what good had they done her?

She bent down to put on her sandals. Her toenails needed clipping, she noticed; they were yellow and looked more like horns than toenails. She stood and walked toward the elevator.

On the radio in Ruth's bedroom, a Brahms piano concerto was coming to an end.

. . . and in just a moment we'll be back with more here at The Golden Age, *Southern California's only truly classical hour of programming* . . .

Ruth stepped from the elevator and, pausing briefly, switched off the radio. A great silence filled the room, pressing up against her ears. Then the sound of distant waves washed through the air around her.

Ruth glanced in the direction of the window: all dark.

She walked past the bed to her chair. She undid the hook-and-eye clasp on her pants and had just started to pull down the zipper when she reminded herself that undressing from the top down would leave her body exposed for the shortest span of time. So she released the pants' zipper and, crossing her arms above the wrists, took hold of the bottom of her vest. Starting with her right hand near the left hip bone, her left hand near the right hip bone, she raised her elbows in front of her and up to her chin.

"Skin the rabbit!" she whispered, and lifted her hands high to pull off the vest. Years ago, she used to say those same words to her boys as she undressed them, and before that, her own mother had used the expression with her: Here we go, Ruthie, skin the rabbit!

She gave a final tug, uncrossing her hands, and the vest popped off. She placed it on the chair. Absently, she undid the top buttons of her blouse and began to skin the rabbit once again. She crossed her wrists, grasped the blouse, lifted her hands high above her head. Except this time something went wrong — a tight pinching at her throat. It took a moment to realize that the cord of her silver locket had twisted up; it was attacking her neck.

"Oh, criminey," she said, "just what I need."

She gave her shoulders a shake. She wiggled her arms and

head, twisted at the waist, but the locket wouldn't budge. The thing had somehow snagged on the button of a sleeve, winding around itself, and the long cord was squeezing her throat like one of those weird African snakes.

Blouse over her head, the stupid locket almost strangling her, she couldn't see a thing. She took a couple of steps in what she supposed was the direction of the door, but almost immediately her pants slithered down around her ankles. She yelped and stumbled; her feet wouldn't work; she couldn't move more than two or three inches at a time.

Still wiggling, arms pinned by the blouse, she began to shuffle forward. Suddenly things got darker.

"For crying out loud," she muttered. She'd ended up inside her closet. She felt the hangers against her arms, the skirts and dresses swishing all around her. A person could vanish, she thought, in a place like this.

For a moment she stood perfectly still.

Disappear, she thought.

The idea was seductive.

It was also disconcertingly familiar.

A streak of white light pierced the pure, black background of Ruth's temporary blindness. Was it a mistake to nurture fantasies of how things should have been? Ruth swayed to the side, then stood motionless again. Life without illusion. Might it have been more bearable, more meaningful, more kind?

Nineteen thirty-six, Washington, D.C. — Hale sequestered in his study with Frank Deeds — and she was listening to the low, conspiratorial hum of their voices from the kitchen, where she stood waiting for the coffee to finish percolating. One more misfortune in the Deeds household, she thought. No doubt something Myrna had done. Poor Frank — she pitied the man, she really did. And Myrna, too. How lucky she was to have Hale. God, she loved him.

Shaking her head, Ruth poured out three cups of coffee. She placed the cups on a tray and then crossed the hall toward the study.

"If only *I'd* married her," Frank was saying.

Ruth paused. She lowered the tray to her left hip and inched toward the door, which stood ajar.

"Charming," Hale said.

She heard an odd chuckle, high and artificial.

"You should have just *seen* her, last year out in Ponca City. Such antics. Such desperation. Just the thought of it sickens me." Another chuckle. "I mean all of it. This marriage."

"My God, man, she's the loveliest woman alive." Frank's voice, ordinarily smooth and commanding, sounded almost bewildered. "And she's crazy about you. Thinks about nothing else."

"Certifiable myopia. Lucky, lucky me."

"Enough, shut up," Frank said.

For a while there was silence.

Then Frank said, "You want to know, I'm jealous as hell."

"Charming once again." Hale's voice was not his own. "Christ!" he said.

There was another brief silence.

Hale said, "Thing is, I adored her."

Then, after a moment: "Couldn't get enough of her, be with her enough. But Christ, I hardly knew her, only six *weeks* before we married, and now . . . Well, now my whole goddamn future . . ." Something hot entered Ruth's throat; somewhere down inside her, the pain of a lifetime was gathering force. "So much *time!*" he said. "I swear to you, Frank. It's killing me."

An angry, hostile silence.

And in that silence, which Ruth would not allow herself to remember for almost sixty years, her heart lost its natural rhythm. Ownerless and free, it floated for a time through the cold, shapeless mass of the universe.

She stepped forward into the room, mumbled something about coffee.

When Hale turned toward her, his features revealed no trace of treachery, nothing at all; he looked just as he had looked every day since she'd met him. The same small, well-formed mouth and crooked nose, the same glowing green eyes with those beautiful flecks of brown. Such splendid eyes.

Frank stood up and reached for the coffee tray. "Now, what was I saying? Ah, yes. Ruthie, my darling, I was just telling Hale how happy any man on earth would be to have you for a wife."

He smiled.

A cocky Frank Deeds smile, yes. But she saw the compassion too. And the pity.

After Hale died, Ruth devoted herself to the watch he had given her, regulating her actions according to its stern requirements; her heart took up the rhythm of that strict metronome; all harmony, all melody, slipped away.

It wasn't betrayal exactly. Maybe not even inexactly. He had only shaken her from a dream, a silly romantic dream.

All that time, he'd said. His whole sad future.

Alone in her closet, Ruth thought of those tapes of airplane pilots screaming "Mama!" as they made their brain-bending surrender to gravity. She thought of Hale's last syllable. "Time!" he'd yelled — part proclamation, part question — the sound of one human voice adding itself to the great electric buzz.

The heat began to rise in her throat — her own electric clamor, her own indelible Ruthness releasing itself to the universe — a vulgar and desperate and angry scream that she'd somehow managed to swallow back all these years.

"Gehr," she said, blouse wrapped around her head, lace collar pressing up against her mouth and nose.

"Gehhhrr!"

A moment later, incredibly, Henry entered the bedroom. She heard him lumber over to the bed, heard him rustle her pillow and sleeping bag. There was some silence, then the sound of drawers opening.

She tried to clap, stretching her arms high, but all she could manage was a muted little pat.

His hand touched her shoulder.

"Well, hey," Henry said, "what's this?"

He fingered her blouse, reaching beneath it to touch her belly, then ran a hand up to her armpit. When he spoke again, his voice seemed full of wonder.

"I'll tell you, Ruthie, we've been married all these years, but I never figured you for a closet person. Shows we're made for each other." His hand moved to the side of her breast. "Like I said once to Douglas, I says, 'Closets are a darn good place to hang out, sort of collect your thoughts and —'"

Ruth spat away some fabric.

"Okay, okay," Henry said.

He took her wrist. He unhooked the locket from her sleeve, pulled the cord over her head, lifted off her blouse.

"Fiend," she said.

"Hey, I just —"

Ruth snatched the blouse from his hands and yanked up her pants. Henry stood gaping. "All *right*," she said, "you saved me, that's no excuse for a peep show." She walked around him to her chair. "Hope you're satisfied."

"Not bad," he said, and smiled at her. A goofy smile, partly, but also calm and tender. It made her glance away.

"Well, anyway," she said. "Thanks."

"That's what I'm here for."

Ruth reached up to smooth her curls. "So I guess you'll be going to bed now?"

"Right," he said. "Guess so."

She waited a moment, almost looking at him. "First, though, you'll set up my breakfast tray? The usual way. I think you know how I like it done."

"Oh, sure," Henry said, and kept smiling. "Quarter cup of bran, no milk till morning. Don't want the stuff mushy." He crossed to the chair and placed the locket on the cushion, still smiling, his mouth wide open. He reached for his tooth, twisted it a couple of times, then turned toward the door.

"Call if you need me," he said.

When she was certain Henry was downstairs, Ruth took off her pants and struggled to hang them underneath her blouse and vest on the hanger. She lay her garters, panty girdle, and camisole over the back of the chair, slipped on her flannel nightgown, stepped into her slippers, and pulled on her bedjacket. Stooping to lift her silver locket from the cushion, she made her way into the bathroom.

Methodically, humming quietly to herself, she lay the locket on the table by the toilet, next to a stack of old bills, then turned to the counter where her laxative was waiting. She picked up the spoon she always used and dipped it deep into the jar to pull out a heaping teaspoonful of brown pellets. She chewed them thoroughly for a full minute — a few dropped to the tile — and while she chewed, she idly took stock of the items around her sink.

Too much, she thought.

Seven bottles of moisturizing lotion were turned upside down, leaning against the medicine cabinet mirror. Their faded labels said "Moondew." Ruth picked up a bottle and pumped its top, but nothing came out. She tried another one, then several more — all empty. Most certainly, Karen and Luzma were right: all the old clutter should be thrown away. Next week, she tried to convince herself, she'd find a place for these bottles in the trash.

The phone rang.

Ruth licked her index finger, popped the fallen laxative pellets into her mouth, and hurried out from the bathroom and over to her bedside table. Wheezing slightly, she reached for the receiver.

There was silence at the other end. Then a shallow whisper: "White Rabbit."

The voice startled her. "Who is this?"

"It's me." There was a quick, high chuckle. "I meant to get you earlier."

"Nora?"

"Not quite."

"Carter? Douglas?"

"Well, no, I'm sorry."

Absently, Ruth sat down on her bed. The voice seemed familiar now.

"Elizabeth? Uncle Stephen — it's you!"

The voice chuckled.

"Frank?" she said. She paused and adjusted her glasses. "*Hale?*"

On the other end there was a delicate, almost feathery sound, not the wind, not the sea, but something in between, something cool and breathy and weightless.

"Who?" she said.

Again, for an instant, she detected that odd feathery sound, then came a sad little sigh.

"Just me. White Rabbit."

Ruth reached for her pillbox. She picked out a Cardizem, studied it for a second, then washed it down with water. Enough, she thought. No need for Tylenol or Naprosyn or pink tranquilizers. She set the box on her bedside table.

She didn't bother to clean her face. She didn't bother to turn out the lamp, nor to take off her bedjacket, nor to pull the bobby pins from her hair. For a few minutes, perfectly still, she listened to the waves whisper through her open window.

Well fine, she thought.

She unfastened her digital watch and put it aside. Then, staring straight ahead, she also took off Hale's wristwatch. She held it firmly, as if to contain time in the palm of her hand, then eased back slowly against her sit-up pillow.